IBERIAN CHIVALRIC ROMANCE

Translations and Cultural Transmission
in Early Modern England

Iberian Chivalric Romance

Translations and Cultural Transmission in Early Modern England

EDITED BY LETICIA ÁLVAREZ-RECIO

UNIVERSITY OF TORONTO PRESS

Toronto Buffalo London

ISBN 978-1-4875-0881-4 (cloth)   ISBN 978-1-4875-3901-6 (EPUB)
                                  ISBN 978-1-4875-3900-9 (PDF)

Library and Archives Canada Cataloguing in Publication

Title: Iberian chivalric romance : translations and cultural transmission in
    early modern England / edited by Leticia Álvarez-Recio.
Names: Alvarez Recio, Leticia, editor.
Series: Toronto Iberic ; 58.
Description: Series statement: Toronto Iberic series ; 58 | Includes index.
Identifiers: Canadiana (print) 20200344404 | Canadiana (ebook)
    20200346385 | ISBN 9781487508814 (hardcover) | ISBN 9781487539016
    (EPUB) | ISBN 9781487539009 (PDF)
Subjects: LCSH: Romances, Spanish – Appreciation – England – History –
    16th century. | LCSH: Romances, Spanish – Translations into English –
    History and criticism. | LCSH: Romances, Spanish – Translations into
    English. | LCSH: English literature – Spanish influences. | LCSH: Books
    and reading – England – History – 16th century. | LCSH: Romances,
    Spanish – History and criticism. | LCSH: England – Intellectual life –
    16th century.
Classification: LCC PQ6042.E5 I24 2021 | DDC 861/.0330903 – dc23

This book has been published with the financial assistance of the Spanish
Ministry of Economy and Competitiveness and the European Union in
the project "The Spanish Romances of Chivalry in English Translation:
Anthony Munday and Early Modern Culture in Europe" (FFI2015-70101-P;
MINECO/FEDER, UE).

University of Toronto Press acknowledges the financial assistance to its
publishing program of the Canada Council for the Arts and the Ontario
Arts Council, an agency of the Government of Ontario.

Canada Council   Conseil des Arts
for the Arts   du Canada

ONTARIO ARTS COUNCIL
CONSEIL DES ARTS DE L'ONTARIO

an Ontario government agency
un organisme du gouvernement de l'Ontario

Funded by the   Financé par le
Government   gouvernement
of Canada   du Canada

Contents

Illustrations and Tables

Illustrations

Tables

Acknowledgments

The present work is the result of a thorough process whose origin goes back to an expert meeting on Iberian chivalric books held in Seville in early 2018. The meeting itself had been regarded as one of the main components of our project "The Spanish Romances of Chivalry in English Translation: Anthony Munday and Early Modern Culture in Europe", funded by the Spanish Ministry of Economy and Competitiveness (FFFI2015-70101-P). It proved to be extremely rewarding, as participants were only too eager to share their latest research findings. I wish to thank them all for their attendance and for having agreed to contribute to this volume.

My heartfelt thanks to my colleagues Jordi Sánchez Martí (University of Alicante) and Goran Stanivukovic (Saint Mary's University), whose sensible advice and constant support have been essential. I must also thank Professor Rafael Portillo (University of Seville) for his ceaseless help and always profitable advice.

Abbreviations

Arber	*A Transcript of the Registers of the Company of Stationers of London: 1554–1640*, ed. Edward Arber. 5 Vols. New York: P Smith, 1950
BBTI	British Book Trade Index, Centre for the Study of the Book, Bodleian Libraries, University of Oxford http://bbti.bodleian.ox.ac.uk/#
Blayney	Peter W.M. Blayney, *The Stationers' Company and the Printers of London, 1501–1557*. 2 vols. Cambridge: Cambridge University Press, 2013
BL	British Library
Duff	*Printing in England in the Fifteenth Century: E. Gordon Duff's Bibliography with Supplementary Descriptions, Chronologies and a Census of Copies by Lotte Hellinga*. London: Bibliographical Society and the British Library, 2009
EEBO	*Early English Books Online*, http://eebo.chadwyck.com. Chadwyck-Healey. ProQuest LLC, 2003–18
EETS o.s.	Early English Text Society, original series
FB	*French Vernacular Books: Books Published in the French Language before 1601*, ed. Andrew Pettegree, Malcolm Walsby, and Alexander Wilkinson. Leiden and Boston: Brill, 2007
IB	*Iberian Books: Books Published in Spanish or Portuguese or on the Iberian Peninsula before 1601*, ed. Alexander Wilkinson. Leiden and Boston: Brill, 2010
McKerrow, *Dictionary*	R.B. McKerrow, ed. *A Dictionary of Printers and Booksellers in England, Scotland and Ireland, and of Foreign Printers of English Books, 1557–1640*. London: Bibliographical Society, 1910

ODNB 2004	*Oxford Dictionary of National Biography*, ed. by H.C.G. Matthew and Brian Harrison, 61 vols. Oxford: Oxford University Press, 2004
ODNB 2020	*The Oxford Dictionary of National Biography*, ed. Sir David Cannadine. Oxford: Oxford University Press, 2020 https://www.oxforddnb.com.
OED	*The Oxford English Dictionary*. Oxford: Oxford University Press, 2020. https://www.oed.com
STC	*A Short-Title Catalogue of Books Printed in England, Scotland, and Ireland and of English Books Printed Abroad, 1475-1640*, ed. A. W. Pollard and G. R. Redgrave, 2nd. ed., rev. W.A. Jacobs, F.S. Ferguson, and Katherine R. Pantzer, 3 vols. London: Bibliographical Society, 1976–91
USTC	*Universal Short Title Catalogue*, Arts and Humanities Research Council, Iberian Books, Brill, Proquest, ICCU, GLN1516, STVC and STCN. St. Andrews: University of St. Andrews, https://www.ustc.ac.uk/index.php

IBERIAN CHIVALRIC ROMANCE

Translations and Cultural Transmission in Early Modern England

Introduction: The Iberian Books of Chivalry in English Translation

LETICIA ÁLVAREZ-RECIO

What a madnes is it of folkes, to haue pleasure in these bokes? Also ther is no wytte in them, but a fewe wordes of wanton lust, whiche be spoken to moue her mynde, with whom they loue, if it chaunce she be steadfast ... Finally though they were neuer so wytty and pleasant, yet wold I haue no pleasure infected with poyson, nor haue no woman quickened vnto vyce.

– Juan Luis Vives, *Instruction of a Christen Woman*

The workes of Poetes, the Fables of Milesius, as that of the golden asse, and in a maner all Lucianes workes, and manye other whiche are written in the vulgar tonge, as of Trystram, Launcelote, Ogier, Amasus [Amadis] and of Artur the whiche were written and made by suche as were ydle and knew nothinge. These bokes do hurt both man & woman, for they make them wylye & craftye, they kyndle and styr up couetousnes, inflame angre, & all beastly and filthy desire.

– Juan Luis Vives, *The Office and Dutie of an Husband*

Deep-rooted attacks against chivalric books of Iberian origin reached English soil at a very early stage, when the works of their most virulent detractors were first published in English translation. Such was the case of *De institutione christianae feminae*, by Juan Luis Vives (1492–1540), first published in Antwerp in 1524 (USTC 442383, 403719). This work, intended mostly for Princess Mary's education, had been commissioned by Queen Catherine of Aragon; it enjoyed enormous popularity in Europe, as the publication of six editions in 1524–66 (Basel, USTC 667563, 667568, 667577; Frankfurt, 611418) and multiple translations into diverse continental languages – French, Italian, Dutch, German, and English – attest. Richard Hyrd (d. 1528), who worked as a tutor at Sir Thomas More's service, translated the original work into English and published it in 1529 (STC 24856, 24856.5); it became a bestseller in the second half of the century, as it had seven editions issued in 1531–92 (STC 24857–24863). Vives's *De officio mariti*, which was not as popular as its predecessor, had four editions of the Latin text published from 1529 to 1542 (USTC 410230, 667559, 667568, 667577), and there were various translations into French, Dutch, Italian, German, and English.[1] All in all, Vives's works were extraordinarily well-known and became standard educational books in sixteenth-century Europe, which can also explain the longstanding negative impact that his opinions had on the perception of chivalric literature in general. Quite ironically, though, Sir Thomas Paynell (d. 1564?), who translated the English version of Vives's *De officio mariti*, and called it *The Office and Dutie of a Husband* (London, 1555?; STC 24855), would also translate some years later the French *Tresor des Amadis* as *The Treasurie of Amadis of Fraunce* (London, 1572?; STC 545). This book contains a selection of passages from Books 1–13 of Nicolas Herberay's version of the Spanish *Amadís de Gaula* (Antwerp, 1560; FB 882). Paynell's engagement in both projects illustrates the somewhat contradictory nature of the Renaissance debate on chivalric literature.

In England, as in Europe, romances of chivalry, either native or Iberian, were criticized for three main reasons. Most of all, their subject matter was alleged to inflame the readers' most basic passions. Thomas Underdowne (1566–87), in his translation of Heliodorus's *An Aethiopian Historie* (1577; STC 13042), vehemently condemns such books as "*Mort Darthure, Arthur of Little Britain*, yea, and *Amadis of Gaule*" that "accompt violente murder or murder for no cause manhood: and fornication and all vnlawfull luste, friendely loue" (iii^r), thus dwelling on those same commonplace topics. Edward Aggas (1564–1601), the translator of *The Politicke and Militarie Discourse of the Lord de la Nouue* (1587; STC 15215), shows a similar concern about readers, whom he believed to be incapable of distinguishing fact from fiction, since the romances "pollute themselues, wening to reape delight, and through loitering in reading of lies, do disdaine those wherein the truth doth most euidently shine forth" (G8^r). De la Noue and his translator go even further when condemning Spanish chivalric books such as *Amadis* for "catching the soules, infecting with a foolish belief, which by little and little carieth them [readers] from God" (G4^v). As Elizabeth Spiller has remarked, the *furor* felt by lovers of chivalric romances was "notably comparable to the physical and emotional dangers that may afflict readers," for the very act of reading could engage people in "the physiological acts that were most likely to disrupt the healthy functioning of the brain."[2] Such ideas about brain pollution permeate most attacks. According to B.W. Ife, "the poison *topos*" served to distinguish fruitful from unhealthy or pernicious reading, and Noue and Aggas warned their reading public against "the poison hidden among the fruits of Amadis delightes" (G6ᵛ).³

The second basis for criticism, connected to the first, was that the corrupt nature of chivalric romances was thought to weaken the religious and moral beliefs of such "unprepared" readers as women and young people, who would be unable to maintain the principles of the true faith in the face of such books. Those prejudices were held by Catholic and Protestant critics alike. Italian Jesuit Antonio Possevino (1534–1611) complained in his *Bibliotheca Selecta* (Rome, 1593; USTC 851076) that the French rendering of *Amadis* had contributed to spreading Protestantism among the French nobility (Bk 1, ch. xxv, p. 113),⁴ while similar arguments were used in England to prevent readers from consuming romance literature, mainly of foreign origin.⁵ In his manual *The Scholemaster* (London, 1970; STC 832), Roger Ascham (1515–68) was in favour of banning native chivalric books as well as romances of Italian origin, since they could "soone displace all bookes of godly learning. For they, carrying the will of vanitie, and marryng good maners, shall easily corrupt the mynd with ill opinions and false iudgement in doctrine: first to thinke ill of all trewe Religion, and at last to think nothing of God hymselfe" (I3ᵛ). Nearly sixty years later, William Vaughan (1577–1641), in his *Golden Fleece* (1626; STC 24609), used a similar argument against chivalric romances, which, in his view, were useless: "Those prodigious, idle, and time-wasting Bookes, called *The Mirrour of Knighthood*, the *Knights of the Round Table*, *Palmerin de Oliua*, and the like rabblement, [were] deuised no doubt by the Deuill to confirme soules in the knowledge of euill" (C2ʳ).⁶ Virginia Krause has incisively explained the connection between useless and immoral reading in the discourse against chivalric romance. In her view, underlying such criticism was the notion of the "sacredness of time," for time belongs to God, not to each individual person. When presenting romance reading as "time-wasting," its detractors were regarding it as an act of simony, and therefore as a sin against God himself.⁷

A third recurrent argument against chivalric literature dwelled on its lack of decorum, since it boasted long, hyperbolic descriptions of improbable events. In his introduction to *L'Histoire Aethiopique* (Paris, 1547; USTC 40569), Jacques Amyot (1513–93) attacked Spanish books of chivalry and their French translations, since they contained "no learning, no knowledge of antiquity, nothing (to put it briefly) from which we can draw some utility." He added that they were "so badly put together and so far from any probability in their appearance, that they seem rather to be the dreams of some sick person struggling in hot fever, than the inventions of a man of wit and ingenuity."[8] Amyot's arguments partly reproduced those of Spanish scholars Juan de Valdés (1509–41) and Juan Luis Vives, who had already painted those books as witless;[9] they also inspired further attacks by English detractors on those same grounds. The Anatomie of the Absurditie (1589; STC 18364) by Thomas Nashe (1567–1601), for instance, found that chivalric books resulted from "the fantasticall dreames of those exiled Abbie-lubbers, from whose idle pens, proceeded those worne out impressions of ... feyned nowhere acts" (A2^r).[10]

Despite such pervasive criticism, chivalric romance, especially of Spanish origin, managed to occupy an important niche in the late-Elizabethan and early-Jacobean book market for prose literature.[11] The early impressive impact of Cervantes's Quixote, both on the stage and the book industry, confirms the genre's popularity in seventeenth-century England. The multiple reprints of Spanish chivalric books in English translation throughout that century are evidence of their market value, even two centuries after the publication of the first Spanish editions. Their status as literary bestsellers in early modern Europe should have made them the subject of scholarly and academic interest, although that has not, unfortunately, been the case.[12]

The eighteenth-century vogue for realistic fiction containing probable facts tended to sideline romance, which was then regarded as second-rate literature. In the nineteenth century, despite the romantic reappraisal of chivalric romances, academics and scholars were still prejudiced against the genre. An exception was poet Robert Southey (1774–1843), who was interested in the English translations of the Spanish Palmerin and Amadis cycles.[13] Otherwise, common opinion insisted that it was a "nonsensical," type of literature and condemned the "extravagant fictions and entangled episodes of the early Romances, without seeking for probability of incident or correctness of idea."[14] Spanish chivalric romances were then considered to break the aesthetic rules of decorum, and this argument, which had originated in the late sixteenth century, was still employed well into the twentieth century, until, at last, various scholars began to view the genre in a different light. Although their contribution to the study of Iberian chivalric romance in English was extremely helpful, they still had a deep-rooted prejudice against the genre – and against the translator who monopolized the market in the early modern period, namely, Anthony Munday.[15] James Fitzmaurice-Kelly regarded Munday as "a dismal draper of misplaced literary ambitions," while Henry Thomas accused him of being a "mercenary" agent who had started "a factory for the translation of chivalresque romances of foreign origin." Thomas openly attacked Munday's method of translation, which he considered "cheaper and inferior."[16] For Donald S. Crane, Munday was no more than the leader of some "obscure men working at the behest of a group of commercial publishers"; to Edwin H. Miller, he was "a patriarch ... of Grubstreet" who "would do anything for money."[17] The first biography of Munday's life, by Celeste Turner Wright, devotes little space to Munday's professional activity as a translator, which the author regards as secondary to his work as a playwright and civic chronicler. Mary Patchell is even harder, arguing that Munday's translations "added little to his reputation or to the dignity of Elizabethan romance" and that the "intrinsic merit of these works ... is so slight that they deserve the oblivion into which they have fallen."[18]

Anthony Munday's contribution to early modern English prose fiction was still being disregarded by scholars in the second half of the twentieth century,[19] just as there was still a general lack of interest in the corpus of Iberian chivalric works in English.[20] That situation was reversed only in the early 2000s, when Munday scholars began to explore his central role in English literature and culture. Tracey Hill and Donna Hamilton put Munday on the map with their respective monographs *Anthony Munday and Civic Culture* and *Anthony Munday and the Catholics*, which offered two thorough studies of the writer's links with the City and his engagement with the culture and politics of late-sixteenth and early seventeenth-century London.[21] Academic interest in the English translations of Spanish chivalric books also increased significantly after the publication of a critical edition of Munday's *Amadis de Gaule* by Helen Moore in 2004.[22] Since then, a growing number of scholars have approached Munday's translations, relating them to late sixteenth- and seventeenth-century editorial and reading practices.[23] Munday's controversial use of Catholic elements present in his sources has also attracted experts on early modern English Catholicism,[24] who have examined the adaptation of chivalric medieval and Renaissance romances to late sixteenth-century English Protestant discourse.[25] Besides, those English versions became the subject of various recent works that deal with early modern translations, both in England and in Europe.[26] The fact that those Spanish chivalry books had already been translated into the main European languages before reaching England has allowed scholars to explore the phenomena of imitation and adaptation of cultural discourses that transcend national boundaries.[27]

The present collection builds upon the work of these scholars and makes a significant contribution to the field, based on new scholarly evidence and methodologies that include comparative readings across different cultures and languages of early modern Europe. Contributors examine the publication and reception history of sixteenth-century Iberian books of chivalry in English translation and explore the impact of that literary corpus on Elizabethan culture, as well as its connections with other contemporary genres such as native English fiction, chronicle, and epistolary writing. They focus on the renderings of the two main Spanish sixteenth-century cycles – Amadis and Palmerin – from such different critical approaches as cultural studies, book history and reception, material history, translation, post-colonial criticism, and gender studies. The fact that these texts may be approached from so many different viewpoints attest to their malleable nature, which in turn becomes particularly useful to apprehend many of the cultural discourses prevailing in early modern England. Although some of the chapters offer a more general view of the whole corpus, others focus on the works that make up the two aforementioned cycles. The contributors' detailed analysis of individual texts also serves to vindicate their literary value beyond the traditional approach and considers each one as links within a long series.

This volume, which focuses largely on Anthony Munday's work as a leading translator,[28] consists of four sections. The first examines the publication of chivalric literature in England from 1570 to 1603, placing special emphasis on Munday's role in the literary book market. The second section, in the manner of case studies, approaches some of Munday's most representative translations – *Palmendos*, *Primaleon*, *Palmerin of England*, and *Amadis* – analysing the contribution of those works to late sixteenth-century cultural debates on sexuality, female individualism, religion, colonialism, and new reading modes. Part 3 offers a broader view of these chivalric works by examining their impact on other contemporary genres such as native English romance, letter writing, and history. The last section considers the influence of those translations on English fiction from the 1590s and throughout the seventeenth century.

Chapter 1 is an extensive introductory essay by Jordi Sánchez-Martí on the publication history of Spanish chivalric romance in sixteenth-century England. The author offers a general panorama of the history of chivalric romance in England from the advent of the printing press to the late 1560s. In his view, the transition from manuscript to print owes a great deal to three early printers who clearly invested on romance – William Caxton, Wynkyn de Worde, and William Copland. They published prose romances of European origin in English translation as well as native medieval verse romances, thus giving rise to a market for this genre that flourished up to the late 1560s, when signs first appeared indicating that the genre had been over-exploited. Sánchez-Martí points out the strange situation produced in England in these years, since customers were prepared to spend money on a kind of literature – chivalric romance – that printers were uninterested in producing and writers were unwilling to compose. The way out was to look for new chivalric material in other countries. The first English translations of Iberian prose romances, which came out in 1578, enjoyed immediate success, as the high rate of reprints attests. In his discussion, Sánchez-Martí explains how the commercial policies adopted by English stationers – mainly Thomas East, John Charlewood, Cuthbert Burby, and Thomas Creede – made it possible for Elizabethan customers to read medievalizing chivalric literature well into the seventeenth century.

The three chapters that make up part 2 offer various analytical approaches to some of Anthony Munday's most popular translations of chivalric books. In chapter 2, Leticia Álvarez-Recio discusses Munday's dedication to Sir Francis Drake in *Palmendos* (1589; STC 18064), which she views in relation to the network of publishing agents who invested in navigation and New World literature in the 1580s. She studies the links between stationers who published works dedicated to Drake and those engaged in the publication of Munday's first translations of the Palmerin cycle. She then compares the episode occurring on the Isle of Delphos in the Spanish, French, and English versions of *Palmendos* and analyses these versions in the context of utopian models for political powers in clear competition for territorial expansion. The chapter also studies the way Anthony Munday reconsiders some of the principles on the just-war and natural-law theories present in his Spanish and French sources. Álvarez-Recio illustrates how chivalric romance was employed in sixteenth-century debates on conquest and foreign intervention. In her opinion, Munday and/or his publishers were actually proposing certain specific standards of conduct for Sir Francis Drake in his confrontation with Spain. Finally, the chapter examines a series of Catholic features present in the Baledon episode as evidence of the support of Munday, his dedicatees, and/or stationers for contemporary colonial English emprises involving non-conformists.

In chapter 3, María Beatriz Hernández-Pérez's considers a book in the Palmerin series – namely, *Primaleon of Greece* (1595; STC 20366) – studying the various social roles played by female characters. She highlights the close connection between the genres of romance and medieval hagiography in relation to the way women make use of their own private space. She explores how notions such as pleasure and space apply both to female characters and readers, as she focuses on the medieval *topos* of the *femme sole* while examining the main characters in the *First Book of Primaleon of Greece*. In the second part of her chapter, Hernández-Pérez links the medieval hagiographic tradition to Munday's portrait of his female protagonist Gridonia, who stands as the alternative model to *femme sole* Flerida. She concludes by underlining the capacity of the romance genre to offer an extraordinary variety of models for female readers seeking to enjoy a private space of their own.

In the last chapter of this section, Louise Wilson studies the significance of material objects in Munday's translation of the first book of *Palmerin of England* (1596; STC 19161). Wilson analyses the ways in which characters read those objects, just as she studies the reader's attitude to the narrative. The artefacts described by Munday in his chivalric translations are strongly connected to the material world of his non-elite readers; thus, the latter's experience of pleasure when reading Munday's romances relies partly on the readers' sense of familiarity with the objects portrayed in those texts. Wilson's choice of *Palmerin of England* is pertinent here, as its publication coincided precisely with Munday's professional engagement in civic entertainments and the lord mayor's shows. She reads this romance alongside Munday's involvement with the City and successfully proves how Munday's detailed descriptions of the "artificial" world in *Palmerin of England* reveal the translator's parallel interest in the artisan work of the City guilds as well as his ability to "customize" the medieval framework of the romance narrative to the contemporary world of his urban readers.

Part 3, on the impact of Iberian chivalric romance on English literature, opens with a chapter by Rocío G. Sumillera that examines how the letter-writing genre – so relevant in all spheres of European life – found its way into the Iberian romance. Letter writing becomes a rhetorical device that proves most useful in the development of both plot and characters. Sumillera's chapter explores the role of the epistolary genre in Herberay's French (1540–43; FB 653, 658, 662, 674) and Anthony Munday's English (1590, 1595, 1618; STC 541–3) translations of the Spanish *Amadís de Gaula*. Sumillera successfully links the theoretical principles of letter writing with actual letter samples taken from the most popular manuals at the time and a selection of *Amadis* letters. In doing so, she explores the development of the *ars dictaminis* in sixteenth-century Europe and the role played by authors and translators of prose fiction in providing proper cases of epistolary exchanges for the middling sort. In this sense, the author stresses the didactic value of chivalric translations and sheds light on the mixing of different genres, so often found in Spanish Renaissance literary works prior to *Don Quixote*. She examines the influence that such blend of genres could have had on early modern French and English fiction as well.

Timothy Crowley devotes his chapter to a study the influence of the Amadis cycle on Philip Sidney's *Arcadia*. This chapter analyses three interlaced motifs – a sequestered princess, love by image, and an Amazonian disguise leading to secret marriage – in Feliciano de Silva's part 2 of *Amadís de Grecia* and part 3 of *Florisel de Niquea*. Such motifs, subtly instilled with Neoplatonic and alchemical references, allowed Silva to explore the ethics of clandestine marriage. Crowley then examines the French version of the first half of *Florisel de Niquea*, translated by Jacques Gohory (1554; FB 779–81), arguing that Gohory turned the Neoplatonic philosophy in Silva's work into a "microcosm of occult allegory," which became a determining influence in Sidney's *Old Arcadia* (comp. 1578–81) and *New Arcadia* (1590; STC 22539) in terms of plot and characterization. Sidney's creative method consisted of adapting Gohory's embellishments within the French source text by steering its dialogue and metaphysical language away from allegorical characterization. In the process, Sidney granted his protagonist lovers a new degree of philosophical and political self-awareness as he infuses the chivalric source's Neoplatonic patterns with Aristotelian premises and Ciceronian and Senecan modes of Stoic discourse on constancy. As Crowley argues, those philosophical registers, together with disguise and secret marriage, prove essential in *Arcadia*'s unique dramatic, political, legal, and intellectual ironies.

The final two chapters in part 3, by Elizabeth Evenden-Kenyon and Donna Hamilton, respectively, present Anthony Munday as an English Catholic deeply engaged in what Brian C. Lockey calls "the transnational Christian Commonwealth."[29] In chapter 7, Evenden-Kenyon reflects on the central role played by Arthurian themes in the confessional debates of the sixteenth and early seventeenth centuries and focuses on the impact of Arthuriana on the Iberian Peninsula. She explores then how Iberian Arthuriana contributed to English Catholic history. In the second half of her chapter, Evenden-Kenyon focuses on Munday's translations of Portuguese and Spanish romances to explore the ways cosmopolitanism was perceived in relation to loyalty to one's own country and monarch in late Elizabethan and Jacobean England. She thus highlights Munday's role as a mediator who succeeded in bringing English readers into close contact with an international community reading Arthurian romances that were still linked to pre-Reformation Anglo-Iberian history.

In Donna Hamilton's view, the various histories Munday wrote are consonant in content and emphasis with the international perspective he represented through his translations of chivalric romance. As she argues, both romance and history were the most useful genres "for transnational European history, ideology, and myth," and so Munday's use of them attests to his commitment to spread a more ecumenical and inclusive view of England in early seventeenth-century Europe. Hamilton focuses on excerpts from Munday's *A Briefe Chronicle, of the Successe of Times* (1611; STC 18263) and from his 1618 and 1633 revisions of Stow's *Survey of London* (STC 23344–5), which she reads alongside some fragments from his romances, such as *Palmerin of England*, Book 1 of *Amadis*, and *Palmendos*, thus illustrating his support of pre-Reformation Christian traditions and values, despite censorship. Hamilton considers Munday's romances and histories in the light of contemporary religious and political controversies on the Oath of Allegiance (1606, 1610), the Spanish Match, and the jurisdiction of the Roman Catholic Church, thus enhancing the translator's decision to authorize, in Hamilton's words, "the Catholic world that Henry VIII and Elizabeth I had dismissed but James and Charles had not."

The last section in the volume deals with the impact of Iberian romance on English fiction. In chapter 9, Goran Stanivukovic argues that Iberian romances brought into England an altogether new kind of fiction associated with modern Renaissance literary production, despite the storytelling, thematic, and even structural anachronisms upon which Iberian romances were based. In his view, the modernity of English romance lies in the way it shifts the narrative focus "from the exteriority of militant chivalry to the interiority of protagonists." He observes the pervasive influence of Iberian chivalric romances in this shift. He focuses on *Amadis de Gaule*, as it clearly shows such emphasis on the characters' emotions and sensual experiences rather than on their knightly deeds. Stanivukovic explores Munday's translations of *Amadis* in connection with two other key Spanish works that employed what he calls "the narrative of interiority" – *Don Quixote* and Montemayor's *Diana* – and he concludes that these three works are connected not just by their Iberian literary origin but by their relevance as "constitutive texts that fundamentally expanded meaning in romance writing in England." In his view, the characters' tendency to self-analysis and articulation of inner thoughts in these works shows a high degree of psychological complexity, which would become a most significant marker of subsequent modern English fiction.

In chapter 10, Helen Cooper considers the influence of Spanish chivalric romance as a key factor in understanding the change in literary taste of the period from 1525, when Rastell began composing his version of Fernando de Rojas's *Celestina*, to 1631, the date of publication of James Mabbe's translation of Rojas's text (STC 4911). Cooper compares both versions and their ascriptions to genre. In her view, if characters (a young man and a young lady), topics (the overcoming of female virtue), and even title (focused largely on the lovers' names) are taken into account, it would not have been difficult for sixteenth-century English readers to regard *Celestina* as a romance, though Rastell eventually transformed Rojas's piece into a didactic interlude on parental discipline, thus departing from that tradition. Mabbe's translation, however, closely followed its Spanish source, as he gives pre-eminence to sex from the very title, thus revealing a clear change in literary taste. In Cooper's view, eroticism had rooted in English literature largely through familiarity with the Iberian chivalric romances that were popular in England from the late 1570s. Her chapter concludes with a reflection on the capacity of Iberian romances to mould English readers' reception of fiction in the seventeenth century.

The afterword by Alex Davis, which closes this volume, wonderfully summarizes its contents and takes its themes in new directions. Davis explores the modernity of Iberian romance and focuses on the interaction between words and deeds by paying attention to the performative function of language in these romances and their effective systematization of those descriptive patterns that make violent scenes almost interchangeable. In his view, such systematization emphasizes the power of deeds (and their consequences) and hints at the affinity between these chivalric narratives and Renaissance handbooks. Iberian romance witnesses the bureaucratic shift of modernity while highlighting an aristocratic ideal still connected with the past. Overall, Davis describes Iberian romance as a genre deeply engaged with the modern period, which cannot be fully understood if separated from a European perspective.

Iberian Chivalric Romance: Translations and Cultural Transmission in Early Modern England offers an insightful approach to the myriad ways in which Iberian chivalric romance permeated English literature and culture for over a century, contributing successfully to the very definition of English native prose fiction. In this volume, those translations are given a centrality they have not enjoyed to this point, thus vindicating their relevance to the study of English Renaissance literature. This work enhances the importance of Anglo-Iberian literary relations, which we deem essential to understand the way in which Elizabethan and Jacobean culture defined itself. Above all, this volume proves that it is not possible to apprehend early modern English literature unless it is done transnationally.

NOTES

1 *Juan Luis Vives. De Officio Mariti: Introduction, Critical Edition, Translation and Notes*, ed. Charles Fantazzi (Leiden: Brill, 2006), introduction.
2 *Reading and the History of Race in the Renaissance* (Cambridge: Cambridge University Press, 2011), 32, 34.
3 For further critiques on romances' "poisonous" nature, see B.W. Ife, *Reading and Fiction in Golden-Age Spain: A Platonist Critique and Some Picaresque Replies* (Cambridge: Cambridge University Press, 1985), 31–4, and Marc Fumaroli, "Jacques Amyot and the Clerical Polemic against the Chivalric Novel," *Renaissance Quarterly* 38, no. 1 (1985): 30.
4 See also Simona Munari, "Translation, Re-Writing and Censorship during the Counter-Reformation," in *Translation and the Book Trade in Early Modern Europe*, ed. José María Pérez Fernández and Edward Wilson-Lee (Cambridge: Cambridge University Press, 2014), 188, and Henry Thomas, *Spanish and Portuguese Romances of Chivalry: The Revival of the Romance of Chivalry in the Spanish Peninsula, and Its Extension and Influence Abroad* (Cambridge: Cambridge University Press, 1920), 217–18.
5 Negative critical assessments of Iberian chivalric romances were directed toward the literary genre rather than at Iberian culture itself. Indeed those attacks did not differ much from those against native chivalric romances of medieval origin. As the Reformation advanced, prejudices against the genre increased when combined with anti-Catholic sentiments. Ascham's is an illustrative case of the pervasive fear among some sectors of the cultural elite for the potential impact of those Catholic or pre-Reformation works in Protestant England.
6 Various ethical and aesthetic problems these critics see may also mask their anti-Catholic stance against these books. I am grateful to Goran Stanivukovic for this observation.
7 Virginia Krause, *Idle Pursuits: Literature and Oisiveté in the French Renaissance* (Newark: University of Delaware Press, 2003), 139.
8 Translation quoted in Fumaroli, "Jacques Amyot and the Clerical Polemic," 30.
9 For different examples, see Ife, *Reading and Fiction*, 13–14.
10 Interestingly enough, Nashe's treatise was printed by John Charlewood, the main printer of Anthony Munday's translations of chivalric books of continental origin.
11 In the last two decades of the sixteenth-century there were forty-one editions of translations of Iberian chivalric books. The number of publications increased significantly in the 1590s, with seventy-one romance editions, thirty-seven of these were chivalric, while thirty-three out of those thirty-seven were of Spanish origin. For further information,

see *A Critical Edition of Anthony Munday's Palmendos, edited with an Introduction, Critical Apparatus, Notes, and Glossary*, ed. Leticia Álvarez-Recio (forthcoming), introduction.

12 Daniel Eisenberg and María del Carmen Marín Pina found up to sixty-five Spanish books of chivalry published in the sixteenth century in 176 different editions. Nineteen of these works have survived only in manuscript form. See *Bibliografía de los libros de caballerías castellanos* (Zaragoza: Prensas Universitarias de Zaragoza, 2000).

13 Southey published an abridged version of *Amadis of Gaul* in 1803 and a four-volume edition of *Palmerin of England* in 1807. For further information, see Leticia Álvarez-Recio, "Provenance and Reception of Iberian Chivalric Books in English from the Seventeenth to the Twentieth Century: The Case of Anthony Munday's *Palmendos* (1589)," *Studies in Medievalism* 30 (forthcoming).

14 Ralph Griffiths and George Edward Griffiths, "Art VI.Palmerin of England by Francisco de Moraes: Corrected by Robert Southey, from the Original Portuguese," *Monthly Review or Literary Journal* (London: Ralph Griffiths, 1809), 159; Sir Samuel Egerton Brydge, "Art. VII. The Honorable, Pleasant and Rare Conceited Historie of Palmendos," *British Bibliographer* 1 (1810): 226.

15 On their contribution, see Álvarez-Recio, "Provenance and Reception of Iberian Chivalric Books."

16 Thomas, *Spanish and Portuguese Romances*, 249. In the previous century, Robert Southey had similarly disregarded Munday's method, whose "errors" he attempted to mend in his *Palmerin* and *Amadis* editions.

17 Donald S. Crane, *The Vogue of Medieval Chivalric Romance during the English Renaissance* (Menasha, WI: George Banta, 1919), 16; Edwin H. Miller, *The Professional Writer in Elizabethan England* (Cambridge, MA: Harvard University Press, 1959), 9; Marchette Chute, *Ben Jonson of Westminster* (New York: E.P. Dutton, 1953), 57. See also Gerald R. Hayes, "Anthony Munday's Romances of Chivalry," *The Library*, 4th ser., 6 (1925): 57–81, 74, and Celeste Turner Wright, *Anthony Mundy: An Elizabethan Man of Letters* (Berkeley: University of California Press, 1928), 123–31. The exception to the rule was Clare Byrne, who vindicated Munday's literary skills in her article "Anthony Munday and His Books," *The Library* 4-I, no. 1 (1920–1): 225–56.

18 Wright, *Anthony Mundy*; Mary Patchell, *The Palmerin Romances in Elizabethan Prose Fiction* (New York: AMS Press, 1966), xii, 17.

19 See, for instance, John O'Connor, *Amadis de Gaule and Its Influence on Elizabethan Literature* (New Brunswick, NJ: Rutgers University Press, 1970), and Margaret Schlauch, "English Short Fiction in the 15th and 16th Centuries," *Studies in Short Fiction* 3 (1966): 393–434.

20 The critical editions of his prose works *Zelauto, the Fountain of Fame*, ed.
    Jack Stillinger (Carbondale: Southern Illinois University Press, 1963) and
    The English Roman Life, ed. Philip J. Ayres (Oxford: Clarendon Press, 1980)
    were quite exceptional in this regard.

21 See Tracey Hill, *Anthony Munday and Civic Culture: Theatre, History,
    and Power in Early Modern London, 1580–1633* (Manchester: Manchester
    University Press, 2004), and Donna Hamilton, *Anthony Munday and the
    Catholics, 1560–1633* (Aldershot, UK: Ashgate, 2005).

22 *Amadis de Gaule. Translated by Anthony Munday*, ed. Helen Moore
    (Aldershot, UK: Ashgate, 2004).

23 See Helen Moore, "Ancient and Modern Romance," in *The Oxford
    History of Literary Translation in English*, vol. 2, *1550–1660*, ed. Gordon
    Braden et al. (Oxford: Oxford University Press, 2010), 333–46; Alejandra
    Ortiz Salamovich, "Anthony Munday's *Palmerin d'Oliva*: Representing
    Sexual Threat in the Near East," *Sederi* 26 (2016): 67–84; Joshua Phillips,
    "Chronicles of Wasted Time: Anthony Munday, Tudor Romance, and
    Literary Labor,' *English Literary History* 73: 781–803 and *English Fiction
    of Communal Identity, 1485–1603* (Farnham, UK: Ashgate, 2013); Jordi
    Sánchez-Martí, "The Publication History of *Palmerin d'Oliva*," *Gutenberg-
    Jahrbuch* 17 (2014): 190–207 and "Zelauto's Polinarda and the Palmerin
    Romances," *Cahiers Élisabéthains* 89, no. 1 (2016): 1–9; Goran Stanivukovic,
    *Knights in Arms: Prose Romance, Masculinity, and Eastern Mediterranean Trade
    in Early Modern England, 1565–1655* (Toronto: University of Toronto Press,
    2016); Louise Wilson, "Playful Paratexts: The Front Matter of Anthony
    Munday's Iberian Romance Translations," in *Renaissance Paratexts*, ed.
    Helen Smith and Louise Wilson (Cambridge: Cambridge University Press,
    2011), 121–32 and "The Publication of Iberian Romance in Early Modern
    Europe," in *Translation and the Book Trade in Early Modern Europe*, ed. José
    María Pérez Pérez and Edward Wilson-Lee (Cambridge: Cambridge
    University Press, 2014), 201–16. See also Leticia Álvarez-Recio, "Anthony
    Munday's *Palmendos* (1589) in the Early Modern English Book Trade:
    Print and Reception,' *Atlantis* 38, no. 1 (2016): 53–69, "Spanish Chivalric
    Romances in English Translation," *Cahiers Élisabéthains* 91, no. 1 (2016):
    5–20, and "Translations of Spanish Chivalry Works in the Jacobean
    Book Trade: Shelton's *Don Quixote* in the Light of Anthony Munday's
    Publications," *Renaissance Studies* 33, no. 5 (2019): 691–711.

24 See Melanie Ord, "Representing Rome and the Self in Anthony Munday's
    The English Romayne Life," in *Travels and Translations in the Sixteenth
    Century*, ed. Mike Pincombe (Aldershot, UK: Ashgate, 2004), 45–61;
    Hamilton, *Anthony Munday and the Catholics*; Christopher Highley,
    Catholics Writing the Nation in Early Modern Britain and Ireland (Oxford:
    Oxford University Press, 2008), 145–50; and Brian C. Lockey, *Early Modern*

Catholics, Royalists, and Cosmopolitans: English Transnationalism and the Christian Commonwealth (Farnham, UK: Ashgate, 2015), ch. 2.

25 See Tiffany J. Werth, *The Fabulous Dark Cloister: Romance in England after the Reformation* (Baltimore: John Hopkins University Press, 2011), and Christina Wald, *The Reformation of Romance: The Eucharist, Disguise, and Foreign Fashion in Early Modern Prose Fiction* (Berlin: Walter de Gruyter, 2014).

26 *Renaissance Cultural Crossroads: Translation, Print and Culture in Britain, 1473–1640*, ed. S.K. Barker et al. (Leiden and Boston: Brill, 2013); Braden et al., *The Oxford History of Literary Translation in English*, vol. 2, *1550–1660*; *English Renaissance Translation Theory*, ed. Neil Rhodes et al. (London: MHRA, 2013); Pérez Fernández and Wilson-Lee, eds., *Translation and the Book Trade*; and Fred Schurink, ed., *Tudor Translation* (Basingstoke, UK: Palgrave, 2011).

27 The Modern Humanities Research Association (MHRA) and the Arizona Center for Medieval and Renaissance Studies (ACMRS) have started publishing a series of critical editions of some of the most representative English translations of the Spanish books of chivalry. The edition of Margaret Tyler's *Mirror of Princely Deed and Knighthood*, by Joyce Boro, was published by MHRA in 2014; Books I and II of *Palmerin d'Oliva*, edited by Jordi Sánchez-Martí, have been published by ACMRS in 2020, while the edition of the first book of *Palmerin of England* by Louise Wilson is expected to be published by MHRA in 2020–21. Leticia Álvarez-Recio has recently completed her edition of *Palmendos* as well. The publication of these editions confirms the current interest of Anglo-Iberian studies in this corpus and will most probably encourage future research on these texts, which are now more easily available to the scholarly community.

28 Munday was the main, though not the only, translator of the Iberian corpus. Margaret Tyler's translation of the first book of *Espejo de príncipes y cavalleros*, published in 1578 as *The Mirrour of Princely Deedes and Knighthood* (STC 18859) was later reprinted in 1580 and 1599 (STC 18860–1). Other books of this cycle, rendered into English by Robert Parry and L.A., were published in different editions from 1583 to 1601 (STC 18863–71). L.A. did also translate *Don Bellianis* in 1598 (STC 1804). Two different versions of the same text were sometimes translated and printed by different authors; such was the case with Munday's *Palmendos* and William Barley's *Celestina The Faire*, the English renderings of *Primaleón de Grecia* (Book 1).

29 Lockey, *Early Modern Catholics*, 8.

PART ONE

Iberian Chivalric Romance in the Early Modern English Book Trade

Chapter One

The Publication of Chivalric Romances in England, 1570–1603

JORDI SÁNCHEZ-MARTÍ

During the manuscript period, chivalric literature exerted a fascination in late medieval England and continued to do so after the introduction of the printing press, whose multiplying effect eventually made chivalric books accessible to all levels of society. The genre's successful circulation in print is, to a certain extent, attributable to the efforts of several generations of early printers, especially William Caxton (d. 1492), Wynkyn de Worde (d. 1535), and William Copland (d. 1569), who relied on two types of source materials: first, prose romances of continental origin that were translated into English in order to be printed; and, second, English traditional verse romances whose manuscript copies were still available and used as copytexts.[1] From 1473, when Caxton published *Recuyell of the Histories of Troie* (STC 15375),[2] his own translation of Raoul Lefèvre's French original, until Copland died in 1569, approximately one hundred editions of thirty-seven different romance texts were printed in English, a clear indication of the strong appeal the genre held among English readers and book buyers.

When Copland passed away, however, there were signs suggesting that English customers were starting to desert chivalric romances, not because the genre had lost its lustre, but because printers had overused their sources of chivalric materials. Between 1547 and 1567, when Copland was active as a printer, a total of forty editions of medieval romance texts were published, all of which had already been printed before 1531.[3] It seems that, in the mid-sixteenth century, printers failed to unearth unprinted medieval romances and instead simply reissued works with previous print circulation, thus diminishing the market value of this literary corpus. As a result, at the end of the 1560s there was a market anomaly: while English readers were willing to spend money on chivalric romances, printers were unable to meet their customers' desire for variety and novelty. This chapter, first, analyses some of the underlying causes that led to the decline of romance texts during the 1560s and to their disappearance in the decade following Copland's death. Next, considering that the literary tastes and preferences of the English reading public changed in the course of the sixteenth century, I examine important social developments of the 1560s and 1570s that affected the book trade in general and the consumption of medieval romances in particular. Finally, I explore some of the decisions and strategies Elizabethan printers and publishers adopted to remove their predecessors' product bottleneck and thus meet the commercial demand for chivalric literature to the end of the sixteenth century and beyond.

Between 19 July 1557 and 9 July 1558, just a few months after the Stationers' Company was incorporated, John King (active 1555–61) was granted a licence to print two Middle English verse romances, namely, "*a Jeste of syr GAWAYNE*" and "*syr LAMWELL*."[4] King, who was one of the original members of the Stationers' Company, registered another two metrical romances on 10 June 1560, namely, "*The squyre of Low degre /* and *syr DEGGRE*."[5] These four verse romances had not appeared in print for quite some time, so the printer was probably hopeful to find a market for them and make a profit.[6] Other printers soon followed King's example and obtained licences to print Middle English verse romances up until 1561.[7] This renewed interest in popular English romances was most likely prompted by Copland, who, from 1553 and throughout the rest of the decade, printed some seven or eight editions of chivalric romances, in both verse and prose. Certainly, he must have been displeased to find other printers competing with him for the same line of business, and he responded quickly by issuing editions of exactly the same romance texts his competitors had already registered. In doing so, Copland was contravening the Stationers' Company's licensing system but also sending a strong message that the entire romance corpus was off-limits to all other printers.[8]

Having thwarted his adversaries' attempts to expand their business into the publication of English medieval romances, Copland effectively obtained a printing privilege over the genre. By restraining all competition, he was also curbing further business activity that could have helped diversify the catalogue of printed romances available, as happened at the turn of the sixteenth century. Then, Wynkyn de Worde had a dominant position comparable to Copland's but could not prevent his competitors from printing the *editiones principes* of various Middle English romances. Eventually, this early competition redounded to De

Worde's benefit, as, later on, he reprinted those same romances his business rivals had first put on the market.[9] Thus, Copland's monopolizing of the market in printed romances, paradoxically, precipitated the genre's commercial decline during the 1560s.

Although Copland contrived to frustrate his competitors' plans, they remained intent on exploiting the English medieval romances and simply postponed any further action until after Copland retired in 1567. John Allde (active 1555–84) and Thomas Purfoot (active 1542?–1615) were quick to react and, before the decade was over, registered three Middle English verse romances, namely, *Bevis of Hampton* – the medieval romance most frequently printed throughout the sixteenth century[10] – together with *Generides* and *Richard Coeur de Lion*, which had not been published since 1518(?) and 1528, respectively (STC 11721.7, 21008).[11] These intended publications suggest that the notion that the romance genre was potentially lucrative continued to exist at least until the end of the 1560s. There is, however, no evidence that either Allde or Purfoot actually printed the romance texts they had registered. Not only did they apparently abstain from publishing these works, but not a single medieval English romance was printed throughout the entire 1570s.[12] With a transmission history of four centuries, it would appear that medieval romances were finally becoming obsolete and out of fashion.

If Allde, Purfoot, and the rest of early printers neglected the entire corpus of Middle English romances during the 1570s, they all must have perceived that the genre's status in the literary book market had changed. The end of Copland's printing career coincided with a period of profound educational transformations that affected England's sociocultural development, altering its literary landscape. The 1560s and 1570s saw an impressive growth in literacy that was not limited to the ruling elite and men of commerce, the sectors of English society that traditionally had more access to formal education, but also reached yeomen, tradesmen, craftsmen, and husbandmen.[13] The members of these various groups did not receive the same standard of education, but instead acquired different levels of literacy skills ranging from passive literacy (the ability to read but not to write) to active literacy (the ability to read and write). The expansion of literacy skills was a concrete result of the so-called educational revolution, which started around 1560, when there was a marked increase in the number of educational foundations that were meant for people belonging to all strata of the social structure.[14] Literacy abilities were acquired in formal contexts, but also in informal ones, such as the family, where the practices typical of institutional settings were used as models.[15] Since

Elizabethan children were taught how to read before they learned to write, and many had their primary education interrupted, passive literacy became not only more common but also a more widespread social expectation.[16]

Reading also made it possible to have a personal and unmediated encounter with the Bible, thus becoming a vehicle for spiritual improvement. In fact, reading instruction generally progressed from Alexander Nowell's *Catechism*, a compulsory textbook in all schools after 1571,[17] to the Bible, a text in prose with a complex narrative design.[18] Ample segments of English society, including the urban popular classes, used prose texts like Nowell's *Catechism* to acquire a reading competence, which became aspirational among less privileged households.[19] The impact of these new cohorts of readers with varying reading skills must have been felt in England's book market, as the numbers of potential bookshop customers increased significantly.

Concurrent with this educational advance, another circumstance started to materialize in the second half of the 1560s – namely, the emergence of prose fiction in English. In contrast to the continent, where prose had been the predominant form for narrative fiction for quite some time, in England the choice of prose was a late development originating in the fifteenth century. The early printers, particularly Caxton, privileged the publication of prose romances, which never actually won the favour of the reading public.[20] When verse romances appeared in print, possibly with the publication of *Guy of Warwick* around 1497–98, the public response was much more enthusiastic,[21] although the production of editions of prose romances was not discontinued.

Initially, the new forays into prose fiction took the form of short narratives or novellas that were part of a story collection or miscellany, as in the case of the earliest exponent of this new fashion, William Painter's (1540?–94) *Palace of Pleasure* (1566; STC 19121),[22] and its closest competitor, Geoffrey Fenton's (ca. 1539–1608) *Certaine Tragicall Discourses* (1567; STC 1356.1). These short narratives soon developed into lengthier prose stories that may be considered as proto-novels, as is the case of George Gascoigne's (1534/5?–77) innovative *Discourse of the Adventures Passed by Master F.J.* (1573), still published as part of a literary miscellany titled *A Hundreth Sundrie Flowres* (STC 11635).[23] This process of narrative experimentation in prose culminated in 1578 when Thomas East (active 1565–1608) published John Lyly's (1554–1606) *Euphues: The Anatomy of Wyt* (STC 17051), a work that marked the beginning of a new era in which "the dominant form of fiction was the single-story book."[24] In short, between 1566 and 1578, writers from Painter to Lyly contributed to sanctioning the use of prose as the preferred form for the expression of narrative fiction.

In such a changing sociocultural environment, as literary fashions and conventions were being redefined, printers had to adapt to new market conditions and be sensitive to their customers' needs, rather than persist in publishing the same age-old narratives. Thus, it is not surprising that, without delay, printers shelved their plans to print the registered Middle English metrical romances and instead explored the market potential of new prose works of fiction. For instance, Thomas Marshe (active 1554–87) never used his licence to print *Bevis of Hampton*, obtained in 1558/9, but grasped the opportunity to publish Fenton's *Certaine Tragicall Discourses*, which appeared in the wake of Painter's *Palace of Pleasure*. The favourable reception of both of these prose works, reprinted on many occasions, opened up possibilities for developing new product lines in prose fiction. With its long-lasting history, chivalric romance seemed an obvious choice, provided that printers managed to attract the traditional consumers of the English verse romances and convince them to transition to prose.

In order to satisfy the resilient market demand for chivalric fiction, Elizabethan printers initially pursued two avenues that resembled the ones frequented by their predecessors at the beginning of the sixteenth century. First, they tried to revive the Middle English romances that the previous generations of English printers had published. Next, they promoted the importation and translation of continental chivalric romances in prose that had achieved commercial success elsewhere. Finally, during the 1590s, printers also added one further source of chivalric fiction and put on the market medievalizing romances freshly composed by English writers.

As mentioned above, no single edition of a Middle English romance was published during the 1570s, but the register of the Stationers' Company, despite being incomplete, records an abiding interest in exploiting this corpus (see table 1).[25] The paradigm shift from verse to prose was also transferred to medieval romances, which before had been predominantly in verse. Of the fourteen licences of medieval romances granted in the last quarter of the sixteenth century, only two refer to texts in verse, namely, *Bevis* and *Eglamour of Artois*. The choice of titles, moreover, suggests that Elizabethan printers wanted to avoid market saturation, since they registered mainly works not printed by William Copland, except for romances with enduring commercial demand such as *Bevis* and Malory's *Morte Darthur*.[26]

Table 1. Licences to print English medieval romances, 1576–1603

Date	Title	Licensee	Arber
17 July 1576	*Prince Apollonius*	William Howe	2:301
15 January 1582	*Eglamour of Artois*	John Charlewood (from Sampson Awdeley)	2:405
	King Ponthus	John Charlewood	2:405
12 March 1582	*Arthur of Little Britain*	Thomas East	2:408
	Bevis of Hampton	Thomas East	2:408
	Four Sons of Aymon	Thomas East	2:408
	Malory, *Morte Darthur*	Thomas East	2:408
	Oliver of Castille	Thomas East	2:408
8 August 1586	*Paris and Vienne*	Thomas Purfoot	2:453
	Valentine and Orson	Thomas Purfoot	2:453
23 June 1591	*Recuyell* [in meter]	Thomas Orwyn	2:586
20 May 1595	*Blanchardine*	William Blackwall	2:298
5 February 1599	*Four Sons of Aymon*	Thomas Purfoot, sen.	3:137
22 February 1599	*Four Sons of Aymon* (last part)	John Wolfe	3:139

The importation and translation of continental romances opened up more exciting business opportunities. A new publication trend was started on 20 May 1577, when John Jugge (active 1576–88) obtained a licence to print *"Gerillion of Englande"* (Arber II, 312), the English translation of Étienne de Maisonneufve's French original. An edition of *Gerileon* was finally printed in 1578 by John Kingston for Miles Jennings (see table 3). This edition appeared in a favourable commercial context characterized, first, by the appetite for continental works in English translation – which peaked at the end of the 1570s – and, second, by the expansionist policies of the metropolitan book trade, which saw "an unprecedented jump in published London titles" in the same decade.[27]

Although Jennings's move seems opportune, his edition of *Gerileon* was never reprinted, probably an indication that it failed to achieve the success he had hoped. The cause for this edition's apparent failure lies not so much in the choice of genre or even of text, but most likely in its poor translation, which was done by "a certaine yonge man, more hardie and venturous in attempte, then luckie and Fortunate in atchieuaunce," as Jennings reveals in the dedicatory epistle (*1ʳ). In order to profit from the unflagging demand for chivalric literature, Jennings was seeking an alternative to English medieval romances, and, in so doing, opened the eyes of other publishers and printers to the possibilities afforded by continental prose romances. The first to follow Jennings's example was

Thomas East, who, on 4 August 1578, registered *The Mirrour of Knighthood and Princely Deedes* (Arber II, 334), translated directly from the Spanish by Margaret Tyler (active 1558–78).[28] Tyler's careful translation must have contributed to the commercial success of East's edition of *Mirrour*, first printed before the end of 1578 (STC 18859) and reprinted again by East in 1580 (STC 18860) (see table 3).

In view of the public reception of East's editions of *Mirrour*, it became apparent to other London stationers that chivalric romances continued to be commercially attractive and viable, even if they were in prose. The printer John Charlewood (active 1553?–93) was quick to react and on 13 February 1581 licensed *Palmerin of England* (Arber II, 388), although he was not yet in possession of a complete translation of this work.[29] In taking such a pre-emptive business action, Charlewood was bargaining for the growth of continental chivalric romances in the English book market and, at the same time, positioning himself advantageously to reap the benefits of anticipating his competitors. He tried to do the same in January 1582 by registering the Middle English romances *Eglamour* and *King Ponthus*, this time provoking an immediate response from East, who just two months later licensed five English medieval romances (see table 1). The concentration of seven licenses to print Middle English romances early in 1582 is indicative of intense competition for the market in chivalric fiction between Charlewood and East. Moreover, it also suggests that English medieval romances still retained sufficient market value to justify going head-to-head with a business rival.

While East did put on the market three printed Middle English romances of those that were licenced to him, we have no evidence that Charlewood printed either of the two medieval texts he had entered in January 1582 (see table 2). Thinking he would be getting only meagre returns from these works, Charlewood got cold feet, whereas East felt more optimistic about his choice of texts, which included Malory's *Morte* and *Bevis*, two works that had been in print since the incunabular period. So confident was East in the case of Malory's *Morte* (STC 804) that he retained the folio format and commissioned six woodcuts for this edition, since he had only two of the twenty-six woodcuts used by Copland in 1557.[30] By contrast, East significantly changed the textual presentation of *Bevis* in order to have it approximate the more fashionable visual rhetoric of prose. Instead of printing each line of verse separately, as was the convention, he printed each couplet as one single line (see figure 1). In an attempt to stop the genre's decline, East experimented with the textual layout of verse at a time when the metrical romances were definitively falling out of favour among English

Table 2. Medieval English romances printed between 1570 and 1603

Date	Title	Printer	Format	STC
1578	Malory, *Morte Darthur*	Thomas East	fol.	805
1582	*Arthur of Little Britain*	Thomas East	4°	808
ca. 1585	*Bevis of Hampton*	Thomas East	4°	1990
1594	*Prince Apollonius*	V. Simmes for E. Newman	4°	709, 709.5
1595	*Blanchardyn and Eglantine*	E. Allde for W. Blackwall	4°	3125
1596	*Recuyell of the Histories of Troy*	T. Creede and V. Simmes	4°	15379
1597	*Blanchardyn and Eglantine*	G. Shaw for W. Blackwall	4°	3126
1601	*Huon of Burdeux*	T. Purfoot for E. White	4°	13999

audiences. Despite all his efforts, the metrical romances' decline was inexorable and most probably explains why in 1586 the London printer and bookseller Thomas Vautrollier (1564–1600?) got rid of a stock of fifty unbound copies of the Middle English verse romance *Squire of Low Degree.* It accounted for the largest number of books contained in the cargo Vautrollier shipped from London to Scotland, as if he felt that this kind of book had more exciting prospects in the Scottish book market, which was less competitive and less saturated than the metropolitan one.[31]

English customers were no longer enthusiastic about medieval romances and, therefore, it is no surprise that, with his edition of *Bevis* of ca. 1585, East discontinued the publication of Middle English romances altogether. The change in the public attitude toward this medieval corpus may be illustrated by Robert Ashley (1565–1641), a translator and book collector with an Oxford education and founder of the library of the Middle Temple. Between ca. 1607 and 1614, Ashley wrote an autobiographical account in Latin, now preserved in the British Library, titled "Vita R. A. ab ipso conscripta" (figure 2).[32] There Ashley recounts the main events in his life, from the very moment of his birth, and pays special attention to his education. At one point, he recalls some of the books he read as a youth, before turning twenty, and admits he became so immersed in the chivalric romances that they kept him away from his school duties, even at the expense of eating and sleeping. The romances he remembers reading before 1584, which he describes as "fictas et futiles fabellas," include "qualia de Bevisio Hamtonensi Guidone Warwicensi Historia Valentini et Orsoni, vita Arthuri Regis Britaniae et equitum orbicularis mensae circumferetur."[33] The fact that, in the late 1570s and early 1580s, these works could be seen

Beuis of Hampton.

That thou ſitteſt vppon there, he was my bꝛothers ſir Grandere.
God knoweth then ſayd Beuis, I choꝛe ſir Grauuders crowne ywis.
When we met laſt in battayle, I made him Deacon withouten fayle.
And if that thou wilt oꝛder take, a Pꝛieſt ſayd Beuis I ſhall thee make.
Alas ſaid the Gyaut foꝛ ſir Grandere, his death is, if thou abide ſƿ here.
To ſir Beuis he ſmote full ſoꝛe, but of Beuis he fayꝺ thoꝛe.
And hit Trunchefice in that ſtound, that he fell dead vnto the ground.
Beuis ſtart vp without reſpite, and to the Gyant gathe ſmite.
Such a ſtroke was not ſeene in no land, ſithen Oliuer dyed and Rouland.
The Gyaunt ſaw y̆ Beuis was ſtrong, he dꝛew out a dart ſharpe & long.

E.i.   Thꝛough

1. *Bevis of Hampton* (Thomas East, 1582). Bodleian Library, University of Oxford, shelfmark S. seld. D. 45.(2), sig. E1ʳ. By permission.

2. Robert Ashley, *Vita*. BL, Sloane MS 2131, fol. 18ʳ. © The British Library Board. By permission.

as suitable reading matter for children and youth is indicative of the genre's devaluation in the public sphere.[34] This growing perception of English medieval romances as children's books explains why printers were reluctant to print them after Copland's death. In addition, owing to its alleged association with the Catholic past, this literary corpus also attracted the censure of other contemporary writers, including Thomas Nashe (1567–1601), who railed against medieval romances in his 1589 *Anatomie of Absurditie* (STC 18364).[35] Consequently, during the 1580s, printers perceived Middle English romances as "worne out," in Nashe's words, and as having no value in the English book market.[36]

East must have also considered Charlewood's licensing of *Palmerin of England* as undue interference and, in August 1582, retaliated by registering "*the seconde parte of the mirror of knighthoode* to be translated into Englishe."[37] It would appear that East closely monitored Charlewood's moves and, in licensing a work that had yet to be translated into English, East was clearly following his competitor's example. Of course, both East and Charlewood were competing and being tactical over the rights to publish chivalric literature, but their manoeuvres also had consequences for the geographical distribution of these works. Between 1577 and 1588, when East was claiming his ascendancy over medieval English romances and the cycle of *Mirror of Knighthood*, he had his premises by Paul's Wharf in the south of London. At the same time and from the opposite end of the city, in Barbican, Cripplegate, Charlewood was jockeying for the right to print chivalric romances, but he concentrated his energies on the cycle of *Palmerin*, of which he printed three separate works.[38] By respecting each other's literary and geographical territories, East and Charlewood showed restraint in their rivalry, probably aided by the licensing system of the Stationers' Company.

If we consider East's and Charlewood's output of chivalric romances, the former published many more editions than the latter, thus suggesting that East had the upper hand, either because he had more capital resources or because he was willing to take more risks than Charlewood. In fact, when Charlewood printed a romance, he did so only after securing the financial support of some bookseller publisher, whereas East could do without involving a publisher. While between 1566 and 1589 East "printed forty-three books, of which sixteen only were for himself,"[39] it is significant that his editions of romances belong to the group that he printed for himself, as if printing the genre was more of a personal choice.

This state of affairs changed significantly after 1587, when East abandoned the publication of romances altogether and instead specialized in printing music as assign of the composer William Byrd, who obtained a royal patent for music printing from 1575 to 1596.[40] In similar fashion, on 30 October 1587, Charlewood secured an exclusive license for "The onelye ympryntinge of *all manner of Billes for players*" (Arber II, 477), which was sufficiently lucrative and provided him with a stable revenue stream, although he did not entirely stop printing romances.[41] After East and Charlewood temporarily withdrew from printing chivalric fiction, the publication of continental chivalric romances was not interrupted, thanks to Anthony Munday (ca. 1560–1633), who translated the entire cycle of *Palmerin* and the opening books of the cycle of *Amadis*, and was probably the inexpert translator of the first part of *Gerileon* too.[42] It would appear that Munday translated these chivalric romances as a freelancer and then convinced various publishers to cover the cost of printing them. This method of working was unusual in Elizabethan England,[43] but Munday used it successfully, owing to his inside knowledge of the London book trade. His father, Christopher Munday (n.d.), was a stationer, and, after he died, Munday became an apprentice to the printer John Allde on 1 October 1576 (Arber II, 69). In addition, Munday's living quarters were in Cripplegate, at least from 1584 to 1589, a location that must have enabled him to build up valuable business contacts among printers and stationers whose premises where in the same neighbourhood, including Charlewood and Edward Allde (active 1584–1627), the son of Munday's former master.[44]

During the 1590s, after East and Charlewood stopped printing romances, the leading figures in the publication of chivalric literature were the bookseller Cuthbert Burby (1592–1607) and the printer Thomas Creede (1578–1619). Burby was apprenticed to William Wright (active 1574?–1624) from 1583 until he took up his freedom on 13 January 1592. During this period, Wright commissioned the publication of Munday's *Palmerin d'Oliva*, and it is likely that Burby began a business relationship with Munday. During the same year that Burby established his own operation, he published the first edition of Munday's translation of *Gerileon II*, and, in the following years up until 1596, he financed the publication of three further chivalric romances translated by Munday (see table 3). It has been contended that Burby's success as a publisher sprang from his astute commercial practices that minimized risk by "investing in titles with proven market records."[45] Yet none of the romances published by Burby had previously appeared in print. He probably had an aversion to risk, but, in his view, printing romances was relatively safe, since the genre had a proven market record. Just like East in the preceding decade, Burby also made an exception with chivalric literature.

Burby's more enterprising strategy contrasts with Thomas Creede's conservative approach to printing romances. Apprenticed to Thomas

Table 3. English translations of continental chivalric romances, 1570–1603

Year	Title	Printer	Translator	STC
1578	Gerileon of England, pt. I	J. Kingston for M. Jennings	A. Munday	17203
1578	Mirror of Knighthood, bk. 1	Thomas East	M. Tyler	18859
1580?	Mirror of Knighthood, bk. 1	Thomas East	M. Tyler	18860
1581–1585?	Palmerin of England, pt. I–II	J. Charlewood? for W. Wright?	A. Munday	–
1583	Mirror of Knighthood, bk. 4–5	Thomas East	R. P[arry]	18866
1585	Mirror of Knighthood, bk. 2	Thomas East	R. P[arry]	18862–2.5
1586?	Mirror of Knighthood, bk. 3	Thomas East	R. P[arry]	18864
1588	Palmerin d'Oliva, pt. I–II	J. Charlewood for W. Wright	A. Munday	19157
1588	Palladine of England	Edward Allde for John Perrin	A. Munday	5541
1589	Palmendos	J. Charlewood for S. Watersonne	A. Munday	18064
1590?	Amadis de Gaule, bk. 1	Edward Allde	A. Munday	541
1592	Gerileon of England, pt. II	T. Scarlet(?) for C. Burby	A. Munday	17206
1595	Amadis de Gaule, bk. 2	A. Islip for C. Burby	A. Munday	542
1595	Primaleon of Greece, bk. 1	J. Danter for C. Burby	A. Munday	20366
1596	Primaleon of Greece, bk. 2	J. Danter for C. Burby	A. Munday	20366a
1596	Palmerin of England, pt. I–II	Thomas Creede	A. Munday	19161
1596	Palmendos (Celestina)	A. Islip for W. Barley	W. Barley?	4910
1597	Palmerin d'Oliva, pt. I–II	Thomas Creede	A. Munday	19158
1598	Amadis de Gaule, bk. 5	A. Islip, sold by H. Jackson	–	542.5
1598	Bellianis	Thomas Creede	L.A.	1804
1598	Mirror of Knighthood, bk. 4–5	Thomas East	R.P.	18867
1598	Mirror of Knighthood, bk. 6	Thomas East	R.P.	18868
1598	Mirror of Knighthood, bk. 7	T. Purfoot for C. Burby	L.A.	18869

(Continued)

Table 3. (Continued)

Year	Title	Printer	Translator	STC
1598–99?	*Mirror of Knighthood*, bk. 3	Thomas East	R.P.	18865
1599	*Mirror of Knighthood*, k. 2	Thomas East	R.P.	18863
1599	*Mirror of Knighthood*, bk. 8	T. Creede for C. Burby	L.A.	18870
1599?	*Mirror of Knighthood*, bk. 1	Thomas East	M. Tyler	18861
1601	*Mirror of Knighthood*, bk. 9	S. Stafford for C. Burby	R. Parry?	18871
1602	*Palmerin of England*, pt. III	J. Roberts for W. Leake	A. Munday	19165

Note: The first edition of *Palmerin of England* is listed because there is evidence that it was indeed printed, although no copy has been pre-served. I attribute this edition to Charlewood, because he entered this title in 1581 (Arber II, 388), and it seems highly probable that Wright was the publisher, since he owned the licence when it was transferred to Scarlet in 1596 (Arber III, 68) and also financed Charlewood's edition of *Palmerin d'Oliva*. Although the translation of *Amadis*, Book 2, was done by a certain Lazarus Pyott, I assign it to Anthony Munday, since Celeste Wright has convincingly argued that Munday used that name as a pseudonym; see "'Lazarus Pyott' and Other Inventions of Anthony Mundy," *Philological Quarterly* 56 (1959): 150–68.

East, Creede preferred to reprint works that had already been tested in the book market, as were, for instance, *Palmerin d'Oliva* and *Palmerin of England*. Only in the case of *Bellianis of Greece* (1598) did he venture to print the first edition of an Iberian romance, but this he did in a context favourable to chivalric fiction, when the genre seemed to be in vogue.[46] So fashionable did chivalric fiction become in the final years of the sixteenth century that, when East temporarily stopped benefiting from the music monopoly, he went back to print various parts of *Mirror of Knighthood*, probably a kind of publication he considered commercially and financially safe and reliable.[47] This renewed interest in *Mirror* also attracted Burby, who decided to profit from it by printing the first edition of *Mirror*'s Books 7 and 9. Likewise, other publishers that had shown no previous interest in the genre decided to cash in on its popularity, as did the booksellers William Barley (active 1591–1614) and Hugh Jackson (active 1572–1616), who published, respectively, *Palmendos* and *Amadis*'s Book 5.[48] The publication of chivalric fiction intensified in the second half of the 1590s, with at least sixteen editions of Iberian romances printed between 1595 and 1600, thus confirming that the market for chivalric romances became particularly vibrant at the end of the Elizabethan period.

During the 1590s, the fascination with English translations of Iberian romances served as a catalyst to encourage the publication of other types of chivalric fiction. All seemed to indicate that Middle English romances fell out of favour after Copland's death and, thereafter, were perceived as old fashioned, even obsolete. It is therefore surprising that this literary corpus resurfaced once again with the publication of five editions of English medieval romances between 1594 and 1601. Printers, however, had to adapt this corpus to new market conditions and expectations; that is why they printed only romances that were in prose, and some works were offered in revised and modernized versions.[49] This medieval corpus continued to be commercially relevant at the end of the Elizabethan period, thus proving once again its resilience and protean nature.

One additional effect of Iberian romances' commercial success was their influence over aspiring English writers, who, in the 1590s, started to reproduce the same narrative modes, copying motifs, plots, and even the style of the continental works (see table 4).[50] For the first time since Malory completed his *Morte Darthur* around 1470, English narrators cultivated the genre of chivalric romance in their own language and not as a translation. The first English writer to experiment with the composition of a new chivalric romance was Henry Robarts (active 1585–1617), whose family connection with the Stationers' Company

Table 4. Chivalric romances composed in English, 1570–1603

Year	Author	Title	Printer	STC
1590	Henry Robarts	A Defiance to Fortune	A. Jeffes for J. Proctor	21078
1595	Henry Robarts	Pheander, the Mayden Knight	Thomas Creede	21086
1595	R[obert] P[arry]	Moderatus	Richard Jones	19337
1596	Richard Johnson	Seven Champions of Christendom, pt. I	J. Danter for C. Burby	14677
1597	Richard Johnson	Seven Champions of Christendome, pt. II	E. Allde(?) for C. Burby	14678
1597	Christopher Middleton	Chinon of England	J. Danter for C. Burby	17866
1598	Henry Robarts	Honours conquest	Thomas Creede	21082
1598	Emanuel Forde	Parismus	Thomas Creede for R. Olive	11171
1599	Emanuel Forde	Parismenos	Thomas Creede for R. Olive and W. Holme	11171.2
1599?	Emanuel Forde	Ornatus and Artesia	Thomas Creede	11168

must have given him an excellent vantage point from which to detect and follow market trends. With this first-hand knowledge, Robarts ventured to write a romance titled *A Defiance to Fortune* (1590; STC 21078), which has been described as "an undistinguished romance" and was never reprinted.[51]

The English romancers started to excite public attention in 1595, when Creede and Burby, at the same time that they were publishing the Iberian books of chivalry, decided also to promote new chivalric fiction in English. Once again, Creede acted as a printer publisher, but this time he had no qualms about producing the *editio princeps* of some of these texts, as he did with *Pheander* (1595; STC 21086) and *Honours Conquest* (1598; 21082) – two other romances by Robarts – and with Emanuel Forde's (n.d.) *Ornatus and Artesia* (1599?; STC 11168). This doesn't mean that Creede was not exercising caution: if he was willing to publish these *editiones principes*, it was because the works of Robarts and Forde had already been tested on the market. Notwithstanding, Creede tried to reduce financial risks whenever he could and, despite having the licence to print Forde's *Parismus* and its sequel, *Parismenos*, he sought the collaboration of the booksellers William Holme (active 1589–1606?) and Richard Olive (1580–1603) to print Forde's works.[52] By contrast, Burby continued displaying entrepreneurial initiative and did not hesitate to finance the first edition of Richard Johnson's (active 1592–1622) *Seven Champions of Christendom*, parts I and II (1596–7; STC 14677–8), which were well received by the reading public.[53] In 1597 Burby also published Christopher Middleton's (d. 1628) chivalric narrative *Chinon of England* (1597; STC 17866), a work that was never reprinted.[54] Finally, the printer Richard Jones (active 1564–1613) produced an edition of *Moderatus, or the Adventures of the Black Knight* (1595; STC 19377), a chivalric narrative composed by Robert Parry (active 1590–1612). It seems probable that Parry was the same individual who translated the *Mirror of Knighthood* for Thomas East during the 1580s, although he was now wearing the hat of writer of chivalric romance, a genre he was well acquainted with and that could earn him some money.[55]

In the final part of the sixteenth century, the economies of the London book trade were transformed and expanded by the rise of new generations of readers and book buyers who had benefited from the educational revolution that began in the 1560s. This new reading class formed a substantial and socially diverse group whose literary tastes and expectations differed from the aesthetic preferences and demands of the book market's traditional clientele. Accordingly, there were great financial gains to be made by those stationers who knew how to cater to these new customers belonging to social strata that were below the level of the elite. Considering that chivalric literature was a favourite of popular audiences since medieval times, it seems natural that printers and publishers considered the romance genre as a potentially profitable option.

During the 1570s, before the effects of the educational advances that began in the 1560s were felt in the market place, Middle English romances vanished from bookstalls; toward the end of the decade, printers started, instead, to successfully publish English translations of Iberian romances. It appeared that these continental narratives were going to entirely displace English medieval romances, thus renewing this age-old romance genre. In fact, from 1578 until the mid-1590s, Iberian romances were published steadily, whereas Middle English romances remained unavailable in print, with the exception of only the three editions produced by East in 1582. Yet, paradoxically, the cultivation of the Iberian books of chivalry and their market penetration, rather than wiping medieval English romances off the map, ultimately ended up by reviving this literary corpus, with editions being printed from 1594 onward. In addition, this revival of interest in chivalric fiction stimulated the composition of new chivalric romances in English for the first time since the introduction of the printing press in England. In sum, printers and publishers recognized that they could gain a commercial advantage by diversifying their range of chivalric fiction, and, as a result, they encouraged the proliferation of printed chivalric materials in three different product lines: medieval English romances, translations of Iberian books of chivalry, and chivalric fiction newly created in English. Thomas Creede clearly exemplifies this commercial strategy, as in 1595–6 he put on the market titles representing each individual product line: Robarts's *Pheander*, in 1595, and the medieval *Recuyell* and the Iberian *Palmerin of England*, in 1596.

With more than thirty separate editions of romances issued during the 1590s, the publication of medieval and medievalizing chivalric romance occupied a prominent place in the English literary book market at the end of the sixteenth century. With such an unprecedented concentration of chivalric publications, the romance genre continued to be the most popular and most successful expression of secular literature at the end of the Elizabethan period. This tremendous enthusiasm for chivalric fiction, however, was not to everyone's liking and was frowned upon, for instance, by Francis Meres (1565/6–1647) in his *Palladis Tamia*, printed for Burby in 1598 (STC 17834).[56] Unfortunately, modern scholarship has also shown prejudice against this literary phenomenon: it has generally focused on those early modern texts that seem sophisticated to modern-day readers, according to anachronistic criteria, but has failed to give due consideration to some of the actual literary texts that were consumed by, and successful among, Elizabethan readers and customers. In order to compensate for the distortions of literary history, both past and present, and establish a more accurate picture of Elizabethan literary culture, it is imperative that we channel more of our energies into determining and scrutinizing the literature read and favoured by the actual Elizabethans.

NOTES

1 Only one prose romance originally composed in English was printed during the first century of printing in England – namely, Thomas Malory's *Le Morte Darthur*, whose manuscript copy (BL, Add. MS 59678) was consulted by Caxton for his 1485 edition; see E. Gordon Duff, *A Century of the English Book Trade* (London: Bibliographical Society, 1905), 283; Lotte Hellinga, "William Caxton and the Malory Manuscript," in *Texts in Transit: Manuscript to Proof and Print in the Fifteenth Century* (Leiden: Brill, 2014), 410–29. The manuscript version of *The Lyfe of Ipomydon*, contained in booklet I of BL, Harley MS 2252, served as copytext for Wynkyn de Worde's edition of ca. 1523–24 (STC 5732.5); see Carol M. Meale, "Wynkyn

de Worde's Setting-Copy for *Ipomydon*," *Studies in Bibliography* 35 (1982): 156–71. For the date of De Worde's edition, see Joseph J. Gwara, "Three Forms of w and Four English Printers: Robert Copland, Henry Pepwell, Henry Watson, and Wynkyn de Worde," *Papers of the Bibliographical Society of America* 106 (2012): 196n47.

2 Duff, *A Century of the English Book Trade*, 242.

3 The only romances printed by Copland that are not preserved in an earlier edition are Lord Berners's *Arthur of Little Britain* (STC 807, 807.5) and *The Knight of Curtesy* (STC 24223). It seems plausible that there existed earlier editions of both these works; see, respectively, Joyce Boro, "Lord Berners and His Books: A New Survey," *Huntington Library Quarterly* 67 (2004): 238 and Ronald S. Crane, *The Vogue of Medieval Chivalric Romance during the English Renaissance* (Menasha, WI: George Banta, 1919), 6.

4 Arber I, 79.

5 Ibid., 128.

6 *Jeste* was printed for the last time in 1540(?) (STC 11691a.7), *Lamwell* in 1531(?) (STC 15187), *Squire* in 1520(?) (STC 23111.5), and *Degare* in ca. 1535(?) (STC 6470.5). For *Lamwell*, I use the date suggested by Blayney, I, 283, II, 1048. For information on King, see Blayney, II, 783–5, and Duff, *A Century of the English Book Trade*, 86.

7 The printers are Thomas Marshe and John Tysdale; see Arber I, 95, 156. For the relation between Marshe and King, see Blayney, II, 784; see also Duff, *A Century of the English Book Trade*, 100. For Tysdale, see Blayney, II, 794–5, and Duff, *A Century of the English Book Trade*, 156.

8 See further in Jordi Sánchez-Martí, "The Publication of English Medieval Romances after the Death of Wynkyn de Worde, 1536–1569," in *Early Printed Narrative Literature in Western Europe*, ed. Elisabeth de Bruijn, Bart Besamusca, and Frank Willaert (Berlin: De Gruyter, 2019), 143–66.

9 Richard Pynson was the first to print *Generides* (1504?; STC 11721), *Torrent of Portyngale* (1505?; STC 24133), *Sir Triamour* (1503?; STC 24301.5), and possibly *Guy of Warwick* (STC 12540) and *Robert the Devyll* (1510?; STC 21071.5); Julian Notary, *Huon of Burdeux* (ca. 1515; STC 13998.5); Jan van Doesborch, *Lyfe of Virgilius* (1518?; STC 24828); John Skot, *Sir Isumbras* (ca. 1530; STC 14280.5) and *Jeste of Sir Gawaine* (1528?; STC 11691a.3); Richard Faques, *Kyng Alisaunder* (1525?; STC 321); John Mitchell, *Sir Lamwell* (1531?; STC 15187). For an overview of sixteenth-century English printers up to 1534, see Tamara Atkin and A.S.G. Edwards, "Printers, Publishers and Promoters to 1558," in *A Companion to the Early Printed Book in Britain, 1476–1558*, ed. Vincent Gillespie and Susan Powell (Cambridge: D.S. Brewer, 2014), 27–44, 29–36.

10 It was licensed to Allde (Arber I, 389). *Bevis* was first printed ca. 1500 (STC 1987.5); see Joseph J. Gwara, "Dating Wynkyn de Worde's Devotional,

Homiletic, and Other Texts, 1501–11," in *Preaching the Word in Manuscript and Print in Late Medieval England: Essays in Honour of Susan Powell*, ed. Martha W. Driver and Veronica O'Mara (Turnhout, BE: Brepols, 2013), 203n17. For a discussion of this romance's textual history with a description of most extant early printed editions, see Jennifer Fellows, "The Middle English and Renaissance *Bevis*: A Textual Survey," in *Sir Bevis of Hampton in Literary Tradition*, ed. Jennifer Fellows and Ivana Djordjevic (Cambridge: D.S. Brewer, 2008), 80–113. One further edition, attributed to Copland, was printed in the second half of the 1560s and is now fragmentarily preserved in the Cambridge University Library, shelfmark 5000.d.144.

11 They were then licensed to Purfoot (Arber I, 389).

12 Note, however, that when Thomas Bassandyne, printer and bookseller in Edinburgh, died, the inventory of all his goods and stock, dated 18 October 1577, mentions 300 printed copies of the Middle English romance *Eger and Grime*. See *Early Metrical Tales; Including the History of Sir Egeir, Sir Gryme, and Sir Gray-Steill* (Edinburgh, 1826), ix–x. For information on Bassandyne, see McKerrow, *A Dictionary of Printers and Booksellers in England, Scotland and Ireland, and of Foreign Printers of English Books 1557–1640* (London: Bibliographical Society, 1910), 25–6. It appears that the Scottish book market for medieval romances differed from the English one; see also n. 31 below.

13 For a graphic representation of this circumstance, see David Cressy, "Levels of Illiteracy in England, 1530–1730," *Historical Journal* 20 (1977): 13. Note, however, that this tendency was reversed during the 1580s and beyond.

14 See Lawrence Stone, "The Educational Revolution in England, 1560–1640," *Past and Present* 28 (1964): 41–80.

15 See Thomas Laqueur, "The Cultural Origins of Popular Literacy in England, 1500–1850," *Oxford Review of Education* 2 (1976): 255–75; see also Cressy, "Levels of Illiteracy," 15, table 4.

16 See David Cressy, *Literacy and the Social Order: Reading and Writing in Tudor and Stuart England* (Cambridge: Cambridge University Press, 1980), 20.

17 *A Catechisme, or First Instruction of Christian Religion* (1570; STC 18708).

18 See Cressy, *Literacy and the Social Order*, 21.

19 As Mark Bland states, "The ability to read some things did not mean that all who did read could read everything; a different level of competency was required for a complex book than a broadside ballad or the catechism" (*A Guide to Early Printed Books and Manuscripts* [Malden, MA: Wiley-Blackwell, 2010], 86).

20 Caxton rejected printing verse romances but never sold out his editions of prose romances. See Helen Cooper, "Prose Romances," in *A Companion to*

Middle English Prose, ed. A.S.G. Edwards (Cambridge: D.S. Brewer, 2004), 215–29. In France, prose was preferred over verse for the composition of romances as early as the thirteenth century.

21 See Jordi Sánchez-Martí, "The Printed History of the Middle English Verse Romances," *Modern Philology* 107 (2009): 1–31. We do not know with certainty whether De Worde's edition of *Guy* (STC 12541; Duff 171) came before or after Pynson's (STC 12540; Duff 170). A now lost edition of *Bevis* is mentioned to have been printed before 1498; see H.R. Plomer, "Two Lawsuits of Richard Pynson," *The Library*, n.s., 10 (1909): 115–33, 122, 126–8.

22 The second part (STC 19124) was printed in 1567. The text is available in *The Palace of Pleasure: Elizabethan Versions of Italian and French Novels from Boccaccio, Bandello, Cinthio, Straparola, Queen Margaret of Navarre and Others*, 3 vols, ed. Joseph Jacobs (London: David Nutt, 1890). For a discussion, see Neil Rhodes, "Italianate Tales: William Painter and George Pettie," in *The Oxford Handbook of English Prose, 1500–1640*, ed. Andrew Hadfield (Oxford: Oxford University Press, 2013), 91–105. For an overview of the emergence of prose fiction, see Paul Salzman, *English Prose Fiction, 1558–1700: A Critical History* (Oxford: Clarendon Press, 1985), 7–21.

23 The text is edited by G.W. Pigman III, *George Gascoigne: A Hundreth Sundrie Flowres* (Oxford: Oxford University Press, 2000). For the publication of Gascoigne's work, see Adrian Weiss, "Shared Printing, Printer's Copy, and the Text(s) of Gascoigne's 'A Hundreth Sundrie Flowers,'" *Studies in Bibliography* 45 (1992): 71–104; and, more recently, Kirk Melnikoff, *Elizabethan Publishing and the Makings of Literary Culture* (Toronto: University of Toronto Press, 2018), 108–17.

24 Andy Kesson, *John Lyly and Early Modern Authorship* (Manchester: Manchester University Press, 2011), 59. The text is edited by R. Warwick Bond, *The Complete Works of John Lyly* (Oxford: Clarendon Press, 1902), vol. 1. William Baldwin's *Beware the Cat* represents a special case. Considered by some as the first English novel, it was composed in the early months of 1553, but its publication was aborted when it became known that the Catholic Mary would be crowned queen. The work appeared posthumously in 1570, in a context that was more favourable to literary prose and at a time when its message could be used as propaganda for the Northern Rebellion. The first edition, now lost, was probably printed by John Allde for John Arnold, and its text is preserved in a transcript in BL, MS Additional 24628; the first edition extant dates also from 1570 (STC 1244). The text is edited by William A. Ringler, Jr. and Michael Flachmann (San Marino, CA: Huntington Library, 1988). See also Thomas Betteridge, "William Baldwin's *Beware the Cat* and Other Foolish Writing," in *The Oxford Handbook of English Prose*, 139–55.

25 The register lacks the period from July 1571 to July 1576, so it is not unlikely that more medieval English romances were entered in the first part of the decade. See Alexandra Hill, *Lost Books and Printing in London, 1557–1640: An Analysis of the Stationers' Company Register* (Leiden: Brill, 2018), 22–3; see also D.F. McKenzie, "Stationers' Company Liber A: An Apologia," in *The Stationers' Company and the Book Trade, 1550–1990,* ed. Robert Myers and Michael Harris (Winchester, UK: St Paul's Bibliographies, 1997), 43.

26 Here I list the licensed romances not printed by Copland, followed by the year when they were last printed: *Apollonius* (1532–34; STC 708.5), *Blanchardine* (1490; STC 3124), *Oliver of Castile* (1518; STC 18808), *Paris and Vienne* (ca. 1505; STC 19208), and *Ponthus* (1511; STC 20108). See Edward Wilson-Lee, "Romance and Resistance: Narratives of Chivalry in Mid-Tudor England," *Renaissance Studies* 24 (2010): 490. For a list of the prose romances printed by Copland, see Sánchez-Martí, "Publication of English Medieval Romances," table 1, p. 153.

27 Melnikoff, *Elizabethan Publishing,* 18. There was a steady and consistent increase in the number of London publications, which began in 1565 and continued in the following decades. For the publication of translations, see Julia G. Ebel, "A Numerical Survey of Elizabethan Translations," *The Library,* 5th ser., 22 (1967): 113 and 126. For Jugge, see Joyce Boro, "Jugge, Richard (*c.* 1514–77)," in *ODNB,* 30:816; for Kingston, see Blayney, II, 773–5; for Jennings, see McKerrow, *Dictionary,* 157.

28 This Spanish romance, authored by Diego Ordúñez de Calahorra, was printed in 1555; see Daniel Eisenberg and Mª Carmen Marín Pina, *Bibliografía de los libros de caballerías castellanos* (Saragossa: Prensas Universitarias de Zaragoza, 2000), no. 1673. Tyler's translation is edited by Joyce Boro, Tudor and Stuart Translations, no. 11 (London: MHRA, 2014). For information on East, see Jeremy L. Smith, "East, Thomas (1540–1608)," in *ODNB.*

29 On Charlewood, see H.R. Tedder, "Charlewood, John (*d.* 1593)," rev. Robert Faber, in *ODNB* 11: 176–7.

30 See Henry R. Plomer, "Thomas East, Printer," *The Library,* 2nd ser., 2 (1901): 307. In the case of Lord Berner's *Arthur of Little Britain,* East exercised more caution and printed it in quarto, reducing the twenty-five woodcuts used by Copland (STC 807) to only fifteen. For a list of the woodcuts used by Copland and East, see Ruth Samson Luborsky and Elizabeth Morley Ingram, *A Guide to English Illustrated Book, 1536–1603* (Tempe, AZ: Medieval and Renaissance Texts and Studies, 1998), I: 32–6. See also Yu-Chiao Wang, "William Copland's and Thomas East's Promotional Strategies for the *Morte Darthur*: A Study of the Origins, Forms, and Contexts of Their Title Pages," *Journal of the Early Book Society* 6 (2003): 83.

31 The printed copies were shipped in the *Scout of Leith* when she was intercepted by English pirates in October 1586, according to an account in the Public Record Office, Ref. HCA 13/26, fol. 188–9 (High Court of Admiralty Examinations); see Donald Robertson, "A Packet of Books for Scotland," *Bibliothek* 6 (1971–3): 52–3. Vautrollier was connected to the Scottish book trade; see Andrew Pettegree, "Vautrollier, Thomas (d. 1587)," in *ODNB*.

32 Sloane MS 2131, fols. 16–20. According to Virgil B. Heltzel, "Robert Ashley: Elizabethan Man of Letters," *Huntington Library Quarterly* 10 (1947): 349n 2, Ashley must have written this account between 1607 and 1610, since he refers in the present to John Harding as president of Magdalene College. Conversely, Ronald S. Crane, "The Reading of an Elizabethan Youth," *Modern Philology* 11 (1913): 269n2, dates it to 9 May 1614, the date that appears at the end of the account. For more information, see John Ferris, "Ashley, Robert (1565–1641)," in *ODNB*; William D. Macray, *A Register of the Members of St. Mary Magdalen College, Oxford*, n.s., 3 (London: Henry Frowde, 1901), 91–101; and Renae Satterley, "'To be unto them as the foundation of a library': The Books of Robert Ashley at the Middle Temple," in *The Book Trade in Early Modern England: Practices, Perceptions, Connections*, ed. John Hinks and Victoria Gardner (New Castle, DE: Oak Knoll Press, 2013), 61–85.

33 "Fabulous and useless stories ... such as those that were widely circulated concerning Bevis of Hampton, Guy of Warwick, the story of Valentine and Orson, the life of Arthur King of Britain and of the knights of the Round Table" (my translation); Crane, "The Reading of an Elizabethan Youth," 271. Crane mentions that Copland printed editions of these texts, although it is not unlikely that Ashley could have read some of them in one of the editions printed by East in 1582. Of course, there were also Tudor readers who took romances more seriously, as did Anthony Foster of Trotton in the marginal annotations he added to a manuscript containing several Middle English romances; see Nicole Clifton, "Anthony Foster of Trotton and London, Lincoln's Inn MS 150," *Yearbook of Langland Studies* 32 (2018): 77–126.

34 H.S. Bennett, *English Books and Readers, 1475 to 1557* (Cambridge: Cambridge University Press, 1969), 26, suggests that the reading of romances might have been used to improve the reading skills of schoolboys. It has also been argued that, during the manuscript period, young readers were already captivated by the English romances; see Phillipa Hardman, "Popular Romances and Young Readers," in *A Companion to Medieval Popular Romance*, ed. Raluca L. Radulescu and Cory James Rushton (Cambridge: D.S. Brewer, 2009), 150–64.

35 Nashe connects the English medieval romances with "Abbie-lubbers, from whose idle pens proceeded those worne out impressions of the feyned

no where acts, of Arthur of the rounde table, Arthur of litle Brittaine, sir Tristram, Hewon of Burdeaux, the Squire of low degree, the foure sons of Amon [sic]," *The Works of Thomas Nashe*, ed. Ronald B. McKerrow, 2nd ed. rev. F.P. Wilson (Oxford: Blackwell, 1958), 1:11.7–11. Note that, while the adventures of Sir Tristram are included in Malory's *Morte Darthur*, no romance of *Sir Tristram* is printed separately. A metrical version exists in manuscript form, although it was never printed; see *Sir Tristrem*, ed. Eugen Kölbing (Heilbronn, DE: Henninger, 1882). Ashley also associates this literary corpus with the Catholic past, though he seems to have assumed this view with hindsight.

36 Note that when, in 1586, Thomas Purfoot, who had registered two verse romances in 1568/69 (Arber I, 389), obtained a licence to print *Paris and Vienne* and *Valentine and Orson*, he described each of these prose romances as an "old booke" (Arber II, 453).

37 Arber II, 414. Cf. Jeremy L. Smith, *Thomas East and Music Publishing in Renaissance England* (Oxford: Oxford University Press, 2003), 180n58.

38 While no copy of the *editio princeps* of *Palmerin of England I–II* has come down to us, there is evidence of its existence. For his edition of *Palmerin d'Oliva*, see Jordi Sánchez-Martí, "The Publication History of Anthony Munday's *Palmerin d'Oliva*," *Gutenberg-Jahrbuch* 89 (2014): 190–207. For *Palmendos*, see Leticia Álvarez-Recio, "Anthony Munday's *Palmendos* (1589) in the Early Modern English Book Trade: Print and Reception," *Atlantis* 38, no. 1 (2016): 53–69.

39 H.S. Bennett, *English Books and Readers, 1558 to 1603* (Cambridge: Cambridge University Press, 1965), 272.

40 See Smith, *Thomas East*, and Katherine Butler, "Printed Borders for Sixteenth-Century Music or Music Paper and the Early Career of Music Printer Thomas East," *The Library*, 7th ser., 19 (2018): 174–202.

41 See Tedder, "Charlewood," 11:176. He accepted commissions to print Iberian prose romances from publishers like William Wright and Simon Waterson; cf. table 3 in the present chapter.

42 See Jordi Sánchez-Martí, ed., *A Critical Edition of Anthony Munday's "Palmerin d'Oliva"* (Tempe, AZ: Arizona Center for Medieval and Renaissance Studies, 2020), 56–8. For an overview of his translations, see Gerald R. Hayes, "Anthony Munday's Romances of Chivalry," *The Library*, 4th ser., 6 (1925): 57–81. For biographical information, see Celeste Turner, *Anthony Mundy: An Elizabethan Man of Letters*, University of California Publications in English 2, no. 1 (Berkeley: University of California Press, 1928). See also Donna B. Hamilton, *Anthony Munday and the Catholics, 1560–1633* (Burlington, VT: Ashgate, 2005).

43 See Melnikoff, *Elizabethan Publishing*, 34–5, 66–70. Before translating an entire romance, Munday probably reached an agreement with a publisher.

Note that, when *Palmerin of England* and *Palladine of England* were registered in the Stationers' Company, the translation was not yet finished. In the case of *Palladine*, we know that Edward Allde obtained the licence on 20 November 1587 (Arber II, 480), but the book was not published until 23 April 1588, after sufficient time elapsed for Munday to translate this short work; cf. the case of *Amadis* in Arber II, 514.

44 See William E. Miller, "Printers and Stationers in the Parish of St. Giles Cripplegate 1561–1640," *Studies in Bibliography* 19 (1966): 15–38; and Louise Wilson, "Playful Paratexts: The Front Matter of Anthony Munday's Iberian Romance Translations," in *Renaissance Paratexts*, ed. Helen Smith and Louise Wilson (Cambridge: Cambridge University Press, 2011): 129–30. For information on Edward Allde, see H.R. Tedder, "Allde, John," rev. Ian Gadd, *ODNB*; and R.B. McKerrow, "Edward Allde as a Typical Trade Printer," *The Library*, 4th ser., 10 (1929): 121–62. It is likely that Edward Allde left his premises in the Long Shop in the Poultry in Cripplegate after he got married on 1 December 1588 and then moved to Fore Street, also in Cripplegate.

45 Melnikoff, *Elizabethan Publishing*, 76. Note that Burby owned the licence to publish a romance only in the case of *Primaleon of Greece I–II*, granted on 10 August 1594 (Arber II, 311). For Burby, see Gerald D. Johnson, "Succeeding as an Elizabethan Publisher: The Example of Cuthbert Burby," *Journal of the Printing Historical Society* 21 (1992): 71–78.

46 For information on Creede, see Akihiro Yamada, *Thomas Creede Printer to Shakespeare and His Contemporaries* (Tokyo: Meisei University Press, 1994); and David L. Gants, "Creede, Thomas," in *ODNB* 14: 128–9. For his edition of *Bellianis*, see María J. Sánchez-de-Nieva, "A Bibliographical Description of the British Library Copy of *The Honour of Chivalrie* (1598)," *Sederi: Yearbook of the Spanish and Portuguese Society for English Renaissance Studies* 24 (2014): 171–9. For Creede's reprints of the *Palmerin* romances, see Wilson, "Playful Paratexts," 126.

47 Note that Byrd's successor, Thomas Morley, was not granted the music patent until September 1598. During the interval between the end of Byrd's patent in 1596 and the moment when Morley exercised his monopoly on music printing, this line of business was open to other printers. As a result, there were "more presses than ever before producing music for English consumers" (Smith, *Thomas East*, 91), and East's finances certainly struggled, as his market share slipped.

48 Note that Barley's edition of *Palmendos* was actually titled *The Delightful History of Celestina the Faire* and contains a translation different from Munday's. The reasons Barley had to disguise the sequel to *Palmerin d'Oliva* as the story of *Celestina* escape us; see also the chapter by Helen Cooper in the present collection. For Barley, see Gerald D.

Johnson, "William Barley, 'Publisher & Seller of Bookes,' 1591–1614," *The Library*, 6th ser., 11 (1989): 10–46. See also Holger Schott Syme, "Thomas Creede, William Barley, and the Venture of Printing Plays," in *Shakespeare's Stationers: Studies in Cultural Bibliography*, ed. Marta Straznicky (Philadelphia: University of Pennsylvania Press, 2013), 28–46. For Jackson, see McKerrow, *Dictionary*, 149.

49   The editions of *Blanchardyn* published in 1595 and 1597 actually contain an adaptation done by Thomas Pope Goodwine (n.d.); the edition of Caxton's *Recuyell* printed by Creede and Simmes (active 1585–1622) was revised by William Phiston (active 1571–1609); Purfoot's edition of *Huon* presents a modernized version.

50   See John O'Connor, *Amadis de Gaule and Its Influence on Elizabethan Literature* (New Brunswick, NJ: Rutgers University Press, 1970), 203–25; and Mary Patchell, *The "Palmerin" Romances in Elizabethan Prose Fiction* (New York: Columbia University Press, 1947), 95–127. For a discussion of the thematic and stylistic characteristic of these romances newly composed in English, see Anne Falke, "'The Work Well Done that Pleaseth All': Emanuel Forde and the Seventeenth-Century Popular Chivalric Romance," *Studies in Philology* 78 (1981): 241–54. For an overview of this corpus of English romances, see John Simons, "Transforming the Romance: Some Observations on Early Modern Popular Narratives," in *Narrative Strategies in Early English Fiction*, ed. Wolfgang Görtschacher and Holger Klein Lewiston (Lewiston, NY: Edwin Mellen Press, 1995), 273–88.

51   Salzman, *English Prose Fiction*, 100. Robarts was the son of a London stationer, named also Henry Roberts, and became free of the company *"per patronagium"* on 18 August 1595 (Arber II, 716). See McKerrow, *Dictionary*, 228–9. For Robarts, sometimes spelled Roberts, see Helen Moore, "Roberts, Henry," in *ODNB*; see also Louis B. Wright, "Henry Robarts: Patriotic Propagandist and Novelist," *Studies in Philology* 29 (1932): 175–99. Note that a second part of *Defiance of Nature* was entered on 7 August 1592 (Arber II, 618), but it was never published. See also John Simons, "Open and Closed Books: A Semiotic Approach to the History of Elizabethan and Jacobean Popular Romance," in *Jacobean Poetry and Prose: Rhetoric Representation and Popular Imagination*, ed. Clive Bloom (London: Macmillan, 1988), 8–24.

52   For these licences, see Arber III, 98, 129. Forde also wrote *Montelyon, Knight of the Oracle*, whose first extant edition was printed in 1633 by Bernard Alsop and Thomas Fawcet (STC 11167). It was first printed ca. 1600, probably by Thomas Creede, one of whose devices appears on the title page of the 1633 edition; see Yamada, *Thomas Creede*, 81, orn. 3. This text is available in a modernized version edited by Anne Falke (Salzburg:

Institut für Anglistik und Amerikanistik, Universität Salzburg, 1981). For the booksellers Holme and Olive, see McKerrow, *Dictionary*, 141 and 207, respectively. The Holme mentioned here must be William Holme, Jr. On Forde, see Helen Moore, "Ford, Emanuel," in *ODNB*. Goran Stanivukovic has edited *Ornatus and Artesia* (Ottawa: Dovehouse, 2003).

53 It was reissued at least five times until 1640; see STC 14677–14680, 14682–14683. The romance is edited by Jennifer Fellows (Aldershot, UK: Ashgate, 2003). For biographical information, see Richard Proudfoot, "Johnson, Richard," in *ODNB*. Johnson also wrote another chivalric romance, *Tom a Lincolne*, which is edited by Richard S.M. Hirsch (Columbia, SC: Newberry Library, 1978); see xix–xx for the printing history. The earliest extant edition is the sixth impression, printed in 1631 (STC 14684), although there is evidence that William White obtained the licence to print this romance from John Danter's widow on 24 December 1599 (Arber III, 153). Therefore it seems likely that it appeared with commercial success before 1603.

54 It is edited by William Edward Mead, EETS os 165 (London: Oxford University Press, 1925). See also John Simons, "Christopher Middleton and Elizabethan Medievalism," in *Medievalism in the Modern World: Essays in Honour of Leslie J. Workman*, ed. Richard Utz and Tom Shippey (Turnhout, BE: Brepols, 1998), 43–60; and Norris J. Lacy, "'Coda': *Chinon of England* (1597), or the Limits of Romance," *Cahiers de Recherches Médiévales et Humanistes* 30 (2015): 441–50.

55 For biographical information, see D. Aneurin Thomas, "Parry, Robert," *ODNB*; see also the chapter by Goran Stanivukovic in the present collection. The work is edited by John Simons (Burlington, VT: Ashgate, 2002). For the printer, see Kirk Melnikoff, "Jones, Richard (active 1564–1613)," in *ODNB*.

56 For biographical information, see David Katham, "Meres, Francis," in *ODNB*.

PART TWO

Iberian Chivalric Romance in Anthony Munday's Translation

Case Studies on Early Modern English Culture and Ideology

Chapter Two

Sir Francis Drake: Conquest and Colonization in Anthony Munday's *Palmendos* (1589)

LETICIA ÁLVAREZ-RECIO

Anthony Munday's *The Honourable, Pleasant and Rare Conceited Historie of Palmendos*[1] is based on the first book of the Spanish chivalric romance *Primaleón de Grecia* (Salamanca, 1512), a sequel to *Palmerín de Olivia* (Salamanca, 1511). The Spanish original, which narrates the adventures of Palmerín's two sons, Polendos and Primaleón, enjoyed an extraordinary editorial success both in Spain and the rest of Europe, as its numerous editions and translations into four different languages attest.[2] Toward the end of 1588, Anthony Munday finished translating the first thirty-two chapters of Vernassal's French version that deal with the deeds of Palmendos[3] in his quest to Palmerin's court in Constantinople.[4] The book was entered by John Charlewood (active 1553?–93) in the Stationers' Register on 9 January 1589,[5] and it must have been available in London bookshops soon afterwards, for Munday's letter to "the courteous reader" is dated 5 February 1589. The translator dedicated his work to Sir Francis Drake (1540?–96), a well-known figure at the time, largely as a result of his travels around the world in the period 1577–80, his subsequent exploits in the Caribbean, and his contribution to the defeat of the Spanish Armada in October 1588. Given his popularity, many of the exploration and navigation manuals published in this decade had been dedicated to Drake, while he had been praised in numerous travel accounts and news pamphlets commending his exploits in the New World.

The research for this essay was supported by funding from the Spanish Ministry of Economy and Competitiveness (ref. FFI2015-70101-P; MINECO/FEDER, UE), whose financial support is herewith gratefully acknowledged. My grateful thanks to Professor Rafael Portillo for his detailed and constructive revision of this essay. Many thanks go as well to the readers who reviewed an earlier version of this work for their helpful suggestions.

This chapter consists of two sections. The first examines Munday's dedication to Sir Francis Drake in *Palmendos* in the context of the publishing agents who invested in navigation and travel literature in the 1580s. It explores the interest of Munday's stationers in this type of work and offers a detailed list of works dedicated to Drake in this same period, coinciding with Munday's early translations of the *Palmerin* cycle. In the second section, I analyse the Isle of Delphos episode in *Palmendos*; it is at this moment that the eponymous hero frees both his beloved Francelina and the islanders from giant Baledon (chapters 6, 7, 8). In these chapters, Palmendos's chivalric aims seem to address his imperial and colonial aspirations, which points to a possible link between the fictional hero and the contemporaneous English hero Sir Francis Drake.

Munday's Dedication to Sir Francis Drake

Munday's dedication is a verse written in Latin, praising Drake's heroic deeds while seeking his protection. The style must have struck Munday's readers, since he had always employed English prose when dedicating his previous literary works – *Zelauto* (1580; STC 18283), *Palmerin D'Oliva* (Book I, 1588; STC 19157), and *Palladine of England* (1588; STC 5541) – to such significant Elizabethan courtiers as the Earl of Oxford (1550–1604) and the Earl of Essex (1566–1601).[6] Munday's dedicatory poem reads as follows:

> Desinat Herculeas iam Grecia vana columnas
> Mirari, aut Minyas, Dulichiumue ducem.
> Amphitryoniadem superas fortissime Drace,
> Iasonaque, et comites, Penelopesque virum.
> Neptunusque suum credit tibi iure tridentem,
> Cedit Sceptra libens, imperiumque maris.
> Palmendos tanto laetus, tutusque Patrono
> Audet in innumeras peruolitare manus.
> Zoilus inuideat rumpantur et ilia Codro,
> Palmendos Draco vindice tutus erit.
> It, volat, et gaudet, spernitque minacia verba,
> Nempe soles tumidas spernere Drace minas.[7]

In an overtly patriotic tone, the author compares his patron to such mythological heroes and gods as Hercules, Ulysses, Jason, and Neptune, thus emphasizing Drakes's strength, skill, and power "over the seas."[8] His last two lines, however, sound disturbing: "[Palmendos] goes, flies and ventures, and despises menacing words, / For you, Drake, are used to despising swollen menaces." Munday probably expected to have his translation censored by some of his contemporaries – chivalric romance had been largely criticized from the early sixteenth century by humanists and scholars alike – but a comparison between potential censorship of his work and threats against Drake looks rather striking. Drake had indeed become a nightmare for Spain since the late 1570s, and the Spanish had often complained to Elizabeth I about him and his piracy ventures, thus leaving him in a difficult position. In Christopher Hodgkins's words, "to many on the Queen's council, particularly Burgley and Walshingham, the idolized mariner was an object of suspicion and his successful thievery a diplomatic embarrassment."[9]

Although his fame at court was tainted by his privateering activities, his reputation as a popular hero grew enormously, especially among the "middling sort."[10] Drake embodied the ideal of "an urban, mercantile model of adventure which," Mark Netzloff argues, "was distinct from that of the aristocratic knightly quest." In Netzloff's view, the political and literary elite's neglect of Drake "did not result from his privateering exploits in themselves" but from the fact that "this form of commercial piracy was a domain unsuitable for gentlemanly adventure."[11] However, Richard Hakluyt (c. 1552–1616), geographer, member of the Skinners' Company, and most significant Elizabethan editor of travel and colonial literature, reinterpreted Drake's piracy as a type of virtuous and patriotic trade, "central to England's imperial and commercial project."[12] In those years, many English merchants, mainly associated with the cloth trade, participated actively in the funding of expeditions in search of new markets. Colonial and travel literature was then a means to encourage financial support for such expeditions, as the multiple links of adventurers and patrons with authors and editors seem to prove. The engagement of the merchant community and various noblemen in both colonial expansion and the publication of colonial-travel literature suggests that both activities were two sides of the same coin, and so many of the intended readers of those literary works were mostly people who invested – or were expected to invest – in such expansion.

Indeed, the boom of travel/colonial literature and navigational works in the London book trade occurred in the late 1570s and lasted up to the early 1590s, coinciding with the first efforts to found English colonies in America.[13] Those literary works were advertised as entertainment pieces for ambitious men interested in sea voyages. Descriptions of the "New World" appealed to readers' sense of wonder, thus prompting a response of pleasure and amazement at the "factual" possibilities that such distant lands offered to English entrepreneurs and adventurers.[14]

The middling people who would read those works would also read English translations of Iberian chivalric romances, as Joan Pong Linton has observed when studying the interplay between romance and colonial discourse in early modern English literature. In her opinion, they both this literature and colonial discourse were the "products of print," as they shared "the means of production and readership." Thus, Linton suggests, history became popularized as a response to the growing "interest in narratives of travel and colonial enterprise in the New World."[15]

Nevertheless, the late sixteenth-century boom of romance literature and, more specifically, that of chivalric romance of Iberian origin were not the result simply of a growing interest in accounts of the New World: they also reflected the colonial ambition of contemporary Englishmen. Translations of Spanish and Portuguese chivalric romances and navigation works, together with narratives of the New World, enticed English readers to imitate the models proposed in the original sources and make the imperial fantasies permeating those accounts come true. To a certain extent, Munday, when dedicating his romance *Palmendos* to Sir Francis Drake, was inviting his patron and readers to cross the boundaries between the fictional deeds of Palmerin's son and Drake's real-life exploits.[16] In doing so, Munday contributed indirectly to a colonial campaign arranged by a complex network of English editors, translators, authors, and publishers collaborating with the main privateers, naval officers, and patrons engaged in colonial enterprises. It is necessary, then, to explore Munday's and his stationers' connections with the colonial project all through the 1580s, as well as their links with other works dedicated to Drake in this same period.

De Schepper has estimated that at least forty-three navigational works and conquest accounts were published in England from 1528 to 1633; if reprints were considered too, the number would increase to ninety-six. Most of these works/accounts and reprints were translations, a third of the former had a Spanish source. In 1575–90 alone, eighteen Spanish texts were translated into English, which accounts for 42 per cent of the complete corpus.[17] In that fifteen-year span, Drake was the dedicatee of eleven works belonging to different genres. These included three navigation manuals: *The New Attractive* (1581), by Robert Norman (fl. 1560–84), the earliest text establishing Drake as a national hero;[18] *A Discourse of the Variation of the Cumpass* (1581), by William Borough (1536–98), usually published together with Norman's work; and *Instructions for Trauellers*, by Albretch Meyer (1528–1603), whose publication in 1589 had been encouraged by Richard Hakluyt himself.[19] Also included in this number were a New World history by Fernão Lopes de

Castanheda (1500–59), translated into English by Nicholas Lichefield (n.d.) and published in 1582,[20] and several travel accounts praising Drake's exploits in the sea: *A Discourse in Commendation of the Valiant and Virtuous Minded Gentleman, Maiester Francis Drake* (1581), by Nicholas Breton (1554–1626); *A Most Friendly Farewell, Giuen by a Welwiller to the Right Worshipful Sir Frauncis Drake Knight* (1585), by Henry Roberts (fl. 1585–1617); *The True and Perfecte Newes of the Worthy Valiant Exploytes, Performed and Done by that Valiant Knight Syr Francis Drake* (1587), by Thomas Greepe (n.d.); *Newes out of the Coast of Spaine* (1587), by Henry Haslop (n.d.); and *A Farewell Intitled to the Famous and Fortunate Generals of our English Forces and Sea, Sir John Norris and Sir Francis Drake* (1589), by George Peele (1556–96). In those same years, Drake was also the dedicatee of two editions of the French chivalric romance by Jean de Cartigny (1520?–78), *The Voyage of the Wandering Knight* (1581, 1584), translated by a merchant from Southampton by the name of William Goodyear (n.d.), and a poem in Latin by Joannes Hercusanus (n.d.), published in 1587 under the title *Magnifico ac strenuo uiro D. Francisco Draco*.[21]

On the whole, these works praised Drake's deeds in the context of specific past or future ventures. Thus, the four pieces published in 1581 – Breton's *Discourse*, Goodyear's *Voyage of the Wandering Knight*, Borough's *Discourse*, and Norman's *The New Attractive* – indirectly celebrated Drake's circumnavigation, since the queen had banned any open commendation of Drake's ventures. Three of these authors, the exception being poet Nicholas Breton, were associated to a greater or lesser extent with the worlds of trade and exploration: Goodyear was a merchant; Robert Norman, a mathematician and hydrographer; and Borough, an explorer and naval administrator. The connections between some of them were quite evident too – for example, Norman signed the dedicatory epistle to Drake in Goodyear's translation – and they all shared some kind of coorporate identity.

The case of the translation by Thomas Nicholas is somehow similar, for he praises Drake as a new, outstanding modern hero, alien to courtly circles: "His paineful trauaile, and maruailous nauigation, was not obtayned with white handes, perfumed gloues, daintie fare or softe lodging: no, no: Honour is not gotten with pleasures, & quiet minds."[22] Such class awareness is also shared by Henry Roberts in his *Most Friendly Farewell* (1585), intended to promote Drake's future expedition to Cartagena in 1586.[23] Roberts attacks Drake's open neglect at court and dwells on the traditional connection between virtue (merit) and true nobility when praising his hero: "The enuiousness of our countreymen is such as they disdaine to giue them the honour they haue gained for their right ... This renowned knight as your worthinesse is more than any I haue knowne, and that you haue so well deserued, I trust some learned which can write, will of their good nature emploie their paines to your praise."[24]

The three works dedicated to Drake and published in 1587 – those by Thomas Greepe, Joannes Hercusanus, and Henry Haslop – showed their support for Drake's violent actions against Spanish ships and against the towns of Lisbon, Sagres, and Cádiz in May–June that same year. The expedition, subsidized by a group of London merchants and the queen herself, had apparently first been intended to place the Portuguese pretender Don Antonio on the throne of Portugal. Quite surprisingly, when Drake was already at sea, the Privy Council sent him a letter banning any attacks on Spanish possessions. No one knows what happened to that letter, and Drake did not follow the Privy Council's orders and instead sacked those possessions. The queen had to apologize to Spain, and Drake was out of favour at court for some time.[25] The accounts by Greepe and Haslop and the poem by Hercusanus may be assumed to be retrieving Drake's lost reputation. There is scant information about those authors, but it may be inferred from their writings that they were not members of aristocratic courtly circles. They addressed their works – ephemeral literature consisting of a short verse work, a news pamphlet, and a broadside poem, respectively – to the common reader. These authors insist on Drake's humble origins when portraying him as a national Protestant hero, as Greepe acknowledges in his letter to the reader: "God be praysed by hys good successe, to the great terror and feare of the enemie, he beeing a man of meane calling, to deale with so mightie a Monarke [Philip II of Spain]."[26]

After being away from the court for a few months, Drake was called back and was appointed vice-admiral of the English fleet in May 1588 in response to the impending attack of the Spanish Armada. Many laudatory poems praising Drake circulated in manuscript form soon after the English victory over Spain in October that same year. Other works on or dedicated to Drake appeared in 1589, not just celebrating the Armada triumph but encouraging Drake and Norris's expedition to Spain the following spring: George Peele's *Farewell*, the translation of Meyer's *Instructions for Travellers* by Philip Jones (n.d.), and Walter Bigges's *A Summarie and True Discourse of Sir Francis Drake West Indian Voyage*.[27] Jones included a laudatory poem in Latin to praise Drake's virtues, while Peele annexed a chivalric poem on Troy to instil in his patron the heroic virtues of his Trojan "ancestors" "in highest aduentures."[28] It is not surprising, then, that Anthony Munday, a free man who, like George Peele, was in search of powerful patrons who might help him make a living, dedicated his work to Drake by means of a laudatory Latin poem, following in the footsteps of various other writers. His patriotic tone and his allusions to mythical heroes who had been surpassed by Drake had already become commonplace by January 1589, when Charlewood entered Munday's translation in the Stationers' Register.

Munday's *Palmendos*, then, might be viewed partly as a work intended to encourage Sir John Norris (ca. 1547–97) and Drake's voyage to Portugal and Spain in April 1589. Both military leaders counted on royal support, for the queen had given them orders to destroy all Spanish warships in Santander and the Bay of Biscay.[29] However, Drake and Norris disobeyed Elizabeth and went to La Coruña and Lisbon instead, in an attempt to place Don Antonio on the throne. The Portuguese pretender had been in England since late 1588, promising Drake and other West Country men large sums of money in exchange for their help to "recover" the crown.[30] Peele's, Jones's, and Munday's romances, published in the months prior to Drake's departure, were possibly intended to gain support for this project.

Two of the aforementioned works, those by Peele and Munday, were printed by John Charlewood, Munday's neighbour and regular printer in the 1580s. Charlewood published up to nine navigational works and travel accounts in the period 1580–89; seven of them were dedicated to or openly praised Drake's colonial exploits.[31] In those same years, Charlewood published seventeen works by Munday, three of which – *Zelauto* (1580), *The First Book of Palmerin D'Oliva* (1588), and *Palmendos* (1589) – were romances.[32] There seems to have been considerable interest among Munday's printers in promoting the exploration ventures organized by important members of the merchant community in association with the Elizabethan court, as was the case of Sir Francis Drake, who lived in between these two worlds.

To sum up, it should be borne in mind that relevant publishers of Iberian chivalric romance, such as Charlewood, East, and, to a lesser extent, Wolfe, also invested in navigational and New World literature in the late 1570s and 1580s, just when the English were first trying to set up colonies in America. Some prominent merchants investing in those ventures were also engaged in the publication and reception of sea accounts and New World histories, which, in turn, very often prompted similar enterprises among urban readers. Those very readers were also the main intended audience of the Iberian chivalric romances. It is not surprising, then, that navigational literature, New World histories, and chivalric romances of Spanish origin became so popular at the time, partly owing to the translation boom that had taken place in the late sixteenth century. The fact that the stationers who invested in travel and New World literature also produced chivalric romances cannot be coincidental, as both genres shared similar cultural discourses. Those similarities made it possible for non-aristocratic English explorers and sea dogs such as Drake to be associated with a new type of romance hero characterized not by birth but by personal worth.

One of those discourses, focusing on the likely influence of sixteenth-century debates on the right of conquest, is analysed in the next section, which discusses chapters 6–8 of *Palmendos*. In those chapters, Palmendos and his men are brought to the Isle of Delphos after a tempest.[33] The reader is informed that the giant Baledon has kept the island under control by subduing its inhabitants and taking away their possessions. Baledon keeps the island isolated from the outside world and spoils, imprisons, or kills any knight or merchant reaching its shores. Although one of the mariners travelling with Palmendos earnestly recommends him not to anchor at Delphos's port, the hero views their arrival as a good omen, and he decides to face Baledon and put an end to his tyranny. The episode ends with Baledon's defeat and Palmendos's subsequent assumption of sovereignty on the island on behalf of Emperor Palmerin, who is willingly accepted by the inhabitants of Delphos as their new lord. Although the hero first regards this adventure as a challenge to prove his worth and punish his enemy's tyranny, his venture finally results in the conquest of Delphos, which is ultimately annexed to Palmerin's empire.

In the idyllic world of romance, Palmendos's colonization of the island is carried out peacefully. However, his rights of conquest, even after liberating the inhabitants of the island from Baledon's evil rule, may have posed a challenge to contemporary readers who had a keen interest in exploration. In this sense, these chapters can be read in relation to late medieval and early modern ideas on the just-war theory and the law of nature, probably the two main legal frameworks to which colonizers resorted when it was necessary to justify such acts. The doctrines were intimately interconnected and were applicable to Christians and non-Christians alike, thus establishing the basis for a law of nations that would regulate international affairs. In this sense, they could offer, at least at a theoretical level, a convincing response to the territorial and commercial ambitions of European powers immersed in an increasing rivalry on the continent and overseas. A comparative analysis of these chapters in the Spanish, French, and English versions can also illustrate the various utopian models that were put forward when having to deal with rival powers seeking territorial expansion as well as considering the colonized others.[34]

Palmendos's Conquest and Colonization of the Isle of Delphos

In his work *War and the Law of Nations*, Stephen C. Neff broadly summarizes the notion of war in the just-war theory as an instrument that "could and should be employed in a socially productive fashion, for the subduing of evil and the promotion of good." Such theory permitted the use of armed force only when it was necessary to vindicate a legal right that had been previously violated or, in a more general sense, to promote the interests of the community.[35] Martin Wight insists on this instrumental, legal notion of just war when distinguishing it from that of the holy war. According to him, in a just war, "all parties have their due rights, and war is the means of penalizing violation of right and ensuring restoration and restitution," while a holy war is a religious conception whose main premise is "that the true believers are right, and that infidels are converted or exterminated."[36] The just-war theory was a clearly regulated legal framework largely developed in the thirteenth century by a number of theologians and lawyers, among them Thomas Aquinas (1224/5–74), Alexander of Hales (1170/85–1245), and Raymond of Pennafort (1175/80–1275), who established five main criteria to declare the justice of war: *auctoritas, personae, res, justa causa,* and *animus.*[37] Such requirements would be extensively discussed in the sixteenth century by members of the Salamanca school headed by Francisco de Vitoria (ca. 1483–1546), who tried to balance the necessity of war and the basic Christian principle of loving one's enemy.

No war is waged by one state against another in the Baledon episode; rather, the conflict consists of violent combat between the main hero and a ruthless tyrant who has unrightfully acquired the lands he rules over. Munday makes it clear in his translation – "he [Baledon] had by force gotten this Island" (F1^{r-v}) – which follows almost word for word the French version by Vernassal – "il eut herité par force de ceste Isle" (C5^v). The Spanish original, however, mentions only that Baledon was made lord of the isle – "fue señor de la isla" (19) – though nothing is said about the illicit nature of his actions. That may be the reason why Vernassal and Munday depict Baledon as a hideous tyrant,[38] in contrast with the Spanish version, which describes him as the bravest knight in the world.[39]

The three editions offer similar explanations for Baledon's dealings with the knights and merchants that reach his port. At this stage, Vernassal and Munday follow the Spanish and do not need to pass open judgment on Baledon's attacks against his visitors, as his actions already show a clear violation of international and natural laws. Francisco de Vitoria had made such laws clear in his *De Indis* (1537–9), in which he underlined man's right of "natural partnership and communication" – that is, his rights to travel, trade, and preach his religion freely."[40] According to Vitoria, a refusal to allow free passage could be used as a reason to conquer, since the law of nations established the necessity to be hospitable to strangers. All individuals were thus allowed to trade freely and lawfully as long as they did not wrong the inhabitants of the lands where they traded.[41] It is precisely this natural right that Baledon infringes, which would permit Palmendos's subsequent actions against the giant and his son. This is made apparent in the first exchange between Baledon's son and Palmendos: "The Gyants Sonne thus spake to him. Howe darest thou Knight be so bold, as to enter our Porte without licence? I dare doo more then that, answered Palmendos, in despight of such disloyall villaines as you are, who by treacherous meanes intrap the innocent, and afterward exercise what crueltie you please upon them: but nowe is the time come, I hope, that shal guerdon you with recompence aunswerable to such brutish behauiour" (F3^v).

This short dialogue is almost identical in the three versions,[42] thus underlining the villains' treacherous behaviour.[43] However, in contrast with the Spanish, the French and English allude to Baledon and his son's brutal conduct – Vernassal speaks of "execrable brutalité" (D1^r). The French term is relevant, as it emphasizes their fierce attitude toward newcomers. Their irrational actions bring them closer to the status of beasts, which, in the just-law theory, must be punished and corrected so that a rational order may be restored.[44] In the rational-law framework, Palmendos's attack would be a fair response to such behaviour. It must be recognized that Palmendos only acts after Baledon's son has tried to invade his ship; all the three editions present his actions as a response to his foe's offensive acts.[45] In the Spanish and French, Palmendos badly injures young Baledon – he slices his arm from his shoulder – but does not kill him. In Munday's version, Palmendos kills his enemy, but only when the latter tries to force his way onto the vessel. Munday seems then less constrained than Vernassal and the Spanish author, who apparently follow more closely the requirements of the just-law doctrine, thus allowing for the use of violence within certain limits – that is, to win and restore order, without having to destroy the enemy.[46] One may hesitate about the just nature of Palmendos's actions in Munday's version, since he resorts to killing young Baledon as the means of preventing his advance. In doing so, he fails to offer a proportional response to his foe's attack and does not entirely comply with the just-law requirements, one of which is a "proportional restraint of force" for charitable reasons.[47]

In this same vein, Munday introduces a less sympathetic view of old Baledon when he is eventually defeated. Though the three versions offer a quite similar description of the fierce combat, Munday presents the antagonist in a different light. In the English text, Baledon acknowledges his evil doings and invokes the pagan gods but does not actually repent: "Now see I well, that myne infinite and wicked offences, committed against men without desert, had throwne this wreakefull sentence on me" (G1r). By contrast, in the French and Spanish versions, the giant openly declares his willingness to save his soul.[48] The combat is then presented as a means of bringing the enemy back to (Christian) order.[49] The Spanish and French views seem to be indebted to the scholastics' doctrine of the just war as a charitable act,[50] a perspective that Munday's translation fails to offer. In Munday's sources, the giant is depicted as a devoted husband who begs to see his wife before dying, but he is able to take leave of his wife only in the Spanish original. In contrast, Munday does away with both Baledon's repentance and farewell to his wife, hence focusing solely on his evil nature.

After his victory over old Baledon, Palmendos frees all of the giant's prisoners and takes control of the island (Sp.23–5; Fr. D5v; Eng. G3v). According to the laws of war, a victor assumes rights over conquered territory and its people.[51] Yet all three versions of the tale are similar in casting Palmendos's control over Delphos as something other than a "real conquest." Rather, they present it as an act of cession of sovereignty from the inhabitants of the island to Palmendos, who assumes it on behalf of Emperor Palmerin. This episode clearly recalls well-known sixteenth-century debates on the rights of native people over their lands, in an age of increasing European expansion. Those debates had been especially interesting in Spain – more specifically, within the School of Salamanca – and had an extraordinary impact on European foreign affairs from the mid-sixteenth century. The official position held by the Spanish crown on its American empire was to regard its native inhabitants as human beings with dominion over their goods and lands, as it was made clear in the 1512 Burgos Statutes and their subsequent amendments in 1513 and 1518.[52] Neo-Thomist theologians, highly engaged in these discussions from the late 1530s to the late 1550s, went beyond such beliefs and generally concluded that the Spanish monarch could claim sovereignty and property rights in America only if "the native Americans themselves could be said to have surrendered their natural legislative authority to the empire voluntarily." Without such voluntary surrender, the Spanish *potestas* could not rightfully be considered as existing for the exclusive benefit of those over whom it was to be exercised.[53]

All these principles, firmly embedded in natural-law theory, seem to permeate the Baledon episode in the three versions, since the inhabitants of Delphos, happy at their release from the giant's tyranny, unanimously accept Palmerin's rule. Thus, the island is conquered and colonized as a result of the bond established between the people of Delphos and their new lord. No violence is exerted on the islanders, for the conqueror requests his subjects to accept their new lord willingly. The conquest is then presented as a cession of sovereignty that is fully accepted by the new subjects.[54] The noblemen of the island, who stand as high representatives of the community, choose a governor who will rule the island until Palmerin decides to appoint one of his own choosing. The provisional election of Guillador as governor suggests that there will be changes in the future when these vassals – not citizens – will have a new ruler appointed by their lord.

Both the Spanish and French versions stress the fact that Palmendos refuses to accept any presents from the islanders; thus, the hero does not seem to receive any material reward for his victory. Munday does not include these lines: there is no reference to Palmendos's refusal of tributes. Instead, he points out that the island will eventually be transferred to one of Palmendos's sons, "beeing a pleasant, fayre and opulent Countrey, nauigable for all passengers whatsoeuer" (K1ᵛ). Munday enhances the commercial worth of Delphos as a source of raw material and because of its strategic ports. Neither the Spanish nor the French version includes this reference. In this sense, Munday's translation seems to commit itself to the principles of contemporary English explorers and merchants, those who were trying to open new commercial routes overseas. His pragmatic views on the possibility of acquiring goods from the inhabitants of Delphos and on Palmendos's disregard of his foe's spiritual good reveal a much less nuanced approach when dealing with rivals: Baledon is not given any positive traits, and therefore the vanquished foe deserves only punishment.

Munday decided to stick to the French and Spanish sources in introducing the idea of a cession in order to explain how a rational free people – the islanders – transferred their sovereignty. By so doing, he could claim the moral authority of neo-Thomist theologians while following in the footsteps of English travel and New World accounts that, in many cases, idealized the conduct of English explorers with regard to native people. In this manner, English colonists might be presented in a far more favourable light than the allegedly terribly cruel Spaniards. An obvious example of such a "white legend" would indeed be Sir Francis Drake, whose supposedly peaceful and respectful treatment of the natives of Nova Albion in 1579 was described in detail in Hakluyt's

Principal Navigations, published ten years later. The transfer of sovereignty over this region is similar to the aforementioned episode in *Palmendos.* In Hakluyt's narrative, the inhabitants of Nova Albion make signs to Drake

> that they would resigne unto him their right and title of the whole land, and become his subjects. In which ... the King and the rest, with one consent, and with great reverence, joyfully singing a song, did set the crown upon his head, inriched his necke with all the chaines, and offered unto him many other things ... which thing our Generall thought not meet to reject, because he knew not what honour and profit it might be to our Countrey. Wherefore in the name, and to the use of her Majestie he tooke the scepter, crowne, and dignitie of the said country into his hands.

Hakluyt quite intentionally stresses the fact that Drake accepted sovereignty over the island in the name of the queen, though it is clear that he did not refuse the natives' presents and that he made substantial private profit from the numerous exploits against Spanish ships. His supposedly gentle manner with regard to the natives stands in sharp contrast with his violent dealings with the Spanish, which suggests a possible parallel between the Spanish enemy and the giant Baledon, who is divested of his island – and his life. Baledon's seizing of all people and goods that reached his island may have reminded English readers of contemporary attacks against Spain's exclusive trading rights over lands that could be of commercial interest to English merchants. Munday's more practical and less troubled view on international affairs may suggest he was addressing a mainly mercantile audience eager to imitate the models proposed by fictional or historical characters – that is, Palmendos or Drake – in late sixteenth-century English romance and travel literature.

As Brian Lockey insightfully comments, "while one might expect religious and legal authorities to have formulated legal rationales for English expansionism, it was actually writers of romance fiction who employed juridical standards to evaluate acts of foreign intervention or conquest." Thus, he adds, "a form condemned for frivolity was able to accommodate the ethical and political issues of transnational justice and the laws of war."[55] This process of cultural accommodation is evident in the case of *Palmendos,* since its translator reconsiders the just-war and natural-law codes present in his French and Spanish sources. What is most striking, however, is that Munday, who was particularly careful about religious references throughout his text, decided to preserve certain pre-Reformation Christian traits present in the Spanish and French editions with regard to this very episode. Thus, the hero, even if he is not yet a Christian, commands Guillador to build a church and a nunnery to honour the Virgin Mary, at the request of his beloved lady (H4ᵛ). This reference, which may have sounded troublesome in Protestant England, has been regarded as possible evidence of Munday's alleged Catholic sympathies.[56] It might rather be viewed as an address to Catholic merchants and explorers interested in colonization. Indeed, Catholic explorer Sir Humphrey Gilbert (1537–83) had been given patents in 1578 to search for a northwestern passage to Asia. In 1582, the queen allowed Gilbert to ally with a group of Catholics led by Sir Thomas Gerrard (1560–1621), Sir George Peckham (d. 1608), and Sir William Gatesby (1547–98), who aimed to establish a colony in the New World. Gilbert died in 1583, and his plan for religious freedom in America failed when Peckham was arrested that same year.[57] The latter had published in 1583 a travel account intended to promote Gilbert's emprise, *A True Reporte of the Late Discoveries and Possession Taken in the Right of the Crowne of England*. Peckham's work was issued by Catholic printer John Charlewood, who had worked jointly with Munday in those same years. One of the prefatory poems commending the project was precisely penned by Sir Francis Drake.

The presence of Catholic traits in Munday's translation might be viewed as proof that he, his dedicatees, or even his publishing agents, supported conquest and colonization of new lands both for commercial and religious reasons, with the sole condition that they remained loyal and contributed significant revenue to the Crown. In any case, the overall prevailing authority in Delphos is that of Emperor Palmerin – an outside figure ultimately responsible for correcting the wrongdoings of other rulers. Such a cosmopolitan ideal is probably the most obvious view of a transnational justice in chivalric romances,[58] a recurrent *topos* largely embedded in the medieval and sixteenth-century doctrines on just war and rational law. Such legal discourses successfully articulated a response to European territorial and commercial ambitions and offered an alternative to religious dissenters who happened to be loyal subjects too. Above all, they contributed a model distinct from the increasingly confessional and nationalist views of the new nation states in early modern Europe.

NOTES

1 Anthony Munday, *The Honorable, Pleasant and Rare Conceited Historie of Palmendos Sonne to the Famous and Fortunate Prince Palmerin d'Oliua, Emperour of Constantinople and the Queene of Tharsus. Translated out of*

French by A.M. one of the Messengers of her Maiesties Chamber (London: John Charlewood for Simon Watersonne, 1589).

2 There were ten Spanish editions printed between 1512 and 1588. Up to six editions of Mambrino Roseo's (d. 1573/80) Italian translation were published from 1548 to 1596, while François de Vernassal's (1520?–60s) French version ran through ten editions and reprints only in the sixteenth century. For a more detailed information, see Leticia Álvarez-Recio, "Spanish Chivalric Romances in English Translation: Anthony Munday's *Palmendos* (1589)," *Cahiers Élisabéthains: A Journal of English Renaissance Studies* 91, no. 1 (2016): 8.

3 The French translator Jean Maugin (n.d.) turned the name Polendos into Palmendos in the first edition of *Palmerin D'Olive* (Paris, 1546; Dd6ᵛ) and its ensuing reprints. Vernassal kept the name Palmendos in his French version of *Primaleón*. Anthony Munday emulated Vernassal.

4 Long-lasting confusion among scholars regarding chapter numbers translated from the French version in Munday's *Palmendos* has recently been clarified in Leticia Álvarez-Recio, "Chapters Translated by Anthony Munday in *The History of Palmendos* (1589): A Long-Standing Error," *Notes and Queries* 62, no. 4 (2015): 549–51.

5 Arber II, 513. The information about the dates when Charlewood was active has been taken from the British Book Trade Index, http://bbti.bodleian.ox.ac.uk/.

6 The exception to the English dedications are his Latin verses dedicated to the Earl of Oxford at the end *The Mirrour of Mutabilitie* (1579; STC 18276), M2ᵛ.

7 The poem follows the dedication "To the most strong and skilful man of the navy, the golden knight, Sir Francis Drake":

> Stop vain Greece admiring Hercules's pillars
> Or the Mynians, or the head of Dulichius.
> You surpass Amphitryonidas, most powerful Drake, and Jason and his
>   comrades, and Penelope's husband.
> Neptune entrusts his trident to you,
> And willingly renders his authority and rule over the sea.
> Palmendos, happy and safe under such a patron
> Ventures to fly to innumerable hands.
> Let Zoidus feel envy and Codrus's flanks break,
> Palmendos will be safe under Drake's protection.
> It goes, flies and ventures, and despises menacing words,
> For you, Drake, are used to despising swollen menaces.

Sincere thanks to Professor Ana Pérez Vega, at the University of Seville, for the rendering of this poem into English.

8 This is a clear case of translation as an act of appropriation. Munday overlooks the Spanish origin of his text while he commends it for

Drake's protection. The words "goes, flies and ventures" suggest an act of liberation that can be carried out only by Drake's English hands. As Barbara Fuchs states, "what contemporary poets choose to praise, and more important, the metaphorics of their praise provide key insights into the valuation of literary appropriation and imitation, understood not as timeless aesthetic categories but as historical constructs deeply embedded in political and social relations" (*The Poetics of Piracy: Emulating Spain in English Literature* [Philadelphia: University of Pennsylvania Press, 2013], 22). In *Palmendos*'s case, Munday anglicized the originally Iberian romance as well as the discourse of exploration and conquest that permeates it. He does not mention his French source either, and, by not doing so, he deprives his text of any explicit connection with England's main rivals – above all, Spain – in the competition for trade and colonization.

9 Christopher Hodgkins, *Reforming Empire: Protestant Colonialism and Conscience in British Literature* (Columbia: University of Missouri Press, 2002), 87. Born into a non-aristocratic family in the West Country, Drake had grown up with his kinsman William Hawkins, who had made a reputation thanks to the slave trade in the 1560s. Following in Hawkins's footsteps, Drake gained a good sum of money with his raids on Spanish ships in the late 1560s and 1570s; he then bought some property and was listed as a merchant in Plymouth. In 1577, he started a journey around the world financed by himself and by such leading figures at the court as Sir Francis Walshingham (ca. 1532–90), Christopher Hatton (1540–91), and Queen Elizabeth herself (1533–1603), with the official purpose of seeking new markets. Drake made huge profits from his capture of Spanish treasure in the Pacific. Back in London, he assured the queen that "his prize was contraband in the eyes of the court in Madrid, since the original owners had not registered most of it." Advised by her counsellors, Elizabeth prohibited any written account of Drake's voyage, and "participants were sworn to silence for fear of Spanish reprisals." Nonetheless, he was knighted, on the *Golden Hinde*, in 1581. Drake's raids on Spanish ports in the West Indies in 1585–86 proved a complete failure, while his attacks on Cádiz in April 1587 without, apparently, the explicit support of Elizabeth, were also a matter of concern for many at the court. His actions, however, did not prevent him from being appointed vice-admiral of the English navy fighting against Spain in 1588. See Mark G. Hanna, *Pirate Nests and The Rise of the British Empire, 1570–1740* (Chapel Hill: University of North Carolina Press, 2015), 44; Bruce Wathen, *Sir Francis Drake: The Construction of a Hero* (Woodbridge, UK: D.S. Brewer, 2009), 9–11; and Harry Kelsey, "Drake, Sir Francis (1540–1596), Pirate, Sea Captain, and Explorer," in *ODNB*, accessed 29 January 2020.

10 As H.R. French notes, "the 'middle sort of people' in the seventeenth
and eighteenth centuries remain elusive, definitions of them continue to
be imprecise, and the resultant groups are still incoherent and untidy"
("The Search for the 'Middle Sort of People' in England, 1600–1800,"
Historical Journal 43 [2000]: 293). The present work follows, mostly, in the
footsteps of Jonathan Barry's approach, as it describes the middle sort as a
"bourgeoisie" characterized by "association and collective action within a
civic, and more merely urban, context." According to Barry, this collective
action strengthened a "shared sense of values" based, among other things,
on "civic involvement, mutual support and common economic interests"
(*The Middling Sort of People: Culture, Society and Politics in England,
1550–1800*, ed. Jonathan Barry and Christopher Brooks [New York:
Palgrave, 1994], 82, 98; see also French, "The Search for the 'Middle Sort of
People,'" 287).

11 Mark Netzloff, "Sir Francis Drake's Ghost: Piracy, Cultural Memory, and
Spectral Nationhood," in *Pirates? The Politics of Plunder, 1550–1650*, ed.
Claire Jowitt (Basingstoke, UK: Palgrave, 2007), 141.

12 Andrew Hadfield, *Literature, Travel and Colonial Writing in the English
Renaissance 1545–1625* (Oxford: Clarendon Press, 2007), 133.

13 Susanna De Schepper, "For the Common Good and for the National
Interest: Paratexts in English Translations of Navigational Works," in
*Renaissance Cultural Crossroads: Translation, Print and Culture in Britain,
1473–1640*, ed. Sara K. Barker and Brenda Honsington (Leiden: Brill, 2013),
187.

14 For further information, see Donald Beecher, "The Legacy of John
Frampton: Elizabethan Trader and Translator," *Renaissance Studies* 20, no. 3
(2006): 331; Peter C. Mancall, *Travel Narratives from the Age of Discovery: An
Anthology* (Oxford: Oxford University Press, 2006), 14; and Philip Tromans,
"Advertising America: The Printing, Publication, and Promotion of
English New World Books, 1553–1600" (PhD diss., De Montfort University,
2015), 349–53.

15 Joan Pong Linton, *The Romance of the New World: Gender and the Literary
Formations of English Colonialism* (Cambridge: Cambridge University Press,
1998), 2.

16 This idea is inspired by Irving A. Leonard's argument in his well-known
works *Romances of Chivalry in the Spanish Indies* (Berkeley: University of
California Press, 1933) and *Books of the Brave* (Cambridge, MA: Harvard
University Press, 1949). Leonard's basic premise is that the Spanish
conquistadors behaved in America in the manner of the heroes found in
contemporary books of chivalry, the latter being the clearest models to
imitate in such an unknown void as America may have seemed to them.
Other critics, such as Henry Thomas, José Torre Revello, Ida Rodríguez

Trampolini, and Alan Deyemond, among others, followed a quite similar line of thought, thus enhancing the didactic use that the Spanish conquistadors may have made of those chivalric stories. See Thomas, *Spanish and Portuguese Romances of Chivalry* (Cambridge: Cambridge University Press, 1920); Torre Revello, *El libro, la imprenta y el periodismo en América durante la dominación española* (Buenos Aires: Jacobo Penser, 1940); Rodríguez Trampolini, *Los Amadises en América: La hazaña de Indias como empresa caballeresca* (Mexico City: Junta Mexicana de Investigaciones Históricas, 1948); Deyemond, *The Middle Ages: A Literary History of Spain* (New York: Barnes and Noble, 1971). In De Armas Wilson's opinion, such parallels between the conquistadors and the heroes of Iberian chivalric romances had already been suggested by Romantic authors such as William Prescott and Washington Irving in the early nineteenth century. See her article "Ocean Chivalry: Issues of Alterity in *Don Quixote*," *Colby Quarterly* 32, no. 4 (1996): 221–35.

17 Susanna L.B. De Schepper, "Foreign Books for English Readers: Published Translations of Navigation Manuals and Their Audience in the English Renaissance, 1500–1640" (PhD diss., University of Warwick, 2012), 45–9.

18 In his preface, Norman associates Drake with the heroes of Classical epic and endows him with a quasi-religious aura. For a close analysis of Drake's characterization in Norman's preface, see Marco Nievergelt, "Francis Drake: Merchant, Knight and Pilgrim," *Renaissance Studies* 23 (2008): 56–7; Richard Helgerson, *Forms of Nationhood: The Elizabethan Writing of England* (Chicago: Chicago University Press, 1992), 173; and W.T. Jewkes, "Sir Francis Drake Revived: From Letters to Legend," in *Sir Francis Drake and the Famous Voyage, 1577–1580*, ed. Norman J.W. Thrower (Berkeley and Los Angeles: University of California Press, 1984), 115.

19 Anthony Payne, *Richard Hakluyt: A Guide to His Books and to Those Associated with Him, 1580–1625* (London: Bernard Quaritch, 2008), 95.

20 *First Booke of the Historie of the Discoverie and Conquest of the East Indias, Enterprised by the Portingales, in their Daungerous Navigations, in the Time of King Don John, the Second of that Name* (London: Thomas East, 1582).

21 For an English translation of this poem, see W. Wright, "To the Magnificent and Valiant Man, Sir Francis Drake, the English Knight,'" *Western Antiquary* 8 (1888), 27. Jorge Cañizares-Esguerra has identified most of the works dedicated to Drake in his book *Puritan Conquistadors: Iberianizing the Atlantic, 1550–1700* (Stanford, CA: Stanford University Press, 2006), 247n62.

22 Agustín de Zarate, *The Strange and Delectable History of the Discovery and Conquest of the Provinces of Peru*, trans. Thomas Nicholas (London: John Charlewood, W. How and John Kingston for Richard Jones, 1581), dedication.

23 This enterprise was financed by the queen, the Earl of Leicester (1532–88), John Hawkins (1532–95), William Hawkins (1519–89), and Sir Walter Raleigh (1554–1618). Drake's violent attempts to capture isolated Spanish towns proved a complete failure; the English settlers at Roanoke Island were demoralized after a year living in the Caribbean and went back to England on Drake's ship. They arrived in Plymouth on 28 July 1586. See Kelsey, "Drake, Sir Francis."

24 *A Most Friendly Farewell, Giuen by a Welwiller to the Right Worshipful Sir Frauncis Drake Knight, Generall of her Maiesties Nauy, which he Appointed for this his Honorable Voiage, and the Rest of the Fleete Bound to the Southward, and to All the Gentlemen his Followers, and Captaines in this Exploite, who Set Sale from Wolwich the xv. Day of Iuly, 1585* (London: Thomas East for Walter Mantell and Thomas Lawe, 1585), A4^v.

25 On this letter, see Julian S. Corbett, *Papers Relating to the Navy during the Spanish War, 1585–1587* (London: Navy Records Society, 1898), 101. For additional information on this episode, see Harry Kelsey, *Sir Francis Drake: The Queen's Pirate* (New Haven, CT: Yale University Press, 1998), 280–304.

26 *The True and Perfecte Newes of the Worthy Valiant Exploytes, Performed and Done by that Valiant Knight Syr Francis Drake* (London: John Charlewood for Thomas Hackett, 1587), A3^r.

27 Bigges's account was dedicated to the Earl of Essex, who was to participate in Drake and Norris's aforementioned expedition.

28 *A Farewell Intitled to the Famous and Fortunate Generals of our English Forces and Sea, Sir John Norris and Sir Francis Drake* (London: John Charlewood for William Wright, 1589), A2^r. STC 19537.

29 Kelsey, "Drake, Sir Francis."

30 A.L. Rowse, *The Expansion of Elizabethan England* (Madison: University of Wisconsin Press, 2003), 283.

31 Among them were Nicholas Breton's *A Discourse in Commendation of the Valiant and Virtuous Minded Gentleman, Maiester Francis Drake* (1581), Nicholas's translation of Zarate's *History of the Discovery and Conquest of the Provinces of Peru* (1581), Greepe's *The True and Perfecte Newes of the Worthy Valiant Exploytes, Performed and Done by that Valiant Knight Syr Francis Drake* (1587), Hercusanus Danus's *Magnifico ac strenuo uiro D Francisco Draco* (1587), Luke Wagenar's *The Mariners Mirrour* (1588), Walter Bigges's *A Summarie and True Discourse of Sir Francis Drake West Indian Voyage* (1589), Peele's *Farewell* (1589), Albretch Meyer's *Instructions for Trauellers* (1589), and Haykluyt's *Principall Navigations*. The last was dedicated to Sir Francis Walshingham but included an account of Drake's circumnavigation.

32 Charlewood's case was not exceptional. Printer Thomas East had also shown considerable interest both in exploration literature and Iberian chivalric romance. He printed six navigation works in the 1580s, including

travel accounts and New World histories, among them, Castanheda's *First Booke of the Historie and Conquest of the East Indies* (1582), Roberts's *Most Friendly Farewell* (1585), Nicholas Thomas's *A Pleasant Description of the Fortunate Islandes Called the Ilands of Canaria* (1583), William Bourne's *A Regiment for the Sea* (1584), a single volume containing Robert Norman's *The New Attractive* and William Borough's *The Variation of the Cumpass* (1585), and Juan González de Mendoza's *New Mexico* (1587). East also printed the medieval fictional travel account *The Voyage and Trauayle of Syr John Maundeuile* (1583) and Cartigny's *Voyage of the Wandering Knight* (1584). Castanheda's, Roberts's, and Cartigny's volumes were dedicated to Drake. East was also responsible for the publication of the five English editions of *The Mirrour of Princely Deeds* that were issued from 1578 to 1586. In addition, printer and bookseller John Wolfe (active 1579–1601) published in 1587 and 1588 an Italian and English translation of Juan González de Mendoza's (1545–1618) *The History of the Great and Mighty Kingdom of China*. He also printed Jones's translation of Meyer's *Instructions for Travellers* (1589), which had been dedicated to Drake. *The History of the Great and Mighty Kingdom of China* was sold by Edward White (active 1572?–1613), who also sold Thomas Saunder's (n.d.) translation *A True Description and Breefe Discourse of a Most Lamentable Voyage, Made Lately to Tripodie in Barbarie* (1587) and *The Voyage and Trauel of M Caesar Frederick, Merchant of Venice, into the East Indies* (1588), both printed by Richard Jones (active 1564–1613). White sold five works by Munday in the 1580s, mostly pamphlet literature printed by Charlewood.

33   Delphos was imagined as one of the two Mykonos islands in the Aegean Sea. In the sixteenth century, the smaller one was generally associated with Delphos, the popular site of Apollo's sanctuary. See Terence Spenser, "Shakespeare's Isle of Delphos," *Modern Language Review* 47, no. 2 (1952): 199–202.

34   For the Spanish edition consulted, see *Primaleón, Salamanca 1512*, ed. Mª del Carmen Marín Pina (Alcalá de Henares: Centro de Estudios Cervantinos, 1998). For the French, see François de Vernassal, *L'Histoire de Primaleon de Grece Continvant Celle de Palmerin D'Olive Empereur de Constantinople son Pere* (Paris: Ian [Jean] Longis, 1550; FB 44732). Most scholarship on Munday's *Palmendos* agrees that the English translator never worked with the Spanish original. However, a detailed collation of the English, French, and Spanish texts has revealed certain coincidences between the English and the Spanish, absent in the French, which suggest that Munday may have actually been familiar with the Spanish source. See, for instance, Álvarez-Recio, "Spanish Chivalric Romances in English Translation," 8–9.

35   Stephen C. Neff, *War and the Law of Nations: A General History* (Cambridge: Cambridge University Press, 2005), 29–30.

36 Martin Wight, *Systems of States*, ed. Hendley Bull (Leicester: Leicester University Press, 1977), 34–5.

37 According to the first criterion, *auctoritas*, a war could be launched only at the command of a sovereign. *Personae* refers to the sort of people who could not be involved in warfare – women, children, the infirm, and the aged. *Res* was the specific war aim – the claim that was made – while the *justa causa* referred to the legal worth of such claim. Finally, the *animus* was the rightful intention of the combatant, who could not fight out of personal hatred but just with the aim of amending the wrongful actions of the foe in order to bring him back to righteousness. See Neff, *War and the Law of Nations* (Cambridge: Cambridge University Press, 2005), 50–2; Frederick H. Russell, *The Just War in the Middle Ages* (Cambridge: Cambridge University Press, 1975), chs 6–7; and Barnes, "The Just War," in *The Cambridge History of Later Medieval Philosophy*, ed. Norman Kretzmann et al. (Cambridge: Cambridge University Press, 1982), 771–84.

38 Munday follows Vernassal literally: "le plus fier & plus grand tyran, qui fust pour lors en toutes les trois parties du monde" (D1ᵛ); "The most fierce and cruel Tirant, that liued in all those three partes of the world" (F1ʳ).

39 Sp. "el más bravo cavallero que avía en todo el mundo" (19).

40 *Vitoria: Political Writings*, ed. Anthony Pagden and Jeremy Lawrence (Cambridge: Cambridge University Press, 2017 [1991]), 278–85.

41 Ibid., xxvi–xxvii, 275–80.

42 Fr. "luy commença dire assez arrogamment: Cheualier as tu bien osé prendre la hardiesse, d'entrer sans licence en nostre port? Ouy certes dit lors Palmendos, & ce pourautant que ie fay peu de cas, deslaches & desloyaux comme vous autres, qui par voz damnables malignitez prenez les gens en trahison, pour après n'exercer sur eux que cruauté & felonie: mais il est temps que vous receuiez le guerdon d'vne tant execrable brutalité" (D1ʳ) (he began to say quite arrogantly: Knight, have you dared to enter our port without a license? Yes certainly said Palmendos, and I do not care about such cowardly and disloyal people as you are who do nothing but inflict cruelty and commit felony: but it is time for you to receive your guerdon for such an execrable brutality [my translation]); Sp. "El fijo del gigante llegó muy cerca y díxole: –Vos, don caballero, ¿cómo fuestes osado de entrar en nuestro puerto sin licencia? – Fízelo yo – dixo Polendos– porque tengo en muy poco tales cavalleros traidores como vosotros sois, que tenéis tales artes fechas que tomáis las gentes a traición y fazéis aquí grandes cruezas. – Venidos sois a tiempo que lo pagaréis caramente" (21) (The giant's son came very close and told him: how did you dare to enter our port without a licence? I did so – said Palmendos – because I hold in very low esteem such treacherous knights as you are,

who commit treason and inflict great cruelties. – The time has come that you will pay dearly for that [my translation]).

43 "Treacherous" should be viewed here in a broad sense as the antithesis of knighthood. This is important, as chivalry was one of the main secular codes regulating warfare and thus contributing to the *jus in bello* in the late Middle Ages. On treason as opposed to knighthood, see Megan G. Leitch, *Romancing Treason: The Literature of the War of the Roses* (Oxford: Oxford University Press, 2015); on the alliance between the chivalric code and the just-war theory, see Brian C. Lockey, *Law and Empire in English Renaissance Literature* (Cambridge: Cambridge University Press, 2006), 30–4.

44 This is especially clear in the first entry for "brutish" in the *OED*, "Of or pertaining to the brutes, or lower animals, as opposed to man." See *OED*, accessed 28 March 2020, http://www.oed.com/view/Entry/24026?redirectedFrom=brutish. The French "brutalité" is associated with the adjective "brut," defined as "animal, brute" in Edmond Huguet, *Dictionnaire de la Langue Française du Seizième Siècle* (Paris: Libraire Ancienne Honoré Champion, 1932), 2: 18.

45 Armed self-defence was considered a just-cause action against an unfair action by others. See James Turner Johnson, *Ethics and the Use of Force: Just War in Historical Perspective* (Aldershot, UK: Ashgate, 2011), 12–14.

46 Vitoria, *Law of War*, in *Political Writings*, 317, 326–7.

47 Johnson, *Ethics and the Use of Force*, 82.

48 Fr.: "Mais puis que par condigne remuneration i'en perdz miraculeusement le corps, ne souffrez ie vous supplie, mõ ame deualler es paluz infernaux, pour y estre de perpetuel suplice foudroyée" (D3ʳ) (but after I lose miraculously my body, I beg you not to let my soul descend into the infernal places and remain there in perpetual torment ([my translation]); Sp.: "yo lo conozco y, pues ansí es, no quiero ir contra la voluntad del Alto Señor, que bien creo que es llegada la mi fin, y pues he perdido el cuerpo, no quiero perder el alma!" (22) (I do not intend to go against God's decision and as my death approaches and I have lost my body, I do not wish to lose my soul [my translation]).

49 As John M. Mattox observes, "the end state to which just war tends is not merely the restoration of 'order' but of God's order. Thus, as important as order is, it is not an end in itself. It is a means to an end; and that end is the salvation of man." See *Saint Augustine and the Theory of Just War* (London: Continuum, 2006), 121.

50 In scholastic just-war theory, war was generally discussed under the heading of charity, as "charity, not justice, was the primary regulative norm in war." In Johan Olsthoorn's words, "the biblical duty to love your neighbor as yourself thus determined when, how, and to what end military force may be used." See "Grotius and the Early Modern

Tradition," in *The Cambridge Handbook of the Just War*, ed. Larry May (Cambridge: Cambridge University Press, 2018), 53.

51 See Sharon Korman, *The Right of Conquest: The Acquisition of Territory by Force in International Law and Practice* (Oxford: Clarendon Press, 1996), 8.

52 Guillermo Céspedes del Castillo, *Ensayos sobre los reinos castellanos de Indias* (Madrid: Real Academia de la Historia, 1999), 150–65.

53 Anthony Pagden, *Lords of All the World: Ideology of Empire in Spain, Britain and France, c. 1500–1800* (New Haven, CT: Yale University Press, 1995), 50–8.

54 For a distinction between conquest and cession, see Korman, *The Right of Conquest*, 44.

55 Lockey, *Law and Empire*, 4.

56 Such is the view held by Donna Hamilton in *Anthony Munday and the Catholics, 1560–1633* (Aldershot, UK: Ashgate, 2005), 91–2.

57 Rory Rapple, "Gilbert, Sir Humphrey (1537–1583), explorer and soldier," in *ODNB*, accessed 28 March 2020, http://www.oxforddnb.com/view/10.1093/ref:odnb/9780198614128.001.0001/odnb-9780198614128-e-10690. See also Linton, *The Romance of the New World*, 48; and Adrian Morey, *The Catholic Subjects of Elizabeth I* (Totowa, NJ: Rowman, 1978), 136.

58 For a thorough analysis of such cosmopolitan ideas in Munday and other late sixteenth-century English fiction writers, see Brian Lockey, *Early Modern Catholics, Royalists, and Cosmopolitans: English Transnationalism and the Christian Commonwealth* (Farnham, UK: Ashgate, 2015). The chapters by Donna B. Hamilton and Elizabeth Evenden-Kenyon essays in the present volume also illustrate Munday's cosmopolitanism in his romance translations.

Chapter Three

The Portrait of the *Femme Sole* in Anthony Munday's *The First Book of Primaleon of Greece*

MARÍA BEATRIZ HERNÁNDEZ PÉREZ

Introduction: Hagiographic and Romance Spaces in the Transition to the Renaissance

The representation of space has been a recurrent topic in discussions concerning readership in late medieval literature from the perspective of gender.[1] As reading practices spread in the transition to the Renaissance and larger sections of the population gained access to a wide variety of texts, the boundaries between certain genres revealed themselves as increasingly permeable. The gradual exposure of the reading public to new features of various genres eventually led to a broadening of expectations among readers. Such was the case with respect to romance and hagiography,[2] two genres that, since their inception, had a clear impact on female readers. In this chapter, I suggest that the common ground shared by these two genres is a metaphoric means of highlighting space. In romances, certain "female qualities" are conveyed or reinforced by spatial means. Due to social practices and age-old gender attributions, ladies dwelling in courts or aristocratic households would learn how to take into account and respond to domestic architecture and interior decoration. Such familiar settings would reinforce the identification of readers with romance heroines in their distinctive capacities and roles. On the other hand, in the formative literature intended for religious women, the need to remain isolated in one's own cell was essential. Shari Horner's coinage of the expression "the discourse of enclosure" refers to an early medieval perception of space whereby

The research for this essay was supported by funding from the Spanish Ministry of Economy and Competitiveness (ref. FFI2015-70101-P).

sacred locations became symbolic of the virginal body of female saints. The celebration of enclosure as a sign of devoutness can be found in late medieval hagiographic accounts that, in turn, would stimulate many secular women to pursue a life of domestic piety. With the growing need for privacy – evidenced by secular architectural innovations – reading itself became a more private and alluring experience for women.[3] Thus, as incompatible as the reading of the two generic types may seem at first, and in spite of ecclesiastical disregard for some of the essential elements in romances,[4] romance and hagiographic texts could, in fact, be perceived as compatible, and many women would simultaneously enjoy both.

The erosion of these generic frontiers and its subsequent effect on female characters in romance texts seemed to be almost a natural development in Catholic countries on their way to the Renaissance. In England, on the other hand, we may guess that this trend was subject to several upheavals as the Reformation took root and fostered animosity toward Catholic models. Tiffany J. Werth illustrates the challenge of adapting romance to Reformation requirements that was carried out in Elizabethan England by male and female authors alike.[5] Bearing such tensions in mind, this chapter is concerned with female readership and the administration of space in Anthony Munday's rendering of the Iberian romance *The First Book of Primaleon of Greece*. Its female characters may not only suggest the hybridization of specific features taken from hagiography and romance, but also allow for gender-specific interpretations as female reading habits expanded. This chapter focuses specifically on the *femme sole* figure, a category with a metaphorical counterpart in romance characters. Through the analysis of this motif, I propose that Iberian romances achieved popularity in sixteenth-century England due not only to Munday's mastery in translation but also to the genre's capacity to adjust to the needs of a renewed female reading community.

The Reading of *Femmes Soles*

The existence of a proper Renaissance for women in Europe has been the subject of significant debate, to which the issue of female literacy and literary patronage in England has contributed. Historians have found acknowledgment of the presence of reading women as early as the 1570s and 1580s, as the range of available works greatly widens and female addressees begin to turn up in dedications. Up to the mid-seventeenth century, over 1,500 works in England would be dedicated to women of various social ranks.[6] It is also worth noting that a considerable proportion of the English population maintained ties with their Catholic past; thus, many recusant women would become acquainted with books that would – either nostalgically or actively – keep them in contact with the Catholic sphere of influence. Apart from devotional pieces and practical guides, there was a growing demand among women for recreational literature. To satisfy this demand, early Renaissance Iberian prose romances, along with late medieval or more recent vernacular landmark works, would make their way into England. In such Iberian books of chivalry, the presence of secular and religious female characters sharing or exchanging personal experiences attests to the degree of freedom the genre had acquired. Such versatility in the presentation of female roles may have attracted English women at a moment when society judged their interpretative aptitude as poor, according to humanistic and Reformation standards. As Newcomb suggests, by reading such books, women would challenge not only those voices disavowing unwanted Catholic traits or immoral attitudes in the romance but also the specific disregard for the genre when associated with women.[7] Critics condemned both the female reader and the romances she read as hazardous and subversive.[8] However, in spite of institutional and personal attempts to control female access to these books, the last decades of the sixteenth century witnessed an unprecedented increase in sales of Iberian romances, for which women may have been partly accountable.

Even though measuring reading skills in the sixteenth century is not an easy task, it is beyond doubt that literacy had spread even among the lower social ranks in Elizabethan times. Irrespective of sex, according to Lucas, "the greatest literacy was found at the top, among the gentry and professional classes, who were almost wholly literate by 1600. The literacy of those living in London – including servants and apprentices – appears to have been substantially higher than anywhere else in the country."[9] If middle-class private tuition at home might guarantee literacy beyond that of the daughters of the nobility, those of less privileged groups might learn the skill in petty schools at an early age.[10] In fact, the very remarks about maids reading romances attest to the male concern about such trend. If – as occasional comments seem to indicate – servants were eager readers,[11] Iberian books of chivalry, sold at a cheap price, would have women not only from the aristocracy, but also from the middle and lower social rungs, as devoted readers.[12] At this time, the legal and social category of the so-called *femme sole* might have inspired or encouraged gender-specific reading.[13] If so, it may have contributed to broaden the generic margins of Iberian romances.

The category *femme sole* cut across a wide range of types and classifications at the time, none of which could fully reflect the complexities of the female condition.[14] The singularity of *femmes soles* consisted in their attempt to demand an independent economic and legal status, which some English women managed to achieve by the early fourteenth century in London and other towns through engaging in their own trading activities.[15] The term was originally applied to married women who sought to escape the limitations of a *femmes couvertes de baron* condition, and it ultimately included single women and widows in their capacity to come before the courts or to trade in their own names. Such women might enjoy this exceptional transitory state, a basic *sole* condition that they would ultimately lose. As McIntosh recaps, "the phrase 'a woman alone' might be used to draw attention to a widow's weak and unprotected state, justifying her ignorance or inability to plead in the common law."[16] I am not proposing that this singularity might be used to support a claim for Renaissance economic gender equality: Kowaleski and Bennet discourage that view by studying the hindrances posed by the general patriarchal context and by underscoring that the period when these women were most active was the fifteenth century, and so the concept hardly related to actual economic activities after 1560.[17] McIntosh, though, specifies that the term did survive as a legal status.[18]

I suggest that the concept may well have had a great impact and may have captured the imagination of Renaissance women from a wide social provenance, since, as Anne Laurence has argued, a significant part of the female English population lived on their own: "two-thirds were on their own, either widowed or having never been married ... It was common to find large numbers of unmarried women in towns, chiefly working in service and in trades connected with service."[19] When Munday's translation was first published in 1595, the very reference to the women who in the story are found alone or occupying a space of their own might have reminded readers not only of conventional damsels in imminent distress or of hermits derived from the Catholic tradition, but also of legally unguarded women.

Since Iberian romances tend to offer an ideal view of chivalric culture, their female characters do not become independent entrepreneurs. Their *femme sole* condition does not respond to a calling for trade or commerce but rather to their partaking in a patriarchal system that barely acknowledges in them any exchange value other than in the marriage contract. Within this literary framework, only some ladies in the upper social ranks maintained the status of women alone. Their capacity to remain alone, if only temporarily or by occupying a particular single space, would be valued by female readers from other social spheres whose condition also placed them in a situation of aloneness. Alex Davis refers specifically to those serving other women: "In particular, the figure of the romance-reading confidant or 'friend' who is placed in a subordinate position to her mistress, but whose reading is somehow linked to the prospect of upward mobility, may prove suggestive."[20] I propose that any reading woman, regardless of rank or degree, could project onto aristocratic female characters her own wish to maintain her private space and basic condition.

Iberian Romances of Chivalry: Munday's *First Book of Primaleon of Greece*

Joshua Phillips underlines Munday's pioneering role in turning Elizabethan stationers in need of unpatented products toward the Iberian romances.[21] Those books had proved to be rather profitable in Spain, Italy, and France, and so Munday considered them a safe bet when undertaking their English translation. As for the weight of female readership in the book market, there is evidence of the impact of the genre among noble Spanish and Portuguese ladies. Inventories of their private collections as well as explicit dedications to many of them confirm their interest.[22] However, although first intended for a higher readership, these romances soon reached the rest of the population and came to be regarded as popular products. In Daniel Eisenberg's words, "the accepted opinion concerning the Spanish romances of chivalry during their heyday, the sixteenth century, is that they were works which were read by all social types, from the highest to the lowest, but with a considerable predominance of the more numerous lower classes."[23] In France, such works were first printed in folio editions for the aristocracy, and later in cheaper quartos to be acquired more widely.

We are given a revealing glimpse of female family circles in Guillaume Landré's dedication of his own French translation of the second book of *Primaleón de Grecia* to Lady Loyse D'Estampes, a commission requiring access to the Spanish source text, a copy of which this lady kept in her cabinet.[24] The dedicatee, along with her sister Marie de la Chastre and her mother, Anne Robertet, not only enjoyed the Spanish edition but also had at home François Vernassal's French rendering of the first book, which Landré read and judged in this dedication. That is precisely the French translation – first edited in 1550 – that Munday would use as the source for his 1595 English edition. Although, in some countries, the genre became outdated by the late sixteenth century,[25] it was having its heyday in England. Munday's translation of Primaleon's story would be sold in popular quarto editions, which made it afford-able to a large section of the English population.[26]

These translations owed their popularity partly to the sense of rhythm in their narratives. Renaissance chivalric books offer a rhyth-mic pattern based on the alternation of departures and encounters, a pulse Patricia Parker presents as inescapably inherent to the threshold nature of romance.[27] *The First Book of Primaleon of Greece* reproduces such cadence. While intent on reaching their destinations, its roving knights get sidetracked along the way: dalliances in love games or knightly duties reinforce the traditional syntax with instant attachments that divide the long-distance journey into a sequence of short-term loops. In the framework of the story, such straying contributes to the density of a narrative pattern based on accumulation. Each new stop on their way spells distraction from those errant knights' main quests. This relentless additive practice, in turn, heralds the disorientation of readers, who can only keep on dutifully reading and veering away from the central plot.[28] The dynamic rhythm of the genre screens the relevance of the women who inhabit these fictional landscapes. Although the genre traditionally leans on the character of the distant woman who exerts all her power to help the male character achieve his aims, that basic plot line blends with subplots in which women seem more approachable. Although, at first sight, the latter seem to stand simply as "ladies in waiting" for male vis-itors, their being alone serves a dilation strategy in the narrative while vividly reflecting wider gender concerns that might be appreciated not only by courtly or rural aristocratic ladies, but also by readers from other rungs of the social ladder. The variety of such episodes in the book allows for a consideration of different situations and characters; I pay particular attention to women involved in "secondary" encounters while, at the same time, examining the spatial performances of the two main female characters, Gridonia and Flerida.

The First Booke of Primaleon of Greece is the title of Munday's transla-tion of a sequence of chapters in Vernassal's *L'Histoire de Primaleon de Grece*.[29] It focuses on the coming of age of Emperor Palmerin d'Oliva's legitimate son, Primaleon, while displaying in its twenty-four chapters several story lines connected thematically by the characters' journey to Constantinople. Its contents may be divided into three major sections. There is first a complex narrative told through the initial thirteen chap-ters, in which some of the main plot lines of Munday's *Palmendos* (1589) are displayed.[30] After a few chapters devoted to various male characters, the narrative focuses on Primaleon, the best fencer at the festive jousts held in the imperial city, who soon becomes the target for a series of for-eign knights willing to challenge him. This point marks the beginning of the second part, devoted to the prince as legatee to his father's past feuds – more specifically, the old debt contracted with the Duchy of Ormeda, whose lord had died when seeking revenge on Emperor Palmerin. Unaware of the existence of such open wounds, Primaleon cannot fulfil his promise of arranging an enjoyable, bloodless tournament, since the grieving widow, the Duchess of Ormeda, encourages her daughter's suitors not only to defeat, but to actually kill, the emperor's heir. The coming of new contenders to Constantinople, stirred by this bloody claim, will plague the innocent prince throughout this first book. In the third section, from chapter 18 onwards, the narrative focuses on a new figure, young Prince Edward of England, whose deeds will turn him into a matchless brave champion always willing to help anyone in distress. Primaleon's prominence is now replaced by that of the new male character, who will eventually become his counterpart.[31] The young English and Constantinopolitan opponents finally join in the lists.

A Female Crucible

The diversity of gender roles associated with the *femme sole* category in this first book is extraordinary. The traditional marital status framework cannot mirror the complexity of the borderline situations Munday presents. A case in point is that of young maidens still to be betrothed or already engaged to a future husband. Such characters usually take up a sisterly role within a family, aiding their brothers or parents in difficult situations or partaking of their common destiny. They are hardly ever found alone or expressing a will to remain single or independent from their family lot. However, at some key moments, these sisters perform the most daring actions and share the male protagonists' adventures.[32]

In general terms, maiden status is normally linked to virginity, itself presented as a transitional stage prior to wedlock, especially in the case of women fully integrated in a family. In contrast, any type of sexual initiation is normally linked to illegitimate relationships. Of paramount relevance in this context are the commentaries on the almost magical ritual that turns the brides Francelina and Philocrista into wives (N3r), or the passages in which young Rene, the Duke of Borsa's daughter, attempts to frame Prince Edward, with her sorceress aunt's support, so as to lure him into her private chamber and from there into forced wedlock. It is only when she realizes that the prince is quite determined not to marry her that she withdraws from secular life and accepts virginity as a permanent state:

> Rene, after shee saw her hope desperate, shee besought her Father to make her a Nunne in the Monastery which had beene cause of her disaster,

protesting neuer to loue any other knight but he: Whereunto her father easily condescended, because this Abbie was within the Country vnder his obedience, and long since founded by his auncestors. In this place the Damsell liuing at her great ease, felt euery day more and more some accesse of the languishing passion which shee indured for her deare and perpetuall friend Prince Edward: who after hee was Crowned King of England, knowing of the austere life she lead after his refusall, came to see her as farre as the Conuent was from him, where hee bestowed great riches on it, for the loue of her and of the Abbesse, who by meanes of his sword which he left there, remembred his promise. (Y3ʳ⁻ᵛ)

In the eyes of Protestant reformists, this, and other cases of religious women visited by and infatuated with knights errant, would reinforce their view of Catholic convents as places that harboured indecent female behaviour or, at best, feelings associated with frustrated love, like Rene's. However, this specific episode is given a proleptic happy ending that dignifies the girl's decision through the king's visit and their sincere friendship. The religious space, which is presented here as being wealthy and comfortable, is not disqualified but rather celebrated as a sacred spot where Rene's virginity – just as the king's sword kept at the abbey – guarantees institutional and personal pledges.

Munday does not present all religious women as zealous virgins, since certain nuns enjoy the luxury of private rooms where they can meet men, thus sharing space and time with male visitors. In chapter 4, Lecefin says farewell to a nobly born abbess who has followed a secular lady's course of life and who, after healing his physical wounds, engages in a long relationship with him. In a metaphoric joyous game, Munday develops the siege motif when alluding to the man's sexual advances, which take place when, in the middle of secret talk, the lady willingly sets her book of hours aside, and a figurative love battle begins (F3ʳ⁻ᵛ).

Similarly, even if the narrative is somewhat subtle, Poncia, who is shown as a virgin who has been raised since birth by a hermit, and likely will become a hermit herself, quickly considers the end of her maidenhood and life in solitude when meeting the duke for the first time. As the hunting lord goes into her cave when chasing a fawn,[33] he accidentally meets the girl:

The grace this Mayden had in her honest tattle, pearced so deepe into the heart of the Duke, that what by promise, by flattery, or otherwise, before an houre was past hee appeased the strife of his passion, making her of a mayden dedicated to Pallas, a wife ready to offer the Seston or Girdle to Venus, to present him her seruice, whereof he was the gladdest man that might bee. (Q1ᵛ)

The violence of the encounter, hinted at here by the "or otherwise" phrase, is then overshadowed by the female mythological allusions that serve the duke's purposes well. This reference, in turn, leads to the moment when the duke's wife hears of her husband's infidelity, dying afterwards "for griefe and rage," a passing reference that is conveniently counteracted by praises of young Poncia's new motherly and spousal duties (Q2^r). The passive female role is simply stated from a male viewpoint in this episode: the hermit girl is denied the capacity to administer her own loneliness once her own sanctuary is occupied and turned into a palace of delights: the hermit role, which had been imposed on her at birth, is surrendered, in a manner parallel to the way in which the sacred nature of the place is incapable of barring such unexpected sexual purposes. But although sex, marriage, and eventual motherhood are presented as Poncia's fate, the place will regain its sacred quality in the future, thus becoming a retreat for her descendant Gridonia.

It is mainly in the cases of widows that the actual Renaissance *femme soles* motif can be found, both in society and in romance literature. Those widows are liable to become easy prey to ruthless visitors, relatives, or feudal lords, and that is why they repeatedly demand justice. Although they are not necessarily presented as weak, they still require the support of champions.[34] In *The First Booke of Primaleon of Greece*, two heartbreaking accounts are told by the widows themselves. In the first one, the grieving woman tells newly arrived Rifarano how she had become a widow: her husband had allowed a traitor knight into their home, only to find him trying to rape her. In the sudden fight that ensued, the host paid for his unwise invitation with his life, leaving his disconsolate wife to find justice: "Now you haue heard word by word Sir knight, the veritie of my disgrace, seeing it hath pleased you to vnderstand it; wherein, beside the disaster of my husband, (which cannot now be remedied,) I account my selfe much disfauored of the heauens and fortune, hauing no meane to finde out one, who will for me enterprise vengeance against the Author of my fatall ruine" (F1^r).[35] The second account is given by another widow, one of whose sons has been killed by another lady's jealous husband, who also holds another younger son of hers in prison. Having nobody to defend her, she asks Tyrendos for his aid to see justice done:

> But I sorrowfull and heauy Widdowe, voyde of kinred and friends, who may for me demaund Justice for this iniury done; hearing the fame of your Prowesse, built some hope to be reuenged by your mean, being as assured as I am to dye, my sonnes were innocent, and iniured without any reason; and therefore would I most humbly pray you faire Syr,

according to the promise you made me, to goe bid him defiance in his
Castell, telling him if he refuse the Combat you will accuse him of treason
before the Emperour. (L3ʳ)

There are two more cases in which the political and economic concerns of harassed widows are made evident: Prince Edward champions
the Lady of Arriace in her claim against her overlord King Frisoll, who
unfairly tries to take possession of the frontier town she guards for her
young son. In the lady's eloquent speech when she is summoned by the
king, she makes her limitations clear while defending her husband's
honour: "Surely sir you may do and say of vs your pleasure, because
you are our Prince and liege Soueraigne: but if I were as good a knight
as I am a woman, I would make good against the hardiest knight of
your Court, that my deceased husband neuer committed any treason
in his life" (Aa3ᵛ).[36] Another widow who must fight her way into the
imperial feuds is the Duchess of Ormeda. When she receives news of
her husband's violent death, her deep sorrow at not being able to have
him duly buried is compared to that of legendary Arthemisia of Caria,
who had dissolved her husband's ashes into the potion she had subsequently drunk, turning herself into his final sepulchre. The reference
metaphorically explains what is about to happen to the pregnant duchess, whose agony causes her to deliver her baby sooner than expected:
the death breath announced by Arthemisia's account seems to reach the
unborn creature, so that the duchess's tears, as an essential liquid, are
transferred to the baby, whose very name, Gridonia, tells of her mother's sorrow and echoes Arthemisia's lament (O2ʳ).

Years later, still craving revenge, the duchess offers her daughter
in marriage to anyone who will champion their cause. When Gridonia's cousin and first suitor, Perrequin of Duas, meets death in combat
against Primaleon as a result of Perrequin's own foul play, Gridonia
is told a false account of Primaleon's treachery during combat. Then
the association of her birth with widowhood is renewed: she outdoes
her mother's promise by offering herself in marriage to anyone who
can avenge her dear Perrequin's death. However, mother and daughter soon realize that disclosing their unprotected status intensifies their
weakness: as a greedy suitor starts harassing them to force Gridonia
into marriage, the duchess sends her to the family castle on a remote
crag once occupied by Poncia, where she is to remain secluded, further
protected from male wooers by an impressive lion (P4ʳ). Her situation
becomes essential to the structure of the romance, and she is to remain
at a distance, while conducting all male traffic to the imperial city, thus
guaranteeing rhythm to the romance narrative.

This brief overview confirms the capacity of romance both to contain and unfold a significant part of the female experience.[37] As Peter Coss points out, "In reading or hearing romances women could recognise their role and internalise what was expected from them; but, more significantly still, they could recognise, and absorb uncritically, what they could expect from men. This included social violence in certain circumstances; even violence against them."[38] Unquestionable as this statement is, reading critically might also have been an option for female readers. Although fully integrated in and subservient to the inherited social and legal order, these female characters still try to accomplish an explicit and autonomous profile; both their silences and their claims would certainly sound differently to modern English ears.

Women at Bay: Gridonia's Portrait and Flerida's Speech

As the story proceeds from the second into the third part of the book, readers become acquainted with Prince Edward of England. At the family palace his father has built, he sees Gridonia for the first time, portrayed in a fresco by a painter recently arrived in England from the dukedom of Ormeda:

> Wherein among many excellent things which hee inuented there by his Art and skill, hauing as yet fresh in his memory the beauties of *Gridonia*, hee pourtrayed her so naturall, that shee seemed a liuing creature, seeming euer to them which behelde her, that shee woulde open her mouth to speake vnto them; and there hee set her in a place as it were in a prison, settuate vpon a Rocke, and a Lyon couched vppon the skyrt of her Coate, holding his heade between this Ladies handes, who did gently stroake his heade and all the rest of hys body. (T1ᵛ)

The portrait offers such a natural resemblance that the image seems to speak, and the prince sometimes addresses it as in a magic spell. The painting seems to come to life and utter some words, as Gridonia holds the lion's head next to her.[39] Her imposing figure towers over the beast and the viewer alike. Since she has not been a sitter for the artist, hers is an ideal, pure image of the lady stroking the lion. Such distant, lofty disposition would be evoked by the earliest Renaissance female portraits and still be fashionable among aristocratic and royal Elizabethan ladies:

> These iron ladies are guardians of virtue controlling and subduing masculine sexuality. Their function is to civilise and check impulses which are understood to be natural: they contain and discipline unruly male desire.

But they do so without abandoning the virtues which are seen as specifically feminine. It is precisely as chaste maidens or model wives and mothers that they exercise the only form of power that patriarchy leaves to women: the right of prohibition. They are thus able to remain objects of desire without themselves being subject to it.[40]

If, in courtly love imagery, the idealization of the lady already embraced the principles of beauty and virtue, here a new meaning is added, that associated with female space: Gridonia is located within a frame to be remembered forever as the painter's invention – one with a lion, the idea of loneliness thus being thus further emphasized. She stands as a peculiar *femme sole*, as the painting vividly verifies. The frame acts as a window for the prince to peep into her story and become mesmerized by the presence of the lion.[41] In wondering about such an enigmatic couple, he falls in *love's alteration* (T2ʳ). Gridonia's power is thus produced and enacted even beyond her own will, through the proxy effect of the painting.[42] The portrait conveys the principles of virtue and beauty as an enticing tandem. In addition, its mimetic force evokes the very power images possess in the medieval tradition: their partaking of the essence of the depicted one, and their working as relics or sacred objects when representing the divine. Effective as Tudor iconoclastic reform may have been, Christian iconography had carved its way into popular memory, entwined with literary and folk topics, so that Gridonia's portrait might irrevocably bring to the fore certain hagiographic features.[43] Among such elements, solitude, much sought after by saintly hermits, would be eased by the presence of animals, the most common of which was the lion.[44]

Ironically, if the portrait motif has been used to keep Gridonia at bay, as an inspiring distant drive for male action, the very narrative of *The First Book of Primaleon* enacts a final twist that sentences her to an even more remote angle of the story. Prince Edward finds his way to Constantinople, inspired by the fixed memory of the painting, only to fall in love with the woman striding along with Primaleon, his sister Princess Flerida. As Emperor Palmerin's daughter, she represents and stands for a clear patriarchal pattern, and is consistently surrounded by her relatives, not having at first a distinct voice of her own. However, as Edward announces his challenge to Primaleon, Flerida interrupts the conversation to protest in favour of her brother's innocence. At that moment, shocked by such female passion and eloquence, all thoughts of the distant Gridonia leave Edward's mind:

She ending her exclamation, turned towards prince Edward her bliew eyes, bedewed with teares, which distilled from her braine, thorough the vehemencie of the anguish which she felt in her brest, seeing her brother whom she loued as her owne soul, so chafed, and so peruerse against her, to performe the battell. The gracious and pittifull regard of these two glistering starres wounded in a moment the heart of the knight in such strange manner, that loosing almost all sense, hee clean forgot Gridonia also, and the passion of this his greene and newe wound was so vehement, that hee found no phisition nor surgion who could vnderstand the method of his cure, except the verie same from whome his wound was inflicted. (Dd1ᵛ)

In this scene, the enthralling power of the portrait is replaced by that of the flesh-and-blood woman, who will thereupon interrupt the ritual fight: just as the princely duel turns endless and the two contenders seem destined to die, Flerida, with her parents' acquiescence and on behalf of the women attending the fight, comes forward and places herself within the lists to entreat the two princes to stop (Dd3ʳ). Certainly, at this moment, not only Edward and Primaleon are confused and defeated by the woman's swift movement and her rhetoric: readers are too, as they attempt to understand how she manages to leave her own space and stand alone between those men. Disorientation conquers: the mimetic energy of the painting reveals itself inoperable as the least expected woman has her saying against the reprisal and counter-reprisal system of romance warfare. At this point, the framework of the story leans solely on the shoulders of the young woman who has thus far been screened by male prominence, and, although her father immediately grasps the occasion to command a halt, it is Flerida's resolve that brings the narrative to a bittersweet end.

We may conclude by stating that, even if the narrative is still inserted within a clear patriarchal pattern, women are granted an undeniably active role in this book. If, on the one hand, the plot relies on a distant lady, necessarily kept at bay, to inspire male journeys and encounters at the jousts, on the other, another woman, the resourceful sister, interrupts and threatens the senseless routine of jousting, thus reversing Gridonia's death wish. By intruding into that purely male business, Flerida comes of age herself and acquires a dramatic size that enables her to match Gridonia's pain and oppose her designs altogether. If the genre sows disorientation through its quest and postponement rhythm, Flerida's sudden choice stands as the ultimate surprise, just as she demands the reader's full identification with a female point of view that brings the quest cycle to an abrupt end. In spite of its suddenness, this change of perspective widens the scope of the account as Flerida proves that the male space can be occupied, and that female needs and opinions can prevail in the public arena.

Munday's rendering of this book in the late sixteenth century presents us with a good example of the expanding and synthetic nature of the genre. The echoes of previous romances and hagiographic stories adjust to modern English patterns, thus making it possible for contemporary readers to identify with the Iberian romances in translation. It is in this context that the motif of the *femme sole* becomes relevant. Munday's success may be due partly to a new awareness in English female reading communities that enables them to adjust their expectations and identify with those *femmes soles*. If, as Joan Kelly suspected, medieval ladies lost much of their independence on their passage to the Renaissance,[45] then the resourcefulness of these characters endows Iberian romances with a Janus-like quality, offering women a somewhat optimistic reading.

NOTES

1　The gender-spatial question received due attention in the field of medieval studies only after Eileen Power published her works in the early twentieth century. The study of medieval women – particularly nuns and religious women – has been given further attention by such historians as Roberta Gilchrist and Bruce Vernarde, while literature and cultural products have been approached as part and parcel of this phenomenon by Carolyn Walker-Bynum, Jocelyn Wogan-Browne, Julie Ann Smith, Jane T. Schulenburg, Barbara Newman, Clare A. Lees, Barbara A. Hanawalt, and D.H. Green, among others.

2　About the blending of both genres, see the collection edited by Brigitte Cazelles, *The Lady as Saint: A Collection of French Hagiographic Romances of the Thirteenth Century* (Philadelphia: University of Pennsylvania Press, 1991). See also Roberta Krueger, *Women Readers and the Ideology of Gender in Old French Verse Romance* (Cambridge: Cambridge University Press, 1993). As for the influence of the genre on Renaissance cultural and artistic expressions, see Julia Reinhardt Lupton, *Afterlives of the Saints: Hagiography, Typology, and Renaissance Literature* (Stanford, CA: Stanford University Press, 1996).

3　Diana Webb, *Privacy and Solitude* (London: Humbledom, 2007). On the other hand, Jane Grenville considers the risk of using the essentialist notion of "female space," since archaeological evidence does not precisely support such a simplistic view: "The social use of space is more nuanced and subtle than a simple male/female dichotomy allows" ("Houses and

Households in Late Medieval England: An Archaeological Perspective," in *Medieval Women: Texts and Contexts in late Medieval Britain, Essays for Felicity Riddy*, ed. Jocelyn Wogan-Browne et al. [Turnhout, BE: Brepols, 2000], 311).

4 We must bear in mind that this was not always the case. The English church's long-standing hostility to romance would cease for a while in the transition to the Renaissance, when heretic messages threatened orthodox doctrines. Catholic preachers would turn a blind eye to romance reading as long as it deterred readers from gaining access to the more damaging Lollard texts. See Helen Cooper, *The English Romance in Time: Transforming Motifs from Geoffrey of Monmouth to the Death of Shakespeare* (Oxford: Oxford University Press, 2004), 90.

5 Tiffany J. Werth, *The Fabulous Dark Cloister: Romance in England after the Reformation* (Baltimore, MD: Johns Hopkins University Press, 2011). The possibility of female authorship for these books and their translations has become an important issue: Spanish and Portuguese women seem to have been clearly driven toward the genre, whereas, in England, the key translation of *The Mirror of Knighthood* carried out in 1578 by Margaret Tyler, a servant in the household of Thomas Howard's parents, speaks for itself. The very origin of the Spanish source of *Primaleon of Greece* is a case in point, since the possibility of female authorship by a wise woman from Augustóbriga is suggested at the end of the book. On authorial controversy, see Mª Carmen Marín Pina, "Nuevos datos sobre Francisco Vázquez y Feliciano de Silva, autores de libros de caballerías," *Journal of Hispanic Philology* 15 (1991): 117–30.

6 See Suzanne Hull, *Chaste, Silent, and Obedient: English Books for Women, 1475–1640* (San Marino, CA: Huntington Library, 1982), 20. It mentions 1,780 works dedicated to patronesses, according to Franklin Williams's *Index to Dedications and Commendatory Verses in English Books before 1641* (London: Bibliographical Society, 1962).

7 Lori Humphrey Newcomb, "Gendering Prose Romance in Renaissance England," in *A Companion to Romance from Classical to Contemporary*, ed. Corinne Saunders (Oxford: Blackwell, 2007), 121. Since female reading practice was perceived as distracting, the object falling into their hands would be instantly disqualified. About the basic instruction given to women, see Roger Chartier, "Labourers and Voyagers: From the Text to the Reader," *Diacritics* 22, no. 2 (1992): 58.

8 Caroline Lucas resorts to Judith Fetterley's concept of "resisting reader" for this particular context, looking beyond and pointing at the possibilities of a subversive interpretation of the patriarchal tenets romances lean on. Ironically, then, in raising a cultural perception of the genre as linked to dangerously pleasurable reading, the moralists' concerns would have provided publishers with an incentive to increase their profits. See Lucas,

Writing for Women: The Example of Woman as Reader in Elizabethan Romance (Milton Keynes, UK: Open University Press, 1989), 35.

9 Ibid., 12. On the rise of literacy in late sixteenth-century England, see also Sánchez-Martí's essay in the present volume.

10 See Margaret Spufford, *Small Books and Pleasant Histories: Popular Fiction and Its Readership in Seventeenth-Century England* (Cambridge: Cambridge University Press, 1985).

11 The most famous cases being Sir Thomas Overbury's reference in his *New and Choise Characters* to the chambermaid who read *The Myrrour of Knighthood* (London: Thomas Creede, 1615, I4ᵛ–I5ʳ; STC 18908) and William Browne's description of the chambermaid who knew the Iberian cycles, found in "Fido, an Epistle to Fidelia" (ca. 1616). See William Browne, *Original Poems*, ed. Sir Egerton Brydges (London, 1815), 137.

12 See Tina Krontiris, "Breaking Barriers of Genre and Gender: Margaret Tyler's Translation of *The Mirrour of Knighthood*," in *Women in the Renaissance: Selections from English Literary Renaissance*, ed. Kirby Farrell et al. (Amherst: University of Massachusetts Press, 1990) 48–68, 56.

13 Cordelia Beattie shows the complexity and overlap of any classifying schemes, and so she presents them under the umbrella "category of difference." See *Medieval Single Women: The Politics of Social Classification in Late Medieval England* (Oxford: Clarendon, 2007), 7.

14 Mainly, those describing civil status, sexual condition, or professional categories associated with women. See Cordelia Beattie, "Married Women, Contract and Coverture in Late Medieval England," in *Married Women and the Law in Premodern Northwest Europe*, ed. Cordelia Beattie and Matthew Frank Stevens (Woodbridge, UK: Boydell, 2013), 133–54. Joan Chandler's focus on marriage tellingly reveals a continuum where cases of separated wives, those with absent husbands, or those who cohabited with men other than their husbands, can be found (*Women without Husbands: An Exploration of the Margins of Marriage* [Houndmills, UK: Macmillan, 1991]). Sharon Farmer tells of genders being structurally constructed within a range of "interlocking inequalities," in a grid-like pattern. She further detects that, in the clerical conceptualization of women, the professional categories of servants and prostitutes may at times be added to the classical triad; thus, the conflation between the professional and the civil-sexual status might lead to a growing confusion ("'It Is Not Good that Woman Should Be Alone': Elite Responses to Single Women in High Medieval Paris," in *Single Women in the European Past, 1250–1800*, ed. Judith Bennett and Amy M. Froide [Philadelphia: University of Pennsylvania Press, 1998], 82–105). To this potential puzzle, the ambiguity of the concept "single women" is added: see, among others, Laurel Amtower and Dorothea Kehler, eds., *The Single Woman in Medieval and*

Early Modern England: Her Life and Representation (Tempe: Arizona Center for Medieval and Renaissance Studies, 2003), and Amy Froide, *Never Married: Single Women in Early Modern England* (Oxford: Oxford University Press, 2005).

15 The *Liber Albus* states: "where a woman *couverte de baron*, follows a craft of her own in the city in which the husband does not intermeddle, such a woman shall be bound as a single woman as to all that concerns her craft" (*Munimenta Gildhallae Londoniensis: Liber Albus, Liber Custumarum et Liber Horn (MGL)*, ed. H.T. Riley, Rolls Series, bk. 3, pt. 1, 204–5 [London, 1859–62], trans. Caroline Barron in "The 'Golden Age' of Women in Medieval London," *Reading Medieval Studies* 15 [1989]: 40). Barron and Goldberg are in favour of a relative, cautious use of the "golden age" paradigm for these late medieval entrepreneurs. See Barron, "The 'Golden Age' of Women," and P.J.P. Goldberg, *Women, Work, and Life Cycle in a Medieval Economy* (Oxford: Clarendon, 1992).

16 Marjorie McIntosh, "The Benefits and Drawbacks of *Femme Sole* Status in England, 1300–1630," *Journal of British Studies* 44, no. 3 (July 2005): 416.

17 Maryanne Kowaleski, "Women at Work in a Market Town: Exeter in the Late Fourteenth Century," in *Women and Work in Preindustrial Europe*, ed. Barbara A. Hanawalt (Bloomington: University of Indiana Press, 1986), 145–64; Judith Bennet, "Medieval Women, Modern Women: Across the Great Divide," in *Culture and History, 1350–1600: Essays on English Communities, Identities and Writing*, ed. David Aers (Detroit: Wayne State University Press, 1992), 147–75. However, women were actually allowed in 1571 to engage in the activity of money lending. See Judith M. Spicksley, "To Be or Not to Be Married: Single Women, Money-Lending, and the Question of Choice in Late Tudor and Stuart England," in Amtower and Kehler, *The Single Woman*, 72.

18 McIntosh, "Benefits and Drawbacks," 427.

19 Anne Laurence, *Women in England, 1500–1760* (Phoenix, AZ: Giant, 1999), 55–6.

20 Alex Davis, *Chivalry and Romance in the English Renaissance* (Cambridge: D.S. Brewer, 2003), 171.

21 Joshua Phillips, *English Fictions of Communal Identity, 1485–1603* (Ashgate, UK: Farnham, 2009), 129. Wilson views Munday's handling of his sources as part of a personal translation enterprise. See "Serial Publication and Romance," in *The Elizabethan Top Ten: Defining Print Popularity in Early Modern England*, ed. Andy Kesson and Emma Smith (Ashgate, UK: Farnham & Burlington, 2013), 215.

22 Recent studies have focused on specific female reception of Spanish and Portuguese books by women such as Mencía de Mendoza – Juan Luis Vives's disciple – who seems to have had access in the humanistic context

of sixteenth-century Valencia to at least thirty of these romances, or Ana de Mendoza, Princess of Eboli, who inherited a collection of some three hundred titles, which included the Amadis cycle. See the special issue of *Tirant* 20 (2017), edited by María Coduras Bruna, which includes several studies dedicated to female readership and authorship in the Iberian Peninsula. In Spain, the vogue for these books can be attested to even by Teresa de Jesús, who acknowledges having read them with zest in her youth.

23 Daniel Eisenberg, "Who Read the Romances of Chivalry?" *Kentucky Romance Quarterly* 20 (1973): 210.

24 Guillaume Landré, *Second livre de l'histoire de Primaleon de Grece, povrsvivant les havts et chevalevrevxfaitz d'armes, &d'Amours, par luy & le Cheualier Giber mis à fin, à l'occasion de l'Infante Gridoine, Duchesse d'Ormede* (Paris: Galliot du Pré, 1576, FB 44737), A3ʳ–A3ᵛ.

25 In Protestant England, Munday would somehow try to lessen the Catholic influence present in those books, while maintaining the theocratic model posed by the Hellenistic emperor, a figure that would suit the political aims of the Anglican monarch. See Donna Hamilton, "Anthony Munday's Translation of Iberian Chivalric Romances: *Palmerin of England, Part 1* as Exemplar," in *Catholic Culture in Early Modern England*, ed. Ronald Corthell et al. (Notre Dame, IN: University of Notre Dame Press, 2007), 286.

26 Munday's *The First Booke of Primaleon of Greece* was printed in 1595 by John Danter for Cuthbert Burby (STC 20366), who also published *The Second Booke* in 1596 (STC 20366ª). As for the third book, no extant copy of a possible 1597 edition has been found. A joint edition of the three books was printed by Thomas Snodham in 1619 (STC 20367). Page references in this chapter are those by signature number found in the 1595 edition of the first book.

27 Patricia Parker, *Inescapable Romance: Studies in the Poetics of a Mode* (Princeton, NJ: Princeton University Press, 1979), 4.

28 Helen Cooper does, however, point out that the implied reader always knows better than the main characters, and that certain disorientation is constrained by generic conventionality. Although we might think that the narrative demands a yielding attitude from readers, other more reassuring psychological effects are also possible (*The English Romance in Time*, 47), and, as John O'Connor suggests, "the repetitions set up mnemonic echoes in the reader and help give an impression of purpose and form that is belied by the rambling structure of the work" (*Amadis de Gaule and Its Influence on Elizabethan Literature* [New Brunswick, NJ: Rutgers University Press, 1970], 117).

29 Both *Palmendos* and *Primaleon of Greece* entered the Stationers' Register to John Charlewood on 9 January 1589 (Arber II, 513). Munday translated the 1550 French version by François de Vernassal (FB 44732) and made two

books out of one. He translated the first thirty-two chapters in *Palmendos* and the remaining twenty-four in *The First Booke of Primaleon of Greece*, which would be published in 1595 by John Danter for Cuthbert Burby (STC 20366). See Álvarez-Recio's chapter in the present collection for the publication history of *Primaleón* and its subsequent English renderings. See also Sánchez-Martí's chapter, 45n45.

30 The main lines derived from *Palmendos* are Turkish King Ocurites's self-imposed starvation to death, and Palmendos's sadness at hearing of his mother's demise. With Palmendos-Francelina and Arnedes-Philocrista's joint weddings, immediate action concentrates on the courtly celebrations held in Constantinople. As for roving knights, the stories of Rifarano and Lecefin get entwined and lead them to the imperial court in Germany. A different thread is that concerning the companions Belcar, Recindes, and Tyrendos, a line that drifts momentarily as Tyrendos decides to split from the group.

31 In this first book they are, in fact, antithetical characters: if Primaleon never leaves the court, the English prince will be clearly introduced as exulting in his search for adventure. Whereas the Greek must comply with the ritualistic arrangement of the tourney, with its single deadly combat pattern, Edward of England is granted just the opposite, the diversity and magic stimulus of the adventures in store for him, till he eventually follows the path into the imperial capital too, to engage in battle against Primaleon.

32 Such is the case of Olymba, who, after being released, together with her own brothers, from a magic spell, becomes Edward's invaluable assistant (Ee1^r).

33 This is a feature deeply ingrained in hagiographic texts, as well as in European folk memory. Various male and female *vitae* include the guiding hart or fawn, sometimes associated with the unicorn, which will alter the destiny of saints or of those linked to them. The motif is likewise found in the Arthurian tradition, after Chrétien de Troyes' *Érec et Énide*. A classical work that approaches all those situations and circumstances is that by William K. Entwistle, "The Adventures of *Le Cerf au Pied Blanc* in Spanish and Elsewhere," *Modern Language Review* 18 (1923): 435–48.

34 On widows, see Sue Sheridan Walker, *Wife and Widow in Medieval England* (Ann Arbor: University of Michigan Press, 1993); Caroline M. Barron and Anne F. Sutton, *Medieval London Widows, 1300–1500* (London: Hambledon Press, 1994); and Sandra Cavallo and Lyndan Warner, *Widowhood in Medieval and Early Modern Europe* (London: Longman, 1999).

35 This case is all the more distressing because the lady will never get news from Rifarano – who had offered his help – as he forgets this enterprise once he finds out that the villain he is chasing is none other than Lecefin, who will join him again on their common journey to Germany. A

reprimand will do between them to settle the feud, and the crime will go unpunished.

36 The context for this episode may be related to the late medieval interregional wars. However, if the story deals with noble ladies and their overlords, parallel situations can be found among English modern humble widows. Dramatically loud and constant as their involvement in legal action may look, some of those grievances would remain unheard. In Barbara J. Todd's view, in England, "the cultural preference for conjugal households" accounted for a larger capacity to enjoy independence from male control ("The Virtuous Widow in Protestant England," in *Widowhood in Medieval and Early Modern Europe*, ed. Sandra Cavallo and Lyndan Warner [Edinburgh: Longman, 1999], 66). Tim Stretton agrees that, in many cases, "rival claimants who alleged they owned title in property violently evicted widows from their marital homes or used force to carry away their movable goods" ("Widows at Law in Tudor and Stuart England," in Cavallo and Warner, *Widowhood*, 200).

37 Not only does the story consider the special bonds between granddaughters and grandmothers, or aunts and their nieces, it also exemplifies the relationship between female servants and their ladies, an instance of which is Zerphira, the Turkish princess sent to serve Christian Gridonia (Aa2ʳ). Female intimacy becomes particularly significant at certain moments – for instance, when the obliging princess Philocrista assists the desperate captive wife Marencida, helping her get dressed (D4ᵛ), or the confidential talk between a married lady and a widow about infidelity (M1ʳ).

38 *The Lady in Medieval England, 1000–1500* (Phoenix Mill, UK: Sutton Publishing, 1998), 174. In this first book, other instances of violence are justified through certain cultural or religious peculiarities.

39 One may wonder at the power of this portrait and relate its naturalistic quality to the advances of Renaissance mimetic arts in fifteenth-century Dutch and Italian contexts. Shearer West explores the allegorical aspect of Renaissance portraits: "The origins of the tendency to view women allegorically can be traced to fifteenth- and sixteenth-century Italy. Here several factors combined to inspire portraits of women that related them to abstract ideas of beauty rather than status or character." See *Portraiture* (Oxford: Oxford University Press, 2004), 49–50.

40 Andre Belsey and Catherine Belsey, "Icons of Divinity: Portraits of Elizabeth I," in *Renaissance Bodies: The Human Figure in English Culture, 1540–1660*, ed. Lucy Gent and Nigel Llewelyn (London: Reaktion Books, 1990), 20.

41 In the Old Testament, the lion symbolizes the power of the kings of Israel as well as the idea of kingship. See Margaret Haist, "The Lion, Bloodline, and Kingship," in *The Mark of the Beast*, ed. Debra Hassig (New York:

Routledge, 1999), 3. The fierceness and untamed nature of the animal plus its allegorical value in resurrection would possibly be assumed in hagiographies. It is a motif that can be found not only in hagiography, but also in the romance tradition, as Chrétien de Troyes's *Y vain ou le chevalier au lion* proves. On the other hand, in the Palmerin cycle, there are several fights between the protagonists and dangerous lions, a motif that even Cervantes himself would employ.

42   Elizabethan readers would not fail to remember the artistic reverberations of marriage policy through this otherwise innocent portrait, for which there are no commissioners or sitters. At a moment when love portraits were fashioned through the miniature technique, this large-size painting might contribute to the distance effect strategy. Patricia Fumerton refers to the decades when the popularity of these romances is at its highest as the time when a new conception of personal depiction linked to love also arises. See "'Secret' Arts: Elizabethan Miniatures and Sonnets," in *Representing the English Renaissance*, ed. Stephen Greenblatt (Berkeley and Los Angeles: University of California Press, 1988), 101.

43   According to Catherine Sanok, "the Catholic legendary offers a double, and inconsistent, argument in response to the dominant historiographic conceit of Protestant nationalist discourses: that history is organized around moments of rupture. On the one hand, it insists on the continuity of English national identity in the continuing physical presence of ancient virgin saints. On the other, it acknowledges the discontinuities of history but suggests that they can be overcome through the exemplary relation linking past and present, as contemporary audiences imitate the ancient devotion of native saints. This double answer is produced through and under the sign of gender: the monumental past is figured by female virgins and martyrs, while the present is gendered masculine through the text's ethical address." See "The Lives of Women Saints of Our Countrie of England" Gender and Nationalism in Recusant Hagiography," in Corthell et al., *Catholic Culture in Early Modern England*, 267.

44   Alison Goddard Elliot traces back the tradition to the lives of early anchorites in which dramatic encounters with lions took place: just as happens to Gridonia, these animals immediately acknowledge the saintly powers and adopt a helpful attitude, as found in some of the lives in *The Golden Legend* collection. The medieval precedent for the hagiographic female collections in England was Osbert Bokenham's fifteenth-century *Legends of Holy Women,* compiled chiefly from Jacobus à Voragine's *Legenda aurea*. See Larissa Tracy, *Women of the Gilte Legende: A Selection of Middle English Saints Lives* (Cambridge: D.S. Brewer, 2003).

45   Joan Kelly, "Did Women Have a Renaissance?" in *Feminism and Renaissance Studies*, ed. Lorna Hutson (Oxford: Oxford University Press, 1999), 44.

Chapter Four

"Such maner of stuff": Translating Material London in Anthony Munday's *Palmerin of England*

LOUISE WILSON

Francis Beaumont's play *The Knight of the Burning Pestle*, a burlesque of popular contemporary entertainments first performed in 1607, advertises in its title a seemingly incongruous image: an object from the mercantile world of early modern London transformed into a heraldic device. The play satirizes the cultural tastes of London citizenry through the characters of the Citizen (George, a merchant), the Citizen's Wife (Nell), and their apprentice, Rafe, all neophytes in the world of private London theatre in which the play is set. The play's wit hinges on the dissonances between the new, fashionable genre of city comedy and the various forms of performance that the Citizen and his wife demand in its place; the first of these – and the one that receives the most extensive treatment in the play – is the chivalric romance. When the Citizen instructs the Prologue about the protagonist he wishes to see in the play – "I will haue a Citizen, and hee shall be of my owne trade"; "I will haue a Grocer, and he shall do admirable things"[1] – his choices are treated as something absurd: according to the logic of the play, grocers cannot be the heroes of chivalric romances. On one level, this is true: romances deal with royalty and aristocracy; yet, in early modern London, the City was self-consciously defining itself through ideological models provided by chivalric narratives; concepts such as "honour" were prevalent in the discourses of the livery companies and civic elites, and tales of merchants enacting charitable practices structured the history of the City.[2] As Tracey Hill has argued in her discussion of citizen honour, "[a] central tenet of the City's self-presentation – the potential for a meritocratic rise through the ranks from apprenticeship to the ultimate 'honour' of the mayoralty" – was also a principle of the chivalric romance narratives and helps to account for their popularity among citizen readers.[3] It is this capacity for chivalric romance to exploit the polytemporal nature of chivalric discourse – representing simultaneously an imagined past and an aspiring present – that I focus on in this chapter to suggest that Munday self-consciously frames his romance translations for a broadening constituency of non-elite readers associated with the livery companies and consumers of the arts and crafts produced by them through the evocation of familiar objects that belong simultaneously to the worlds of chivalric romance and early modern London.

When the Citizen's Wife proposes that a pestle be used to kill a lion in the alternative romance plot of *The Knight of the Burning Pestle*, it is a comically egregious example of a displaced object; a tool of her husband's trade as a grocer, it suggests an attempt to blend the everyday world of the citizens with the wondrous world of chivalric romance[4] – a scheme that *The Knight of the Burning Pestle* suggests is irreconcilable, as it contrasts the contemporary social, material, temporal, and topographical specificity of city comedy with the supposedly geographically and temporally distant generic spaces, character types, and episodes of chivalric narratives. The Citizen's Wife's inappropriate suggestion of the pestle as a weapon adds to the sense that these are two worlds that do not naturally coalesce. While a pestle may not be accommodated equally in the worlds of the romance and the City, civic London did appropriate the most recognizable romance objects as part of its self-expression: shields, banners, and portraits were part of the ceremonial and corporate world of the livery companies, and I examine those narrative artefacts that would have been familiar to early modern Londoners to present a new perspective on the relationship between chivalric romance and its early modern readership. Attention to the translation of the material world of the romance reveals strong connections to the contemporary material and social world of London's citizens and suggests that what that emerging community of readers took from romance was the pleasure of familiarity alongside the outlandish episodes for which the romances are more usually famed.

This chapter takes as its focus the chivalric romance that appears as a prop in *The Knight of the Burning Pestle*: Anthony Munday's translation of *The First Part of Palmerin of England*.[5] The romance was an early modern bestseller,[6] and, in the play, it exemplifies the crude and outmoded literary tastes of the Citizen and his wife. The introduction of the romance and its consumers relies for its comic effect on contemporary stereotypes about the genre. By the mid-sixteenth century, chivalric romance was repeatedly characterized by its detractors as a genre suffused with anachronism and Catholic superstition, whether imported from the Middle Ages or from more recent continental models.[7] Moreover, it was thought to lack verisimilitude and sophistication, if not to promote pernicious moral values, and was seen as the reading matter of choice of citizens, such as George the grocer in *The Knight of the Burning Pestle*, and the lower denizens of society. Modern critical readings of concerns about the popularity of romance in early modern England often centre on the model of narrative pleasure set out by sixteenth-century commentators such as Roger Ascham in his dismissal of romance readers as ones who seek "bold bawdry and bloody manslaughter" and implausible narratives.[8] The supernatural marvels, gore, and excess of medieval romance are, of course, present in *The First Part of Palmerin of England* and undoubtedly remain a large part of the genre's attraction, but such critical focus on anachronism, exoticism, and the marvellous in the romances has obscured the extent to which they also capture the material world of early modern London and speak to its readers in surprisingly local and contemporary ways.

In recent years, the "material turn" in literary studies has produced a wealth of insight into the significance of things in early modern culture, and, through this, we can train attention on the artefacts in romance that were also part of the texture of everyday life for early modern readers.[9] Jonathan Gil Harris and Natasha Korda have argued for the importance of paying attention to the relationship between the material world in drama and the lived world of the audience by noting that early modern stage properties "encode networks of material relations that are the stuff of drama and society alike."[10] In his study of the shifting signification of stage properties in early English drama, Gil Harris also suggests that one conception of the material props of Elizabethan theatre was as *"membership* within a corporate body."[11] His interpretation traces the development of stage properties from medieval guild drama, in which products were incorporated to advertise the artisanal skill of their producers, into the emergence of the object as a personalized capital asset; Gil Harris notes that early modern objects take on new significance as part of the inventories of goods owned by the investors and sharers in theatre companies but that they nonetheless retain their status as agents of social identity. A similar dynamic appears to be at work in Munday's romance translations: as someone whose long writing career encompassed the theatre, civic pageant, and civic description (among many other occupations), he betrays a significant interest in the materials, processes, and values of objects associated with the guilds and their makers.

Munday's extensive literary output ranges across many genres, and critical studies tend to treat these genres in isolation: for example, his civic pageants, his revisions to John Stow's *Survey of London*, or his chivalric romance translations.[12] Critical work on Munday's translation

practice predominantly focuses on the political and religious dimensions of the work or on piecing together its publication history. Donna
Hamilton suggests that, through his translations, Munday was involved
"directly in the importation – smuggling, if you will – of material that
carried foreign ideologies."[13] Moreover, as critics such as Andrew Pettegree have pointed out, Munday made alterations to his Catholic sources
in an attempt to "de-Hispanise" the texts, omitting, for example, references to the Virgin Mary and the Mass.[14] However, instead of seeing
Munday's translation practice as one of subtraction and generalization,
it is also productive to focus on what he adds, alters, or emphasizes in
order to craft a richly textured world that speaks to the cultural and professional interests of his readers. This chapter reads his romance translation in conjunction with his civic preoccupations at the turn of the seventeenth century. While the religious and political tensions that were
negotiated in the process of translation remain salient critical issues,
attention to Munday's London, and a study of the translation of artefacts and craft practices in the romance, shows that the growing readership would recognize the arts, crafts, and labours of their own everyday
urban experience in its vivid and detailed descriptions of things.

Munday's London preserved and transformed tropes of chivalry in
the course of its emergence as a modern city. The early modern City
of London bore the social and material legacies of the medieval trade
guilds; the livery companies – early modern developments of the guilds –
were so named because of the distinctive uniforms trade guilds had
adopted in the fourteenth century to differentiate themselves from
others, and, as Tracey Hill has noted, their participation in Lord Mayors' Shows and other forms of civic commemoration forged a sense of
"history and corporate identity" through the display of coats of arms
and other heraldic devices on their banners and shields.[15] A.L. Beier
observes that, in the sixteenth and seventeenth centuries, nearly three-
fifths of London's trades were involved in producing goods.[16] The
social stratification of early modern London placed craftspeople and
manual labourers at the bottom of the scale. Thomas Smith (1513–77), in
his *De Republica Anglorum*, lists those who "have no voice nor authoritie in our common wealth" as "day labourers, poore husbandmen, yea
marchantes or retailers which have no free lande, copyholders, and all
artificers, as Taylers, Shoomakers, Carpenters, Brickemakers, Bricklay-
ers, Masons, and c."[17] As Laurie Ellinghausen notes in her summary of
social descriptions and the prevalence of trades named in them, "ideas
of art and craft are pulled into the service of reinforcing hierarchy."[18]
Much critical work has focused on the endurance of chivalry in London
and the complex ideological as well as aesthetic functions this system

of values and representation performed in relation to social hierarchy: it follows the influential model of Arthur Ferguson, who posited that craftsmen and merchants in the City "had not yet developed a consciousness of class in the sense that they had a set of values peculiarly their own."[19] Lawrence Manley has argued that chivalry fitted a society "still being imagined in quasi-feudal terms, according to which service and tribute were exchanged for liberty, privilege and honor."[20] While these earlier critical accounts read this social discourse as a form of indoctrination of the lower ranks of society, such as artisans and labourers, entrenching the privilege of the elite,[21] Munday's emphasis on the beauty of artisanal objects and the skill involved in producing them speaks to a more sensitive appreciation of the contribution of company members to the evolving City.

Munday's life and career were intertwined with the City; his father, Christopher, was a member of the Drapers' Company but, like many members of this company, worked as a stationer. Anthony followed his father's pattern, first becoming apprenticed to the printer John Allde in 1576 and receiving the freedom of the Drapers' Company by patrimony on 21 June 1585. On the title pages of his published Lord Mayor's Shows, Munday styles himself "Citizen and Draper," foregrounding his free status and company connections.[22] Evidence from December 1615 suggests that he had also received the freedom of the Merchant Taylors' Company by this date.[23] During his varied and prolific literary career, Munday's translation of numerous chivalric romances spanned from at least the late 1580s to the early 1600s. His translation of *The First Part of Palmerin of England* in particular appears to coincide with an intensification of his civic writing. Munday translated *The First Part of Palmerin of England* from the second French edition of 1574 (FB 40412) by Jacques Vincent (d. 1556?) and printed by Jean D'Ongois in Paris; there had also been an earlier French edition printed by Thibault Payen in Lyon in 1552–53 (FB 40400–1). Vincent had translated from the Castilian edition of 1547 (IB 16732) translated by Francisco de Moraes (ca. 1500–72), itself a translation from medieval Portuguese manuscript origins. Although *Palmerin of England* was entered in the Stationers' Register to John Charlewood on 13 February 1581,[24] it is unclear whether a first edition of this particular volume appeared in the 1580s. The first extant edition is from 1596 (STC 19161), but there is a possibility that an edition was printed in the 1580s and has since been lost. Charlewood had also printed two earlier volumes of the *Palmerin* cycle translated by Munday in the late 1580s: *Palmerin d'Oliva* for William Wright in 1588 (STC 19157), and *Palmendos* for Simon Waterson in 1589 (STC 18064). *Palmerin of England*'s title was transferred to Thomas Creede on 9 August 1596, and

Creede's name appears on the title page of the first extant edition of the romance, from 1596. This later publication date fits with the sequence of the romances and also places the romance translation squarely alongside Munday's emerging professional associations with civic entertainments and interest in Stow's project to document the City's topography and traditions in the *Survey of London*.[25]

The Iberian romance translations and the forms of writing practised by Munday to document and praise the City stood in opposition to the classically inflected humanist historiography that was emerging in the 1590s. Ian Archer notes that chroniclers and annalists such as Grafton, Stow, and Holinshed began to be singled out for their interest in the apparently trivial day-to-day matters of the City; Thomas Nashe complained that "lay chronographers ... write of nothing but of Mayors and Sheriffs, and the dere yere, and the great frost," and John Donne ridiculed what he called their interest in "triviall household trash."[26] Nonetheless, in spite of this mockery, these "lay" forms of writing were very popular. Stow's antiquarian emphasis on contrasting past and present through the City's artefacts resonates with the material world of the romances in which objects carry deep historical narratives and express what Gil Harris terms the "polytemporal."[27] Stow's particular focus on the destruction of tomb monuments and the associated loss of cultural memory finds an analogue in an episode in *The First Part of Palmerin of England*, when Palmerin travels to London to deliver a challenge at court to the Knight of the Savage Man. Shortly after entering the city, he seeks rest at a hermitage and, afterwards, desires to see the "ruinated" monuments in the chapel. Among these is one particularly eye-catching tomb. Munday translates this as "an ancient Sepulchre, which was cunningly framed in workmanship, albeit long continuance of time, had both wasted and dimmed the workes and figures thereof, so that one could hardly reade what was engrauen about it."[28] The hermit also points out that not only time but also invading forces had caused the destruction of the sepulchre: "when the Infidelles did inuade this Lande, they did ruinate and spoyle this Tombe aboue all the rest."[29] Munday does not depart substantially from the French in either of these cases, but the loss of a monument through religious difference would no doubt resonate with his English readers. Stow's *Survey of London* is a nostalgic text, aiming to foster a sense of continuity across four hundred years of London's history, from the late twelfth century until the Reformation, and mourning the cultural and social losses of the decades immediately preceding its publication. Episodes such as this one at the hermitage show how readily the narrative of the romance could speak to the historical moment in which it was translated and connect it to the visual landscape of the city.[30]

Heraldry, as a salient feature of both chivalric romances and the livery companies' performance of corporate chivalry, proved to be a popular subject for cheap print at that moment too. In 1596, the same year in which *The First Part of Palmerin of England* was first published, the map engraver Benjamin Wright (active 1596?–1613) published a broadsheet engraving entitled *The Armes of All the Cheife Corporatons of England wt. the Companees of London Described by Letters for ther Seuerall Collores* (STC 26018). Gerard Leigh's (d. 1563) *The Accedens of Armory*, first printed in 1562 by Richard Tottell, went through five further editions until 1612 (STC 15388–93); John Bossewell's *Workes of Armorie* was printed by Richard Tottell in 1572 and by Henry Ballard in 1597 (STC 3393–4); and John Guillim's (1565–1621) *A Display of Heraldrie* was first printed in 1610/11 (STC 12500–1) and was regularly reprinted until 1724.[31] Ian Gadd argues that the development of printed catalogues of corporate coats of arms attests to the popular interest in the livery companies, as these catalogues were "primarily visual rather than textual, usually ephemeral and hence cheaper" and they "did not need to rely on a reasonably literate, reasonably wealthy and reasonably historically-minded readership in the same way as a Stow or Strype did."[32] He also suggests that these catalogues may have prompted the inclusion of corporate heraldic illustrations in the 1633 *Survey* and its successors; Munday's additions to this edition included a long section on medieval coats of arms. In this context, the long catalogues of arms described in such elaborate detail in *The First Part of Palmerin of England* could be interpreted as part of its attraction for non-elite readers of the period.

Chivalry is a culture that embraces ostentatious display. Moreover, the extensive dwelling on the materials from which the knights' armour is made relates *The First Part of Palmerin of England*'s material objects to those who produced and traded them. The French and English translations of the *Palmerin* romances are thick with descriptions of knights' armour and weaponry, and it is on the surfaces of these objects that artistic ingenuity is given free rein: descriptions of arms and shields embellished with precious metals, brilliantly executed portraits and emblems, and heavily pigmented materials and the skill of the artisans are all brought to the fore. Munday sometimes adds more than his French source: for instance, as Dramusiande watches Don Rosuel and Gracian approach in chapter 63, he observes that one's armour has "diuers borders of Gold finely wrought vpon it, bearing in his Shield for his deuice, a murthered body in a campe of Sinople";[33] this expands on the French, "le bord desquelles estoit doré, & dans l'escu estoit pourtrait vn corps meurdri sur vn champ de gueulles" (the edge of which was gilded and on the shield was pictured a murdered body in a field of gules).[34] The other knight's armour is described as "very thicke beset with Lyons of Gold"[35] from the French's slightly diminished in comparison "semé de leonceaux" (covered with lion cubs).[36] The added emphasis on materials ("borders of Gold"; "Lyons of Gold") and on process ("finely wrought") suggests a shift toward connecting heraldry with its producers.

While the examples I have discussed so far attend more to the ways in which episodes and descriptive passages already found in the French translation of *Palmerin of England* were able to speak serendipitously to the current moment for the romance's London readers, translation choices that Munday made also demonstrate the ways in which he relates the text to the material world, particularly in his much-favoured use of the terms "artificial" and "artificially," allied to the trade of artificer, another term for artisan. On the title page of *The Gentlemans Exercise* (STC 19508) – a treatise on drawing and the making of pigments, printed for John Brown in 1612 – Henry Peacham (ca. 1576–ca. 1643) claims that production of the stuff of heraldry provided work for "divers Trades-men and Artificers, as namly Painters, Ioyners, Free-masons, Cutters and Caruers &c."[37] As David Bergeron discusses in his study of civic pageants, the term "artificer" could also refer to "the chief artisans involved with the physical aspects of the pageant, instrumental in causing the 'word' to take on flesh."[38] They also worked alongside playwrights in the theatre to create stage properties. Gil Harris quotes Thomas Dekker (ca. 1572–1632) in *The Magnificent Entertainment* (1603), who complained that plays were "at the hard-handed mercy of Mycanitiens [i.e., mechanicals] ... Carpenters, Ioyners, Caruers, and other Artificers sweating at their Chizzells." Gil Harris comments, "The attention Dekker focuses here not only on the materials of stage performance, but also on their histories of manufacture by callous, sweating "Mycanitiens" and "Artificers," underscores how stage properties potentially introduce into any play a plurality of makers, a multiplicity of meanings, and alternate tales of the body or of artisanal labour."[39] As heads of the body of craftsmen involved in pageant making, artificers worked closely with the dramatists in the production of pageants, and Munday, as a writer of civic pageants, was very familiar with their role.

A further instance in which Munday's translation of the *Palmerin* cycle and his involvement with civic entertainments and Lord Mayor's Shows overlapped can be seen in his choice of dedicatees for his texts. He explicitly connected his chivalric romance translations with contemporary civic culture when he dedicated the first edition of *The Third and Last Part of Palmerin of England* to John Swinnerton in 1602.[40] Guild records show that Munday was also responsible for the Lord

Mayor's Show that year, his first documented involvement with civic pageantry.[41] Swinnerton was a wealthy merchant who would become lord mayor in 1612. He was appointed sheriff in 1602, and this appears to be the occasion that prompted Munday to dedicate three works to him in that one year; alongside the third part of *Palmerin of England*, these were his translation of Philippe de Mornay's translation of Xenophon, *The True Knowledge of a Mans Owne Selfe*, printed by James Roberts for William Leake, and a manuscript, *The Heauen of the Mynde, or The Myndes Heauen* by Isabella Sforza.[42]

The dedicatory epistle to Swinnerton in *The True Knowledge of a Mans Owne Selfe* offers an insight into the value placed by Munday on the visual arts, crafts, and monuments. It includes the following analogy for observing the world and "the wonderful thinges therein contained." The term "artificiall" in its early modern sense of "expert" or "artistically adept" makes a notable appearance here: "If wee looke upon any curious picture drawne to the life: wee immediately conceive, that the same was the work of some rare and artificiall Painter. If wee gaze upon the goodly Monuments and stately erected Pallaces, fulle of arte, industry, and many exquisite perfections: wee presently apprehend, that some ingenious Maister was the contriver thereof, and that it proceeded from a skilfull workman."[43] The epistle exemplifies Munday's approach to describing things as "curious," "rare," "ingenious," "full of ... industry," "skilfull," and, in particular, "artificiall," which emphasises the "biography"[44] of the objects and foregrounds their status as products of skilled makers. These terms correspond directly to his descriptions of similar artefacts – portraits, effigies, devices on shields, castles, and so on – in *The First Part of Palmerin of England*. He favours these terms when called on to translate descriptions of craftsmanship from the French: for example, Don Edward approaches the castle of the giant, Dramusiande, with a shield "in the middest whereof, was *curiously* painted the Image of a sadde conceyted minde, so *artificially framed*";[45] this is from the French's "au milieu duquel estoit pourtraite la tristesse si subtilement & par industrie si fort grande"[46] (in the midst of which sadness was painted so subtly and with such great skill). When Palmerin enters Eutropa's castle, he is astounded by the sight of a courtyard with pillars of jasper and paved with marble "with euery thing so *curious* and *ingeniously framed* about the castle, that the prince supposed it the most excellent thing that euer he had seen."[47] The French reads, "Lequel estoit si industrieusement composé, & d'inuention tant moderne & subtile que homme n'eust sceu iuger le commencement de l'edifice, encores moins congnoistre où il venoit terminer"[48] (Which was so skilfully made and of such modern and ingenious invention that one could not judge

where the castle began, much less know where it came to and end).
Munday's love of the term "artificial" is apparent in his description of
a tournament in which every knight is required to have a portrait of
his lady painted on his shield, the indifferent French "feit pourtraire sa
Dame"[49] (had painted the portrait of his lady) becomes "had his Lady
to be artificially figured,"[50] once again reminding his readership of the
artisanal skill involved in the creation of heraldic devices. Throughout the descriptions of objects in the text, Munday's additional details
direct attention to the skill of the maker: to give just two of numerous
examples, the statue of the dead Altea placed on her tomb is described
as a "rare piece of workmanship,"[51] and the tears depicted on Prince
Berold's shield are "cunningly" sprinkled.[52]

In chapter 29 of *The First Part of Palmerin of England*, Munday aug-
ments his French source with a substantial original passage that likewise reflects the interest in handiwork and artificers that permeates his
translation. The emperor counsels Floraman, the Knight of Death, to
end his mourning for Altea with the following words:

> if a man applie himselfe to any exercise, as eyther trauayle, for the hon-
> our of himselfe, and fame of his Countrey, or spending his time in mar-
> tiall exploytes, or according as his estate is, the poore to take paine, the
> riche, paine with pleasure, the Artificer and such, to their handy crafts,
> the noble minde, the Courtly Gentleman, eyther to the exploytes of the
> fielde, or such exercise as may auoide idlenesse. Then is the eye directed,
> the sence quickened, the minde preserued, the heart quieted, the con-
> science unpolluted, affection gouerned, loue bridled, and lust banished,
> the good name perfected, virtue established, honour wel exercised, and
> Fame eternized.[53]

Notwithstanding the moral exhortation of this passage, with its emphasis on "honour," "Fame," and "virtue," the advice is as suitable for the
martial world of the romance as the chivalric-minded civic world of
London; the acknowledgment that each man act "according as his
estate is" additionally underscores the way in which Munday adapts
the romance to his broad readership.

One of the most striking examples of Munday's alteration to his source
material to foreground artisanal labour occurs in chapter 49, when the
emperor of Germany, the king of England, and their entourage travel
to an enchanted castle just outside of London. While going through the
Forest of Great Britain, they happen upon a cave in which Palmerin and
his twin brother, Florian, had been raised by a savage man and his lions.
This is, of course, a familiar trope of romance, but, entering the cave,

they are met with a surprising scene of artistic ingenuity: "they began euery one to be greatly amazed, seeing this Caue to containe so large a breadth and length: which made them suppose it to bee in manner an intricate Dedalus."[54] This description underwent a number of changes in its translation from the Castilian through the French to the English. The first printed edition of the romance, in Castilian by Francisco de Moraes in 1547, introduces the idea that the cave is like a labyrinth: "alláronla tan grande que parecía un laborintio"[55] (finding it so large that it appeared to be a labyrinth); Munday's French source introduces the term "Dedalus": "Vous asseurant qu'ils furent aucunement esbahis, trouuans ceste crotte fort spacieuse & de grande estendue, tellement qu'au iugement d'vn chacun on eust estimé ce lieu estre vn vray Dedalus"[56] (I assure you that they were somewhat amazed, finding this cave very spacious and of a great breadth, so much that, in each of their judgments, one would have reckoned the place to be a true Dedalus). "Dedalus" was a synonym for a labyrinth or other ingenious design, after the creator of the Cretan labyrinth. The use of the eponymous noun in the French translation foregrounds the semblance of human agency in the design of the cave.

Once inside the cave, the party is met by a further peculiar sight:

> All about on the walles was hanged Tapistrie, not of Gold, Silke, Caddis, or such maner of Stuffe, but the skinnes of Beastes, which the two Princes had slaine, very finely laboured into an artificiall frame, and so decked foorth the Chambers, that the Knights marveyled in so desart a place, to finde such a fayre dwelling.[57]

This alters the French translation, which states "alentour duquel estoit tendue à force tapisserie, qui n'estoit faite n'y tissue d'or, soye & filo-selle: car c'estoyent les peaux des bestes sauuages que ces deux Princes Anglois auoyent occis durant le temps qu'ils prindrent nourriture en ceste cauerne"[58] (all around which was hung many tapestries, which were made neither of gold cloth, silk, or thread; for they were the skins of wild beasts that the two English princes had killed during the time when they were raised in this cave). The French elaborates greatly on the Castilian description of the walls as clad in "pieles de alimañas" (animal skins), contrasting the wall hangings with the kinds of materials one would expect to find in domestic interiors. But, in the English, the skins are "finely laboured into an artificiall frame," and the process by which they are turned from their original state into their new decorative function once again foregrounds the skill and effort typical of Munday's praise of artisanal work in the romance.

One further particular use of the term "artificial" in *The First Part of Palmerin of England* is in relation to portraiture and the figuring of people. In these instances, it is often paired with the term "lively" to indicate that the image is especially lifelike. Primaleon is moved to tears at the mock funeral Pandritia is holding for Don Edward when, lifting up the hearse, he "beheld the liuely Portrait of his deere friend Don Edoard: so artificially drawne, that he doubted whether he had bene slaine therabout or no."[59] This reads in the French: "il apperceut l'image de Dom Edoard, si bien tiree au naturel, qu'il doubta plusieurs fois que Don Edoard avoit esté occis en ce lieu"[60] (he viewed the picture of Don Edward, so true to life that he questioned several times if Don Edward had been killed in this place). In chapter 19, after Altea is poisoned, her father, the duke of Sicily, "caused the Anatomie of his Daughter to be artificially figured, which he placed upon a tombe, representing her Funerals, and thereupon in golden verses, write [sic] the Epitaph of her rare and vertuous life, and by her was the image of Death very liuely drawn in perfect proportion."[61] His "very liuely drawn in perfect proportion" is a rendering of the French "figuree au naturel, & tellement diapree, comme les paintres sont coustumiers de la representer"[62] (drawn to life and so lustrous, as painters are accustomed to represent). The French's text's emphasis on early modern representational style is adopted by Munday too. When Palmerin accompanies the magician, the Sage Aliart, to the sage's castle in the Obscure Valley, he is shown "many rare and excellent Monumentes, the liuely shape of Men and Women, in fayre Portraitures, which gaue a great delight to his noble minde, so that he thought this Castle, the fayrest that euer he had seene in all his life";[63] and, when Aliart sends Palmerin his shield, we are told the palm tree on it is "so liuely framed, as if it had beene a naturall Tree."[64] In these and many other examples throughout the romance, the representational style described reflects that which had recently developed in Europe.

In *Wonders and the Order of Nature*, Lorraine Daston and Katherine Park discuss what they call an "economy of astonishment"[65] in relation to early modern art and show that early modern Europe witnessed a vogue for mimetic objects, designed to imitate nature completely, and that visual pleasure was also intended through marvelling at the *trompe l'oeil* effects of images replicating objects. This was not merely a movement in the visual arts: it had its analogue in the debate on visual communication in the natural, anatomical, and botanical sciences, with debate raging as to whether images were in fact necessary to complement the verbal description of things. Pamela Smith, in her discussion of the evolution of botanical and anatomical illustration, argues that "artisanal skill in naturalistic representation gave rise to a new aesthetic and engendered a lively demand for lifelike representation."[66] And accordingly, as Daston and Park note, what came to be valued in the decorative arts were objects "emphasizing technical polish over soaring fantasy,"[67] which, as result, remained closer to craft practices. This emphasis on technical polish can be applied to the artefacts in *The First Part of Palmerin of England*, rooting the text in artisanal London and celebrating the representational skill on display.

Early modern polemics on chivalric romance made much of its supposed anachronism, but, in Munday's hands, the genre was entwined with the quotidian world of its readers. Its critics emphasized its temporal and geographical estrangement from its readers in manoeuvres that explicitly connected the texts with their medieval Catholic and continental roots. Such attacks effectively continue to frame the critical terms in which we discuss the genre's attraction for readers. I have suggested that Munday's translations are alive to the "polychronicity" of things in romance and the ways in which, through them, the ostensibly medieval narrative world is at once conserved and customized to contemporary London. J.F. Merritt suggests that, when editing Stow's *Survey of London*, Munday "found it possible to engage with the medieval past while placing it in a triumphalist celebration of continuity with the present."[68] As Munday had been engaged in both the book trade and the livery companies throughout his career, his various writings might usefully be read as contingent; his chivalric romance translations show a marked interest in the material world of the early modern City, while their imaginative world of heraldry, skilful decoration, and corporation feeds the fantastic tableaux of London he depicts in his pageants and the nostalgic vision of the City he depicts in his continuation of Stow.

The First Part of Palmerin of England calls attention to characters' affective engagement with these artefacts; the process of looking is foregrounded as the characters are struck by the skill and beauty on display. By considering what it is that the characters read when they encounter these things, and what fascinates them and gives them so much pleasure in their reading of them, we can then think more carefully about the ways in which the pleasure of reading is both imagined and activated in these long narrative cycles. *The First Part of Palmerin of England* provides a way to pose fresh questions about readerly pleasure among the broadest range of readers in early modern London as common vocabulary, imagery, and values place the cosmopolitan medieval romances squarely within the walls of the Elizabethan City.

NOTES

1   Francis Beaumont, *The Knight of the Burning Pestle* (London: [Nicholas Okes] for Walter Burre, 1613; STC 1674), B1ᵛ.
2   For a detailed analysis of social relations in early modern London, see, for example, Ian W. Archer, *The Pursuit of Stability: Social Relations in Elizabethan London* (Cambridge: Cambridge University Press, 1991); Michael Rappaport, *Worlds within Worlds: Structures of Life in Sixteenth-Century London* (Cambridge: Cambridge University Press, 1989); Joseph P. Ward, *Culture, Faith and Philanthropy: Londoners and Provincial Reform in Early Modern England* (New York: Palgrave Macmillan, 2013); and Edward T. Bonahue Jr., "Citizen History: Stow's *Survey of London*," *Studies in English Literature, 1500–1900* 38, no. 1 (1998): 61–85.
3   Tracey Hill, "'The Grocers Honour': or, Taking the City Seriously in *The Knight of the Burning Pestle*," *Early Theatre* 20, no. 2 (2017): 162.
4   William Hunt suggests that Rafe wields the pestle as a club, a weapon associated with apprentice riots. See "Civic Chivalry and the English Civil War," in *The Transmission of Culture in the English Civil War*, ed. Anthony Grafton and Ann Blair (Philadelphia: University of Pennsylvania Press, 1990), 210.
5   In Act One, when Rafe makes his first appearance as an actor onstage, the stage direction states "Enter Rafe like a Grocer in's shop, with two Prentices Reading Palmerin of England" (C1ᵛ). The extract Rafe then reads aloud is, in fact, from *Palmerin d'Oliva*, the first volume of the cycle of Palmerin romances, also translated by Munday in 1588.
6   On the publication of Munday's translation, see, for example, Louise Wilson, "Serial Publication and Romance," in *The Elizabethan Top Ten: Defining Print Popularity in Early Modern England*, ed. Andy Kesson and Emma Smith (Farnham, UK: Ashgate, 2013), 213–21.
7   Alex Davis provides an excellent account of the responses to chivalric romance in the early modern period in his *Chivalry and Romance in the English Renaissance* (Cambridge: D.S. Brewer, 2003), 1–19; Tiffany Jo Werth explores the relationship throughout *The Fabulous Dark Cloister: Romance in England after the Reformation* (Baltimore: Johns Hopkins University Press, 2011), 1–27. See also Nandini Das, *Renaissance Romance: The Transformation of English Prose Fiction, 1570–1620* (Farnham, UK: Ashgate, 2011), 18–27.
8   The seminal article that has shaped approaches to romance reading is Robert P. Adams, "Bold Bawdry and Open Manslaughter: The English New Humanist Attack on Medieval Romance," *Huntington Library Quarterly* 23, no. 1 (1959): 33–48.
9   See, for example, Douglas Bruster, *Shakespeare and the Question of Culture: Early Modern Literature and the Cultural Turn* (New York: Palgrave

Macmillan, 2003); Margreta de Grazia, Maureen Quilligan, and Peter Stallybrass, eds., *Subject and Object in Renaissance Culture* (Cambridge: Cambridge University Press, 1996); and Lena Cowen Orlin, ed., *Material London, ca. 1600* (Philadelphia: University of Pennsylvania Press, 2000).

10 Jonathan Gil Harris and Natasha Korda, "Introduction: Towards a Materialist Account of Stage Properties," in *Staged Properties in Early Modern English Drama*, ed. Gil Harris and Korda (Cambridge: Cambridge University Press, 2002), 1.

11 Jonathan Gil Harris, "Properties of Skill: Product Placement in Early English Artisanal Drama," in Gil Harris and Korda, *Staged Properties*, 37 (emphasis in original).

12 See, for example, Tracey Hill, *Anthony Munday and Civic Culture: Theatre, History and Power in Early Modern London 1580–1633* (Manchester: Manchester University Press, 2004). An exception to this is Donna B. Hamilton, who ranges across Munday's writing career to argue for his covert Catholicism in her *Anthony Munday and the Catholics, 1560–1633* (Aldershot, UK: Ashgate, 2005).

13 Hamilton, *Anthony Munday and the Catholics*, 75.

14 Andrew Pettegree, *The French Book and the European Book World* (Leiden: Brill, 2007), 212–13.

15 Tracey Hill, *Pageantry and Power: A Cultural History of the Early Modern Lord Mayor's Show, 1585–1639* (Manchester: Manchester University Press, 2011), 9.

16 A.L. Beier, "Engines of Manufacture: The Trades of London," in *London, 1500–1700: The Making of the Metropolis*, ed. A.L. Beier and Roger Finlay (London: Longman, 1986), 150.

17 Thomas Smith, *De Republica Anglorum* (London: Henry Middleton for Gregory Seaton, 1583; STC 22857), A4^v.

18 Laurie Ellinghausen, *Labor and Writing in Early Modern England, 1567–1667* (Aldershot, UK: Ashgate, 2008), 3.

19 Arthur B. Ferguson, *The Chivalric Tradition in Renaissance England* (Washington, DC: Folger Shakespeare Library, 1986), 78.

20 Lawrence Manley, *Literature and Culture in Early Modern London* (Cambridge: Cambridge University Press, 1995), 129. See also William Hunt, "Civic Chivalry," 208–10.

21 See, for example, Manley, *Literature and Culture*, 126–31.

22 These are *The Triumphes of Re-United Britania* (William Jaggard, 1605); *Chruso-thriambos. The Triumphes of Golde* (William Jaggard, 1611); *Himatia-Poleos. The Triumphs of Olde Draperie* (Edward Allde, 1614); *Metropolis Coronata, the Triumphes of Ancient Drapery* (George Purslowe, 1615); *Chrysanaleia: the Golden Fishing* (George Purslowe, 1616); *Sidero-Thriambos. Or Steele and Iron Triumphing* (Nicholas Okes, 1618); and, *The Triumphs of*

the Golden Fleece (Thomas Snodham, 1623); STC 18279, 18267, 18274, 18275, 18266, 18278, 18280.

23 Charles Forker, "Two Notes on John Webster and Anthony Munday," *English Language Notes* 6 (1968): 30–1.

24 Arber II, 383.

25 See Donna Hamilton's essay in this volume for a more detailed analysis of Munday's histories in relation to his romance translations.

26 Quoted in Ian W. Archer, "John Stow, Citizen and Historian," in *John Stow (1525–1605) and the Making of the English Past*, ed. Ian Gadd and Alexandra Gillespie (London: British Library, 2004), 13.

27 Jonathan Gil Harris, in *Untimely Matter in the Time of the Renaissance* (Philadelphia: University of Pennsylvania Press, 2009), argues for attention to the fact that an object is never "of a singular moment but instead combines ingredients from several times" and materializes diverse relations among past, present, and future (4).

28 Anthony Munday, trans., *The First Part of Palmerin of England* (London: Thomas Creede, 1609), K8ᵛ. All quotations are taken from this edition. Although there is an earlier extant edition from 1596, the only surviving copy is not complete.

29 Ibid.

30 Stow's antiquarianism is, of course, inflected by his religious beliefs, and the desecration of the City's monuments is linked to the loss of community as well as the suppression of Catholicism during the Reformation. For further reading on Stow, see the two valuable collections Ian Gadd and Alexandra Gillespie, eds., *John Stow (1525–1605) and the Making of the English Past: Studies in Early Modern Culture and the History of the Book* (London: British Library, 2004); and J.F. Merritt, ed., *Imagining Early Modern London: Perceptions and Portrayals of the City from Stow to Strype, 1598–720* (New York: Cambridge University Press, 2001).

31 Ian Anders Gadd, "Early Modern Printed Histories of the London Livery Companies," in *Guilds, Society and Economy in London, 1450–1800*, ed. Ian Anders Gadd and Patrick Wallis (London: Centre for Metropolitan History, Institute of Historical Research in assoc. with Guildhall Library [Corporation of London], 2002), 35.

32 Ibid., 35.

33 Munday, *The First Part of Palmerin of England*, S8ᵛ.

34 Vincent, *Palmerin d'Angleterre*, Eviiiʳ.

35 Munday, *The First Part of Palmerin of England*, S8ᵛ.

36 Vincent, *Palmerin d'Angleterre*, Eviiiʳ.

37 Henry Peacham, *The Gentlemans Exercise* (London: John Browne, 1612), tp, quoted in Gadd, "Early Modern Printed Histories," 37.

38 David Bergeron, ed., *Pageants and Entertainments of Anthony Munday: A Critical Edition* (New York: Garland, 1985), 238.

39 Gil Harris and Korda, "Introduction," 6–7.

40 Anthony Munday, trans., *The Third and last part of Palmerin of England* (London: J[ames] R[oberts] for William Leake, 1602; STC 19165). Munday writes a dedicatory epistle to Swinnerton and his wife (A2^r), followed by a dedicatory sonnet to Swinnerton (A2^v), and a dedicatory ode to his son, Henry (A3^r).

41 Bergeron, *Pageants and Entertainments*, xi.

42 For further discussion, see Hill, "'The Grocers Honour,'" 166; Louise Wilson, "Dedication," in "In Brief," ed. Irina Dumitrescu and Bruce Holsinger, special issue, *New Literary History* 50 (2019), 483–6; and Leticia Álvarez-Recio, "Translations of Spanish Chivalry Works in the Jacobean Book Trade: Shelton's *Don Quixote* in the Light of Anthony Munday's Publications," *Renaissance Studies* 33, no. 5 (2019): 691–711. Álvarez-Recio remarks that the stationers engaged in the publication of the second run of Munday's romance translations also published most of the chronicles of these Jacobean civic pageants.

43 Anthony Munday, trans., *The True Knowledge of a Mans Owne Selfe*, by Philippe de Mornay (London: J[ames] Roberts for William Leake, 1602), A3^v; STC 18163.

44 Arjun Appadurai, "Introduction: Commodities and the Politics of Value," in *The Social Life of Things: Commodities in Cultural Perspective*, ed. Arjun Appadurai (Cambridge: Cambridge University Press, 1986), 3–63.

45 Munday, *The First Part of Palmerin of England*, D5^{r-v} (my emphasis).

46 Vincent, *Palmerin d'Angleterre*, dviii^r.

47 Munday, *The First Part of Palmerin of England*, R6^r (my emphasis).

48 Vincent, *Palmerin d'Angleterre*, Cvi^r.

49 Ibid., Ni^v.

50 Munday, *The First Part of Palmerin of England*, Z2^r.

51 Ibid., F8^r.

52 Ibid., L8^r.

53 Ibid., I2^v.

54 Ibid., P1^r.

55 Francisco de Moraes, *Palmerín de Ingalaterra* (Libro 1), ed. Aurelio Vargas Díaz-Toledo (Alcalá de Henares: Centro de Estudios Cervantinos, 2006), 104.

56 All quotations from the French are taken from the edition that Munday used as his source: Jacques Vincent, trans., *Histoire du prevx, vaillant et tres-victorievx chevalier Palmerin d'Angleterre* (Paris: Jehan Ruelle, 1574; FB 40409), yiiii^r. Quotations have been silently expanded to include omitted "m" and "n".

57 Munday, *The First Part of Palmerin of England*, P1^r.

58 Vincent, *Palmerin d'Angleterre*, sig. yiiii^r.

59 Munday, *The First Part of Palmerin of England*, C5^v.

60 Vincent, *Palmerin d'Angleterre*, ciiii^r.

61 Munday, *Palmerin of England*, F8^r.

62 Vincent, *Palmerin d'Angleterre*, Ii^{r-v}.

63 Munday, *The First Part of Palmerin of England*, K1^r.

64 Ibid., E6^v.

65 Lorraine Daston and Katherine Park, *Wonders and the Order of Nature, 1150–1750* (New York: Zone Books, 2001), 284.

66 Pamela Smith, "Art, Science, and Visual Culture in Early Modern Europe," *Isis* 97, no. 1 (2006): 90.

67 Daston and Park, *Wonders and the Order of Nature*, 284.

68 J.F. Merritt, "Introduction: Perceptions and Portrayals of London, 1598–1720," in *Imagining Early Modern London: Perceptions and Portrayals of the City from Stow to Strype, 1598–1720*, ed. J.F. Merritt (Cambridge: Cambridge University Press, 2001), 5.

PART THREE

The Impact of Iberian Chivalric Literature on English Literature

Chapter Five

The Rhetoric of Letter Writing: The *Amadís de Gaula* in Translation

ROCÍO G. SUMILLERA

In a seminal article published in 1985,[1] Sylvia Roubaud discusses the letters that appear inserted in the four books of the *Amadís de Gaula*, and affirms that the inclusion of epistolary texts in chivalric novels had been a common practice since the second half of the fifteenth century. In total, Roubaud counted nine letters in *Amadís de Gaula*, which she arranged into three categories according to their subject: informative letters to make announcements; letters of request of military support; and letters sent by a lady to her beloved either to declare her love, to inform him she was upset or disappointed with him, or to remind him of their shared past romantic relationship. Roubaud observes that the letters are short, few in number, and limited in their thematic variety – so limited that she asserts they are ultimately concerned either with war or with love.[2] In addition, she remarks that the insertion of epistles within the narrative evinces a link between chivalric novels and sentimental fiction, even if the latter contains a far greater number of epistles and heavily relies on them as structural strategies to construct and develop plots.[3] As Françoise Vigier notes,[4] the occasional use of letters in novels of chivalry greatly differs from the multiple functions they have not only in works such as Juan de Segura's *Proceso de cartas de amores* (1548), written in its entirety as an epistolary exchange, but even in the foundational sentimental romance *Siervo libre de amor* (ca. 1440) by Juan Rodríguez del Padrón.[5] Not at all coincidentally, Juan Rodríguez had previously translated Ovid's *Epistulae heroidum* – that is, the *Heroides* – under the title of *Bursario*, to which he appended three fictional letters, considered by some scholars to be "a first step towards literary originality."[6] In other words, it was precisely Rodríguez del Padrón's training in epistle translating and epistle inventive writing that ultimately accounted for many of the features of the sentimental romance genre.[7] The use of letters in sentimental romances has been described as a "realistic narrative" technique in that, for instance, in *Proceso de cartas de amores*, the "missive format lends a great degree of verisimilitude to its characters and the world in which they move," partly because "the reader proceeds under the illusion that he is perusing actual letters." Furthermore, because its epistolary form allows "the analysis of feeling and the portrayal of subjective states of mind," *Proceso de cartas de amores* has been interpreted as an "important link between the sentimental romance, of which it is the last chronological example, and the later psychological novel."[8] The presence of comparatively few epistles in chivalric novels is illustrated by *Olivante de Laura* (1564; IB 18516), written by Antonio de Torquemada (ca. 1507–69), who also authored the letter-writing manual *Manual de escribientes*, written ca. 1552 but never published. Even if one might imagine that Torquemada would include in his novel various samples of letters to showcase his letter-writing skills as well as to illustrate his theories, there are only six epistles in his long volume, and these are of the expected sort, which suggests that the genre accepted only a reduced number of letters, and that more would be inappropriately excessive.[9] Of course, this does not prevent letters in general, and love letters in particular, from bearing a strong emotional charge and a salient role in the development of the action in novels of chivalry without ever constituting, as in sentimental fiction, a true epistolary exchange.

Years before Roubaud, Kany had already noted that the presence of letters in romances of chivalry was scarce, except in cases such as *Tirant lo Blanch* (with thirty letters, "an average of one letter to every fifty-two pages"),[10] and yet, for Marín Pina, the work that sets the paradigm in terms of the insertion of letters in novels of chivalry is Montalvo's *Amadís*.[11] In this regard, Marín Pina puts forward a fourfold thematic taxonomy of the letters included in chivalric novels, namely: 1) love letters, focused on either reproach and breakup, or declarations of love and reconciliation; 2) letters of request; 3) letters of warning and prophetic letters; and 4) war and battle letters. In her view, the inclusion of letters enables authors to explore various narrative possibilities, for epistles not only facilitate characterization and reveal a character's innermost thoughts and emotions, but also make it easier for an author to open and close stories, and to unleash tensions and conflicts – and eventually to mitigate and solve them.[12]

It should be noted that, in the *Amadís*, there are more than the nine letters counted by Roubaud. Indeed, I have counted a total of fourteen: to those discussed by Roubaud, there ought to be added Arbán's letter to King Lisuarte (II.LVII.817–8); Urganda's letter to King Lisuarte (III.LXXI.1108–9); Grasinda's letter to King Lisuarte (III.LXXVIII.1242);

Amadís's letter to Briolania, Queen of Sobradisa (IV.LXXXIX.1340–2); and the letter sent by Queen Brisena to Amadís (IV.CXXXIII.1748).[13] Because critics have already explored the letters included in the *Amadís* with regard to the function they perform in the work, the purposes that motivate their inclusion, and the topics they cover, I will not delve into any of these issues. Neither will I reflect on what the letters can tell us about the genre of the chivalric romance, or how they behave with respect to plot or characterization. Rather, my approach to the study of these letters focuses on what their translations into French and English reveal about the development of the rhetoric of epistle writing through-out the sixteenth century. In other words, my goal in this chapter is to take the letters as a means to reflect on the evolution of the epistolary genre by specifically considering the ways in which they were treated and translated in the renderings into French and English of the *Amadís*. Their translation offers insight into how the rhetoric of epistle writing evolved in the sixteenth century, and how, in this process, the publica-tion of manuals on letter writing in accordance with Renaissance prin-ciples altered the beginning-of-the-century conventions displayed in the text of the *Amadís* in Spanish.

The sixteenth-century translations into French and English of Garci Rodríguez de Montalvo's (ca. 1450–ca. 1505) *Los cuatro libros de Amadís de Gaula* (published as a single volume in Saragossa in 1508; IB 16414) were carried out by, respectively, Nicolas de Herberay des Essarts (d. ca. 1557) and Anthony Munday (1560–1633). From 1540 onwards, Her-beray published a book of the *Amadís* cycle yearly, and to the original four books of the series he added translations of Rodríguez de Mon-talvo's *Las Sergas de Espladián* (1510; IB 16416), Rui Páez de Ribera's (b. 1460/70) *Florisando* (1510; IB 16415), Feliciano de Silva's (ca. 1490–1554) *Lisuarte de Grecia* (1514; IB 16420), and, by the same author, *Amadís de Gre-cia* (1535; IB 16438). Previously, he had translated Diego de San Pedro's (ca. 1437–ca.98) *Tractado de amores de Arnalte y Lucenda* (1491; IB 17160) under the title *L'amant mal traicté de s'amye* (1539; FB 47362). It was from Herberay's French translation, and not from the text in Spanish, that Munday carried out his English rendering of the *Amadís*; his four books of the *Amadis of Gaul* were published between 1595 and 1619 (STC 542, 542.5, 543–4).[14] Analyses of Herberay and Munday's translations of the *Amadís* have revealed, for example, that Herberay deviates at times so much from the Spanish source that his translations rather seem versions or adaptations instead[15] – for instance, he reduces moralizing comments and increases courtly scenes at will.[16] At no point did he ever deny or attempt to mask these flights from the source; much to the contrary, in the prologue to his translation, Herberay writes the following: "And if you observe in some part that I have not forced myself to translate it word by word, I beg you believe that I did so because some things I deemed little in accordance with the characters, considering current uses and customs, as well as the opinion of some of my friends who have thought appropriate to free me from the common superstition of translators, especially as it [the book] touches on a matter which does not require scrupulous respect."[17]

His aim was rather to adapt and update the text to a specific readership and its national and historical context – namely, the high aristocracy of France in the first half of the sixteenth century, whose values differed from those of Rodríguez de Montalvo.[18] As for the translation of the work into English, it has been said that "Munday, who elsewhere translated rather freely, in this work followed Herberay closely."[19] Helen Moore also states that "Munday's translation of *Amadis* is faithful to Herberay's original," even if there are some discrepancies: Munday's "main departure lies in removing almost all the details reminiscent of Roman Catholic diction or practice"; "Munday also compresses the narrative, for example by removing formulaic battle motifs, ... moving straight to a summary of the end result of the battle," and, consequently, "the adventures follow more rapidly upon one another in the English text." Finally, according to Moore, "in general he omits the more risqué elements in the French, and tones down the manner in which sexual relations are described."[20] That Herberay took many liberties with the text in Spanish, and that Munday closely followed his decisions, appears evident in the analysis of the letters included in the *Amadís*. Thus, the greatest textual differences are found between the Spanish and the French texts, and the differences between the French and the English are comparatively minor, even if significant and revealing, as I will argue.

The ending of the second letter from Oriana to Amadís illustrates some of the differences between the letters in the three languages. The following extracts show the transformation of the final sentence of the letter in Spanish. The italicized items are additions by the French translator that also appear in the English version:

... assí que mi leal amigo, como de persona culpada que con humildad su yerro conosce, sea recebida esta mi doncella, que más de la carta le fará saber en el estremo que mi vida queda, de la cual, no porque ella lo merezca, mas por el reparo de la vuestra, se debe haber piedad. (II. LII.745)[21]

Pourtant doncques mon loyal amy, ie vous supplie affectueusement recepuoir ceste mienne damoyselle (comme de la part de celle qui recognoist en toute humilité la grande faute qu'elle a commise en vostre endroit) laquelle vous fera entendre mieux que ma lettre l'extremité de ma vie: dont vous deuez auoir pitié, non pour merite, mais pour vostre reputation, *qui n'estes tenu cruel ne vindicatif, làou vous trouuez repentance & fubiećtion. Mesmement que nulle poenitance ne seauroit venir de vous plus rigoreuse, que celle que moymesmes me suis ordonnée: & que ie porte patiemment : esperant que vous la remettrez, me rendant vostre bonne grace, & ensemble ma vie en depend.* (II.X.F2^v–F3^r)[22]

Therefore my constant friend, I beseech you bartely to receiue this Damosell (as beeing sent from her, who acknowledgeth in all humility, the great fault which she hath committed against you) who shall (better then my letter) acquaint you with the extremitie of my life, whereof you ought to haue pittie, not for any of mine own desert, but for your owne reputation, *who are neither accounted cruell, nor desirous of reuenge, where you finde repentance and submition, especially seeing that no penance may proceede from you more rigorous, then that which I my selfe haue ordained for me, and the which I doe bare patiently, hoping that you will release it, restoring vnto me your good fauour and my life together, which thereupon dependeth.* (II.X.F4^v)[23]

Although on this occasion the French version is longer than the Spanish, typically the opposite happens in Herberay's translations of epistles, for he often cuts down long fragments and condenses their message. For example, the letter from Amadís to Briolania, Queen of Sobradisa, possibly the longest epistle in the four volumes of the *Amadís*, is strikingly reduced in the French (and consequently in the English version too) to a single paragraph in which Amadís says the following: "Ie ne vous ennuyray à vous donner peine de lire plus longue letter" ("I will not be troublesome to you, in reading over a tedious long Letter").[24] Herberay justifies thus the extensive cutting down of the Spanish letter. Similarly, the letter from Queen Brisena to Amadís is reduced to a minimum, and, even if in this case there are no explanatory remarks, we can assume that the French translator must have also deemed this letter unnecessarily long, and hence potentially boring for his readership, or perhaps he thought it interrupted the narration and the advancement of the plot and broke the pace of the novel.

Other noticeable differences between the source and the translations concern the rhetoric of the epistles, particularly the *salutatio* and the *conclusio*. Traditionally, letters have been understood to have five parts: *salutatio, exordium, narratio, petitio,* and *conclusio*. The first two received the lion's share of attention in the medieval *ars dictaminis*, partly because they were the most fixed and formulaic sections of all, and therefore they lent themselves to codification. The *salutatio* was what generally comprised "the bulk of each *ars dictandi*,"[25] and, compared to the "the *salutatio* or even the *exordium*," there was not such an "elaborate a scheme for the conclusion of the letter" in fifteenth-century Spain, to the degree that "the ending of the letter, technically the eschatocol, appears to have been a matter of personal preference for each individual letter."[26] As the fifteenth century progressed, salutations became gradually shorter "omitting the sender's name and carrying only the receiver's name and attributes," relegating the sender's name to the end of the letter and eliminating the greeting itself or meshing it "with the exordium which follows."[27] Subsequent Spanish chivalric novels do not strictly follow the norms prescribed by the medieval treatises either, as Bernardo de Vargas's (n.d.) *Cirongilio de Tracia* (1545; IB 16523) evinces; none of the thirty-nine letters that this work contains closely observe the medieval rules regarding the *salutatio*.[28] In the letters of the *Amadís*, it is precisely in the *salutatio* and the *conclusio* where the most interesting divergences between the source and the translations can be found. A first glance suggests a more formal and formulaic rhetoric in the French and the English letters, whereas, in Spanish, often letters sound very forthright. This directness might have made Herberay uneasy, and perhaps, believing it inadequate for his French readership, he made his letters much more reverential toward social hierarchies. The acute awareness of social distances and positions manifests in the opening and the closing of the letter sent by Urganda to King Lisuarte:

A ti, Lisuarte, Rey de la Gran Bretaña, yo Urganda la Desconocida, te embió a saludar, y fágote saber que ... Cata, Rey, lo que farás, que lo que te embió dezir se fará sin duda ninguna. (II. LVII.813)

A Vous Lisuart Roy de la grand' Bretaigne, *salut cōdigne à vostre maiesté*, le Vrgande la descogneue, *vostre humble seruante*, vous faitz sçavoir ... *Et soyez seur, Sire, que tout ce aduiēdra sans doubte: pourtant pouruoyez saigement à voz affaires.* (II.XV.K3ᵛ)

Vnto you Lisuart king of great Brittaine, *such health & happinesse as beseemeth your Royall Maiesty*. I Vrganda the Vnknowne, *your humble seruant*, doe certifie you ... *And be your Maiesty assured that without doubt all this shal happen therfore prouide for al your affairs with good aduise.* (II.XV.K4ᵛ–K5ʳ)

Other differences reflect a change in the arrangement of the *salutatio* and the concluding formulae, by which certain expressions that appear at the beginning of the letter in Spanish are moved to the end in the French version (and, consequently, also in the English one). Consider the letter from the Infanta Celinda to King Lisuarte:

Muy alto Lisuarte, Rey de la Gran Bretaña: *Yo, la infanta Celinda, fija del rey Hegido, mando besar vuestras manos.* Bien se vos acordará, ... Y tomando de la vuestra el gran ardimien[t]o y de la mía el muy sobrado encendimiento de amor que yo vos tuve, mucha esperança se debe tener que todo será en él muy bien empleado. (III.LXVI.996–7)

Respuissant & excellent prince, lisant cette lettre, il vous pourra peult estre souuenir ... lequel ie vous renuoye, aussi en tesmoing de la promesse que vous feites à *vostre humble seruante Celinde, fille du Roy Hegide, qui baise les mais de vostre royalle maiesté.* (III.III.C1ᵛ–C2ʳ)

Most mighty and excellent Prince, by reading this Letter, it may be, you will remember, ... in the testimony of the faithfull promise you then made to *your humble seruant Celinda, Daughter to King Hegide, who kisseth the hand of your Royall Maiestie.* (III.III.D1ʳ)[29]

The same happens in the letter sent by Oriana to her mother: in this case, in the French translation (and therefore also in the English), Oriana's formal *salutatio* to her mother is deleted and somewhat rephrased as a farewell and a subscription:

Muy poderosa reina Brisena, mi señora madre: yo la triste y desdichada Oriana, vuestra hija, con mucha humildad mando besar vuestros pies y manos. Mi buena señora, ya sabéis cómo la mi adversa fortuna ... y no quiera poner en condición el gran estado en que la movible fortuna hasta aquí con mucho favor le ha puesto, pues que mejor él que otro alguno sabe la gran fuerça y sin justicia que, sin lo yo merescer, se me fizo. (IV.XCV.1364–5)

Madame, encores que vous soyez desia auertie (comme ie croy) de mon infortune ... ma Dame vous m'ayderez s'il vous plaist, & à mettre paix aussi à si grande guerre ia commencée par le malheur, qui est en ceste:
Vostre tres humble & tres obeyssante fille Oriane.[30] (IV.VIII.D3ʳ⁻ᵛ)

Madame, although you cannot but be (alreadie) aduertised of my misfortune, such as it is ... Herein Madame, according as I haue giuen charge to Durin, hee will further instruct you at his arriuall, and lend a helping hand, to plant peace (if you can) to such a dangerous warre begun by misfortune; for her sake, who remaineth:
Your most humble and obedient Daughter, Oriana. (IV.VII.D5ᵛ)

On other occasions, nonetheless, what is added in French and English appears in the *salutatio,* as in the letter sent from Queen Brisena to Amadís. In Spanish the letter begins without a *salutatio* ("Si en los tiempos passados, bienaventurado cavallero, esta real casa"), even if, halfway through the letter, Oriana's mother does say "Sabréis, mi muy amado hijo y verdadero amigo." In French (and English), this idea is moved to the opening of the letter ("Monsieur mon filz" / "My Lord and Sonne").[31]

Still, it is the ending of the letters that acquires special importance in both the French and English texts in comparison to the Spanish. In the case of the letter from Amadís to Briolana, Queen of Sobradisa, the French translator adds a subscription, which Munday then renders into English. The letter in Spanish, by contrast, lacks such an elaborate farewell:

> Y a la Reina mi señora besa las manos por mí, y le suplica mande venir aquí a mi hermana Melicia, que tenga compañía a Oriana, y porque su nobleza y gran hermosura sea conoçida de muchos por vista assí como lo es por fama. (IV. LXXXIX.1342)

> Ie ne vous ennuyray à vous donner peine de lire plus longue lettre : mais ie vous prieray bien (apres l'auoir creu) me tenir tousiours en vostre bonne grace, à laquelle desire tant qu'il viura auoir bonne part,
> *Cestuy Amadis qui est vostre*. (IV.IV.C2^r)

> I will not be troublesome to you, in reading ouer a tedious long Letter. But earnestly entreat you, that (crediting him) you will alwaies containe mee in your gracious fauour, whereof I desire to pertake so long as I liue.
> *That Amadis, who is yours*. (IV.IV.C5^r)

Interestingly, the letters in English also vary from their French source, particularly in regard to the *salutatio* and the *conclusio*. For example, in the letter sent from Urganda to Lisuarte, on top of the additions to the Spanish text that the French version makes at the beginning and at the end of the letter (and that the English reproduces), Munday adds a subscription (which I underscore) that did not exist in the French text:

> Al muy alto y muy honrado rey Lisuarte: Yo, Urganda la Desconoscida, que os mucho amo, os consejo de vuestro ... Y ahún más te digo, buen Rey, que este donzel será occasion de poner entre ti y Amadís y su linaje paz que durará en tus días, lo cual a otro ninguno es otorgado. (III.LXXI.1108–9)

> Treshault & trespuissant prince, Vrgande la descogneue qui vous ayme & *desire faire seruice*, vous aduise & cōseille, pour vostre tresgrād proffit, ... Et qui plus est, luy seul sera cause de mettre paix immortelle entre vous, Amadis, & toute sa lignée: *Pourtant bon Roy, retenez mon conseil, & bien vous en prendra*. (III.VIII.H1^r–H1^v)

Most high and powerfull Prince, Vrganda the vnknowne, who loues and *desires to doe you any seruice*, doth aduise and councell you to your great benefit ... And that which exceedeth all the rest; he will prooue the onely cause, of planting immortall peace betweene you, Amadis, and all his Linage. *Therefore good King accept my counsell, and you will finde it for the best.* Yours in all seruices, Vrganda the vnknowne. (III.VIII.I1ʳ)

If, for the French translator, the text in Spanish seemed to end too abruptly, in the eyes of Munday the same appears to be true in regard to the French text; hence Munday's final addition to cushion what must have felt like a sudden closing of the letter. Another example of Munday's additions to end letters, which (perhaps not coincidentally) become more common in Books III and IV, appears in the epistle from Grasinda to King Lisuarte:

Y si el cavallero que por las donzellas se combatiere fuere vencido, venga el Segundo, assí el tercero, que a todos manterná campo con la su alta bondad. (III.LXXVIII.1242)

... & s'il deffait le premier, vienne le second, le tiers, *le quart, & tous ceulx qui se vouldront esprouuer l'vn apres l'autre.* (III.XVI.N6ᵛ)

And if hee chance to vanquish the first, then let a second, yea, third, *fourth, and fift, or so many (one after another) as shall haue the courage to contend against me and my Knight.* Your Maiesties in all seruices else to bee commanded. GRASINDA. (III.XV.O5ᵛ)

Consider as well the ending of the letter sent by Amadís to the Emperor of Constantinople:

... le suplico mande dar fe y aya su embaxada aquel efeto que yo con mi persona y todos los que han de guardar y seguir pornían en vuestro servicio. (IV.LXXXVIII.1338)

... Or est l'occasion auenue, que vous auez moyen, s'il vous plaist, d'acomplir ceste vostre promesse, auec la plus iuste querelle qu'il est possible d'entreprendre, ainsi que vous dira maistre Helizabel, lequel ie vous suplie, *Sire croire entierement, de la part de celuy qui baise les mains de vostre maiesté.* (IV. IV.C1ᵛ)

According as Maister Elisabet shall further impart vnto you: whom I humbly entreate you to credit, *on the behalfe of him, that (in all dutie) kisseth the hand of your Imperiall Maiestie.* Your Highnesse loyall Knight and seruant, Amadis de Gaule. (IV.IV.C4ᵛ)

In the letter written by Amadís and addressed to Taffinor, King of Bohemia, there are again extra final additions by Munday:

> ... y porque este cavallero que de mi parte dirá el caso más por estenso como passa, le pido, después de le mandar dar fe, aya aquel efecto su embaxada que habría la que de vuestra parte a mí embiada fuesse. (IV. XCI.1346)

> ... il vous dira, vous supliant, Sire, le croire comme moy mesmes, & commander sa depesche la plus prompte qu'il seroit posible, *pour mettre hors de peine celuy qui voudroit pour vous hazarder la vie, qui est Amadis de Gaule surnommé en plusieurs lieux le Cheualier à la verde Espée.* (IV.IV.C3^v)

> I beseech you Sir to credit him, euen as my selfe, and to command his dispatch with all possible speed: *to rid him out of all dread, that is readie to sacrifice his life for you. And that is Amadis de Gaule, sirnamed in many places, The Knight of the greene Sworde,* <u>euermore by you and yours to be commanded.</u> (IV.IV.C6^v)

Another subscription is inserted by Munday in the letter sent from Queen Brisena to Amadís:

> Y porque el caso es tan doloroso que las fuerças ni el juizio podrían star a lo escrevir, remitiéndome al mensajero doy fin en ésta, y en mi triste vida, si el remedio dél presto no viere. (IV.CXXXIII.1748)

> ... ie vo' en ay bien voulu auertir par Brandoyuas present porteur, qui a le tout ve & entendu: & lequel vous dira l'ennuy & fascherie ou ie suis, mieux que ie ne le vous sçaurois escrire: *parquoy ie vous prie le croire comme moy mesmes, & auiser au surplus.* (IV.XXXVIII.v1^r)

> I haue sent to aduertise you there-of by Brandoynas this bearer, who hath seene and vnderstands all, and who can acquaint you with my instant aistresse, better then I am able to set it downe in wrighting. *Wherefore I pray you to credit him as my selfe, and consider on the rest.*
> <u>Your wofull Mother Queene Brisena.</u> (IV.XXXVIII.R5^v)

By contrast, it was common in Spanish chivalric novels and sentimental romances for letters to appear unsigned and without a subscription.[32] For example, none of the letters contained in Diego de San Pedro's *Cárcel de amor* (1492) are signed, and in *Los siete libros de la Diana* (1559; IB 13240) by Jorge de Montemayor (1520–61), the most representative Spanish pastoral novel, all the epistles are unsigned.[33] Lack of a subscription and a signature eventually became the norm in the letters included in fifteenth- and sixteenth-century Spanish prose fiction, to the degree that their absence was not only taken for granted but also understood as part of the defining traits of the inserted epistles in those genres. Proof of this can be found in the *Quixote*, for some of the full epistles contained in it are modelled after those that appear in chivalric and sentimental romances.[34] Significantly, in chapter 11, when Don Quixote retires to Sierra Morena, after the manner of Amadís in Peña Pobre to fulfil his penance, he writes a letter to Dulcinea in imitation of Amadís. To Sancho's question, "And how shall we doe for want of your name and subscription?" Don Quixote replies as if he were addressing an obvious matter: "Why ... *Amadis* was neuer wont to subscribe to his Letters."[35] In other words, Don Quixote's letter could not have a subscription because none of those by his hero did. The relevance of this observation cannot be underestimated: Sancho understands that a subscription is a must in an epistle, whereas Don Quixote takes its absence as one of the conventions of letters written by knights. No subscription is, thus, a requirement to comply with the demands of the chivalric code for letter writing established by Amadís.

Claudio Guillén, in his discussion of seven types of Renaissance letters, among which he distinguishes the category "letters inserted within other genres," argues that "the Renaissance letter makes an important contribution to the dissolution of that strict division into styles (*Stiltrennung*), according to genre."[36] For his part, Roberto González believes that, in the case of epistles inserted in novels, the rules of letter writing become subordinated to the conventions of the novel, given that the latter is, of the two, the dominating genre in the case of books of chivalry. As a result, he claims, the conventions of the epistle adapt to the new discursive circumstances.[37] However, this explanation does not account for the rhetorical processes that occur in the French and English translations of the letters of the Spanish *Amadís*. On the contrary, in the translations of the *Amadís* into French and English, the conventions of letter writing strengthen and acquire greater prevalence and visibility, for the status of the letter as a letter becomes obvious also in terms of its layout on the page. Indeed, while the letters in the Spanish *Amadís* are camouflaged in the layout, not drawing attention to themselves, in the translations into French and English they are systematically printed as letters in a way that helps the reader acknowledge the presence of an inserted text regulated by its own rhetorical norms. The letters are given headings that make explicit the sender and the recipient, and they are separated from the text that precedes and follows them. Thus, rather than the letters discreetly adapting to the discourse of the novel, their presence is highlighted and their specific rhetoric vindicated by means of subscriptions and signatures. This change of trend, already evident in the French translations of the 1540s, later goes in crescendo, as Munday's translation decisions evince.

Of course, the particular story of the publishing of Herberay's translation might have helped initiate this trend in terms of layout, for the thoughtful typography and the lavish illustrations of the French *Amadis* did set a precedent: "it was printed in roman type, not gothic, and employed a long line across the page, rather than being split into columns as romances traditionally had been."[38] Denis Janot's typographical atelier, which from 1540 to 1544 (the year of Janot's death) printed the first five books of Herberay's *Amadis*, was certainly unique among its kind, mostly because of Janot's deliberate determination to break with the traditional way of publishing chivalric novels and presenting their texts on the page.[39] Potentially initiated by Janot, then, the phenomenon of presenting letters manifestly as letters on the printed page caught on and, with time, influenced the genre of chivalric novels as a whole. Proof of this appears in other early sixteenth-century Spanish novels translated into French and into English later in the century, among them, *Palmerín de Olivia* (1511; IB 16737), published in English in 1588 in a translation by Munday from the French version by Jean Maugin (1546; FB 40395); and *Primaleón* (1512; IB 19157), translated into French by François de Vernassal as *Il Primaléon de Grèce* (1550; FB 44731), and from the French version rendered into English by Munday as *The honorable, pleasant and rare conceited historie of Palmendos Sonne to the famous and fortunate Prince Palmerin d'Oliua* (1589; STC 18064). In the Spanish text of *Palmerín de Olivia*, there are no reproductions of the contents of the many letters that the characters are said to exchange throughout the book: none are transcribed; rather, their contents are explained and discussed and the processes of sending, receiving, and reading them narrated. Yet, in both the French and the English versions, there are two full letters, rhetorically constructed as such and inserted in the layout of the page as proper letters, which were made up by the French translator and which Munday also translated.[40] The same can be said about *Palmendos*, which contains two letters that did not exist as such in the Spanish text.[41] The letter that the Queen of Tharsus sends to the Emperour Palmerin exemplifies how a mere account of the existence of a letter in the Spanish text is transformed into a fully fledged one. The Spanish text simply refers the existence of a letter in a conversation between Polendos and the queen, where she bids him to take it together with a ring, and Polendos is said to obey and depart.[42] In the French text, this letter is invented by Vernassal, and Munday ultimately translates it into English. In both cases the subscription reads "The most humble of your freendes, the Queene of *Tharsus*."[43] In the letter of Prince Palmerin to the Princess of Assiria in *Palmerin D'Oliua*, the letter invented by the French translator ends with no subscription, and Munday does not hesitate to add one himself to complete the epistle:

> Vous asseurant aussi, que plus tost i'aymerois mourir, que vous addresser en cest endroit vn homme indigne de vostre personne.[44]

> Assuring you withall, that more gladly would I die the death, then sollicite the cause of him, whome I would not imagine vnworthie my person.
>   Your Knight, Palmerin d'Oliua.[45]

My hypothesis to explain the phenomenon of the systematic addition of concluding elements to a letter in translations is unrelated to the dynamics and tensions between the genre of epistle writing and the genre of the novel when they enter in contact with each other but is, rather, linked to the astonishing commercial success of a wave of letter-writing manuals published throughout Europe in the sixteenth century. These manuals quickly established themselves as the new authorities on the matter in place of the previous medieval ones. The publication of letter-writing manuals was, moreover, in itself a pan-European phenomenon greatly determined by processes of translation. *Opus de conscribendis epistolis* (1522; VD16 E 2506) by Erasmus (1466–1536), who had also authored *Conficiendarum epistolarum formula* (1521; VD16 E2060), and *De conscribendis epistolis* (1536; VD16 V 1816) by Juan Luis Vives (1492–1540) became the sixteenth-century landmarks in epistle writing.[46] Francesco Sansovino's (1521–86) *Del Secretario di M. Francesco Sansovino Libri VII. Nel quale si mostra et insegna il modo di scriver lettere acconciamente e con arte, in qualsivoglia soggetto* (1564; EDIT 16 59638), modelled after Erasmus's work, became one of the most influential treatises of the century in a vernacular tongue, undergoing seventeen editions until 1625 and, in turn, becoming the model for many other works in other vernaculars.[47] In Spain, the pioneers in composing letter-writing manuals in Spanish were Gaspar de Tejeda (n.d.) and Juan de Icíar (c.1523–c.1572), authors of, respectively, *Cosa nueva. Éste es el estilo de escrevir cartas mensageras sobre diversas materias* (1547; CCPB 000400067-6) and *Nueuo estillo d'escreuir Cartas mensageras sobre diuersas materias* (1552; CCPB 000013508-9). Their treatises proved to be an extraordinary editorial success: Icíar's work was reprinted on four occasions, and Tejeda published a second part to his in 1553 (CCPB 000358376-7). These manuals were eminently practical in nature, and offered a great variety of models of letters covering all sorts of circumstances. Other works of this kind had tremendous success: Juan Vicente Peliger's (n.d.) *Formulario y estilo curioso de escrivir cartas missivas* (1594; IB 14478), reprinted twelve times between 1594 and 1631; Jerónimo Paulo de Manzanares's (n.d.) *Estilo y formulario de cartas familiares* (1582; IB 12315);[48] and the manuals by Antonio de Torquemada (ca. 1507–69), Gabriel Pérez del Barrio Angulo (ca. 1560–ca.1650), and the Portuguese Juan Fernandes Abarca (n.d.), which specifically addressed professionals such as secretaries.[49]

In France, among the first letter-writing manuals in the vernacular that stand out are Pierre Fabri's (1450–1535) *Grant et vray art de pleine rhetorique* (1521; FB 33498) and Étienne Dolet's (1509–46) *Le prothocolle des secretaires* (1550; FB 16435), both of them predecessors of the anonymous and more comprehensive *Le stile et manière de composer, dicter, et escrire toute sorte d'epistres, ou lettres missives, tant par response que autrement* (1553; FB 17948).[50] In the next decade, Gabriel Chappuis (ca. 1546–ca. 1613) would publish his successful *Secretaire, comprenant le stile et methode d'escrire en tous genres de lettres missives* (1568), an adaptation into French of Sansovino's work. In England, William Fulwood's (d. 1593) *The Enimie of Idlenesse* (1568; STC 11476), reprinted ten times by 1621, and, in reality, a translation of the abovementioned *Le stile et manière de composer*, and Abraham Fleming's (ca. 1552–1607) *A Panoplie of Epistles* (1576; STC 11049) were the most important vernacular treatises on letter writing before the appearance of Angel Day's (active 1575–95) *The English Secretorie* (1586; STC 6401), reprinted ten times before 1635. Fulwood, Fleming, and Day followed the steps of humanists such as Erasmus rather than the principles of the medieval *ars dictaminis*.[51]

All these letter-writing manuals insisted on clear rules for salutations, modes of address, and subscriptions. This insistence was due partly to their relevance in rendering into the letter form the all-important power relations and the acknowledgment of social status, and partly to their formulaic character and hence to how comparatively easy these structures to open and close letters were to codify.[52] Not coincidentally, Fulwood opens the first book of his treatise with the section "Instructions how to endyte Epistles and Letters.[53] Day remarks that, "in writing of all maner of Epistles, foure especiall contentes are alwayes continuallye incident," namely, "the maner of Salutation, an order of taking leaue or farewell, the Subscription, and the outwarde direction."[54] Subscriptions, Day affirms, should be "consonant" and in agreement with "the state and reputation of the same partie to whome he wryteth," and he recommends that writers pay special attention to the letter's layout on the page, for that as well serves as an indication of the dignity of the addressee.[55] The special significance of subscriptions is also made apparent in the pages-long list of examples that Day provides, from which the following are but a small sample:

> Your L. most deuoted and loyally affected. Your Honours moste assured in whatsoeuer seruices. Your L. in whatsoeuer to be commanded. The most affectionate vnto your L. of all others. He that hath vowed to liue and die in your Honorable seruice. Your L. most faithfull and obedient Sonne. Your Lad. louing and obedient Daughter.
>
> UUho but by your L. is only to be commaunded. UUhose heart is your honours, and his lyfe by your L. to bee disposed.
>
> He that lyueth not but for your worship, and to doe you seruice.
>
> UUhose regarde stretcheth vnto your worship more then vnto any others.
>
> He that vnto your worship hath vowed to becomme most assured.
>
> UUhom none haue euer so much bound, as the desertes of your L.
>
> Your Lordsh. in all humblenes. Your honours euer to bee commaunded. At your worships gentle commaund. Your Lad. moste bounden and affectionate. At your honourable direction. Alwayes attendaunt vpon your L. pleasure.
>
> Your worships in all good accompt. Yours euer louing and moste assured.[56]

Subscriptions were not only intended as a means to show respect for the recipient, but they also constituted tools to end letters in a manner that was not brusque. This function becomes evident in George Snell's (d. 1656) *The Right Teaching of Useful Knowledg, to Fit Scholars for Som Honest Profession* (1649), which strongly recommends "to conclude letters not insulsly and abruptly, but with words leading to a mature cessation, and, as the manner now is, with a close and wittie phrase of transition leading to the Subscription," which in turn should "bee filled with verie affectuous, and vigorous words, expressing all fullness of thanks, of dutie, of honor, of service, and of all other omnimodous observance."[57]

In effect, as research has shown, "where early modern letters most closely adhere to the epistolary norms outlined in letter-writing manuals ... is in the use of conventional opening and closing modes of address, and in the rendering of forms of salutation, subscription and superscription."[58] These are precisely the elements that received the greatest emphasis in letter-writing manuals, and precisely those in which the greatest divergences manifest in the Spanish, French, and English versions of the *Amadís* letters. Through these variations, the Spanish texts and their French and English translations attest to the growing relevance of the teachings contained in these letter-writing treatises over the course of the sixteenth century. If Garci Rodríguez de Montalvo's work bears testament to the rhetoric of letter writing at a time when the medieval *ars dictaminis* was in decline in Spain, and the new wave of humanist letter-writing manuals had not yet peaked,[59] Herberay's translations show how seriously and quickly mid-sixteenth-century France was taking up the advice of this body of works, and how a printer thoroughly engaged with the new humanist agenda could make a significant difference in strengthening the status of letters included in a long novel.[60] Finally, it shows how, by the time Munday translates the cycle of the *Amadís* in the final years of the century and the turn of the next, the new guidelines on the composition of epistles had been embraced to such a degree in England that it would have been most likely perceived as an instance of bad writing not to follow their precepts – particularly the shaping of the farewells – irrespective of the rhetoric employed by an acclaimed source.

NOTES

1 Sylvia Robaud and Monique Joly, "Cartas son cartas: Apuntes sobre la carta fuera del género epistolar," *Criticón* 30 (1985): 103–25.
2 Ibid., 106.
3 For more on this, see Vicenta Blay Manzanera, "La convergencia de lo caballeresco y lo sentimental en los siglos XV y XVI," in *Literatura de caballerías y orígenes de la novela*, ed. Rafael Beltrán Llavador (Valencia: Universitat de València, 1998), 259–87. As for the merging between the Arthurian novel and sentimental fiction in Spanish works, Sharrer, by way of an analysis of the epistles inserted in both, interprets this "fusion or interdependence" as generic "cross-fertilisation." Harvey L. Sharrer, "La fusión de las novelas artúrica y sentimental a fines de la Edad Media," *El Crotalón: Anuario de Filología Española* 1 (1984): 157. See also, by the same author, "Letters in the Hispanic Prose Tristan Texts," *Tristania* 7 (1981–2): 3–20, and Renée L. Curtis, *Tristan Studies* (Munich: Wilhelm Fink Verlag, 1969), 55–7.
4 Françoise Vigier, "Fiction epistolaire et *novela sentimental* en Espagne aux XVe et XVIe siècles," *Melanges de la Casa Velázquez* 20 (1984): 235. The links and chronologies of sentimental and pastoral fiction and chivalric novels are also tackled in Antonio Cortijo Ocaña, *La evolución genérica de la ficción sentimental de los siglos XV y XVI: Género literario y contexto social* (Woodbridge, UK: Tamesis, 2001), 288–91.

5   Indeed, many scholars have argued that the sentimental romance in Spain evolved "into an entirely epistolary genre," as the *Proceso de cartas de amores* would evince. E. Michael Gerli, "Toward a Poetics of the Spanish Sentimental Romance," *Hispania* 72, no. 3 (1989): 477.

6   Olga Tudorica Impey, "The Literary Emancipation of Juan Rodríguez del Padrón: From the Fictional 'Cartas' to the *Siervo libre de amor*," *Speculum* 55, no. 2 (1980): 307.

7   Ibid., 315–16. See also Olga Tudorica Impey, "Ovid, Alfonso X, and Juan Rodríguez del Padrón: Two Castilian Translations of the *Heroides* and the Beginnings of Spanish Sentimental Prose," *Bulletin of Hispanic Studies* 57 (1980): 283–97.

8   Gerli, "Toward a Poetics," 478.

9   Robaud and Joly, "Cartas son cartas," 112.

10 Charles E. Kany, *The Beginnings of the Epistolary Novel in France, Italy, and Spain* (Berkeley: University of California Press, 1937), 36.

11 María Carmen Marín Pina, "De los géneros y diferencias de las cartas caballerescas," *Páginas de sueños: Estudios sobre los libros de caballerías castellanos* (Saragossa: Institución Fernando el Católico, 2011), 172.

12 Ibid., 216. See also, in this regard, Patricia Esteban Erlés, "Cartas de caballeros: Usos epistolares en el *Floriseo* de Fernando Bernal," in *"Amadís de Gaula": Quinientos años después. Estudios en homenaje a Juan Manuel Cacho Blecua*, ed. José Manuel Lucía Megías and María del Carmen Marín Pina (Alcalá de Henares, ES: Centro de Estudios Cervantinos, 2008), 204–27. For an alternative taxonomy of epistles, see Javier Roberto González, "Propuestas para una tipología epistolar en los libros de caballerías castellanos," in *Hispanismo en la Argentina en los portales del siglo XXI*, tomo 1, *Literatura Española Medieval, Renacentista y del Siglo de Oro*, ed. César Eduardo Quiroga Salcedo et al. (San Juan, AR: Universidad Nacional de San Juan, 2002), 115–26. Roberto González argues against thematic arrangements of the letters (which, he believes, lead to confusion and to overlaps), and for a classification based on their inner rhetorical structure and their structural relation with what he calls the macrotext in which they are inserted. The thirty-nine letters of Bernardo de Vargas's *Cirongilio de Tracia* (1545) are his corpus.

13 All quotations from the Spanish text throughout this chapter refer to Garci Rodríguez de Montalvo, *Los cuatro libros de Amadís de Gaula*, 2 vols., ed. Juan Manuel Cacho Blecua (Madrid: Cátedra, 1987–8).

14 For the chronology of Munday's translations, see Donna B. Hamilton, *Anthony Munday and the Catholics, 1560–1633* (Aldershot, UK: Ashgate, 2005), 199–206.

15 Jacques Boulanger, "Amadis de Gaule," in *Dictionnaire des lettres françaises, le XVIe siècle*, ed. Albert Pauphilet et al. (Paris: Fayard, 1951), 38; Mario

Martín Botero García, "De Montalvo a Herberay des Essarts: El *Amadís de Gaula* en Francia, entre traducción y adaptación," *Literatura: teoría, historia, crítica* 12 (2010): 25.

16 Sebastián García Barrera, *Le traducteur dans son labyrinthe: La traduction de l'Amadis de Gaule par Nicolas Herberay des Essarts (1540)* (Soria, ES: Diputación Provincial de Soria, 2015), 274.

17 My translation. In French: "Et si vous appercevez en quelque endroict que je ne me soye assubjecty à le rendre de mot à mot : he vous supplye croyre que je l'ay fait, tant pource qu'il m'a semblé beaucoup de choses estre mal seantes aux personnes introuictes, eu regard es meurs et façons du jourd'huy, qu'aussi pour l'advis d'aulcuns mes amys, qui ont trouvé bon me delivrer de la commune superstition des translateurs, mesmement que ce n'est matiere où soit requise si scrupuleuse observance." Nicolas de Herberay, trans. *Le premier livre de Amadis de Gaule* (Paris: Denis Janot, 1540), a3ᵛ.

18 Botero García, "De Montalvo a Herberay des Essarts," 33. See also Mireille Huchon, "Traduction, translation, exaltation et transmutation dans les Amadis," *Camenae* 3 (2007): 1–10. For more on the readership of Herberay's *Amadis*, see Marian Rothstein, *Reading in the Renaissance: Amadis de Gaule and the Lessons of Memory* (Newark: University of Delaware, 1999), 13 and 116–17.

19 Peter France, ed., "Medieval Spanish Literature," in *The Oxford Guide to Literature in English Translation*, ed. Peter France (New York: Oxford University Press, 2000), 407.

20 *Amadis de Gaule*, translated by Anthony Munday, ed. Helen Moore (Burlington, VT: Ashgate, 2004), introduction.

21 To facilitate identification and comparison of these long quotations from letters, immediately after each quotation I include in parentheses the book number and then the chapter number, both in Roman numerals, followed by the page reference.

22 Quotations from Book II refer to Nicolas de Herberay, trans., *Le second livre de Amadis de Gaule* (Paris: Denis Janot, 1541).

23 Quotations from Book II refer to Lazarus Pyott [Anthony Munday's pseudonym], *The Ancient, Famous and Honourable History of Amadis de Gaule* (London: Nicholas Okes, 1619).

24 In Spanish (IV.LXXXIX.1340–2); in French, *Le tiers livre de Amadis de Gaule* (Paris: Denis Janot, 1542), C2ʳ; in English, *The Fourth Booke of Amadis de Gaule* (London: Nicholas Okes, 1618), C5ʳ.

25 Carol A. Copenhagen, "Salutations in Fifteenth-Century Spanish Vernacular Letters," *La Corónica* 12 (1984): 256.

26 Carol A. Copenhagen, "The Conclusio in Fifteenth-Century Spanish Letters," *La Corónica* 15 (1986): 214.

27 Carol A. Copenhagen, "Salutations in Fifteenth-Century Spanish Vernacular Letters," *La Corónica* 12 (1984): 254–64. See also by Carol A. Copenhagen, "The *Exordium* or *Captatio Benevolentiae* in Fifteenth-Century Spanish Letters," *La Corónica* 13 (1985): 196–205, and her "Warratio and *Petitio* in Fifteenth-Century Spanish Letters," *La Corónica* 14 (1985): 6–14.

28 Javier Roberto González, "La *salutatio* epistolar: De la preceptiva latina medieval a la praxis de un libro de caballerías (*Cirongilio de Tracia*, 1545)," *Stylos* 11 (2002): 83–96. See also by the same author, "Las *virtutes narrationis* en las cartas de los libros de caballerías: El caso de *Cirongilio de Tracia*," in *Nuevas tendencias y perspectivas contemporáneas en la narrativa: Actas del Segundo Simposio del Centro de Estudios de Narratología (Buenos Aires, 13 al 15 de junio de 2001)* (Buenos Aires: CEN, edición electrónica en CD, 2001).

29 In English, all quotations from Book III refer to *The Third Booke of Amadis de Gaule* (London: Nicholas Okes, 1618).

30 References to Book IV are to *Le quatriesme livre de Amadis de Gaule* (Paris: Denis Janot, 1543).

31 In Spanish, IV.CXXXIII.1748; in French, IV.XXXVIII.V1[r]; in English, IV.XXXVIII.R5[v].

32 Diego Clemencín, "Introducción," in Miguel de Cervantes, *El ingenioso hidalgo Don Quijote de la Mancha*, ed. Diego Clemencín (Valencia: Alfredo Ortells, 1966), 1255.

33 The translations into English of these works, respectively by John Bourchier (1467–1533) and Bartholomew Yong (bap. 1560–1612), do not have added signatures. I will argue that this is due to the fact that they were translated before the publication of the first letter-writing manuals in the vernacular in England.

34 Amalia Pulgarin, "Función novelística de las cartas en el *Quijote*," *Anales cervantinos* 24 (1986): 77–91. See also on this topic, Giuseppe Grilli, "Don Quijote escribe cartas," in *Siglos dorados: Homenaje a Augustin Redondo*, ed. Pierre Civil (Madrid: Castalia, 2004), 613–27.

35 Thomas Shelton, *The History of the Valorous and Vvittie Knight-errant, Don-Quixote of the Mancha Translated out of the Spanish* (London: William Stansby, 1612), R1[r].

36 Claudio Guillén, "Notes toward the Study of the Renaissance Letter," in *Renaissance Genres: Essays on Theory, History, and Interpretation*, ed. Barbara Kiefer Lewalski (Cambridge, MA: Harvard University Press, 1986), 74, 80.

37 González, "La *salutatio* epistolar," 92.

38 Helen Moore, "Introduction," to *Amadis de Gaule*, xvii–xviii.

39 Jean-Marc Chatelain, "L'illustration d'*Amadis de Gaule* dans les éditions françaises du XVIe siècle," in *Les Amadis en France au XVIe siècle* (Paris: Presses de l'École Normale Supérieure, 2000), 41–52. See also Stephen

Rawles, *Denis Janot (fl. 1529–1544), Parisian Printer and Bookseller: A Bibliography* (Leiden: Brill, 2017), 44.

40 "The Letter of Prince Palmerin, to the great Soldane of Babylon" and "The Letter of Prince Palmerin, to the Princesse of Assiria," which appear one after the other in chapter 54. Anthony Munday, *Palmerin D'Oliua The Mirrour of Nobilitie, Mappe of Honor, Anotamie of Rare Fortunes, Heroycall President of Loue* (London: I. Charlewood, 1588), Y4^v–Y5^v. In French these are found in *L'histoire de Palmerin d'Oliue, filz du roy Florendos de Macedone, et de la belle Griane, fille de Remicivs Emperevr de Constantinople* (Paris: Pour Jean Longis, 1553), Fol. CCLVIII^{r-v}.

41 "The Letter of the Queene of Tharsus, to the Emperour Palmerin" and "The Letter of Zephira, wife to the Soldane of Persia, to the Emperour Palmerin" in, respectively, E4^{r-v} and I3^{r-v}, *The Honorable, Pleasant and Rare Conceited Historie of Palmendos Sonne to the Famous and Fortunate Prince Palmerin d'Oliua, Emperour of Constantinople and the Queene of Tharsus* (London: I[ohn] C[harlewood], 1589). In French, these appear in C4^{r-v} and E6^r, François de Vernassal, *L'Histoire de Primaleon de Grece* (Paris: Estienne Groulleau, 1550).

42 *Primaleón: Salamanca, 1512*, ed. María Carmen Marín Pina (Alcalá de Henares: Centro de Estudios Cervantinos, 1998), 18–19.

43 *The Honorable, Pleasant and Rare Conceited Historie of Palmendos*, E4^v.

44 *L'Histoire de Palmerin d'Oliue*, Fol. CCLVIII^v.

45 Munday, *Palmerin D'Oliua The Mirrour of Nobilitie*, Y5^v.

46 J.R. Henderson, "Defining the Genre of the Letter: Juan Luis Vives' *De conscribendis epistolis*," *Renaissance and Reformation* 7 (1983): 89–105, and, by the same author, "Erasmus on the Art of Letter-Writing," in *Renaissance Eloquence: Studies in the Theory and Practice of Renaissance Rhetoric*, ed. James Jerome Murphy (Berkeley: University of California Press, 1983), 331–55. See also Jamile Trueba Lawland, *El arte epistolar en el Renacimiento español* (Madrid: Tamesis, 1996).

47 Pedro Martín Baños, *El arte epistolar en el Renacimiento europeo, 1400–1600* (Bilbao: Universidad de Deusto, 2005), 460.

48 See, for instance, Antonio Castillo Gómez, "Del tratado a la práctica: La escritura epistolar en los siglos XVI y XVII," in *La correspondencia en la Historia: Modelos y prácticas de la escritura epistolar*, ed. Carlos Sáez and Antonio Castillo Gómez (Madrid: Calambur, 2002), 79–107, and, by the same author, "Del tratado a la práctica epistolar," in *Entre la pluma y la pared: Una historia social de la escritura en los Siglos de Oro* (Madrid: Akal, 2006), 19–57. See also Donald W. Bleznick, "Epistolography in Golden Age Spain," in *Studies in Honor of Gerald E. Wade*, ed. Sylvia Bowman et al. (Madrid: José Porrúa Turanzas, 1979), 11–21.

49 See C. Serrano Sánchez, "Secretarios de papel: Los manuales epistolares en la España moderna (siglos XVI–XVII)," in *Cinco siglos de cartas: Historia y prácticas epistolares en las épocas moderna y contemporánea*, ed. Antonio Castillo Gómez and Verónica Sierra Blas (Huelva, ES: Universidad de Huelva, 2014), 77–95, and Rocío G. Sumillera, "Secretarios reales: Plurilingüismo y manuales de escritura epistolar en la edad moderna," in *La carta: Reflexiones interdisciplinares sobre epistolografía*, ed. Ana Gallego Cuiñas, Aurora López, and Andrés Pociña Pérez (Granada: Editorial Universidad de Granada, 2017), 427–36.

50 G. Gueudet, "Archéologie d'un genre: Les premiers manuels français d'art épistolaire," *Mélanges sur la littérature de la Renaissance: À la mémoire de V.-L. Saulnier* (Geneva: Droz, 1984), 88. See also Sybille Grosse, *Les manuels épistolographiques français entre traditions et normes* (Paris: Honoré Champion éditeur, 2017).

51 James Daybell, *The Material Letter in Early Modern England: Manuscript Letters and the Culture and Practices of Letter-Writing, 1512–1635* (Houndmills, UK: Palgrave Macmillan, 2012), 63, 64.

52 Ibid., 91.

53 William Fulwood, *The Enimie of Idlenesse Teaching the Maner and Stile How to Endite, Compose and Write All Sorts of Epistles and Letters* (London: Henry Bynneman, 1568; STC 11476), A8ʳ.

54 Angel Day, *The English Secretorie VVherin is contayned, a Perfect Method, for the Inditing of All Manner of Epistles and Familiar Letters* (London: Robert Walde-graue, 1586; STC 6401), B8ʳ.

55 Ibid., C3ᵛ, C2ʳ.

56 Ibid., C2ᵛ. The list of examples runs on C3ʳ.

57 George Snell, *The Right Teaching of Useful Knowledg, to Fit Scholars for Som Honest Profession* (London: W. Du-gard, 1649), 106.

58 Daybell, *The Material Letter*, 71.

59 How the changes to later *Amadís* editions in Spanish after the humanist *ars dictaminis* began to influence epistolary culture in Spain (in terms of content, rhetoric, and layout) deserves a separate in-depth study, one that would have to consider, among others, José Manuel Lucía Megías, *Imprenta y libros de caballerías* (Madrid: Ollero y Ramos, 2000); Juan Manuel Cacho Blecua, "Los grabados del texto de las primeras ediciones del *Amadís de Gaula*, del *Tristán de Leonís* (Jacobo Cromberger, h. 1503-1507) a *La coronación* de Juan de Mena (Jacobo Cromberger, 1512)," *RILCE: Revista de filología hispánica* 23, no. 1 (2007): 61–88; and several chapters included in the commemorative volume *Amadís de Gaula, 1508: Quinientos años de libros de caballerías* (Madrid: Biblioteca Nacional de España; Sociedad Estatal de Conmemoraciones Culturales, 2008).

60 The letters of Herberay's translation became in themselves models; as such, they were, for instance, included in the compendium *Le Thresor des douze livres d'Amadis de Gaule*, successfully published between 1559 and 1606. Véronique Benhaïm, "Les *Thresors d'Amadis*," in *Les Amadis en France au XVIe siècle* (Paris: Presses de l'École Normale Supérieure, 2000), 157–81. In Spain, the love letters included in sixteenth-century chivalric romances also became models in themselves. María Carmen Marín Pina, "Las cartas de amor caballerescas como modelos epistolares," in *La recepción del texto literario*, ed. Jean Pierre Etienvre and Leonardo Romero Tobar (Saragossa, ES: Publicaciones de la Universidad de Zaragoza 1988), 24.

Chapter Six

Philosophizing the *Amadís* Cycle: Feliciano de Silva, Jacques Gohory, and Philip Sidney

TIMOTHY D. CROWLEY

This volume commemorates a lively literary genre best known for being parodied by Cervantes (1547–1616). In first describing Don Quixote's voracious appetite for chivalric romances, Cervantes's narrator specifies that this ingenious gentleman of La Mancha favours stories by "el famoso Feliciano de Silva" (the famous Feliciano de Silva [ca. 1490–1554]) because of "la claridad de su prosa y aquellas entricadas razones suyas" (their prose style and intricate narrative logic).[1] The narrator then waxes poetic with a purported example of Silva's style in rhetoric and thought: "La razón de la sinrazón que a mi razón se hace, de tal manera mi razón enflaquece, que con razón me quejo de la vuestra fermosura" (Reasoning out the reason of the irrationality weakens my reason, such that it is with good reason that I complain of your beauty).[2] Here Cervantes playfully imitates Silva with high literary self-consciousness, as a means to establish distance between paradigm and parody. By evoking a brief impression of the rhetorical and conceptual density in Silva's late works, particularly regarding the Spanish words and themes *razón* (reason/justice) and *sinrazón* (folly/injustice), *Don Quixote* concocts a rationale for justifying both its own straightforward style of narration and its characterization of the protagonist as mentally addled. At the same time, the pseudo-quotation pays a backhanded tribute to Silva's literary art and conveys a competitive edge for Cervantes in imitating Silva's virtuosic wit. This Cervantine sentence has been associated with Silva's *Celestina* sequel of 1534 and with the shepherd Darinel's language in Silva's chivalric romances of the early 1530s for the *Amadís* cycle of stories.[3] Yet, in both style and concept, Cervantes's imitation better suits Queen Sidonia's rhetoric in describing her conundrum involving love and vengeance in one of Silva's works from the *Amadís* cycle, *Florisel de Niquea, Part Three* (1535; IB 16442), chapter 2:

> ¡O, amor, y para qué me quexo yo de tus sinrazones, pues más fuerça en ti la sinrazón tiene que la razón! Por do no es justo quexarse de ti el que conoce, en ti, que no saliendo de tu natural usas de tu oficio ... ¡Ó, que quiero dar fin a mis razones por la sinrazón que hago de quexarme de aquel que no la guarda en sus leyes![4]

> Oh, love! Why do I complain about your irrationalities, for irrationality holds more sway in you than reason? For surely it is not just that those of us who know you complain about you, in you (i.e., in your presence), that without escaping your nature you exercise your office ... Oh, how I wish to end my reasons for irrationality, which I make in complaining about that which does not uphold the laws of reason.[5]

This lamentation proves rich conceptually, given the layered meanings of *razón* as both "reason" and "justice," and *sinrazón* as both "irrationality" and "injustice." The verbal wit establishes a nuanced characterization while Sidonia speaks self-consciously of her own vexed motives as a jilted lover. She commissions the construction of two magical towers designed with a dual purpose: to protect her daughter Diana in a leisurely captivity while also luring and slaying Diana's father, Florisel, who in Silva's *Florisel de Niquea, Parts One and Two* (1532; IB 16435) had duped Sidonia into a false presumption of secret marriage in order to free his lost son Falanges from her captivity. This thematic interplay of reasonable passion and impassioned reasoning pervades Silva's *Florisel de Niquea, Part Three*, for which Sidonia's vengeance scheme with the towers serves as the foundational plot premise. In the late sixteenth century, two and a half decades before Cervantes's masterpiece of parody, the narrative and conceptual intricacies of this particular chivalric romance by Silva were imitated and adapted more seriously and scrupulously, though indirectly via French translation, by the influential English author Philip Sidney (1554–86).

Here I trace a strand of innovation and adaptation from Silva to Sidney. For more than a century, it has been known that central plot lines in Sidney's *Arcadia* resemble diverse episodes within the *Amadís* cycle.[6] It always has been assumed that Sidney knew French translations of the relevant stories, but neither the specific French translators nor the original Spanish authors have received critical focus. What Sidney drew from the *Amadís* cycle for his *Arcadia* consists primarily of three interlaced motifs: a sequestered princess, love by image, and Amazonian disguise. Traditional source criticism has discussed these and other motifs separately across different stories from the *Amadís* cycle and has distanced Sidney's *Arcadia* from such chivalric narratives in terms of character and structure, while recognizing shared comical ironies.[7] Based on those observations, a select few studies of the *Arcadia* have theorized analogues from the *Amadís* cycle as discourse of illicit aristocratic sexual licence.[8] Some such accounts incorporate this theorized source connection into arguments for systematic political or moral allegory.[9] A separate approach has theorized the Spanish chivalric romance genre more diffusely as discourse of transnational justice, claiming political allegory in Sidney's *Arcadia* while eliding entirely narrative source connections.[10] Here, by contrast, I analyse how the unusual trio of shared motifs was invented and then reinvented by Feliciano de Silva in the 1530s within two different works of the *Amadís* cycle. To scholarship on Spanish chivalric romance, I add an emphasis that Silva infused each version of these interlaced motifs with distinct but complementary philosophical implications for the ethics and politics of clandestine marriage. From there, I note how Sidney adapted those same motifs, which appeared in a French translation laden with philosophical embellishments, as his primary template for inventing the *Arcadia*'s central characters, plot lines, and philosophical premises. In this regard, to use Helen Cooper's terminology, the shared device constitutes a discrete romance "meme" within a specific "lineage" of literary invention.[11] My argument on Sidney's creative method revises long-standing critical assumptions about moralism and political allegory in the original version of *Arcadia*, known as the *Old Arcadia*.

Silva invented the interlacement of these unusual motifs within Part Two of his *Amadís de Grecia* (1530; IB 16433). In Part Two, the titular hero's love story from Part One with the Sicilian princess Luscela becomes complicated by a new interest in the Middle Eastern princess Niquea. Niquea has been quarantined at home by her father (the sultan of a land also called Niquea) in response to a prophetic warning about his daughter's beauty. Niquea and the young knight Amadís of Greece fall in love, partly by reputation but mainly by viewing each other's images via magical means. Then, for the sake of social access to her, he disguises himself as an Amazonian warrior; he woos her successfully in female disguise amid comical amorous advances upon him by her elderly father; he wins her hand in secret marriage, and (eventually) he gains a public position as her spouse. Thus, this second love interest supersedes the first, though not without significant internal conflict for the protagonist knight. The narrative justifies this inconstancy by Amadís of Greece only tacitly, through a Neoplatonic love logic built into this unique trio of interlaced motifs Silva invented here in Part Two: a sequestered princess, love by image, and courtship via Amazonian disguise leading to clandestine marriage. In this case, the philosophical implications of honour and truth in love hinge especially on the protagonist lovers' perception of the magical images. These innovations in Part Two of *Amadís de Grecia* mark a crucial turning point within the *Amadís* cycle: regarding ideology of love, comic humour, and representations of gender and religious difference amid heroic actions in both love and military conquest.[12]

Silva wrote three of the four works that followed in the Spanish *Amadís* cycle – *Florisel de Niquea, Parts One and Two* (1532), *Part Three* (1535), and *Part Four* (1551; IB 1645–6) – and all of these expand upon various aspects of his *Amadís de Grecia*. In *Florisel de Niquea, Part Three*, Silva builds the entire work's narrative trajectory around an alternate version of the three interlaced motifs from *Amadís de Grecia*, Part Two. As noted above, this later story begins with the jilted and vengeful Queen Sidonia commissioning a pair of magical connected towers, which (she expects) will protect her daughter Diana from male society while also enacting vengeance upon Diana's father, Florisel of Niquea, son to Amadís of Greece by his wife, Niquea. Sidonia's revenge scheme involves circulating portraits of her daughter, one of which incites the love of young Agesilao, prince of Colchos. In the complex genealogies Silva invented for the *Amadís* cycle, Agesilao descends from Amadís of Greece on both the paternal and maternal sides. Here, in contrast with *Amadís de Grecia*, the means of love-by-image proves non-magical, and Silva shifts the realm of high enchantment to the mode of quarantine. To infiltrate the magical towers, Agesilao and his cousin Arlanges both cross-dress as Amazonian warriors. Therein, they woo and win the princess Diana and her friend Cleofila. In this story, while increasing the number of secret lovers, Silva invents various dramatic ironies of same-sex female intrigue to replace the more bluntly sexualized dramatic irony of Niquea's father pursuing the cross-dressed Amadís in *Amadís de Grecia*.[13] This new mode of irony fits the symbolism and philosophical implication built into Silva's new version of the sequestered-princess motif.

At the beginning of *Florisel de Niquea, Part Three*, Silva bedecks the two magical towers with metaphysical symbolism. They are called the Towers of Phoebus and Diana. Prophecies etched into these towers use imagery of the sun and moon to foreshadow from the beginning that Agesilao and Diana will be united in marriage.[14] One hundred and sixty-five chapters later, the work's prophecies about these lovers' marriage and offspring reiterate the names Phoebus and Apollo as labels for Agesilao.[15] For readers familiar with Aristophanes's account of the androgyne in Plato's *Symposium* – or with Neoplatonic Christian ideas of the spiritual androgyne, complementing certain exegetical commentary on the Book of Genesis – these early chapters of *Florisel de Niquea, Part Three* would have suggested that Agesilao and Diana represent two halves of a single soul seeking their original unity.[16] The symbolic structure of these magical towers also bears alchemical implication. The Tower of Diana protects Sidonia's daughter Diana in a comfortable female court; access to her for male suitors must be gained via the Tower of Phoebus, and such access demands the beheading of Diana's father, Florisel of Niquea. In this manner, the adjoined Towers of Phoebus and Diana represent a vessel in which solar and lunar elements may be mixed and transformed in union. By combining this symbolism of Apollo and Diana with towers and beheading, as well as with a *tour de force* of dramatic and verbal ironies regarding androgynous Amazonian identity, Silva's narrative plays upon the Hermetic notion of a metaphysical sublimation through a chemical wedding.[17] Such Hermetic thought circulated in Spain via Marsilio Ficino's works, and Silva's imagery marks an early phase of this occult symbolism in sixteenth-century Spanish literature.[18]

The narrative poetics of Silva's works, though, remain essentially non-allegorical. From start to finish, amid a wide array of playful ironies, Agesilao proves an admirable hero in love and war, reason and folly. From its inception, this young lover's seeming "sandez de sentimiento de amor" (folly in loving emotion) proves only circumstantial in relation to the extreme scenario imposed upon Diana by Sidonia.[19] The narrative construes these protagonists' amorous devotion as morally just in the face of Sidonia's vengeful folly in love, which constitutes a manifestation of "sinrazón" (irrational injustice) that is both egregious and understandable.[20] Silva generates compassion for her, too, though at a greater critical distance than with the protagonist lovers. Sidonia's agency ironically prompts and facilitates both protagonist couples' unions in clandestine marriage. The marriage of Agesilao and Diana functions as a hallmark of virtue; and, in the end, when it is revealed publicly and condoned by their parents, this marriage also mends personal and political rifts that Silva's own earlier stories had introduced within the vast and complex dynastic empire begun by Amadís of Gaul and Oriana of England.

Agesilao and Diana prove admirable in comparison with Sidonia's folly in love, and this characterization complements that of Amazonian Agesilao when pursued by both members of a royal couple in the middle of *Florisel de Niquea, Part Three*, chapters 80–3. When visiting the kingdom of Galdapa, Agesilao (under the pseudonym Daraida) must evade the sexual advances of King Galinides, who takes him for a woman, and Queen Salderna, who sees through the female disguise. The king's thwarted lust proves so powerful that he loses his full mental faculties, and this circumstance of Galinides's perceived insanity incites an invasion of his realm by the neighbouring king of Gelda.[21] Queen Salderna has imprisoned Agesilao for thwarting her sexual advances, but, as the Geldan army enters the city, her guards release the cross-dressed knight, who protects the realm of Galdapa by slaying the invading king and his brother.[22] Here we see sexualized comic humour akin to that of the sultan wooing Amazonian Amadís in *Amadís de Grecia*. Yet, with the political consequences involved, which highlight Agesilao's prowess amid unwavering constancy to Diana in love, here Silva imposes an even greater ethical distance between the protagonist knight in female attire and the hapless sexual aggressor Galanides. This dynamic of character contrast constitutes the central narrative poetics of Silva's chivalric romances. Throughout *Florisel de Niquea, Part Three*, for instance, Agesilao's constancy in love also distinguishes him from his cousin Rogel of Greece, who achieves comparable feats in arms but remains (until Silva's *Part Four*) a shameless scoundrel in love amid many amorous encounters.[23] Metaphysical symbolism associated with Agesilao and Diana adds a figurative texture to the ethics and politics of *Florisel de Niquea, Part Three* across a wide canvas of variegated exemplary characterization.

In French translation, however, Silva's *Florisel de Niquea, Part Three* takes two different directions in the hands of separate translators. The first half, chapters 1–84, was translated by Jacques Gohory (1520–76) as *Book Eleven* of the French *Amadis* cycle, first published in 1554 (FB 779). The second half, chapters 85–170, was translated by Guillaume Aubert (1534–97) as *Book Twelve* of the French *Amadis* cycle, first published in 1556 (FB 815). Both French halves of Silva's story entail significant embellishment. Aubert's alterations prove mainly structural in episodic narration. To accommodate picking up where Gohory leaves off, Aubert rearranges the order of certain chapters at the beginning of his instalment. Then, at the end of Silva's story, Aubert appends a sequence of new adventures for Agesilao and Rogel, recounted in parallel but occurring separately from each other. There, in chapters 84–97 of the French *Book Twelve*, Aubert closely imitates episodes from Ariosto's *Orlando Furioso* and from Virgil's *Aeneid*, including a new love affair undertaken by Rogel that mimics the infamous story of Aeneas and Dido to the point of direct translation at times.[24] As for the first half of *Florisel de Niquea, Part Three*, Gohory amplifies not plot lines but figurative language and symbolism. At the beginning, he adds a full chapter describing the Towers of Phoebus and Diana with extensive new occult symbolism.[25] Another new chapter concludes Gohory's half-translation with a song of Arlanges's Neoplatonic enrapture with Cleofila after they have consummated their secret marriage.[26] Gohory – who translated *Books Ten, Eleven*, and *Thirteen* of the French *Amadis* cycle, often adding lyric poetry, as in this case – was a scientist and occult philosopher. He proved an influential French disciple of Ficino's Neoplatonic and Hermetic Christian thought, of the medical and alchemical theories of Paracelsus, and of other contemporary theories on chemical healing and music.[27] Gohory's choice of structure for *Book Eleven* and his localized embellishments reshape the Neoplatonic and Hermetic symbolism of Silva's fiction into a microcosm of occult allegory.[28] The allegorical subtexts revolve around Silva's distinctive trio of motifs that establish the narrative logic of four protagonist lovers' secret courtships and clandestine marriages.

Sidney knew and drew upon both French segments of Silva's *Florisel de Niquea, Part Three*; yet, Gohory's portion proved more instrumental than Aubert's, especially for inventing the *Old Arcadia*, which Sidney composed between 1578 and early 1581 and allowed to circulate via manuscript copies.[29] With Aubert's *Book Twelve*, Sidney might have adapted certain episodes, although a firm connection remains unclear.[30] Given Sidney's fluid definition of literary forms in the *Defence of Poesy* (ca. 1580), he probably appreciated Aubert's blending of ancient epic and sixteenth-century chivalric romance.[31] His incomplete expansion of the *Arcadia* between 1583 and 1585, known as the *New Arcadia* and printed posthumously in different versions from 1590 onward, expands its narrative scope more toward chivalric epic. Yet, Sidney attended far more thoroughly and precisely to Gohory's distinct rendition of Silva's fiction in *Book Eleven*. Indeed, that first half of *Florisel de Niquea, Part Three*, as translated by Gohory, served as Sidney's primary creative template for inventing the *Old Arcadia*'s central characters, its foundational plot, and its core philosophical discourse. By re-evaluating this literary connection with an eye to Gohory's agency as a translator, we gain a new understanding of Sidney's creative method and his *Old Arcadia*'s essential nature as philosophically charged but non-allegorical exemplary fiction.

In the *Old Arcadia*, as in *Florisel de Niquea, Part Three* and Gohory's half-rendition, the story begins with a sequestered-princess motif. Arcadia's sovereign duke, Basilius, removes himself from political rule to protect his two daughters, Pamela and Philoclea, in response to a prophecy. Like Silva's narrative and Gohory's translation, Sidney's *Old Arcadia* provides readers with its prophetic text from the beginning.[32] As with Agesilao and Diana, Pyrocles falls in love with Philoclea toward the beginning of the narrative by means of a non-magical portrait, then promptly adopts Amazonian disguise to woo her. Musidorus, like Arlanges, follows his cousin in this adventure (here disguised as a shepherd rather than another Amazon) and falls in love within the secluded courtly setting. Sidney replaces Silva's two magical towers with two pastoral huts. This scenario of verisimilitude lends itself to new diversity in comic irony: Musidorus dupes the rustic protectors of Princess Pamela, while Pyrocles must evade the two princesses' parents, Basilius and Gynecia, who simultaneously pursue him sexually as did Galanides and Saldana with Agesilao in Silva's fiction and Gohory's translation. Although the elderly father comedy with Basilius generally resembles that of the sultan in Part Two of Silva's *Amadís de Grecia* (and its French translation by Nicolas de Herberay as *Book Eight*), Sidney adapts details of rhetoric and circumstance from the encounter with Galanides and Salderna in Gohory's *Book Eleven*.[33] Gohory's half-translation of *Florisel de Niquea, Part Three* ends with the Galanides-and-Saldana episode in Galdapa, followed immediately by the protagonist cousin Arlanges's success in wooing Cleofila; thus, this French instalment of the *Amadís* cycle associates the subsidiary plot line of Agesilao in Galdapa with the protagonist lovers' courtship even more closely than in Silva's full work. Sidney's imitation with Basilius integrates the two storylines much more tightly: the structural function of Sidonia's folly in love takes the non-vengeful form of a Galanides, whose mis-guided pursuit of an Amazonian visitor imperils his realm politically. In the *Old Arcadia*, too, the cross-dressed prince's presence inadvertently incites both the ruler's folly and, from there, a political threat to the realm. In this case, the armed conflict constitutes an insurrection of drunken subjects from within Arcadia, and, as with the Geldan inva-sion of Galdapa in Sidney's chivalric source narrative, the cross-dressed prince quells the political turmoil.[34] Thus, in Books One through Three of the *Old Arcadia*'s five-book structure, Pyrocles's Amazonian disguise arises logically from the circumstance of Basilius's political folly and then comically produces new private and political chaos, while also preserving political stability amid Arcadian rebellion.

As in the chivalric source model, the idea of Amazonian disguise arises shortly after the portrait episode and involves a dialogue between the two young princes. Silva's version of the conversation is short. Arlanges proposes that they both infiltrate the towers by cross-dressing, and Agesilao instantly embraces the plan with gratitude.[35] Gohory's translation amplifies this moment of dialogue with a rather long speech by Arlanges in the form of a medical consultation.[36] Sidney creatively exploits the rhetoric of Gohory's Arlanges, expanding the exchange into a much lengthier dialogue of give-and-take between Pyrocles and Musidorus. This narrative and rhetorical imitation includes a playful allusion to tarantism, a mode of occult medicine involving tarantulas and music, probably adapted from the more serious reference to tarantism that Gohory added to Silva's text in a later context with Agesilao and Diana.[37] The light-hearted nature of Sidney's allusion reflects the essence of his rhetorical imitation in this crucial dialogue. Here, as elsewhere, Sidney's text redirects Gohory's philosophical and medical language away from an allegorical poetics of metaphysical implication, toward immediate effects of individual characterization.

Sidney's creative variation alters both the motive and the narrative function of the lovelorn prince's dialogue with his cousin. Here, in contrast with the chivalric source paradigm, the love-struck young prince conceives the idea of Amazonian disguise for himself before his conversation with a slightly elder cousin. Amid that dialogue, Musidorus argues against the prospect of cross-dressing, unlike Arlanges, who proposes that strategy for Agesilao and himself. These creative variations extend beyond moralism and situational comedy.[38] Sidney's innovation with Pyrocles here, as with Musidorus in adopting pastoral disguise shortly afterward, posits for the *Old Arcadia* what becomes a recurrent emphasis: that true love productively fuels mental "invention."[39] In this initial dialogue of the princes, Sidney invents for Pyrocles an enhanced philosophical self-awareness and resolution. Musidorus aims to dissuade Pyrocles from undertaking any rash action, deploying arguments on constancy that constitute a Stoic extension of the Aristotelian premise on virtue and vice as matters of habituation, concerned mainly with the Ciceronian idea of private and public decorum as a matter of ethical consistency.[40] Yet, Pyrocles wins the discussion with counterarguments of his own. To justify his intent for apparent gender transformation as a means to pursue genuine love, he reflects upon his own experience in Neoplatonic terms, valorizing it as "heavenly love," identical to the idea of "true love" that Musidorus has condoned in contrast with the purely sensual "bastard love" Musidorus has assumed Pyrocles feels.[41] This philosophical self-consciousness complements Pyrocles's earlier ethical defence of his own resolution in love with a quasi-Senecan idea of heroic constancy. He argues that an Amazonian guise with a pretext of seeking marriage allows him to retain both his virtue of military prowess and his "noble desire" to court Philoclea and covertly marry her within the extreme domestic and political circumstances Basilius has imposed upon her and Pamela.[42] He does not know what will happen but trusts that, as he puts it, "fortune, occasion, and mine own industry" may lend themselves to the beneficent circumstance of "new secret helps" amid contingencies to come.[43] This claim suggests for Pyrocles a faith in grace distinct from the deification of human resolution in Seneca's essays *De Constantia, De Clementia,* and *De Providentia.* He experiences melancholy only while he still anticipates the action of undertaking the female persona Cleophila, which he deems necessary strategically, also fitting for his new identification of selfhood with love for Philoclea. Hence his focus in the *Old Arcadia's* first lyric poem, "Transformed in show, but more transformed in mind," which he sings (as Cleophila) immediately after adopting the disguise in this episode.[44] Musidorus has conceded the argument out of compassionate friendship, but when he, too, experiences love upon first viewing Pamela shortly afterward in Book One, he embraces the logic of Pyrocles's perspective on ethical constancy amid social metamorphosis, vocalizing that consciousness in song ("Come shepherd's weeds, become your master's mind") before explicitly recanting his inexperienced rational resistance to his younger cousin's earlier argument.[45]

These philosophical registers linked to the logic and motive for disguise prove essential for the *Old Arcadia's* unique dramatic, political, legal, and intellectual ironies. In Books One through Three, Pyrocles and Musidorus outmanoeuvre the princesses' domestic captors and win the hands of Philoclea and Pamela, who exchange with them secret present-tense vows of marriage.[46] Pyrocles and Philoclea consummate those vows.[47] Pamela, as Basilius's heir-apparent, wisely asks Musidorus to defer consummation until they have eloped to his realm of Thessaly, where they will validate their currently clandestine marriage politically.[48] Although Musidorus almost falters once in upholding this agreement of temporary chastity in secret marriage, chaotic political circumstances, ironically, not only thwart his "approaches" upon Pamela while she sleeps (aiming at least to kiss her and likely more) but result in a mutual strengthening of this couple's resolution for chastity and defence of each other's lives, honour, and political positions.[49] This character development occurs within Books Four and Five, which impose a sudden seeming death for Basilius (from the perspectives of all characters and also first-time readers). For the duke's apparent demise, the two visiting princes and the duchess Gynecia are prosecuted by Basilius's deputized governor, Philanax, with misguided charges of treasonous conspiracy. That legal circumstance prompts factional division and prospective armed conflict regarding the Arcadian succession, due to Pamela's insistence on Musidorus's political rights as her husband. This conflict stems from the secret nature of the lovers' marriages, because Arcadian law imposes a death penalty for clandestine marriage, and the only indisputable recourse to merciful reprieve resides in the duke, who is presumed dead. To avert civil war, Philanax deputizes as a temporary foreign magistrate a visiting king, Euarchus of Macedonia, who is internationally renowned for justice. Euarchus happens to be Pyrocles's father and Musidorus's uncle but does not know their identities at first, due to their pseudonyms adopted upon arrest plus the fact that they were in Thessaly and he away at war while they grew up. Even after learning their identities, though, Euarchus sentences them to death by a legalistic judgment according to Arcadian law. With tragic irony, he imprudently endangers Arcadia, Thessaly, and his own realm of Macedonia through a rigidly rational and self-contradictory emphasis on social decorum and ethical consistency, including a Stoic idea of heroic constancy that he attaches to his own personal sacrifice for what he purports to be the public good. The Arcadian populace resents Euarchus for this decision. Pyrocles advises his father publicly that such refusal to allow mitigating circumstances proves imprudent politically, and readers can infer that this imprudence contradicts the principles of international jurisprudence upon which Euarchus acts. Those principles entail the Ciceronian philosophies of *constantia* and *decorum* evoked by Musidorus's initial rhetoric to Pyrocles in Book One, as well as the ethos of a Senecan-style *constantia* implied by Pyrocles's resolution there. In the end, even Philanax and Euarchus rejoice when the princes' imminent deaths are averted at the last minute. Basilius awakens from a deep sleep perceived as death; he grants clemency to both princes and to his wife; and he publicly sanctions the protagonist lovers' clandestine marriages.[50]

Even this brief synopsis of philosophical unity in characterization and dramatic irony calls for a redirection of long-trodden critical pathways in Sidney studies. Since the mid-1960s, this narrative structure and sudden happy ending have been perceived as vexed in one way or another. Modern critics have read the lovers' courtships as premarital affairs; yet, within the text (as well as by Elizabethan English law), they are technically secret marriages.[51] All characters in the story agree on that fact, including Philanax and Euarchus. Although rhetoric points in different directions for different reasons amid the legal prosecution and defence, clandestine marriage – not premarital sex or abduction per se – remains the focus of severe Arcadian law and therefore also of Euarchus's judgment. The dramatic and intellectual ironies of Sidney's fiction do not come at the protagonist princes' expense, neither as moralism nor as ethical ambivalence, as has been assumed (one way or another) for the past half century.[52] Certain critics have recognized that the *Old Arcadia* favours its protagonist princes aesthetically and ideologically, but even they have assumed for the young lovers generalized notions of ethical and political fault amid social privilege.[53] From start to finish, though, Pyrocles and Musidorus boldly embrace metamorphosis amid political chaos as a means of ethical constancy that emerges as virtuous not only by their own philosophical standard but by those of Philanax and Euarchus.[54] This shared ethos in love and friendship proves fortuitous (indeed, providential), both ethically and politically. Sidney's fiction, like Silva's (via Gohory), features ironically but genuinely heroic lovers.

Connecting Sidney indirectly with Silva in this manner calls for a broader and more nuanced appreciation of both authors' inventions and influence within European literary tradition. Consider, for instance, my perspective above on the manner and motives of Cervantes's narrator disparaging Silva's work in the opening chapter of *Don Quixote*. By citing Silva's fantastical fiction and playfully imitating its prose style as a point of departure, Cervantine parody distinguishes itself only superficially from the prose genre of Spanish chivalric romances. Beyond that first chapter, Part One of the *Quixote* imitates with staunch verisimilitude Silva's innovations in generic hybridity and meta-generic parody.[55] Interlaced plot lines in Part One of the *Quixote* also adapt the intricate narrative logic of Silva's works. Cervantes's creative variation includes nuanced characterization amid love stories involving clandestine marriage, especially that of Dorotea and Don Fernando. This invention comes after the Council of Trent's seminal and controversial revision of Roman Catholic marriage law in 1563, optimistically reflecting Spanish legal mitigation of that revised Roman law in the early seventeenth century, defending the rights of women in Dorotea's position. Thus, Cervantes's fiction conveys an ideological sympathy for companionate clandestine marriage akin to that of Silva's works and other Spanish chivalric romances of the early sixteenth century, as does Sidney's fiction in adapting Silva (via Gohory) with a distinct mode of verisimilitude.[56] In the case of Dorotea and Don Fernando – that is, the daughter of a wealthy farmer and the second son of a grandee (the highest level of Spanish nobility) – Cervantes extends this chivalric romance ideology across traditional boundaries of social class. Recognizing this central dimension of continuity and adaptation requires a departure from a long-standing modern critical bias in favour of verisimilitude and Cervantine parody that has precluded serious attention to Spanish chivalric romances in relation to origins of the modern novel.[57] Even amid the rise of specialist scholarship in recent decades, accounts on the *Amadís* cycle have remained tentative regarding Silva's artistry – reluctant to grant his innovations the status of significant literary inventions in their own right due to a residual privileging of certain critical voices within the *Quixote*.[58] Cervantes, like Sidney, perceived the ingenuity of dramatic and intellectual ironies within Silva's chivalric romances, imitating them with a competitive edge.

Sidney's fiction, like Silva's, deserves a more prominent place within critical histories of the modern novel and its early modern origins. The influence of Sidney's *Arcadia* in England and beyond came chiefly in print through its revision as the *New Arcadia*, which retains and expands the *Old Arcadia*'s manner of non-allegorical exemplary characterization while chastening the protagonists' clandestine marriages sexually and heightening these four lovers' consciousness of their own secret unions' ethical virtue and political import.[59] From the 1593 edition onward, *The Countess of Pembroke's Arcadia* – shepherded into print by Sidney's sister as a five-book narration intended as such, though left incomplete by Sidney's untimely death – was reproduced continually and shaped English literature (including stage plays) to a degree only partly approximated by critical surveys to date.[60] William Shakespeare drew upon it most directly in *King Lear* but likely began his consistent dramatic emphasis on companionate marriages (often clandestine unions) at least partly in response to the 1593 *New Arcadia*.[61] By 1660, unusually for early modern English fiction, Sidney's *New Arcadia* was translated into multiple European languages: three times into French (twice fully, once in part) and once each into German, Dutch, and Italian.[62] English novelists wrote continuations and adaptations of the *New Arcadia* for a century and a half after 1593, and a nineteenth-century editor, Hain Friswell, provided notes and glosses defending its continued relevance for English gentry of the Victorian era.[63] In the mid-eighteenth century, Samuel Richardson – who knew Sidney's *Arcadia* directly, having contributed as a printer to the 1725 edition in octavo format – paid tribute to it by borrowing the still-unusual name of Arcadia's heir-apparent for his heroine in *Pamela*.[64] This connection to Sidney's fiction should not be lost in assessing the heated debate on literary theory that ensued, wherein Richardson defended his emphasis on novelistic interiority against Henry Fielding's preference for a Cervantine style of presenting externalized worldly experience laced with ironic commentary by a third-person narrator.[65] At least to some degree, especially regarding the famous captivity episode with Pamela that Sidney added for the *New Arcadia* and Richardson clearly bore in mind, this seminal English debate from the mid-eighteenth century can be viewed as a microcosm of the distinct Sidneian and Cervantine legacies that spawned from Silva's innovations within the Spanish genre of chivalric romances in prose (mediated by Gohory's embellishments in the case of Sidney's artistry). Sidney's innovative fiction resists any singular categorization by genre while lending itself to diverse generic labels. One of them, "proto-novel," should be applied to the *Arcadia* itself, both *Old* and *New*, rather than only to the *New Arcadia*'s eighteenth-century legacies.[66] This chapter's brief re-evaluation of the *Old Arcadia*'s central characters, plot, and philosophical investments signals a need to reassess more broadly the *Arcadia*'s texts and literary legacies (domestic and international) alongside those of Silva beyond Sidney's creative imitation.

NOTES

1 Miguel de Cervantes, *El Ingenioso Hidalgo Don Quijote de la Mancha*, ed. Martín de Riquer (Barcelona: Planeta, 1998), 34. English translations are my own.
2 Ibid.
3 For comparison with the *Segunda Celestina*, see Francisco Márquez Villanueva, *Fuentes Literarias Cervantinas* (Madrid: Gredos, 1973), 27n17, 56n56; Joachim Harst, "Making Love: Celestinesque Literature, Philology, and Marranism," *Modern Language Notes* 127, no. 2 (2007): 180; William Hinrichs, *The Invention of the Sequel: Expanding Prose Fiction in Early Modern Spain* (Woodbridge, UK: Tamesis, 2011), 73–4. For comparison with Darinel, see Sydney Cravens, "Feliciano de Silva and His Romances of Chivalry in *Don Quijote*," *Inti: Revista de Literatura Hispánica* 7 (1978): 28–34, esp. 31–2.
4 Feliciano de Silva, *Florisel de Niquea (Tercera Parte)*, ed. Javier Martín Lalanda (Alcalá de Henares, ES: Centro de Estudios Cervantinos, 1999), 10a. Citations with letters indicate columns on the page.
5 My translation. The pronoun "la" in this final line refers to "la razón" (reason/justice) in the preceding sentence, omitted here, in which Sidonia asks what reason or justice could have allowed Helena to enjoy Florisel's love other than the fact that love involves little reason or justice.
6 See, especially, William Vaughan Moody, "An Inquiry into the Sources of Sir Philip Sidney's *Arcadia*" (1894), Sohier Prize Essay, Harvard manuscript HU 89.365.20, 34–47; John J. O'Connor, *"Amadis de Gaule" and Its Influence on Elizabethan Literature* (New Brunswick, NJ: Rutgers University Press, 1970), 183–201, cf. 121; and Paul E. Rockwell, "Comic Elements in Sidney's *Old Arcadia*" (PhD diss., University of Maryland, 1980), 150–69.
7 O'Connor, *"Amadis de Gaule,"* 186–95, esp. 192; Robert W. Parker, "Terentian Structure and Sidney's Original *Arcadia*," *English Literary Renaissance* 2, no. 1 (1972): 72–3; Rockwell, "Comic Elements," 164–9. A.C. Hamilton's claims to that general effect attend to the wrong *Amadís*

narrative: "Sidney's *Arcadia* as Prose Fiction: Its Relation to Its Sources," *English Literary Renaissance* 2, no. 1 (1972): 38–42, and *Sir Philip Sidney: A Study of His Life and Works* (Cambridge: Cambridge University Press, 1977), 45–7. Otherwise, Hamilton's synopsis of narrative sources proves useful.

8 See, especially, Joshua Scodel, *Excess and the Mean in Early Modern English Literature* (Princeton, NJ: Princeton University Press, 2002), 159–61; also Margaret M. Sullivan, "Amazons and Aristocrats: The Function of Pyrocles' Amazon Role in Sidney's Revised *Arcadia*," in *Playing with Gender: A Renaissance Pursuit*, ed. Jean R. Brink, Maryanne Cline Horowitz, and Allison P. Coudert (Urbana: University of Illinois Press, 1991), 70; David Norbrook, *Poetry and Politics in the English Renaissance*, rev. ed. (Oxford: Oxford University Press, 2002), 90; Victor Skretkowicz, *European Erotic Romance: Philhellene Protestantism, Renaissance Translation, and English Literary Politics* (Manchester: Manchester University Press, 2010), 202–3, 182–3; and Kenneth Borris, "Sir Philip Sidney's *Arcadias*," in *The Ashgate Research Companion to the Sidneys, 1500–1700*, vol. 2, *Literature*, ed. Margaret P. Hannay, Mary Ellen Lamb, and Michael G. Brennan (Farnham, UK: Ashgate, 2015), 94–5.

9 Skretkowicz, *European Erotic Romance*, 168–224, esp. 199, 202–3; Borris, "Sir Philip Sidney's *Arcadias*," 93–105, esp. 95, 99, 100.

10 Brian C. Lockey, *Law and Empire in English Renaissance Literature* (Cambridge: Cambridge University Press, 2006), 17–79.

11 Helen Cooper, *The English Romance in Time* (Oxford: Oxford University Press, 2004), 3, 8. Cooper's study notes briefly that the *Arcadia*'s Amazonian-disguise trope derives from Spanish sources, not English tradition (258).

12 For these perspectives, see Timothy D. Crowley, "Neoplatonic Love Logic in Feliciano de Silva's *Amadís de Grecia* (1530)," *Intertexts* 20, no. 1 (2016): 1–24. My analysis there of proto-modern characterization complements the emphasis on interiority in the contribution to this volume by Goran Stanivukovic.

13 See Marie Cort Daniels, *The Function of Humor in the Spanish Romances of Chivalry* (New York: Garland, 1992), 202–7, 211–26. On aesthetics of disguise in these two works, see also José Jiménez Ruiz, "De Feliciano de Silva al *Persiles*: La Metamorfosis del Hombre en Mujer como Recurso de Estructura y Género," in *Poéticas de la Metamorfosis: Tradición Clásica, Siglo de Oro, y Modernidad*, ed. Gregorio Cabello Porras and Javier Campos Daroca (Malaga: Universidad de Málaga, 2002), 117–62; and Emilio J. Sales Dasí, "Princesas 'desterradas' y caballeros disfrazados: Un acercamiento a la estética literaria de Feliciano de Silva," *Revista de Literatura Medieval* 15, no. 2 (2003): 85–106.

14 Silva, *Florisel de Niquea (Tercera Parte)*, 10b–11a, cf. 9a.

15 Ibid., 495a, 498b.

16 On the intellectual contexts, see Marian Rothstein, *The Androgyne in Early Modern France: Contextualizing the Power of Gender* (New York: Palgrave Macmillan, 2015), 5–26.

17 For conceptual context, see the discussion of the following terms in Lyndy Abraham, *A Dictionary of Alchemical Imagery* (Cambridge: Cambridge University Press, 1998): "Hermes Trismegistus" (100–1), "chemical wedding" (35–9), "distillation and sublimation" (55–6), "tower" (203–4), "peace and strife" (141), "beheading" (20–2), "Apollo" (8), and "Diana" (54–5). Given Agesilao's and Diana's kinship through distinct branches of the Amadís-Oriana dynasty, one might also consider an alchemical notion of "incest": "The fact that the two participants in the wedding are personified as coming from the same family emphasizes the essential similarity of the substances being joined even though they appear to be opposites of unlike nature" (ibid., 106). The Amazonian-disguise motif might have been read in terms of a "perfect integration of male and female energies," with the protagonist lovers' marriage as "complete, undivided unity" ("hermaphrodite," 98). See also "elements'" (68–9) and, given the lovers' geographic origins, "east and west" (65). On Hermetic ideas of the hermaphrodite, see also Kathleen P. Long, *The Hermaphrodite in Renaissance Europe* (Aldershot, UK: Ashgate, 2006), 109–36.

18 See Susan Byrne, *Ficino in Spain* (Toronto: University of Toronto Press, 2015), esp. 142–64 on imagery in poetry of later decades.

19 Here I quote from Arlanges's rhetoric to Agesilao, who has fallen in love with Diana: Silva, *Florisel de Niquea (Tercera Parte)*, 40a. Agesilao has prayed to the Virgin Mary regarding his own confusion of "*razón*" and "*sinrazón*," which he characterizes to Arlanges as a form of "*locura*" (madness) (39a, 39b–40a).

20 Ibid., 10a (see 9a–11a), 57a, 401a, 494b (cf. 417a), 495b.

21 Ibid., 258b, 261a.

22 Ibid., 260b–2b.

23 On Rogel in this regard, see Daniels, *Function of Humor*, 149–57, 174–90.

24 *Le Dovziesme Liure d'Amadis de Gaule*, trans. Guillaume Aubert (Paris: Estienne Groulleau, 1556), fols. CCVI^v–CCXXXVII^v; John J. O'Connor, "Virgil, Ariosto, and Book XII of *Amadis de Gaule*," *Journal of the Rutgers University Library* 37, no. 2 (1974): 29–41.

25 *L'Onzieme Livre d'Amadis de Gavle*, trans. Jacques Gohory (Paris: Vincent Sertenas, 1554), fols. II^v–IIII^v (chap. 2); see Rosanna Gorris, "Pour une lecture stéganographique des *Amadis* de Jacques Gohory," in *Les Amadis en France au XVIe siècle* (Paris: Éditions Rue d'Ulm, 2000), 132–44.

26 *Onzieme Livre*, fols. CLII^r–CLV^v (chap. 89); see Jeanice Brooks, "Music as Erotic Magic in a Renaissance Romance," *Renaissance Quarterly* 60, no. 4

(2007): 1243–6. The text of this concluding song by the French Arlanges has been reproduced in O'Connor, *"Amadis de Gaule,"* 239–41.

27 The most comprehensive account remains Willis H. Bowen, "Jacques Gohory (1520–1576)" (PhD diss., Harvard University, 1935). For Gohory on Ficino and Paracelsus, see also D.P. Walker, *Spiritual and Demonic Magic from Ficino to Campanella* (London: Warburg Institute, 1958), 96–106; and Alan G. Debus, *The French Paracelsians: The Chemical Challenge to Medical and Scientific Tradition in Early Modern France* (Cambridge: Cambridge University Press, 1991), 26–8.

28 Gorris, "Pour une lecture stéganographique"; Rosanna Gorris, "Diane de Guindaye, Pentasilée et les autres, ou les Diane de Jacques Gohory," in *Le mythe de Diane en France au XVIe siècle*, ed. Jean-Raymond Fanlo and Marie-Dominique Legrand (Paris: Librairie Honoré Champion, 2002), 291–332; Brooks, "Music as Erotic Magic"; Magali Jeannin-Corbin, "Jacques Gohory ou l'alchimisation du Moyen Âge," in *Accès aux textes médiévaux de la fin du Moyen Âge au XVIIIe siècle*, ed. Michèle Guéret-Laferté and Claudine Poulouin (Paris: Honoré Champion, 2012), 221–4.

29 For dating the *Old Arcadia*'s composition, see *The Countess of Pembroke's Arcadia (The Old Arcadia)*, ed. Jean Robertson (Oxford: Clarendon, 1973) (hereafter *Old Arcadia*), xv–xix. On its circulation, see H.R. Woudhuysen, *Sir Philip Sidney and the Circulation of Manuscripts, 1558–1640* (Oxford: Clarendon, 1996), 8, 299–355; with John Gouws, "Sidney's 'Old' *Arcadia* as Polymorphous Text: A Case Study of the Phillipps Manuscript," *Text* 17 (2005): 93–116.

30 O'Connor, *"Amadis de Gaule,"* 189–90, 195.

31 O'Connor, "Virgil, Ariosto, and Book XII," 41.

32 Sidney, *Old Arcadia*, 5.15–21. Cf. Silva, *Florisel de Niquea (Tercera Parte)*, 9a, 10b–11a (chaps 1, 2); *Onzieme Livre*, fols. VII^{r-v}, II^{r-v} (chaps 4, 1).

33 Rockwell, "Comic Elements," 153–4, 161–3.

34 Sidney, *Old Arcadia*, 120.30–132.19.

35 Silva, *Florisel de Niquea (Tercera Parte)*, 40a–b.

36 *Onzieme Livre*, fols. XXIX^{r-v} (chap. 15); see Brooks, "Music as Erotic Magic," 1232–3.

37 Sidney, *Old Arcadia*, 17.10–11; cf. O'Connor, *"Amadis de Gaule,"* 198–9. O'Connor's comparison of the two sentences detaches them from rhetorical contexts and makes no reference to Gohory or his intellectual motives. For Gohory's reference, see *Onzieme Livre*, fol. LXXXX^r (chap. 56); with Brooks, "Music as Erotic Magic," 1233.

38 Those interpretive emphases appear in Rockwell, "Comical Elements," 165–9, which usefully revises the speculative and heavy-handed premise of moralism in Mark Rose, "Sidney's Womanish Man," *Review of English Studies* 15, no. 60 (1964): 353–63. Rose's premise marginalized the chivalric

source connection (357n3) and proved influential, most directly for Franco Marenco, *Arcadia Puritana: L'uso delle tradizione nella prima* Arcadia *di Sir Philip Sidney* (Bari: Adriatica Editrice, 1968), 49–88, esp. 52–59, 93–128, 136–70; and Andrew Weiner, *Sir Philip Sidney and the Poetics of Protestantism* (Minneapolis: University of Minnesota Press, 1978), 60–87, esp. 70, 205n48, cf. 163–85.

39 Sidney, *Old Arcadia*, 12.27 (see 11.35–12.29); also 18.7–23, 113.30–2, 206.31–207.2, 215.3–8.

40 Ibid., 13.1–14.6 (esp. 13.9–17), 15.34–17.9, 17.22, 18.32–20.30 (esp. 19.13–16, 19.28–32), 23.32–24.12 (esp. 24.1–3). For these intellectual contexts, see Aristotle, *Nicomachean Ethics*, 1103a–b, and Cicero, *De Officiis* (On Duties), esp. I.66–7, I.72–3, I.90, I.111–12, II.32.

41 Sidney, *Old Arcadia*, 21.6–23.5 (quoted at 22.25–6). The phrases quoted from Musidorus appear at 20.13, 19.37.

42 Ibid., 18.812, cf. 22.33–23.5 (quoted at 23.5).

43 Ibid., 18.18–21.

44 Ibid., 28–9; cf. *Poems of Sir Philip Sidney*, ed. William A. Ringler (Oxford: Clarendon, 1962), 11–12. This is the first lyric poem apart from the Delphic oracle.

45 Sidney, *Old Arcadia*, 40.3–12, 42.19–24; cf. *Poems*, 13. Here I redirect the distinct emphasis on Musidorus's rhetorical concession in Wendy Olmsted, "The Gentle Doctor: Renaissance/Reformation Friendship, Rhetoric, and Emotion in Sidney's *Old Arcadia*," *Modern Philology* 103.2 (2005): 156–86.

46 Sidney, *Old Arcadia*, 122.9–11, 197.5–16, cf. 172.23–173.3.

47 Ibid., 237.9–243.6.

48 Ibid., 172.23–173.16, 196.5–197.28, esp. 197.3–28.

49 Ibid., 201.7–202.16 (quoted at 202.6), 306.10–320.2 (esp. 310.31–314.21, 315.25–36, 319.13–30), 396.34–398.6 (esp. 397.19–24), 400.23–403.2 (esp. 402.1–4).

50 Detailed analysis of the narrative logic, including these dramatic and intellectual ironies, will appear in my book, *Feigned Histories of Secret Marriage*.

51 Only one study even hints at this cultural context beyond the text, claiming a socially biased moral ambivalence in the story (Scodel, *Excess and the Mean*, 155–63). For the context itself, see R.H. Helmholz, "The Legal Regulation of Marriage in England: From the Fifteenth Century to the 1640s," in *Marriage in Europe, 1400–1800*, ed. Silvana Seidel Menchi and Emlyn Eisenach (Toronto: University of Toronto Press, 2016), 122–52.

52 The most extreme arguments for moralism are Marenco, *Arcadia Puritana*, and Weiner, *Sir Philip Sidney*, which build upon Rose, "Sidney's Womanish Man," as noted above. The most influential arguments for ethical ambivalence are Richard Helgerson, *Elizabethan Prodigals* (Berkeley:

University of California Press, 1976), 133–41; Hamilton, *Sir Philip Sidney*, 34–41; and Richard McCoy, *Sir Philip Sidney: Rebellion in Arcadia* (New Brunswick, NJ: Rutgers University Press, 1979). The two general premises have shaped subsequent scholarship pervasively.

53 See Margaret Dana, "The Providential Plot of the *Old Arcadia*," *Studies in English Literature, 1500–1900*, 17, no. 1 (1977): 43–4, 49; Norbrook, *Poetry and Politics*, 86, 89–90, cf. 92; R.S. White, *Natural Law in English Renaissance Literature* (Cambridge: Cambridge University Press, 1996), 142–3, 147; Debora Shuger, "Castigating Livy: The Rape of Lucretia and *The Old Arcadia*," *Renaissance Quarterly* 51, no. 2 (1998): 526–8, 531–3, 542–4; Scodel, *Excess and the Mean*, 155–63; Jeff Dolven, *Scenes of Instruction in Renaissance Romance* (Chicago: University of Chicago Press, 2007), 99–133; Wendy Olmsted, *The Imperfect Friend: Emotion and Rhetoric in Sidney, Milton, and Their Contexts* (Toronto: University of Toronto Press, 2008), 20–53; and, in allegorical terms, Skretkowicz, *European Erotic Romance*, 179.

54 My emphasis on the princes' self-consciousness in characterization revises Dolven's theory of "metamorphosis" as aesthetic discourse construed in opposition to discourse of "constancy" tied to Musidorus and Euarchus.

55 This topic needs further investigation. For useful starting points, see Sydney P. Cravens, *Feliciano de Silva y los antecedentes de la novela pastoril en sus libros de caballerías* (Madrid: Castalia, 1976); Cravens, "Feliciano de Silva and His Romances of Chivalry"; Daniels, *Function of Humor*, 137–47, 237–82; and Emilio J. Sales Dasí, "El humor en la narrativa de Feliciano de Silva: En el camino hacia Cervantes," *Literatura: Teoría, Historia, Crítica* 7 (2005): 115–57.

56 On relevant literary and legal context for Silva in the early sixteenth century, see Justina Ruiz de Conde, *El amor y el matrimonio secreto en los libros de caballerías* (Madrid: Aguilar, 1948); Crowley, "Neoplatonic Love Logic," esp. 6–7, 12–13, 15; and *Florisel de Niquea (Tercera Parte)*, xxxi–xxxii. For the Spanish legal context relevant to my emphasis here on Cervantes, see Cristano Rodríguez-Arano Díaz, "El matrimonio clandestino en la novela cervantina," *Anuario de la Historia del Derecho Español* 25, no. 1 (1955): 731–34; with Abigail Dyer, "Seduction by Promise of Marriage: Law, Sex, and Culture in Seventeenth Century Spain," *Sixteenth Century Journal* 34, no. 2 (2003): 439–55. This dimension of legal mimesis in Part One of the *Quixote* receives no mention in Roberto González Echevarría, *Love and Law in Cervantes* (New Haven, CT: Yale University Press, 2005), which privileges picaresque affinities and theorizes a systematic opposition between love and law.

57 On this issue, see Juan Manuel Cacho Blecua, "Novelas de caballerías," in *Orígenes de la novela: Estudios*, ed. Raquel Gutiérrez Sebastián and

Borja Rodríguez Gutiérrez (Santander, ES: Universidad de Cantabria and Sociedad Menéndez Pelayo, 2007), 133–224.

58 See especially Emilio J. Sales Dasí, "¿Continuador o creador? 'Las Entricadas Razones del Famoso Feliciano de Silva,'" in *La escritura inacabada: Continuaciones literarias y creación en España, siglos XIII a XVII*, ed. David Álvarez and Olivier Biaggini (Madrid: Casa de Velázquez, 2017), 145–61.

59 See my *Feigned Histories of Secret Marriage*.

60 *The Covntesse of Pembrokes Arcadia. Written by Sir Philip Sidney Knight. Now since the first edition augmented and ended* (London: John Windet, for William Ponsonby, 1593; STC 22540). The truncated prior edition appeared in 1590, subsequent early editions in 1598, 1599, 1605, 1613, 1621, 1622, 1623, 1627, 1629, 1633, 1638, 1655, 1662, 1674, 1725, and 1739. Surveys of literary influence include Herbert Wynford Hill, "Sidney's *Arcadia* and the Elizabethan Drama," *University of Nevada Studies* 1 (1908): 1–59; Felicina Rota, *L'Arcadia di Sidney e il teatro* (Bari: Adriatica, 1966); Mary Ellen Lamb, *Gender and Authorship in the Sidney Circle* (Madison: University of Wisconsin Press, 1990); Stephen B. Dobranski, *Readers and Authorship in Early Modern England* (Cambridge: Cambridge University Press, 2005), 63–96; Gavin Alexander, *Writing after Sidney: The Literary Response to Sir Philip Sidney, 1586–1640* (Oxford: Oxford University Press, 2006); Natasha Simonova, *Early Modern Authorship and Prose Continuations: Adaptation and Ownership from Sidney to Richardson* (Basingstoke, UK: Palgrave Macmillan, 2015); cf. Simonova, "'A book that all have heard of … but that nobody reads': Philip Sidney's *Arcadia* in the Eighteenth Century," *Journal of Medieval and Early Modern Studies* 50, no. 1 (2020): 139–59. See also Joel B. Davis, *"The Countess of Pembrokes Arcadia" and the Invention of English Literature* (Basingstoke: Palgrave Macmillan, 2011).

61 See the Epilogue in my *Feigned Histories of Secret Marriage*.

62 Bent Juel-Jensen, "Sir Philip Sidney, 1554–1586: A Check-List of Early Editions of His Works," in *Sir Philip Sidney: An Anthology of Modern Criticism*, ed. Dennis Kay (Oxford: Clarendon, 1987): 306–8. See also the French stage adaptation by André Mareschal, *La Cour Bergère, ou L'Arcadie de Messire Philippes Sidney: Tragi-comédie* [1640], ed. Lucette Desvignes, 2 vols. (Saint-Etienne: Université de Saint-Etienne, 1981).

63 For the primary texts, including narratives and editorial commentary, see *Continuations to Sidney's* Arcadia, *1607–1867*, ed. Marea Mitchell, 4 vols (London: Pickering & Chatto, 2014); with Anna Weamys, *A Continuation of Sir Philip Sidney's* Arcadia [1651], ed. Patrick Cullen (New York: Oxford University Press, 1994); and Martin Garrett, ed., *Sidney: The Critical Heritage* (London: Routledge, 1996). On complementary visual art and biography, see Michael G. Brennan, "The Nineteenth-Century Rediscovery of Sir Philip Sidney," *Sidney Journal* 34, no. 2 (2016): 117–53.

64 See Ian Watt, "The Naming of Characters in Defoe, Richardson, and Fielding," *Review of English Studies* 25, no. 100 (1949): 325–30; Jacob Leed, "Richardson's Pamela and Sidney's," *Journal of the Australasian Universities Language and Literature Association* 40, no. 1 (1973): 240–5; and, on Richardson's investment in Sidney's fiction as a printer, Simonova, "Sidney's *Arcadia* in the Eighteenth Century," 140, 147.

65 For this context, see Thomas Lockwood, "The *Pamela* Debate," in *Prose Fiction in English from the Origins of Print to 1750*, ed. Thomas Keymer (Oxford: Oxford University Press, 2017), 548–62.

66 Here I redirect in a manner different from Simonova ("Sidney's *Arcadia* in the Eighteenth Century," 147) the premise of Peter Lindenbaum, "Sidney's *Arcadia* as Cultural Monument and Proto-Novel," in *Texts and Cultural Change in Early Modern England*, ed. Cedric C. Brown and Arthur F. Marotti (Basingstoke, UK: Macmillan, 1997), 80–94.

Chapter Seven

Portuguese and Spanish Arthuriana: The Case for Munday's Cosmopolitanism

ELIZABETH EVENDEN-KENYON

Earth is the common Mother, every ground
May be one's Countrey, for by birth each man
Is in this World a Cosmopolitan.
> – James Howell, "The Vote, or A Poem Royall …"

As a New Year's gift in 1642, James Howell (1594?–1666) presented a poem to King Charles I, entitled "The Vote, or A Poeme Royall …," which recounts a supposed discussion between the poet and his muse.[1] Howell was an historian and political writer, born in Wales and educated at Jesus College, Oxford. After graduation, he found employment through Sir Robert Mansell, the uncle of his former tutor, as steward of a glass factory located in Broad Street, London. In this position, he was granted three years' travel under a warrant issued by the Privy Council, whereby he was sent in search of materials for the factory. During these years, he became a proficient linguist and, upon return, vacated his position at the factory, falling ill shortly afterwards.

He was attended to by Dr William Harvey, and, upon his return to good health, Howell was sent on warrant to Spain and Sardinia to negotiate the release of an impounded English vessel, and he remained in Madrid throughout 1623–24, during negotiations over the Spanish Match. His usefulness to the English court was duly noted: his linguistic abilities and familiarity with the continent made him a useful tool. He would subsequently find work assisting in the registration of strangers living in England, but he found his vocation in writing about the merits of foreign travel. His writing reveals his attempts to "steer a safe course between royalist and parliamentarian alternatives."[2] "The Vote" and other writings therefore recount both the benefits of foreign travel and its utility in steering a path between polar positions, in an attempt to promote commonalities above disagreements.

The *Oxford English Dictionary* cites Howell's use of the word "cosmopolitan" as the first recorded in the English language.[3] Of course, Howell, like other university-educated men of his age, would have probably become familiar with the word's root in the ancient Greek κοσμοπολίτης, or *kosmopolitês* ("κοσμος" meaning world or universe, and "πολίτης" meaning citizen or of the city).[4] Its first known use is usually credited to the cynic philosopher Diogenes of Sinope, who described himself as "a citizen of the world." The word "cosmopolitan" and the concept of being "a citizen of the world," in the English language, has an uncanny ability to appear at moments of national crisis and collective questioning of identity. It surfaces at moments when what it means to be "English" is brought into question, and when questions of allegiance are brought to bear. Which means more: your national or your global identity? More often than not, the word and concept become aligned with questioning an individual or group religious and/or political affiliation in moments of flux.

Howell, for example, cites his "cosmopolitanism" on the eve of the English Civil War. In our times, British prime minister Theresa May, in her speech to the Conservative Party conference in the wake of the 2016 Brexit referendum vote, declared, "today, too many people in positions of power behave as though they have more in common with international elites than with the people down the road, the people they employ, the people they pass in the street. But if you believe you're a citizen of the world, you're a citizen of nowhere. You don't understand what the very word 'citizenship' means."[5] Her comments were nothing if not incendiary, spurring one philosopher to note that May did not understand the meaning of "cosmopolitan."[6] The word has become associated with calls to "choose your side": "Are you with us or against us?" In short, it explicates a juxtaposition of individual choice with the primeval "pack" mentality. In the former prime minister's case, you are either with the individual in the street (in your home nation) or with the metropolitan, globalist elite.

Yet there is an earlier instance – even before Howell – in which this choice between "national" and "cosmopolitan" came to the fore: in post-Reformation England. During the reign of Elizabeth I and under the Stuarts, Anthony Munday was embroiled in questions over national identity and loyalty. One way in which these questions were explored was through the literary, theological, and political discussions of "British" national heritage, and concepts of loyalty to faith, country, and monarchy. These explorations frequently turned to the nation's past – in particular to the relevance of King Arthur as a warrior king and role model for past, present, and future generations.

Arthur, as we shall see, became synonymous with explorations of "British" identity during periods of political and confessional turmoil. Anthony Munday's translation, recreation, and dissemination of key works of "Arthuriana" raise interesting questions about perceptions of national identity and cosmopolitanism under the Tudor and Stuart monarchies. English Catholics who remained in England would maintain that they could both be loyal to the reigning monarch of England and remain true to the Catholic Church: their religion was a matter of conscience that did not necessarily negate their loyalty to their monarchy. They could be both loyal, "British" citizens *and* a citizen of the world. In this context, this chapter will consider what role Arthurian history and "Arthuriana" played in defining British and Catholic history, both at home and abroad.

Arthuriana and the Matter of Britain in an Early Modern Context

Arthuriana

The term "Arthuriana" is applied both to literary creations (be they wholly original, translated, or rewritten from a foreign source) and historiographical writings (including genealogy). Their contents include elements drawn from the earliest series of texts about King Arthur and his court, people, entities (non-human), objects (such as the Holy Grail and the Round Table), locations, and events associated with them. They can vary in how they incorporate such material: they can be closely or loosely associated with any number of these categories, be it in detail or in passing. The most popular creations of Arthuriana hail from the Iberian Peninsula.[7]

Imitation and adaptation of earlier Arthurian tales and sources can provide us with valuable insights into how these "British" narratives penetrated the peninsula, both geographically and culturally. Our knowledge of this corpus of material migration and evolution on the Iberian Peninsula is frequently being challenged and reassessed, even today. New materials – whether complete texts or fragments (such as those revealed in bindings during conservation) – continue to be discovered.[8] Thus, this remains a vibrant and evolving field, as the present volume affirms.

In the sixteenth century, tales of Arthur as the "Hope" of the "British" – as a king who would return to save his people – became fused with

Portuguese "Sebastianism" and the messianic world-view of Philip II of Spain.[9] The first mention of Arthur's potential return occurs in the chronicle by William of Malmesbury: "The sepulchre of Arthur is no where to be seen, whence ancient ballads fable that he is still to come."[10] The belief that Arthur was merely injured in battle and would return subsequently merged with tales of a monarch who would come to release the British from persecution and bondage.

R.S. Loomis's survey of Arthurian literature and its impact provided the anecdotal claim that Philip II of Spain, around the time of his marriage to Mary I of England (1554), swore that he would abdicate if Arthur returned to his rightful seat.[11] Unsurprisingly, Philip did not relinquish his position until the untimely death of his English bride; yet, unlike for Sebastian, no early modern contenders came forth. The "British," Portuguese, and Spanish, therefore, were all familiar with the messianic connotations and national hopes associated with Arthurian tales and Arthuriana. For English-, Spanish-, and Portuguese-language readers, Arthurian themes linked monarchy and just rule together but in different ways. As we shall see, when Spanish and Portuguese Arthuriana arrived in England, their continental pedigree was associated with both their homelands' long-standing relationship with England, and with Catholicism.

The Matter of Britain

The "Matter of Britain" refers to the corpus of medieval literature associated with Great Britain (and, on occasion, with Brittany also), that details the legendary kings and knights associated with Britain, of which Arthur is the most prevalent figure. It refers to one of three medieval narrative cycles, along with the Matter of France, detailing stories concerned with Charlemagne, and the Matter of Rome, which focuses on materials derived from classical mythology.

The Matter of Britain played a central role in early modern Anglo-Portuguese and Anglo-Spanish relations, since it reinforced historic ties, and bound multinational readers together, through the creation, and cultural associations resonant in the creation, of Arthuriana on the Iberian Peninsula. The earliest texts associated with the Matter of Britain are grouped into two categories: "Vulgate" and "Post-Vulgate." It is important that we gain a basic understanding of their central themes and characters, since they take on new life in the subsequent Arthuriana.

"Vulgate" refers to the *Lancelot-Grail Cycle*, composed over roughly a twenty-year period beginning in 1210.[12] This French-language cycle depicts the Arthurian world from the time of the Crucifixion (for the

introduction of the Holy Grail) to the death of Lancelot and the destruction of the Round Table. It consists of five volumes in prose, the first two
in the cycle actually being written last, in order to introduce the origins
of the Holy Grail quest.

The cycle encompasses the following five parts. Part 1 is the *Estoire
del Saint Grail* (*The History of the Holy Grail*), which details how Joseph
of Arimathea and his son, Josephus, brought the Holy Grail to Britain.
Part 2 is the *Estoire de Merlin* (also known as the *Prose Merlin*), which
introduces the early history of King Arthur and Merlin's involvement
in his conception and early life. This second section can be subdivided:
the first is the *Merlin propre* (or *Merlin Proper*), coming from Robert de
Boron's *Merlin*, while the second is the *Suite du Merlin* (or the *Merlin Continuation*, sometimes referred to as the *Livre d'Artus*), which details more
about Arthur's early life. Part 3, the *Lancelot propre* (the *Lancelot Proper*),
is the longest section, accounting for around half of length of the entire
Vulgate cycle. It focuses on its titular character and other knights of the
Round Table, and details the love affair between Lancelot and Arthur's
queen. Part 4 is the *Queste del Saint Graal* (*Quest for the Holy Grail*), which
sees the quest through to its completion by Galahad. Finally, part 5, the
Mort Artu (*Death of Arthur*), details the death of Arthur at the hands of
Mordred, and the subsequent demise of his kingdom.[13]

The "Post-Vulgate" Cycle, also known as the "Pseudo-Boron" Cycle,
is a further collection of French medieval literary texts, which deal
with Arthurian legends (rather than Arthurian "history" per se).[14] This
continuation was written between 1230 and 1240 and provides innovative plot lines and characters, while at the same time reinforcing or
refashioning elements from the original cycle. This cycle places greater
emphasis on Christian history than its predecessor. The Post-Vulgate
Cycle does not survive intact, but materials do survive in French, Portuguese, and Castilian.[15]

The Post-Vulgate Cycle can be divided into four sections, comparable
to the Vulgate Cycle. Part 1, the *Estoire del Saint Grail* (*The History of the
Holy Grail*), details the journey of Joseph of Arimathea to Great Britian,
bringing the Holy Grail with him. It is essentially the same narrative
as the Vulgate version, with minor modifications. In part 2, the *Estoire
de Merlin* (*The History of Merlin*), the story of Merlin and his early dealings with Arthur are very similar to the Vulgate account. Part 3, the
Queste del Saint Graal (*The Quest of the Holy Grail*), details the quest for
the Holy Grail by Sir Galahad and differs considerably from the Vulgate
accounts, including additional knights in its narrative. Lastly, part 4, the
Mort Artu (*The Death of King Arthur*), details the death of Arthur at the
hands of his son, Mordred, and the subsequent demise of his kingdom.

It is the Post-Vulgate Cycle that proved most popular in the Iberian Peninsula, stimulating the creation of and market for Arthuriana.[16]

The Significance of King Arthur in the Confessional Debates of Early Modern England

W.R.J. Barron once described Arthur as "a secular St George emblematic of nationhood."[17] It is this appeal to the nation's people – and the avoidance of any associated hagiography – that made Arthur, for a time, a perfect exemplar to be exploited by the Tudor dynasty. From the accession of Henry VII, throughout Henry VIII's tumultuous break with the Rome, and particularly amid late Elizabethan fears of Spanish invasion, the Tudor dynasty and its apologists turned to Arthurian "history" in order to define their national heritage and their place on an international stage.[18] During Elizabeth's reign, tales of romance and chivalry became central to the cross-confessional polemics as to who was a true, loyal subject. As we shall see, Arthurian "history" and Arthuriana had the potential to polarize readers into those who put their home nation *before* any international community.

English understanding of Arthur came primarily from the writing of Geoffrey of Monmouth in the twelfth century.[19] His *Historia Regum Brittaniae* was first issued in 1138 and, in 1191, King Arthur's remains were said to have been located in Glastonbury Abbey.[20] For Geoffrey, Arthur was a champion fighting to protect his realm from foreign invaders.[21] Along with Geoffrey's account, antiquarians turned to William of Malmesbury's *De Rebus Gestis Regum Anglorum* (1125), which detailed how Ambrosius had been able to thwart the barbarians only with the help of the warlike Arthur.[22] At the siege of Mount Badon, according to William, Arthur wore an image of the Virgin Mary on his armour, which was said to have protected him as he fought 900 Saxons single-handedly.[23] Geoffrey's account also claimed that Stonehenge, fewer than fifty miles from Glastonbury, had been designed by Merlin at the behest of Aurelious Ambrosius, as a memorial to those who had fallen in battle against the invading Saxons.[24]

Materials such as these, and any that supported Gregory and William's narrative, were sought out by Elizabeth I's archbishop of Canterbury, Matthew Parker, during his "great searching out of books" – a project to recover lost manuscripts, scattered by the Dissolution, but now essential to proving the pristine state of the Church in England.[25] Geoffrey's narrative remained at the heart of disagreements over the lineage of the Church in England, including the polemical exchanges surrounding Elizabeth's excommunication in 1570.[26]

Geoffrey of Monmouth was also important to those seeking to prove "British" superiority over other nations, since he presents Arthur in a military context only, focusing on his role as defender of the nation against the Saxons.[27] As with Shakespeare's subsequent, albeit challenging, portrayal of "war-like Harry" in *Henry V*, Arthur did not hesitate to put hostages to death when the Saxons broke their oaths.[28] Further evidence for his ruthlessness when necessitated was provided by Geoffrey in his account of Arthur's repulsing of the Irish and his decimation of the Picts and Scots. It is understandable how the Elizabethans, in particular, could have considered Arthur as their exemplar of good leadership. As Christopher Dean perceives, Arthur is presented in these twelfth-century sources as "unabashedly seek[ing] empire."[29] Geoffrey even goes so far as to equate Arthur with Alexander the Great. For many then, Arthur suited English expansionism, its nationalistic pride, *and* the defence of its confessional choice.

Yet the sixteenth century also witnessed a change in attitude toward Arthur as a credible figure in the history of Britain. The central figure leading the debunking of Arthur as a reliable exemplar in British history was the Italian humanist scholar Polydore Vergil. The published edition of his *Anglica Historia* (1555) well and truly kicked the English historiographical hornets' nest, resulting in a swarm of protest: he had branded most of Geoffrey's narrative as fiction. Detractors railed at his debunking of a British lineage that could be traced back to Brutus, and his denying of any credibility to the vast majority of Geoffrey's account of Arthur.[30]

Vergil's assaults necessitated a counterattack, since, in the words of James Carley, his "diminution of Arthur struck at the very identity of the English nation."[31] Since its first edition in print, Vergil's debunking of Britain's Arthurian past began to eat away at the credibility of English attempts to situate the country's faith within its ancient lineage. Year after year, edition after edition, the belief in the existence of a genuine king named Arthur began to be torn away from English national identity on a European stage.

By 1544, from his exile on the Continent, the churchman, historian, and theological-fight-picker John Bale called on learned Englishmen to write a thorough, if not exhaustive, history of the English and their faith, one that could parry Vergil's lunge at the credibility of Protestant claims for their church and lineage.[32] Enraged at his audacity, Bale claimed that Vergil – a foreigner – could not possibly comprehend the intricacies of extant English chronicles and their contents. A remise ensued from Protestant pens and presses, but at the head of this counter-attack stood one man, whose research skills and abilities went beyond even those of Polydore Vergil: the English poet and antiquary John Leland (1503?–52).

During a long and complex war of words over Arthur's existence, Leland devoted a section to Geoffrey of Monmouth in his *De viris illustribus*, a substantial biographical and bibliographical study of British authors, which was close to completion when ill health prevented any further historical labours by Leland in 1547.[33] The text remained in manuscript form but proved profoundly influential among his fellow and subsequent Protestant scholars in defining their national heritage.[34]

Since Arthur was central to "the foundations of English nationalism," something that became crucial to understanding what defined "a loyal Englishman" in the latter half of the sixteenth century, an apologist for Geoffrey was certainly needed in the eyes of many.[35] Leland launched himself into the fray with his *Assertio inclytissimi Arturij Regis Britanniae* (1544).[36] In just thirty-nine leaves of text, Leland's assault listed various Arthurian remains extant throughout the kingdom and, in doing so, recreated what he believed was a coherent, succinct account of Arthur's legitimacy, substantiated by archaeological evidence.

As Carley's extensive researches have revealed, Leland's collective manuscript and printed challenges to Vergil's dismissal of Arthur as a credible character in English history provide "the modern reader [with] a detailed statement of intelligent sixteenth-century English opinion about the Arthurian legends and … [show] just what historical and archaeological resources (many subsequently lost) existed at the time." Yet, Carley notes, even Leland "lamented the *fables* which had crept into the historical accounts," declaring that "It is no noueltie, that men mixe trifling toyes with true thinges …"[37] Leland's notes and manuscripts would become substantiating materials for Protestants such as John Foxe, in defence of the English Church.[38]

Early in Elizabeth's reign, Anglo-Saxon history was utilized in particular by defenders of her royal supremacy.[39] Catholics who refused to take the Oath of Supremacy faced difficult decisions: face (at the very least) fines for non-attendance at church (recusancy), attend church but maintain private devotion to the old faith (Nicodemism), or go into exile. As time progressed, the enforcement of penalties (and the penalties themselves) became more severe.[40] As soon as the oath came into force, a "battle of the books" ensued. Authors such as John Jewel, William Fulke, Robert Horne, and John Bridges defended the oath on the Protestant side, thereby locking horns with the likes of Thomas Harding, Nicholas Harpsfield, Thomas Stapleton, Nicholas Sanders, and John Rastell on the other. Their battles revolved around a central issue:

the relationship between temporal rulers and the church, as established historically in England.[41]

What it is important to comprehend from all this confessional sparring over Arthur is that, on the Continent, the "problem" of Arthur was essentially a British one. Insularity came at a cost, and many Catholics chose exile over the Oath of Supremacy. Many chose the Iberian Peninsula as their destination, where Arthuriana maintained its association with Arthur more loosely, but where such texts were firmly grounded in the Catholic faith, a faith inextricably linked to an Arthurian past. As such, Munday's dissemination of such texts was a potential cause for alarm, as we shall see.

Iberian Arthuriana in an Early Modern Context

Garci Rodríguez de Montalvo, a servant to the "Catholic Monarchs," was tasked in 1508 with providing a new version of the chivalric romance *Amadís de Gaula*, one that maintained the central ideas of earlier incarnations of this text but also payed greater attention to a new, contemporary audience.[42] This meant a merging of the traditional and the newly fabricated. In his prologue to *Amadís*, Montalvo highlights the different formats for "history" and their relationship with "the truth": there are those who "narrate the truth," those who "mingle reality and exaggeration," and those who "invent everything."[43] This prologue is addressed to the Catholic Monarchs, and compares their deeds with those of the heroes of antiquity.[44] He claims not to dare to challenge the veracity of the chronicles, and insists that he is merely correcting the three books of *Amadís* and emending the fourth (the *Sergas de Esplandián*). In doing so, he addresses older readers, familiar with previous editions, and a new, younger audience, meeting with Amadís for the first time. Carlos Alvar makes an important observation here: "This consideration of the readership is a clear revelation of the interest of the narrator in transmitting his message and in ensuring that it reached the circles to which it was directed."[45] In doing so, Alvar argues, Montalvo "converts himself into an historian comparable to Sallust or Livy."[46] Montalvo, however, was a Catholic historian.

This emphasis on the Catholicism is at the heart of his *Amadís* narrative: it is a Catholic tale for a Catholic audience. In Book II, the continuation of the narrative is justified through claims about a newly discovered book, found in an ancient tomb ("este libro que oculto y encerrado se hallo en aquella muy Antigua sepultura"), which provides important details about the "Catholic and virtuous Prince Esplandián," Amadís's son ("se haze mención de aquel cathólico y virtuoso príncipe

Esplandián, su hijo").[47] As Alvar points out, like Galaz, the son of Lancelot, Esplandián is "a Christian knight, fundamentally religious."[48] Through such a character, Montalvo creates a narrative appropriating the virtues (he maintains are) synonymous with the text's patrons, the Catholic Monarchs. He also imbues the work with their Providentialism: the son is destined to undertake godly deeds rather than patricide. This plot change and continuation – covering the life of Esplandián as emperor – permeate Montalvo's work, leading to its reputation as something of "a manual of education of princes."[49]

In his consideration of Isabel of Castile's response to chivalric literature within the royal collection, and the potential impact of a new edition of *Amadís* under the auspices of the Catholic Monarchs, Ian Michael observes how chivalric texts "encapsulated ... her own clear political vision: the quest for an identity, the concept of service, the recovery of a kingdom, the establishment of an empire, the perfect ways of honour."[50] On the eve of the Reformation, Montalvo's *Amadís* also established a quintessentially *Catholic* and *Castilian* dynastic way of achieving these aims.

At the heart of this rewriting and overt Christianization of *Amadís* are two key themes of which we should take note: identity and history. Both are explored, promoted, and ultimately disseminated by Montalvo and subsequent reproducers of his text (editors, translators, copyists, or printers), in order to attract and educate readers and auditors. In order to understand such an intention, we must look beyond popularity and profit, and consider the ways in which these two themes speak within the context of their production.

In Spain, Arthuriana persisted within a reading public, stimulated by a printing industry prepared to feed their tastes. This interest in Post-Vulgate texts includes the *Baladro del sabio Merlín* and the *Demanda del Santo Grial*, plus at least eight Spanish editions of *Tristán de Leonís* before the mid-sixteenth century.[51] But, by the 1550s, Spanish printers had become more focused on producing what are known as the "sons of Amadís." These new narratives were seen as "transcending, and thereby renewing, chivalresque narrative" for a new generation.[52]

In Portugal, England's oldest ally, Arthurian themes retained a "far more limited and precarious persistence, both in terms of the variety of Arthurian works involved and in terms of the number of editions" produced during the sixteenth century.[53] The *Baladro del sabio Merlín* and the *Demanda del Santo Grial*, which were printed in Spain (the former in Burgos in 1498 and the latter in Seville in 1535), made their way to readers in Portugal, but no editions of these two texts are known to have been printed in Portugal in the first hundred or so years of printing in that country.[54] The only explanation for such a dearth of materials in Portuguese is that the Portuguese printers simply did not print them. Certainly the Portuguese book trade was not as extensive or as established as that in Spain, and Spanish copies do appear to have made an impression on surviving Portuguese collections.

Yet the Portuguese continued – and perhaps preferred – to interact with and to disseminate tales of Arthurian exploits via *manuscript*.[55] Certainly this was the case with the Portuguese nobility, for whom understanding of the chivalric world of Arthur was so deeply embedded within Portuguese culture as to render it an essential "ideology," with Arthur – a British king – being seen to represent "a just monarch." It is therefore worthy of note that, for the Portuguese during their annexation to Spain (1580–1640), their model king is foreign, but not Spanish. Remembrance of "no tratado de amizade e aliança defensive" (the treaty of amity and defensive alliance) stands firmer than Luso-Hispanic bonds. Such nostalgia for history and alliances is exemplified, by way of example, in the *Crónica do imperador Maximiliano* of the mid-sixteenth century, whose great conqueror, "Artur," is considered a just and honest sovereign.[56]

Perhaps the greatest expression of the link between a chivalric past and monarchy that is expressed in Portuguese literature of the early modern period is that in the *Memorial das proezas da Segunda Távola Redonda* by Jorge Ferreira de Vasconcelos.[57] The first edition was probably printed in 1554 in Coimbra, although it no longer survives; the first surviving edition is that printed in Coimbra in 1567. It features the war between Arthur and Mordred, the Order of the Round Table, and even extends to a second order, which combines "ideological continuity with an awareness of cultural distance."[58] The *Memorial* blurs "the boundaries between fiction and reality" and reinforces the links between Arthuriana and the Portuguese monarchy.[59] Arthur's hereditary knights, in a sense, become the nobles of sixteenth-century Portugal.

Whereas the Spanish *Amadís de Gaula* acts as a predecessor to Arthur's Britain, Portuguese authors chose to locate their texts as descendants of Arthur's world, creating a stronger link between the Portugal of the present and their allies in England. In *Palmerim de Inglaterra* (ca. 1547–48), Francisco de Moraes, who was secretary of the Portuguese ambassador to Paris, Count de Linhares, between 1541 and 1543, depicts the ideological debt owed by the Portuguese to their allies of Arthurian descent. In its original incarnation, *Palmerim de Inglaterra* comprised two books; the earliest known printed edition of Book 1 was produced in Toledo in 1547, with Book 2 appearing the following year. The oldest known Portuguese edition dates to 1567, when it was produced under the title *Crónica de Palmeirim de Inglaterra*.[60] The quality and popularity of the Portuguese edition far outstripped its Spanish counterpart, and it was reprinted for the Portuguese-reading market in 1592.[61] The content of *Palmeirim de Inglaterra* owes much to the *Amadís de Gaula* narrative and was part of a series of "Palmeirim" texts. Chronologically, it is the fourth in this Spanish-Portuguese cycle (the first being the 1511 *Palmerín de Olivia*). We shall now turn our attention to the Iberian Arthuriana from these cycles that was chosen by Anthony Munday, and what his choices might tell us about his perception of insular and international narratives and communities, and of the uses of fiction in exploring connections between history and faith.

Arthuriana in English Translation

In the autumn of 1578, when he was in his late teens, Anthony Munday left his printer's apprenticeship with John Allde and set off for the Continent in the company of Thomas Nowell.[62] Their final destination was in Rome – the English College on Via di Corte Savella (now Via di Monserrato), which had just opened its doors to scholars. Munday was accepted but did not go so far as to take the missionary oath. Speculation abounds as to the possibility that he went there to spy on – rather than join – the community, but there is no definitive evidence to prove the stimulus for his decision to depart for Rome, nor what lay behind his subsequent decision to return to England in the summer of 1579.[63] We only have Munday's own account of his time at the college, which appeared in print in 1582.[64]

Upon his return, many questions arose as to the real motive behind his trip to the Continent: Was he a Catholic? Was he a Protestant spy? Was he truly a loyal English subject? His actions created much speculation in their day (and they continue to do so in academic debate today).[65] Upon his return to England, Munday found paid employment that has been the impetus for differing opinions of Munday's faith and trustworthiness: working as an intelligencer for Richard Topcliffe, the Elizabethan government's chief enforcer of the penal laws against the practice of Catholicism. Munday also worked, subsequently, for Sir Thomas Heneage, treasurer of the chamber.[66] In *A banquet of daitie conceits*, first entered into the Stationers' Register in 1584, Munday describes himself as a "Servaunt to the Queenes most excellent Majestie."[67]

Despite these protestations of fidelity to the Protestant regime, Munday's trustworthiness was frequently brought into question. In 1582, for example, Thomas Alfield attacked Munday as being the antithesis of Edmund Campion: unlike Munday, Campion's erudition was exceptional. He accuses Munday of being nothing more than a charlatan who, he claims, was "never admitted in the seminary as he pleseth to lye."[68] Munday counters this accusation with further detail and proof of his and Nowell's appearance on college records, emphasizing that his forthcoming *The English Romayne Lyfe* would do much to discredit Alfield.[69]

Whatever conditions had prompted Munday's Roman sojourn, upon his return he turned his hand to translation, rather than to religious controversy. Munday dedicates his original work *Zelauto* (1580) to the Earl of Oxford; the author presents himself in the guise of a travelling knight, and indicates to his patron that he has commenced work on a translation of *Palmerin of England*.[70] Clearly, his decision to translate Iberian materials – albeit from French editions – was made quickly upon his return to London.

Peter Burke has emphasized the curious position inhabited by early modern translators: their knowledge of languages – and so often of associated terrains – meant that they could act as "renaissance go-betweens" for Catholic states. I agree with Burke when he asserts that a translator's profession and experience often ensured they were considered a "people out of place," while, at the same time, they could act as conduits between communities.[71] As a man whose motivations and faith were under scrutiny after his time on the continent, Munday's choice to work on Arthuriana is an interesting one, to say the least.

During the years 1595 to 1619, Munday's translations of parts or all of the following works appeared in print: *Amadis de Gaule*, *Palmerin d'Oliva*, *Palmerin of England*, and *Primaleon of Greece*.[72] From the outset, these translations appear to have caused concern, at the very least among members of the Stationers' Company. An entry in their register for 13 February 1581 provides evidence for the company's monitoring of his textual output. The entry for *Palmerin of England* comes with the requirement that the text be examined fully before being released: "uppon Condicon that if there be anie thinge founde in The booke when it is extante worthie of Reprehension that then all the Bookes shalbe put to waste and Burnte."[73]

The original text, *Palmeirim de Inglaterra*, contains numerous references to Catholic religious practices, all of which would make its choice – at this tense time – highly questionable.[74] Although many such scenes would be removed in Munday's translations of the *Palmerin* cycle (the same holds true for his *Amadis*), these texts remained associated with continental and Catholic acts of reading.

As I discuss at length elsewhere, expunging pious formulae in a Protestant realm did not necessarily hinder their mnemonic functionality within an oral society that was more than capable of perpetuating earlier practices in private, since it is apparent in the texts where such passages have been removed.[75] Private readings of key passages within these texts certainly happened, stimulating both discussion and memory, among a variety of communities, including the English Bridgettine nuns in Lisbon during the late sixteenth century.[76]

Catholic Loyalty, Toleration, and the Cosmopolitan Literary Space

Text and language, as Brian Cummings has demonstrated, are active participants in the forging of meaning and comprehension, particularly in periods of religious and political tension and repression.[77] The religio-political tensions that reached fever pitch in England in the 1580s had an impact on the very acts of reading and writing: authors, translators, and readers sought to traverse and comprehend the options presented by conformism, loyalty, and dissent, but they had to tread carefully, for their passage could be perilous.

I contend that the uses and reuses of Arthurian and post-Arthurian settings and themes by Munday are situated among what Alexandra Walsham has described as "the subtle alterations in sensibility" that took place over the centuries, in the quest for a clear demarcation between "truth" and "fiction."[78] They are a moment in time where, thanks to increased literacy and dissemination via print, searches for "truth" – perhaps even universal truths – in texts became a facet of confessional *and* national self-fashioning. Early modern accounts of a nation's past became mediatory texts for explorations of national – and international – history and faith. Protestants had attempted to situate their past in Arthurian heritage; authors of Spanish and Portuguese Arthuriana utilized Britain's pre-Reformation heritage to inextricably link national loyalty with Catholicism. Yet, as English Catholic communities would argue, loyalty to both was possible on home soil.

Reading communities – how they were created and how they perceived themselves – are also crucial to these late sixteenth-century alterations in sensibility. Munday repeatedly positioned himself as the traveller, the "go-between"; Brian Lockey describe this strategy as something undertaken "obsessively," in order to grant "authority" to his voice.[79] His description of Munday's actions and motives suggests that Lockey agrees with Nora Johnson's interpretation that this positioning is nothing more than self-promotion.[80] But could it be something more than that? Could Munday be promoting the dual national loyalty and cosmopolitan outlook of figures such as Amadis and Palmerin?

Translations of continental texts extended reading communities by bringing them together through shared tropes, shared "histories," and even a shared nostalgia. Such nostalgia within Iberian Arthuriana – be it an Anglo-Spanish past or an Anglo-Portuguese present – invites consideration of what were once international communities of faith that were now fractured at the seams. The *saudade* of the Portuguese – an almost untranslatable word, but one pertaining to a sense of loss and longing – is redolent on the pages of these texts, particularly when placed in an English context. Their blurring of faith, loci, history, and fiction create both a past and a present community, locked in appreciation of all that these international tales imbue.

For a Catholic gentry, stripped of their heritage and standing in an increasingly insular and nationalist "Britain," I find it hard to believe that these texts did not stir up both a pride in British heritage and an acknowledgment of a much wider community – of readers, of friendships, of faith. In this sense, Arthuriana speaks to both national loyalism and internationalism. English Catholics' attempts to situate their loyalism to their monarch alongside their universal faith speak volumes in such a context: it is an attempt at coexistence, a universal humanity.

Alexandra Walsham raises a crucial point in *Cultures of Coexistence*, in her own contemplation of the road to religious toleration, which assesses the utility of modes of expression in textual sources:

> The atmosphere of anxiety and the culture of surveillance by which contemporaries perceived themselves to be surrounded acted as a catalyst for important innovations in technique and experiments in genre. It fostered the use of allusion, allegory, and metaphor; it encouraged literary versions of the casuistry, equivocation, and dissimulation to which religious minorities resorted in the face of official pressure to conform; and it compelled many artists, poets, and playwrights to encode criticism in compliment and to disguise admonition of their rulers under the sugar-coating of flattery and praise.[81]

Tracing the routes of religious toleration culminates in a view central to our understanding of Catholic Portugal and Spain, and the uses of Arthuriana: "If the topical resonance of early modern calls for liberty of conscience and of the practical strategies contemporaries devised for accommodating difference has been a valuable spur to scholarly investigation, it is simultaneously our greatest obstacle to clear thinking about the contours and complexities of sixteenth- and seventeenth-century religious coexistence."[82] Could it be, then, that, in extending these reading communities across the Channel, Munday was attempting to offer a literary observation – albeit through translation – on how different communities might be able to coexist and retain collective loyalty to a monarch, as they had once done on the Iberian Peninsula? To argue that English men and women can be both English and part of a wider community – in this instance, of faith – certainly suggests a level of cosmopolitanism at work. Spain and Portugal already had a long history of contemplating how and if coexistence could be achieved, and their approaches – like their literature – reflected their national nuances, even with the passage of time.

From the 1570s onwards, the Portuguese and Spanish Inquisitions began to focus their efforts on the menace of Protestantism and heresy from *within* Old Christendom; in so doing, they left behind their earlier preoccupations with Jews and Conversos, Muslims and Moriscos. At the same time, in England, in the wake of Elizabeth's excommunication, the regime was increasingly under pressure from both sides of the Christian confessional divide to consider its stance on Catholic loyalty. The number of English Catholic exiles on the Iberian Peninsula steadily increased – rising sharply in the late 1580s and into the 1590s, building upon and reinforcing pre-existing "Anglo-Iberian" networks. Textual witnesses could encourage, motivate, activate, and console those who chose to remain faithful to the Old Faith, and they could be explored and exported safely when encapsulated within traditional, familiar narratives. In bringing these texts to the English, Munday may have sought to bring English readers into Arthuriana's international reading community, making him – the travelled translator – a go-between for cosmopolitans who read them. If we cannot pin down Munday's faith with certainty, there remains at least a case for his cosmopolitanism.

NOTES

1 J. Howell, "The Vote, or A Poeme Royall, Presented to His Maiestie for a New-Yeares-Gift. By Way of Discourse 'twixt the Poet, and his Muse. Calendis Ianuariis 1642" (London, 1642), B1ʳ.

2 D.R. Woolf, "Howell, James (1594?-1666)" in *ODNB* 2004.

3 "Cosmopolitan, adj. and n.," *OED* 2020.

4 See Søren Frank, "Globalization, Migrant Literature, and the New Europe," in *Cosmopolitanism and the Postnational: Literature and the New Europe*, ed. César Domínguez and Theo D'haen (Leiden: Brill, 2015), 108.

5 See "Theresa May's Speech in Full," *Telegraph*, 5 October 2016, accessed 29 March 2020, at https://www.telegraph.co.uk/news/2016/10/05/theresa-mays-conference-speech-in-full/.

6 In his 2016 Reith Lecture, Kwame Anthony Appiah responded to Theresa May's comments, and was subsequently interviewed by the BBC: "'Mrs May, We Are All Citizens of the World, Says Philosopher," *BBC News Online*, 29 October 2016, accessed 29 March 2020, at https://www.bbc .co.uk/news/uk-politics-37788717.

7 The creation and uses of Arthuriana in Spanish and Portuguese territories is covered in detail in *The Arthur of the Iberians: The Arthurian Legends in the Spanish and Portuguese Worlds*, ed. David Hook (Cardiff: University of Wales Press, 2015). Here I have used "Palmeirim," in line with the Portuguese spelling of the name, rather than "Palmerin," more commonly associated with Spanish and English renderings of the tale. See Elizabeth Evenden-Kenyon, "Introduction," in *Amadís and Palmeirim in England, Portugal, and Spain: Anglo-Iberian Relations and the Uses of Medieval and Early Modern Arthuriana* (forthcoming).

8 For an English-language assessment of the ongoing research across this field, see Hook, *Arthur of the Iberians*.

9 See Weimin Gu, "Sebastianism, Messianism and Nationalism of Portuguese Overseas Expansion in the Sixteenth Century," *Chinese Journal of Theology*, no. 40 (2011): 53–78. On the messianic view of Philip II of Spain and its impact on Tudor England, see Geoffrey Parker, "The Place of Tudor England in the Messianic Vision of Philip II of Spain," *Transactions of the Royal Historical Society* 12 (2002): 167–221.

10 William of Malmesbury, *William of Malmesbury: Gesta Regum Anglorum, The History of the English Kings*, vol. 1, ed. R.A.B. Mynors, R.M. Thomson, M. Winterbottom, et al. (Oxford: Clarendon Press, 1998), bk. III, 287. On William of Malmesbury and the writing of history, see Sigbjørn Olsen Sønnesyn, *William of Malmesbury and the Ethics of History* (Woodbridge, UK: Boydell Press, 2012).

11 R.S. Loomis, ed., *Arthurian Literature in the Middle Ages* (Oxford: Oxford University Press, 1959), 64–71; Victoria E. Flood, "Exile and Return: The Development of Political Prophecy on the Borders of England, c.1136–1450s" (PhD diss., University of York, 2013), 71.

12 The *Lancelot-Grail Project* at the University of Pittsburgh provides summaries, useful data on the thematic links between the Vulgate texts, as well as high-resolution images: www.lancelot-project.pitt.edu/. See also Norris J. Lacy, ed., *The Lancelot-Grail Reader* (New York: Garland, 2000).

13 See *La mort le Roi Artu (The Death of Arthur), from the Old French "Lancelot" of Yale 229 with Essays Glossaries, and Notes to the Text*, ed. Elizabeth Moore Willingham (Turnhout, BE: Brepols, 2008).

14 See *The Old French Arthurian Vulgate and Post-Vulgate in Translation*, 10 vols, ed. Norris J. Lacy (Martlesham, UK: D.S. Brewer, 2010). For a discussion of the influence of the Post-Vulgate Cycle, see the preface to volume 9

(produced with Martha Asher). For an overview of the evolution of the Vulgate and Post-Vulgate Cycles, see Norris J. Lacy, "'The Evolution and Legacy of French Prose Romance," in *The Cambridge Companion to Medieval Romance*, ed. Roberta L. Krieger (Cambridge: Cambridge University Press, 2000), 167–82.

15 See Elizabeth Evenden-Kenyon, *Amadís and Palmeirim*, chaps 2 and 3 (forthcoming).

16 Rafael M. Mérida Jiménez, *Transmisión y difusión de la literatura caballeresca: Doce estudios de recepción cultural hispaánica (siglos XIII–XVII)* (Lleida: Edicions de la Universitat de Lleida, 2013).

17 W.R.J. Barron, "Introduction," in *The Arthur of the English: The Arthurian Legend in Medieval English Life and Literature*, ed. W.R.J. Barron (Cardiff: University of Wales, 2011), xiii.

18 Kenneth Hodges, "Prince Arthur's Archers: Innovative Nostalgia in Early Modern Popular Chivalry," in *Arthurian Literature XXVII*, ed. Elizabeth Archibald and David F. Johnson (Woodbridge, UK: D.S. Brewer, 2010), 186.

19 For a detailed discussion of medieval and early modern Arthurian historiography, see Evenden-Kenyon, *Amadís and Palmeirim*, chap. 1.

20 For an overview of Geoffrey's account of Arthur, see W.R.J. Barron, Françoise Le Saux, and Lesley Johnson, "Dynastic Chronicles," in Barron, *Arthur of the English*, 11–18; for a more comprehensive survey of medieval dynastic chronicles detailing Arthur, see ibid., 11–46.

21 For the first (Latin and abridged) edition of Geoffrey of Monmouth to be printed in England see *Pontici Virunnii viri doctissimi Britannicae historiae libri sex magna et fide et diligentia conscripti: ad Britannici codicis fidem correcti, & ab infinitis mendis liberati: quibus praefixus est catalogus regum Britanniae: per Dauidem Pouelum, S. Theolog. Professorem* ... (London, 1585; STC 20109). For a modern translation, see *Geoffrey of Monmouth: The History of the Kings of Britain; an Edition and Translation of De Gentis Britonum (Historia Regum Britanniae)*, ed. Michael D. Reeve, trans. Wright, Arthurian studies vol. 69 (Woodbridge, UK: Boydell Press, 2007).

22 No English edition of William of Malmesbury's text was printed during this period, although Henry Saville's Latin compilation did make some of his writing available in England during 1596: *Rerum Anglicarum scriptores post Bedam praecipui, ex vetustissimis codicibus manuscriptis nunc primum in lucem editi. Willielmi monachi Malmesburiensis de gestis regum Anglorum lib. V. Eiusdem Historiae nouellae lib. II. Eiusdem de gestis pontificum Angl. lib. IIII. Henrici Archidiaconi Huntindoniensis Historiarum lib. VIII. Rogeri Houedeni Annalium pars prior & posterior. Chronicorum Ethelwerdi lib. IIII. Ingulphi abbatis Croylandensis historiarum lib. I. Adiecta ad finem chronologia* (London, 1596; STC 21783).

23 Geoffrey of Monmouth, *Historia Regum Brittaniae*, bk. 9, chap. 4. For an online modern American English edition (based on a nineteenth-century edition), see that provided via Indiana University Bloomington, at http://www.indiana.edu/~dmdhist/arthur_gm.htm.

24 For a discussion of this, see Alexander Walsham, *The Reformation of the Landscape: Religion, Identity and Memory in Early Modern Britain and Ireland* (Oxford: Oxford University Press, 2011), 297–8.

25 Elizabeth Evenden, *Patents, Pictures and Patronage: John Day and the Tudor Book Trade* (Abingdon-on-Thames: Routledge, 2008), 80–4 and Evenden, "Agendas and Aesthetics in the Transformation of the Codex in Early Modern England," in *Libraries, Literatures, and Archives*, 2nd ed., ed. Sas Mays (London: Routledge, 2017), 97–114.

26 See Harriet Archer, *Unperfect Histories: The Mirror for Magistrates, 1559–1610* (Oxford: Oxford University Press, 2017), 57–58; Paulina Kewes, "Romans in the Mirror," in *A Mirror for Magistrates in Context: Literature, History, and Politics in Early Modern England* (Cambridge: Cambridge University Press, 2016), 126–46.

27 See Christopher Dean, *Arthur of England: English Attitudes to King Arthur and the Knights of the Round Table in the Middle Ages and the Renaissance* (Toronto: University of Toronto Press, 1987), 4. Dean notes the paucity of information provided by Geoffrey on his household and personal affairs.

28 Geoffrey of Monmouth, *Historia Regum Brittaniae*, bk. 9, chap. 3. William Shakespeare, *Henry V*, Arden Shakespeare, ed. T.W. Craik (London: Routledge, 1995), 4.6.37 and 4.7.62. On the execution of "prisoners" by command of Henry V, see the discussion of Froissart's account of these executions in Adam J. Kosto, *Hostages in the Middle Ages* (Oxford: Oxford University Press, 2012), 202–3.

29 Dean, *Arthur of England*, 5–6.

30 See James P. Carley, "Polydore Vergil and John Leland on King Arthur: The Battle of the Books," in *King Arthur: A Casebook*, ed. Edward Donald Kennedy (New York: Routledge, 2002), 186.

31 Ibid.

32 John Bale, *A Brefe Chronycle Concernynge the Examinacyon and Death of the Blessed Martyr of Christ syr Iohan Oldecastell the Lorde Cobham, Collected Togyther by Iohan Bale . ..* (Antwerp, 1544; STC 1276), fo. 5[r].

33 See Carley, "Polydore Vergil," 185, 198n11.

34 The text was first published in 1709, with a recent, much-awaited (and justly lauded) edition by James Carley appearing in 2010. Carley's research sheds invaluable light on the methodologies and reach of Leland's research. John Leland, *De viris illustribus / On Famous Men*, ed. James P. Carley (Oxford: Bodleian Library, 2010). On the genesis of Leland's argumentation see Carley, "Polydore Vergil," 185–204.

Portuguese and Spanish Arthuriana 177

35 Carley, "Polydore Vergil," 187–8.
36 John Leland, *Assertio inclytissimi Arturij Regis Britanniae* (London, 1544; STC 15440).
37 Carley, "Polydore Vergil," 187.
38 See Elizabeth Evenden and Thomas S. Freeman, *Religion and the Book in Early Modern England: The Making of John Foxe's Book of Martyrs* (Cambridge: Cambridge University Press, 2011), 48–51.
39 See Norman L. Jones, *Faith by Statute: Parliament and the Settlement of Religion, 1559* (London: Royal Historical Society, 1982), esp. 88–9, 90, and 93–4; Michael C. Questier, *Catholicism and Community in Early Modern England: Politics, Aristocratic Patronage and Religion, c. 1550–1640* (Cambridge: Cambridge University Press, 2006), 117–24, 136–41.
40 We will return to this subject in the next section. There is a substantial amount of scholarship available covering these options and penalties for English Catholics. See, merely by way of example, Michael C. Questier, *Conversion, Politics and Religion in England, 1580–1625* (Cambridge: Cambridge University Press, 1996); Adam Morton, ed., *Getting Along? Religious Identities and Confessional Relations in Early Modern England: Essays in Honour of Professor W.J. Sheils* (Abingdon, UK: Ashgate, 2012); Katy Gibbons, *English Catholic Exiles in Late Sixteenth-Century Paris* (London: Royal Historical Society, 2011).
41 Again, many a forest has been felled for this topic too. But Carley's "Polydore Vergil" remains an excellent starting point for inquiry.
42 Juan Bautista Avalle-Arce, *Amadís de Gaula: El primitivo y el de Montalvo* (Mexico City: FCE, 1990); and his chapter "La Intervencion de Montalvo," in *Amadís: Heroísmo mítico cortesano*, ed. Juan Manuel Cacho Blecua (Zaragoza: Universidad de Zaragoza, 1979), 366–88; Alberto Montaner Frutos, "Del *Amadís* primitivo al de Montalvo: Cuestiones de emblemática," in *Amadís de Gaula: Quinientos Años Después. Estudios en homenaje a Juan Manuel Cacho Blecua*, ed. José Manuel Lucía Megías and María del Carmen Marín Pina (Madrid: Alcalá de Henares, 2008), 525–38.
43 My translation. "Estos son los que compusieron las historias fengidas en que se hallan las cosas admirables fuera de la orden de natura, que más por nombre de patrañas que de crónicas con mucha razón deven ser tenidas y llamadas." See Garci Rodríguez de Montalvo, *Amadís de Gaula I*, ed. Juan Manuel Cacho Blecua (Madrid: Cátedra, 1998), 223.
44 Ibid., 220–1.
45 Carlos Alvar, "The Matter of Britain in Spanish Society and Letters from Cluny to Cervantes," in Hook, *Arthur of the Iberians*, 187–270, 212.
46 Ibid.
47 Garci Rodríguez de Montalvo, *Amadís de Gaula*, 2 vols., ed. Juan Manuel Cacho Blecua (Madrid: Cátedra, 1987), II: 1302.

48 Alvar, "The Matter of Britain," 213.

49 On Montalvo's novel conclusion, see (by way of example), Elroy R Gonzalez, *La conclusion del Amadis De Gaula: Las Sergas de Esplandian de Garci Rodriguez de Montalvo* (Potomac, MD: Scripta Humanistica, 2001).

50 Ian Michael, *"From Her Shall Read the Perfect Ways of Honour:* Isabel of Castile and Chivalric Romance," in *The Age of Catholic Monarchs, 1474–1516: Literary Studies in Memory of Keith Whinnom*, ed. A. Deyermond and I. Macpherson (Liverpool: University of Liverpool Press, 1989), 109.

51 Santiago Gutiérrez Garcia, "Arthurian Literature in Portugal," in Hook, *Arthur of the Iberians*, 107.

52 Ibid.

53 Ibid., 105.

54 Ibid., 107.

55 See Evenden-Kenyon, *Amadís and Palmeirim*, chap. 3 and Gutiérrez García, "Arthurian Literature in Portugal," 107.

56 *Crónica do imperador Maximiliano. Cód. 490, Col. Pombalina da Biblioteca Nacional*, ed. João Palma-Ferreira, Luís Carvalho Dias, and Fernando Filipe Portugal (Lisbon: Imprensa Nacional – Casa da Moeda, 1983).

57 Jean Subirats, "Les sortilèges du rêve chevaleresque. Propos sur Jorge Ferreira de Vasconcelos et son *'Memorial' das proezas da Segunda Távola Redonda*," *Culture, História e Filosofia* 5 (1986): 219–37.

58 Gutiérrez García, "Arthurian Literature in Portugal," 109.

59 Ibid.

60 Manuel Calderón Calderón, "Printing Licences and the Trade in Fiction in Spain in the First Half of the Seventeenth Century," in *A Maturing Market: The Iberian Book World in the First Half of the Seventeenth Century*, ed. Alexander Samuel Wilkinson and Alejandro Ulla Lorenzo (Leiden: Brill, 2017), 204.

61 Ibid.

62 See Elizabeth Evenden-Kenyon, "Anthony Munday: Eloquent Equivocator or Contemptible Turncoat?" in *Reformation Reputations: The Power of the Individual in English Reformation History*, ed. David Crankshaw and George Gross (Basingstoke, UK: Palgrave Macmillan 2020).

63 Ibid.

64 Anthony Munday, *The English Romayne Lyfe* (London, 1582; STC 18272). It was reprinted in 1590 (STC 18273). There is also a modern edition *The English Roman Life*, edited by Philip J. Ayres (Oxford: Clarendon Press, 1980).

65 I explore the various attempts to pin down in motives – and just how heated arguments can become – in "Anthony Munday."

66 Heneage died in 1595. See Michael Hicks, "Heneage, Sir Thomas (*b.* in or before 1532, *d.* 1595), Courtier" in *ODNB*.

67 See Hamilton, *Anthony Munday and the Catholics, 1560–1633* (Aldershot, UK: Ashgate, 2005), xx–xxi. Anthony Munday, *A Banquet of Daintie Cconceits. Furnished with Verie Delicate and Choyse Inventions, Either to the Lute, Bandora, Virginalles, or anie other Instrument* (London, 1588; STC 18260). Munday appears to have made good use of this role and was rewarded on 17 July 1587 with some financially profitable "leases in reversion of crown property." (TNA, E351/352 [1579–1596], fol. 83ᵛ).

68 Thomas Alfied, *A True Report of the Death & Martyrdome of M. Campion Iesuite & Prieste, & M. Sherwin, & M. Bryane Priestes, at Tiborn the First of December* (London, 1582; STC 4537), E1ʳ.

69 Anthony Munday, *A Breefe Aunswer Made unto Two Seditious Pamphlets* (London, 1582; STC 18262), D4ʳ⁻ᵛ. See also Joshua Phillips, "Chronicles of Wasted Time: Anthony Munday, Tudor Romance, and Literary Labor," *ELH* 73, no. 4 (2006): 793–6.

70 Anthony Munday, *Zelauto. The Fountaine of Fame* (London, 1580; STC 18283), *4ʳ.

71 See Peter Burke, "The Renaissance Translator as Go-Between," in *Renaissance Go-Betweens: Cultural Exchange in Early Modern Europe*, ed. Andreas Höfele and Werner von Koppenfels (Berlin: Walter de Gruyter, 2005), 17–31.

72 See Hamilton, *Anthony Munday and the Catholics*, 202–6, for full details as to when each part was printed, and when each text was entered onto the Stationers' Register.

73 Arber II, 383.

74 Arthur Golding, in his dedication to the Earl of Oxford in *The Psalms of David and Others. With J. Calvins Commentaries* (London, 1571; STC 2725), juxtaposed chivalric and religious orders (*2ʳ⁻ᵛ) in order to "emphasize the value of right religion to political and social life." See Donna B. Hamilton, "Anthony Munday's Translations of Iberian Chivalric Romances: *Palmerin of England, Part 1 as Exemplar*," in *Catholic Culture in Early Modern England*, ed. Ronald Corthell et al. (Notre Dame, IN: University of Notre Dame Press, 2007), 283.

75 For a detailed discussion of Munday's manipulation of these texts, and evidence for how they were read, see Evenden-Kenyon, *Amadís and Palmeirim*, chaps 6 and 7.

76 See Roger Dalrymple, *Language and Piety in Middle English Romance* (Stroud: D.S. Brewer, 2000), 141–2 on eliding physical and mnemonic text to evoke devotional consciousness. On Catholic exile communities reading Iberian "romance" in translation see Evenden-Kenyon, *Amadís and Palmeirim*, chap. 7.

77 Brian Cummings, *The Literary Culture of the Reformation: Grammar and Grace* (Oxford: Oxford University Press, 2009).

78 Alexandra Walsham, "Cultures of Coexistence in Early Modern England: History, Literature and Religious Toleration," *Seventeenth Century* 28 (2013): 118.

79 Brian C. Lockey, *Catholics, Royalists and Cosmopolitans: English Transnationalism and the Christian Commonwealth* (Aldershot, UK: Ashgate, 2015), 104.

80 Nora Johnson, *The Actor and Playwright in Early Modern Drama* (Cambridge: Cambridge University Press, 2003), 84–121.

81 Walsham, "Cultures of Coexistence," 122.

82 Ibid., 116.

Chapter Eight

Anthony Munday, Romance Translations, and History Writing: Church Rights, Toleration, and the Unity of Christendom, 1609–1633

DONNA B. HAMILTON

A writer whose publications spanned fifty-five years (1577–1633) and included some eighty-two titles,[1] Anthony Munday (1560–1633) has often been known by only a small portion of his output – his works related to Rome and Edmund Campion, plays contemporary with Shakespeare, early translations of chivalric romance, and Jacobean City pageants. Basing conclusions on this early output, both supporters and detractors of Munday have tended to castigate him for testifying against Catholics, lying, and working as a spy, activity concentrated in the reign of Queen Elizabeth. Meanwhile, the evidence for Munday's Catholic sympathies has often gone unrecognized or been denied, despite our knowledge of what Alexandra Walsham has called "the shadowy world of Catholic recusancy and occasional conformity."[2] Those systems for enforcing religious conformity were systems of oppression and persecution that required silence and equivocation. Self-defined as conforming and loyal, Munday lived and worked within that system. In *Lying in Early Modern English Culture*, Andrew Hadfield, who used Henry VIII's Oath of Supremacy and King James's Oath of Allegiance as the bookends of his study, commented: "As the religious nature of the Tudor regime changed with bewildering speed and with differing forms of brutality and tolerance, the parameters of lying became a central question. Could one avoid taking oaths? How permissible was it to bend the truth? Was what passed for truth now the same as it had been a year or two ago?"[3]

I am grateful to Leticia Alvarez-Recio for the opportunity to continue to refine my research and thinking about Munday's work. This chapter is particularly indebted to the work of Michael C. Questier published in 2006, 2008, and 2009, as indicated in the notes, and to discussions with the contributors to this volume.

Our developing a satisfactory narrative for Munday's place in literary history is important to Munday scholarship, and relies on extending our work to his writing during the last two dozen years, 1609–33,
the years that included the reigns of King James I (1603–25) and King
Charles I (1625–49), as well as Munday's continued translations and
reprinting of chivalric romances and his history writing.[4] His romance
translations, originally printed in 1588–1602, came into view again with
reprintings of *The [first] Seconde Part, of the no lesse Rare, Historie of Palmerin of England* (1609, 1616; STC 19162-3), *Palmerin d'Oliva* (1615, 1616;
STC 19159-19159a), *The Third Booke of Amadis de Gaule* (1618; STC 543),
Amadis de Gaule (1619; STC 544), and *The Famous and Renouned Historie of
Primaleon of Greece* (1619; STC 20367). The historical works at issue are *A
Briefe Chronicle, of the Successe of Times* (1611, STC 18263) and Munday's
two revisions of *The Survey of London* (1618, 1633; STC 23344-5), all dedi-
cated to officials of the City of London.

These two revered genres – romance and history – had been the
most significant vehicles for communicating transnational European
history, ideology, and myth. As I argue in this chapter, Munday's handling of these genres in these later years attests to his resourcefulness
and dedication in promulgating notions of the unity of Christendom,
with a view that England belonged to the history and religion of the
Continent. His romance translations presented accounts of adventurers across Catholic pre-Reformation Europe, many of whom regularly
engaged with or returned to England. These adventurers were part of a
complex interconnected, international whole. In *A Briefe Chronicle* and
in his revisions of Stow's *Survey*, Munday did the work of a historian
with a Stow-like perspective. He provided favourable representation of
aspects of the pre-Henrician church, especially in regard to church-state
relations and the role of monarch and emperor in relation to the papacy.
In *The Survey*, there is extensive material on pre-Henrician notions of
church rights, church property, tithes, and sanctuary, along with the
authority for these practices. As a practising antiquarian, Munday was
preserving for his city and country the record of their Catholic history,[5]
buttressed with notions of ecclesiastical authority and church rights that
implicitly defended the ongoing Catholic presence in England, as well
as toleration for that presence.[6] In these historical works, the authority
of which was undergirded by the romance narratives, Munday's rigorous contextualizing of church rights testified to long-established traditions, enlisted not to reverse what Henry VIII had set in motion, but to
explain and defend the English Catholic citizen's right to continue to
worship as Catholic in England and to be understood as one with the
unity of Christendom.

Munday's engagement with what Iberian romance might offer his English readers had begun with the translation of *Palmerin of England*, licensed 13 February 1581, in the Stationers' Register to printer John Charlewood.[7] As an early indication of what Munday was up against, a censorship warning accompanied that licensing: "uppon Condicon that if there be anie thinge founde in The booke when it is extante worthie of Reprehension That then all the Bookes shalbe put to waste and Burnte."[8] Stark in itself, such a warning might carry little significance today without some idea of what may have motivated it. As Elizabeth Evenden-Kenyon has acknowledged, a chivalric tale was traditionally "a Catholic tale for a Catholic audience," with "Catholicism ... at the heart of the narrative."[9] In Munday's case, there were also the growing anxiety about Jesuit priests entering England, suspicion about his own religious loyalties, and his book *The English Roman College*.[10] No copies of the first printing of *Palmerin of England* are extant,[11] and the only copy of *Palmerin of England* from the next printing in 1596 is missing both its front and back pages, signs of deliberate mutilation. Lacking all paratextual matter – title page, dedication, commendatory verses, beginning, and ending – this Elizabethan book loses its identity and becomes merely a scrap of something. In contrast, when *Palmerin* was reprinted in 1609, during the reign of King James, when censorship practices had relaxed, suddenly a whole range of paratextual materials comes into view, a dedication, commendatory verse, and concluding paratext, all most likely originating from the earliest attempt to print, with their earlier repeated omission serving as evidence of persistent censorship during the reign of Elizabeth. The commendatory verse by R.W. (perhaps Robert Wilson) urged Munday to continue despite detractors, and, in the concluding paratext, Munday announced, "let the Author passe uncontrowled" (Ee1^v),[12] both items indicating resistance to censoring authorities.

At the time of the 1609 printing, England was embroiled in the international paper war set off by King James's Oath of Allegiance. Enacted in 1606 in response to the Gunpowder Plot of 5 November 1605, the Oath of Allegiance required Catholics to swear allegiance to the king as their temporal ruler and to swear that the pope did not possess the power either to depose temporal rulers or to absolve an English subject of the Oath of Allegiance. In this oath, James had virtually declared himself to possess a supremacy equal to that of the pope, with the right to govern the church: "The result was to turn a denial of the deposing power into what could plausibly be regarded as a rejection of the papal primacy."[13] In the absence of "normal ecclesiastical structures" representing the Catholic community, the oath could thus be interpreted as confirming that the church was "subject to temporal rulers," rather than that the state "found its end in subordination to the Church."[14] James defended his position in two major works, *Triplici nodo, triplex cuneus or An Apologie for the Oath of Allegiance* (1608; STC 14404) and *A Premonition to All Most Mightie Monarches, Kings, Free Princes, and States of Christendome* (1609; STC 14401). Robert Persons (1546–1610) responded with *The Judgment of a Catholicke English-man Living in Banishment* (1608; STC 19408). Robert Bellarmine (1542–1621) was among the Catholics who joined the argument on the Catholic side, and, at James's request, Lancelot Andrewes (1555–1626) and William Barlow (1544–1625) wrote defending the king's position. Many in England and abroad participated in the quarrel,[15] writing new works and issuing new editions of earlier works, among them the first collected edition of the *Works of John Jewel* (1609; STC 14579), ordered to be placed in the churches together with the Bible and Foxe's *Actes and Monuments*;[16] a revised edition of *Actes and Monuments* (1610; STC 11227); Richard Field's (1561–1616) *Of the Church, Five Books* (1606, 1610; STC 10857, 10857.7); John Speed's (ca. 1552–1629) *History of Great Britaine* (1611; STC 23045); and a new edition of Edmund Spenser's (ca. 1552–99) *Faerie Queene* (1609; STC 23083), followed by Spenser's collected works (1611; STC 23083.3).[17]

In juxtaposition to the polemic driven by conflict over political and religious allegiance, *Palmerin of England* features an expansive international scene that represents England as belonging to that world. In *Palmerin*, the action regularly moves back and forth from England to the Continent, where knights from England, Germany, Poland, Hungary, France, Flanders, and Constantinople engage each other, fight almost to the death, champion their ladies, engage with giants, fight yet another opponent, return to and leave Constantinople, and return to England. In a pointed tract from the time of Elizabeth I, *The Copy of a Letter, Lately Written by a Spanishe Gentleman, to his Friend in England* (1589; STC 1038), Richard Verstegan (ca.1548–ca.1636) had warned against the punitive social and economic hardships being delivered upon the English Catholic people. Given the anti-Catholic restrictions on travel, publishing, and the sale and purchase of foreign books, along with fines, imprisonment, and death for noncompliance, the people were being denied knowledge of "how thinges do ordinarily passe in the world abrode," and not allowed "to demaunde, heare, read, or write, any news of any matter whatsoever, be it true or untrue" (C1^v); "You are cutt of from all trade and trafique, with the moste ritche, and opulent countries aboute you, retaining no hope of any outward comoditie, other then can be gotten by robbery and piracie" (C2^r). Contrasting with this view, Munday's *Palmerin of England* provided an account of an English world conjoined to and enmeshed in life on the continent. That integration with all nations is what King James had also sought through his "requiring, as he contended, only an expression of civil obedience in the Oath of Allegiance, and by treating peaceable Roman Catholics more leniently than the harsh penal laws specified."[18] That integration also offers a view of the cosmopolitanism with which Elizabeth Evenden-Kenyon has associated Munday.[19]

In 1610, the assassination of Henri IV of France raised the stakes. James reissued the Oath of Allegiance with stricter rules for enforcement. When the oath had been published in 1606, noblemen and noblewomen were exempt from having to take it. Following the assassination, the oath was required of everyone eighteen years of age and older. Across the years, compliance and enforcement varied by individual, family, and community, but was broadly applied. Following the proclamation of 1610, tendering the oath increased, with reports circulating that "'the prisons are filled againe' and the Oath 'is more exacted than ever'."[20] Many Catholics of every station took the oath; others refused. Enforcement was more vigorous in the south than in the Catholic stronghold of the north, and more severe among those less wealthy and of lower station.[21] Punishments for refusal could result in confiscation of property, loss of position in Parliament or a household, deprivation of all civil rights, imprisonment, and, for some, execution.[22] Dodd recorded executions for religion during 1610–18, of both clergy and laymen, with four in 1610, four in 1612, five in 1616, and one in 1618.[23] Relenting under this pressure, Ben Jonson (ca.1572–1637) conformed in 1610. In 1610 and 1611, John Donne (1572–1631) contributed two anti-Catholic works, *Pseudo-Martyr* (STC 7048) and *Ignatius His Conclave* (STC 7027). In 1611, "on a single day," London justices of the peace committed thirty recusants to prison.[24] In 1614 in London alone, "a total of 90 individuals [were] confined for their religion" in the three prisons of Newgate, the Clink, and the Gatehouse.[25]

The varying forms of punishment and resistance draw our attention as we try to understand the degrees of extremity or laxness.[26] Among those who took the oath were some who attempted to qualify their responses through mental reservation or direct negotiation with authorities.[27] Some proposed variant or hybrid versions of the oath.[28] Whatever the strategy, a dominant response was debate over its meaning and implications. Such discussion included speculation that the oath would lead to toleration of Catholics, with the Catholic community allowed to retain a separatist identity, and, alternatively, that the oath would result in general conformity of all Catholics.[29] In short, the oath had "fractured English catholic ideological unity into an uncontrollable variety of opinion."[30]

It was at this time – in the aftermath of the assassination of Henri IV, the reissuing of the Oath of Allegiance, and the publication of the works by Donne – that Munday dedicated *A Briefe Chronicle of the Successe of Times* (1611; STC 18263) to City officials, including the lord mayor and Sir Henry Montagu (1563–1642), the recorder of London and a devoted Catholic.[31] Years later, Munday would dedicate to Montagu again in his publications of Thomas North's translation of Antonio de Guevara's *Archontorologion, or The Diall of Princes* (1619; STC 12430), originally dedicated by North to Mary Tudor in 1557, and of André Favyn's treatise on chivalry, *The Theater of Honour of Knight-hood* (1623; STC 10717).[32] As Tracey Hill has indicated, *A Briefe Chronicle* is "extensively based on Stow's historical works and cross-references its source in places."[33] In *A Briefe Chronicle*, a work of 613 pages, Munday tracked a broad range of topics across long periods of time, material that, in the context of the international paper war set off by King James's Oath of Allegiance, also had an immediate relevance. Only superficially a work uninterested in religious-political controversy, *A Briefe Chronicle* carries implicit support for both ecclesiastical authority and toleration for Catholics.

Not a chronicle history like that of Raphael Holinshed or John Speed, and not presented as a polemical work, *A Briefe Chronicle* seems more like a history handbook – over 600 pages long, made up of lists and brief paragraphs on a host of topics, all handled discontinuously. Munday began with the Flood and continued through the monarchies of Persia, Greece, Syria, Egypt, and Rome; the emperors of the West and of the East; Ottomans, Sarcens, bishops and popes of Rome, knights of St. Johns of Jerusalem; and then on to Persia, Tunis, Poland, Italy, Venice, Spain, Germany, France, Holland, Ireland, Scotland, and finally Britain and London. Apparently, England itself was finally the topic of the entire book, with the preceding sections representing its context.

As we work through *A Briefe Chronicle*, we find that Munday, without labelling it as such, inscribed some content with a Catholic perspective that stands in opposition to Protestant anti-Catholic polemic. Munday chose his list of emperors of the West to include those who had opposed the use of images and then fallen on bad ends. He told that Constantine V, who was an enemy to images and to their relics, died a leper, and Leo of Armenia, who defaced images of saints, was "slaine in a Church" (F8[r]). When he discussed the Saracens, the Muslims who had been driven from Spain, he credited Ferdinand, the great-grandfather to Philip II of Spain, with having saved Europe for Christianity, informing the reader that "all *Europe* wold (at this instant) haue bin haunted with those people, if they had not beene formerlie expelled and spoiled" (J5[r]). Munday had reiterated a similar perspective in *Palmendos* (1589), where again it is the secular hero and emperor who take action to preserve right religion. In that romance, Palmendos's keenest desire was to be reunited with his father, the emperor Palmerin d'Oliva, and become Christian. After his baptism, in the Church of St. Sophia, Palmendos pledged himself to marry Francelina, but first joined forces with the Spanish to free the people from the false religion of the Giant Baledon.[34] In Munday's list of the bishops and popes of Rome, from 44 to 1611, he made no mention of dissension between popes and English monarchs, but dwelt on the years 1592 to 1611, and characterized the popes as peacemakers among Catholic nations in Europe, including Clement VIII (reigning 1592–1605) and Leo XI (1–27 April 1605). Pursuing a line of thought that would have meshed easily with King James's ecumenism, Munday exercised a judicious silence on anything to do with Paul V (1605–21), who in 1606 had ordered English Catholics not to take the Oath of Allegiance.[35]

As for his list of English monarchs, Munday wrote with brevity as he surveyed the "success of times" from the reign of Henry VII to that of James I. Henry VII built religious houses; Henry VIII "banished the Popes authority out of England"; Edward VI "caused the Masse to be utterly abolished, Images to be defaced" and devised "good orders" for the "poores reliefe"; Mary, the "eldest daughter" to Henry VIII, married the "prince of Spain"; Elizabeth, the second daughter to Henry VIII, was "Virgin Empresse and matchlesse Queene"; and James – the "onley inheritour" of the line of Henry VII – united England and Scotland "in one sole Monarchy of Great Britaine" (Mm2^r–Mm4^r). For Queen Elizabeth, he reprinted one of the laudatory inscriptions included on monuments in virtually every church (Mm4^r). Beginning and ending the section on monarchs with references to Henry VII, Munday suggested the recurring and cyclical nature of change over time. His brief elaboration in the cases of Mary ("eldest daughter") and James ("onley inheritour" of the line of Henry VII) emphasized pointedly their legitimacy in succession.

Munday again took up the matter of legitimacy in succession in his list of the Princes of Wales (Mm4^v–Mm6^r). Beginning with Edward I, and including Mary and Elizabeth – made Princesses of Wales – Munday named each in order, ending with Prince Henry, son of King James. Munday emphasized that each prince or princess came to the title by way of Parliament – that is, had been "created … by and in Court of Parliament, except three," Richard II, Edward V, and Edward, son to Richard III, all of whom, he noted, had come to bad ends (Mm6^r). In making this point, Munday called attention to the role of Parliament, the voice of the commonwealth, in certifying the legitimacy of the succeeding ruler.[36]

Election along with heredity was what conferred legitimacy, a point of view common to republican thought of the period. In *A Conference about the Next Succession to the Crowne of Ingland* (1594; STC 19398), Robert Persons had written at length on this issue, explaining that a monarch does not fully hold the royal power until the coronation ceremony is complete: "after the prince hath sworne divers times to governe well and iustly, then do the subjects take othes of obedience and allegiance and not before, which argueth that before they were not bounde unto him by allegeance" (K8ᵛ). After discussion of the special reverence in which the people held Henry V, a fact attested to in a quotation Persons furnished from Stow, Persons concluded: "except the admission of the common wealth be joined to succession, it is not sufficient to make a lawful king, and of the two, the second is of far more importance, to wit the consent and admission of the realme, then nearness of blood by succession alone" (L1ʳ). In its monarchomach form, such thinking included a notion that a republican system of elected monarchy could allow for the choice of monarch and for the monarch's removal from power.[37] That thinking is related to Persons's next section, Cap. VII, where he cited numerous examples of the people rejecting for rule someone who could have succeeded "by propinquity of blood," but who had been "put back, by the commonwealth" (L3ᵛ) as unsuitable to rule, with others given the place instead. In later pages, when Munday wrote about Venice, he acknowledged the Venetians' religion – "Catholique Religion they so singularly commended ... that it augmented ... a common affection to piety" (T4ʳ) – and then took up again the matter of election of the monarch. Considering also the Venetians' good government, he explained that it depended on "Dignities, being ... elective, and not hereditary" (T5r–T5v). He then listed the elective systems in Poland and France, emphasizing that in the case of the first king of France, the people could both make and unmake a ruler (Y5ʳ).

To clarify my points here: in Munday's selective list of emperors who respected images, he represented a preference for secular rulers who submit to the ways of the church. In his similarly selective list of popes, he showed papal power, the Roman Catholic Church, as the creator of peace and stability in the temporal world. Both points contradict the versions of history and religion represented in the works of Jewel, Foxe, and Spenser. Similarly, and more radical, in Munday's examples of election, he illustrated the authority that rests in the people and how badly things go awry when that authority is bypassed. In these brief sections, he took on the crux of the Oath of Allegiance controversy by representing a relationship between temporal and ecclesiastical authority that put ecclesiastical authority first. In so doing, he spoke implicitly

on behalf of contemporary English Catholics, whether recusant or conformed, who knew an alternative historical and religious tradition in
England. In these sections, he was representing the validity of and a
certain unequivocal authority in Catholic traditions. What was right
within that tradition stood, especially in the special circumstances of
1611 and later, as testimony to the Catholic right to exist as Catholics, to
be free from persecution, and to have the security of toleration.

In the years following the publication of *A Briefe Chronicle*, several
of Munday's romances were reprinted, *Palmerin d'Oliva* (1615, 1616),
Palmerin of England (1616), *The Third Booke of Amadis de Gaule* (1618),
Amadis de Gaule (1619), and *The Famous and Renouned Historie of Primaleon of Greece* (1619).[38] These are the years after the death of Prince
Henry in 1612, the marriage of Princess Elizabeth to Frederick the Elec-
tor Palatine in 1613, and, from 1613, negotiations for the marriage of
Prince Charles to the Spanish princess. Suitable also for this later time,
the emphasis in *Palmerin of England* is on succession and the problems
posed by the loss of an heir to the throne. In *Palmerin*, these issues are
further entangled as suitors from across Europe seek the favour of Mira-
garda, the beautiful princess of Spain. Finally, conciliation is reached
with the banding together of knights from across Europe who come to
Britain's aid, a powerful representation of the benefits of alliance with
European nations. The *Amadis* editions that had caused such suspicion
in the 1580s and 1590s were now newly authorized and repackaged
as elegant folios with dedications to Philip Herbert, Earl of Montgom-
ery, including references in three of them to his wife, Susan.[39] Susan
was daughter to Munday's early patron the Earl of Oxford, recently
deceased, and had been Anne of Denmark's lady-in-waiting since
1604, with the distinction that she had danced in all of Queen Anne's
masques.[40] *Amadis*, Book 1, emphasizes marriage alliances and the securing of an heir to the throne. And it represents the tension caused by the
preference of Great Britain's King Lisuart for a rule focused on inclusion
rather than isolation. In both *Palmerin* and *Amadis*, the emphasis on marriage leans in a direction supportive of the negotiations for a Spanish
match.[41] The emphasis on inclusion argues against the isolationism that
England had chosen under Elizabeth, and for an ecumenism embracing
a united Christendom, as promulgated by King James, who, in 1618,
freed imprisoned priests and halted harassment of Catholics, and, in
1622, restricted anti-Catholic attacks in sermons and print.[42] The printer
of the *Amadis* volumes in 1618 and 1619 was Nicholas Okes, a printer
with a record of allowing Catholic language in his books. In Munday's
Amadis, Book 3, this permissiveness shows itself in the appearance of
prayers to the Virgin Mary and references to attending mass and to

doing acts of penance, language that had been mainly purged from earlier translations of other romances.[43]

During the several years following publication of *A Briefe Chronicle*, Munday was preparing his first revision of Stow's (1524/5–1605) *Survey of London* (1618; STC 23344).[44] In the preface, he recorded Stow's desire that he be the one to continue his work. We are familiar with the resistance among scholars to accept that Stow was Catholic. Others have insisted that we take Stow's Catholicism for granted, especially Patrick Collinson, but also Ian Archer, David Kastan, and Annabel Patterson.[45] Describing Stow's *Survey* as "born out of the old religion and its values," Collinson concluded that Stow had mostly kept his Catholic religion out of sight, although his library and his writing gave it visibility.[46] Munday's situation was similar. As a conformed Protestant but nevertheless writing regularly in the direction of Catholic loyalism, Munday's signature move in every work written under Queen Elizabeth was always a formal profession of loyalty to the queen, a bedrock move that kept him safe in a tumultuous time of fear and persecution. During the reign of King James, Munday worked primarily for the City of London, not the Crown, a context that also put him closer to Stow.

Each of Munday's two editions of *The Survey* has unique characteristics. To the 1618 edition, he added details on the history and structure of London's government, along with records of monuments and charitable gifts. Stow, avenging Protestants for having defaced Catholic monuments, had refused to record Protestant tombstones. Unlike Stow, Munday proceeded with equanimity, updating the missing records and adding new ones. Treating antiquarian work with great respect, he was similarly accurate and detailed in recording all gifts of charity.[47] It was to London's credit that so many had given so much to benefit others.

In the 1618 edition, Munday documented the City's ability to maintain order among its citizens and to deal with City-Crown jurisdictional disputes. Expanding Stow's narration of the Peasants' Revolt, Munday provided an evenhanded report that covered the economic causes of the rebellion, mentioned the tax collector's abuse of Wat Tyler's daughter, and concluded with the justice meted out by King Richard II.[48] Munday avoided the recriminations against Catholics that other accounts had included. When Henry Howard, Earl of Northampton, had written about the Gunpowder Plot, Northumberland had recalled the Wat Tyler story and linked the rebellion to a notion of ongoing Catholic subversion, blaming Tyler's supposed adviser "Ball a Masse priest." Munday made no reference to the priest. In relating the details from Raphael Holinshed's account of Evil May Day, Munday avoided Holinshed's xenophobic language when he attributed the disturbances to "strangers."[49] Maintaining a nonpolemical style, the 1618 edition is conciliatory, aimed at satisfying the community at large, including the Catholic community.

In succeeding years, Munday published no additional editions of chivalric romances, although other publications registered continuing interests in chivalry and ecclesiastical history and tradition. He again dedicated works to Montagu – first, the folio edition of North's translation of Guevara's *Archontorologion, or The Diall of Princes* (1619), and next Favyn's treatise on chivalry, *The Theater of Honour of Knight-hood* (1623).[50] In further revision of *The Survey*, for what would become the 1633 edition, Munday repeatedly engaged with matters having to do with the restoration of religious traditions, buildings, and monuments.

A central feature of this later edition is the massive amount of new information that Munday was to include, along with the system of cross-referencing that kept track of additions. These additions were primarily of two types: records of the rebuilding of London's churches,[51] and records of historical events and precedents that Stow had not included or, in some cases, that had occurred after his death. There is a precision and purposefulness in these revisions that reward our attention. Commenting on the degree to which historians have not always acknowledged "the religious dimensions of Tudor historical writing," and have been more focused on their technique than on "what these writers are actually saying," David Womersley suggested that "the chronicles are undoubtedly ... intellectually alert in ways that scholars have been slow to recognize ... What we need now is to know much more about individual Tudor historical books."[52] We might make this point in regard to the historical work of Stow and Munday.

While the rebuilding of churches had begun earlier, more recent restoration was spurred on by the ambitious religious program of Archbishop Laud (1573–1645), who wanted the churches returned to the decorated style of pre-Edwardian England, when there was more emphasis on church ceremonies. In Laud's view, churches should offer rich representation of what was termed "the beauty of holiness." In his account of the rebuilding, "A Returne to London," Munday enumerated the extensive refurbishment of churches throughout the city, the newly installed pulpits, baptismal fonts, communion tables, pews, as well as the rich materials such as alabaster and cedar of which they were made. As Kenneth Fincham and Nicholas Tyacke remark, "according to the 1633 edition of Stow's *Survey* over a third of London churches were rebuilt, repaired, or beautified in the years of Laud's episcopate (1628–33)."[53] Merritt found in Munday's descriptions of the rebuilding a writer who added "a more specifically Protestant agenda to the

Survey."[54] I suggest a different emphasis, one more in tune as well with Munday's other publications. In his detailed recording of church building, one can see that Munday celebrated the acts of restoration for their effectiveness in erasing the iconoclasm that Protestants had practised from the time of Edward VI. London churches were being returned to their originally intended condition.

Between Munday's first revision in 1618 and this later one, there had been many changes in England in addition to church building. In 1623, the attempted Spanish Match for Prince Charles had deeply stirred Protestant anti-Catholic animus and unleashed a flood of anti-papal works.[55] The Parliament of 1624 again abolished the right of sanctuary and renewed its efforts to enforce penalties against Catholics and occasionally Puritans. On 6 May 1624, James issued a proclamation charging all Jesuits to "depart the land." In August, he issued "A Proclamation against Seditious, Popish, and Puritanicall Bookes and Pamphlets."[56] Arrangements to secure a marriage for Charles to the French Catholic Henrietta Maria caused more anxiety. Then on 27 March 1625, King James suddenly died. Newly crowned, King Charles I ordered "that, on the pretext supplied by the impending marriage, all the crown's officers should be directed to suspend proceedings against Catholics."[57] Through all this turmoil, and despite efforts running in the opposite direction, Catholic hopes for relaxed penalties and toleration remained strong.

A moment in the 1633 edition that seems to acknowledge this context is Munday's addition to the section on Blackfriars, a precinct long independent of temporal authority of both City and Crown, and still under the pre-Henrician ecclesiastical protections that belonged to tithes and sanctuary.[58] Placing this material within Stow's section on Farington Ward Within, the ward of Blackfriars, Munday documented the limitation of City authority over Blackfriars[59] by citing nearly a century's worth of precedents, from 1484 to 1582, thus extending well after the dissolution of the order of Black Friars (Kk2r–Kk4v).

With this groundwork in place, Munday included in the 1633 edition a report on an incident that had occurred on 26 October 1623, involving a worship service for 300 Catholics on an upper floor of a building next to the French ambassador's residence in Blackfriars. Unable to support so large a crowd, the floor had collapsed, and eighty people were killed. Hearing of the disaster, some Protestants rushed to the scene to inflict further violence on the wounded. As Alexandra Walsham has discussed, numerous pamphlets and sermons were printed interpreting the event.[60] One standard interpretation combined notions of providentialism with anti-popery; hard on the heels of the failed Spanish

Match, the event was viewed by some as the hand of God destroying the papists and saving the church for Protestants. Avoiding that tone, Munday reprinted a tract, *The Fatall Vesper, or A True ... Relation of that Lamentable and Fearefull Accident, Hapning on ... 26 of October*, that Arthur Freeman has described as written by someone, "if not Catholic, certainly closer to Rome than any other contemporary ... pamphleteer."[61] Declaring that his report would not favour either the "Protestant or Papist," this author of the tract explained matter of factly that the floor had collapsed because there were more people in the room than the floor could support. He described the horrors of the accident and listed the names of those who had been killed. Munday inserted this pamphlet, with names of the dead appended, undeterred by the fact that officials had immediately withdrawn from circulation its earlier printed version as a stand-alone tract. Munday thus bypassed the Protestant polemic the event had stirred, and offered an account that represented a group of Catholics in a part of the city that had been declared off-limits to City and Crown temporal authority. Implicit here is an argument for Catholic right to worship, at least in private and, more broadly, for ceasing penalties against Catholics and for granting toleration. It is notable that the pamphlet's author, W.C., actually directed the reader to just these complexities of the moment when he remarked that "the times as yet not serving for such assemblies, the Kings pardon being not yet published, which was granted, as they say, unto all the Romane Catholickes" (F2^r–F2^v).[62]

Munday's method of instruction and argumentation relied on reader awareness. The Catholic perspective was not carried by any statement that Munday added in his own voice, but by the proximity to each other of certain kinds of information – in regard to this section on Blackfriars, the rehearsal of historical precedents that showed the pre-Henrician authority on which practices rested. Munday then clinched this argument by inserting the contemporary example of the Fatall Vesper. Munday followed the same system elsewhere in his revisions of *The Survey*, revisions that included three additional beliefs and practices that foregrounded the historical authority of the Roman Catholic Church: the practice of tithing, the right of the church to its property, and the right to provide sanctuary – rights and authorities that had been abrogated by Henry VIII and Edward VI in their dismantling of church buildings and elimination of ceremonies, and by later laws.[63]

Sir Henry Spelman (ca. 1564–1641), the antiquarian to whom Munday often referred, was writing extensively during this period on the importance of tithes and the protection of church property, citing not papal authority but the Bible, ancient church fathers, and church councils. In

De non temerandis ecclesiis: Of the Rights and Respects Due unto the Church (1616; STC 23067.6), Spelman had explained that these rights are "contained under the name of a Rectory or Parsonage," which is a "*Spirituall living*, composed of *Land, Tythe,* and other *Oblations* of the people" (B1ᵛ). Further, "the ordinary living or revenew of a Parsonage, is of 3 sorts: the one in Land, commonly called the Glebe: another in Tithe, which is a set and regular part of our goods rendered to God: the third, in other offrings and oblations bestowed vpon God and his Church, by the people" (B2ᵛ). When Munday recorded the extensive church rebuilding, he commented frequently that the rebuilding had been paid for "at the cost of the parishioners," an indication of their devotion to the local parish church and to the preservation of its property.

On the matter of tithes, there existed strong support for the practice in various papal bulls. Recognizing the tension in any reliance on papal authority, both John Selden (1584–1654), the historian of English law, and Richard Montague (1577–1641), a clerical supporter of Archbishop Laud, objected to the use of papal bulls to make this case, arguing that the precedents set by temporal courts carried the needed authority.[64] Without acknowledging these opinions, Munday inserted pre-Henrician documents that represented the primacy of Roman ecclesiastical authority on the topic of the responsibility for the financial support of the church. In the section titled "Customes and Orders," the material on tithes is presented under the prominent subsection title "The Copy of the Bull for the Offerings to the Curates of the parishes of the City of London … Chap. Lxxxvi," with the following documents printed next: "The Copy of the Bull of Pope Nicholas for the same matter," "The Letters of Innocent Bishop," and "Thomas Archbishop of Canterbury, Primate of England to the Mayer, Sheriffes, Aldermen, and Citizens of London." Becket's instructions are unambiguous: "Almighty God … commaundithe that tenthis sholde be given him," a rule to be applied to "every persone dweller and inhabitant in any houses in London, or suburbis of the same" (Sss2ʳ). Becket (1118–70) had made the further point that the authority to require the payment of tithes resided in the church, a jurisdiction that no temporal authority might contravene.

Citing Thomas Becket on the matter of church-state authorities had a certain boldness to it. Murdered by the servants of Henry II in 1170 for challenging the king's authority, Becket had subsequently been discredited in 1538 by way of a proclamation of Henry VIII that denounced him "as a maintainer of the enormities of the Bishop of Rome, and a rebel against the King," declaring that "he was no longer to be esteemed as a saint, and his images and pictures were to be 'put down and avoided out of all churches, chapels and other places.'"[65] Munday was aware of this order, as he noted when, at a different point in *The Survey*, he explained that the seal of the Bridgehouse had been changed as a result of a proclamation of Henry VIII ordering the removal of the names of the pope and of Thomas Becket from all books and monuments, "which is the reason that you shall see them so blotted out, in all old Chronicles, Legends, Primers, and Service bookes printed before those times" (Kkkk4ᵛ).⁶⁶ In earlier decades, Munday had translated the story of Palmerin's discovering that many of the tombs in a London chapel had been spoiled, and that Eutropa's policies had resulted in knights having to disguise their identities. Working on a new edition of *The Survey*, Munday now pulled back the veil and, writing more directly, told his London readers to look around them for evidence of what had been blotted from their daily view of their own historical record.

Munday was also precise on the matter of the church's immemorial right to give sanctuary. This right, long disputed by City and Crown for the protection it gave to those who had committed crimes, had endured despite numerous challenges. As Sir John Baker (ca. 1489–1558) explained, sanctuary was available to any within the bounds of a sanctified place, including excommunicates, bigamists, and heretics, even, for some time, someone guilty of treason: "The protection extended to the whole of the sanctified area of church and cemetery, including the steeple, and it was held sufficient to place any part of the body within the sanctuary or merely to grasp the door-ring."⁶⁷ As I.D. Thornley emphasized, "sanctuary … was a very tough privilege which survived more than one legal abolition."⁶⁸ The difficulty in eliminating the privilege was due both to the state struggle to achieve authority over the church, and persistent community support for sanctuary in the face of "the severity of royal law" and the "untrustworthiness of lawyers."⁶⁹ In the reign of Henry VIII, eliminating this right was linked to the goal of establishing the king's ecclesiastical supremacy,⁷⁰ but even Henry, who did eliminate sanctuary for treason, did not abolish sanctuary. Instead, his regime "introduced a system of eight national sanctuaries, to which alone a refugee for stipulated causes might flee."⁷¹ One of these was Westminster, which included St Martin's le Grand in Aldersgate Ward, the sanctuary particularly at issue for Stow and Munday.

Stow had defended sanctuary by citing an incident from the time of Henry VI (1422–61) in relation to claims of sanctuary at St Martin's le Grand that the City had disputed. Before 1503, St Martin's had been governed by the canons of the College of St Martin, but had then been "absorbed into the lands attached to Westminster Abbey and ruled by the abbot."⁷² Bolstering Stow's defence, Munday expanded Stow's section by three folio pages devoted to presenting the eleven articles of Henry VI on the City's violation of sanctuary (Ff2ʳ–Ff3ᵛ).

Munday returned to the issue again for the final section of *The Survey*, "The Remaines," where a decorated headpiece and separate heading – "Additions out of severall Charters of Kings, &c. concerning the ancient Liberties, bounds and privileges, of Saint Martins le Grand in Aldersgate Ward" – call attention to the topic. Here, he added articles and charters from across the centuries, including from William the Conqueror, Henry III, Edward II, Henry VI, Henry VII, and even Sir Henry Spelman, whom Munday named "the learnedest Antiquary of our nation, yea … of all Europe" (Iiii1ʳ–2ᵛ). Not finished, next he placed another three-folio section, "A Declaration of William, Abbot of the Monastery of St. Peter of Westminster, concerning his title to the Privilege and Sanctuary St. Martins le grand" (Iiii2ᵛ–3ᵛ). This addition names the kings, from William the Conqueror to Henry VII, who had confirmed the bounds of St. Martin's sanctuary "for Debt, treason, and Felony" (Iiii3ʳ). Finally, Munday inserted a full folio page, the details of which had been explained by the abbot (Iiii3ᵛ), devoted to the plat outlining the boundaries for sanctuary in St Martin's, including the placement of boundary posts.⁷³ In the centre of that page, Munday put these words: "All the Bounds and Limits about this Plat mentioned, beene contained in the Abbots claime: and is well proved to be good Sanctuary, by divers Witnesses sworne in the Chancery, as well Freemen of the City, as other credible persons" (Iiii4ʳ). As relentless as he had been on the subject of tithes, here again Munday maintained this foregrounding of pre-Henrician Catholic ecclesiastical precedential authority, this time in regard to sanctuary and the right of the church to control its property.

There are 939 pages in the 1633 *Survey*. The section on St Martin's ends on page 923. In the pages that remain, Munday devoted three pages to "the founding of Trinity Church within Aldgate, and of the beginning of the Canons Regular, and Augustine Fryers," material that returns to the topic of the church's right to its property. Indicating that this section was to be inserted "in page 145," a page in the section on Aldgate Ward, Munday identified King Henry I's wife Maud as the founder of Trinity Church. He recorded that some of the lands that King Henry I had given to the church had been "encroached" by the constables of the Tower of London, but that King Stephen, who had also given lands, had declared that the "Church and Canons shall … forever possesse the said lands, acquitted from all secular exaction." Queen Maud had also confirmed the church "to be free and acquitted from all subjection" (Kkkk2ᵛ). Early in the volume, at "page 145," where Stow's section proper on Aldgate

Ward had begun, Stow had provided a briefer narration of the queen's gift to the church. After a pause to insert a list of monuments, Stow had then turned to what had happened to Trinity Church under Henry VIII, action identified in the margin as "surrendered and suppressed." Henry VIII had given the church to Sir Thomas Audley, speaker of Parliament, who then had it dismantled piece by piece – "stones, timber, lead, iron" – so that he could build a house in that place (O1^v). In writing an addition to the history of this church that focused solely on the right of the church to its property, Munday illustrated once more what was at stake. The church rights had been established and protected by successive kings and a queen, and the actions of Henry VIII had violated those rights.

Munday's 1633 revisions of *The Survey* pose various problems of interpretation. We do not know how Munday shared the work with Henry Dyson, his Protestant collaborator. A statement by "C.I." in the address "To the Reader" suggests some tension existed between them, "whether out of difference in Judgement, or want of Information, I dispute not" (A5^r). Munday practised highly controlled writing. His routine omission of sentences that would explicitly explain the purpose of his having included one or another historical topic or detail kept his intention out of focus, without erasing the aggressiveness of his tactics. This style suited well the practices of censorship during the 1620s and 1630s. As Anthony Milton has noted, "apparent challenges to prevailing orthodoxies were legion, but were seldom picked out for regulation unless they were in direct, explicit, and self-conscious conflict with an orthodoxy, or with government policy."[74] It is difficult to estimate whether or to what extent Laudian policies may have influenced Munday's decisions, even given him a sense of greater freedom at a time when Laudian innovations could be thought by some to smack of popery.[75] The policies of King Charles toward Catholics in combination with the Catholic court of Henrietta Maria made anti-popery less acceptable.[76] In Munday's many references to the pre-Henrician church of Roman Catholicism, he referred repeatedly to what he understood as the "unity of the Christian Church," the "unity of Christendom."[77] He may have harboured the notion that England would one day return to Catholicism. More immediate would have been the concern that Catholicism be recognized as fully within the "unity of Christendom," with toleration, the right to worship, and freedom from persecution available to its English adherents. Munday's history writing in *A Briefe Chronicle of the Successe of Times* and in the revisions of *The Survey of London*, in combination with his several chivalric romances, made that argument. These works offered his English readers a pan-European perspective that authorized the Catholic world that Henry VIII and Elizabeth had dismissed, but that James and Charles had not.

NOTES

1 For Munday's vast network of writers, printers, poets, dramatists, members of the nobility, and city officials, see Tracy Hill, *Anthony Munday and Civic Culture: Theatre, History and Power in Early Modern London, 1580–1633* (Manchester: Manchester University Press, 2004); Donna B. Hamilton, *Anthony Munday and the Catholics, 1560–1633* (Aldershot, UK: Ashgate, 2005); Louise Wilson, "'I marvell who the diuell is his Printer': Fictions of Book Production in Anthony Munday's and Henry Chettle's Paratexts," in *The Book Trade in Early Modern England: Practices, Perceptions, Connections*, ed. John Hinks and Victoria Gardner (London: Oak Knoll Press and the British Library, 2014), 1–17; and the chapter by Elizabeth Evenden-Kenyon, in this volume. Helen Moore commented on Munday's expertise as a translator: "There is no justification for the vilification that Munday's translations have received in the past" (*Amadis de Gaule, Translated by Anthony Munday*, ed. Helen Moore [Aldershot, UK: Ashgate, 2004], xxv).

2 Alexandra Walsham, "The Parochial Roots of Laudianism Revisited: Catholics, Anti-Calvinists and 'Parish Anglicans' in Early Stuart England," *Journal of Ecclesiastical History* 49, no. 4 (1998): 621. See also Walsham, *Church Papists: Catholicism, Conformity and Confessional Polemic in Early Modern England* (Woodbridge, UK: Boydell Press for the Royal Historical Society, 1993); Michael C. Questier, *Conversion, Politics and Religion in England, 1580–1625* (Cambridge: Cambridge University Press, 1996); Alison Shell, *Catholicism, Controversy and the English Literary Imagination, 1558–1660* (Cambridge: Cambridge University Press, 1999); Arthur F. Marotti, *Catholicism and Anti-Catholicism in Early Modern English Texts* (New York: St Martin's Press, 1999); Katy Gibbons, "'When he was in France he was a Papist and when he was in England ... he was a Protestant': Negotiating Religious Identities in the Later Sixteenth Century," in *Getting Along? Religious Identities and Confessional Relations in Early Modern England: Essays in Honour of Professor W.J. Sheils*, ed. Nadine Lewycky and Adam Morton (Farnham, UK: Ashgate, 2012), 169–84.

3 Andrew Hadfield, *Lying in Early Modern English Culture: From the Oath of Supremacy to the Oath of Allegiance* (Oxford: Oxford University Press, 2017), 1–2.

4 For a chronological list of Munday's publications, see Hamilton, *Anthony Munday and the Catholics*, 199–206.

5 This preservationist argument is a feature in ibid., xvi–xix. On the use of history for polemic, see Felicity Heal, "Appropriating History: Catholic and Protestant Polemics and the National Past," in *The Uses of History in Early Modern England*, ed. Paulina Kewes (San Marino, CA: Huntington Library, 2006), 105–28.

6 On toleration and community, see Michael C. Questier, *Catholicism and Community in Early Modern England: Politics, Aristocratic Patronage and Religion, c. 1550–1640* (Cambridge: Cambridge University Press, 2006); W.J. Shiels, "'Getting on' and 'Getting along' in Parish and Town: Catholics and Their Neighbors in England," in *Catholic Communities in Protestant States: Britain and the Netherlands, c. 1570–1720*, ed. Benjamin Kaplan et al. (Manchester: Manchester University Press 2009), 67–83; Lewycky and Morton, "Introduction," in *Getting Along?*; Alexandra Walsham, "Supping with Satan's Disciples: Spiritual and Secular Sociability in Post-Reformation England," in ibid., 30–55; Gibbons, "'When he was in France.'"

7 I have also discussed *Palmerin of England* in *Anthony Munday and the Catholics*, 36, 80–6, 95–8; in "Anthony Munday's Translations of Iberian Chivalric Romances," in *Catholic Culture in Early Modern England*, ed. Ronald Corthell et al. (Notre Dame: University of Notre Dame Press, 2007), 303. See also "Palmerin of England," in *La difusión impresa de los libros de caballerías castellanos en Inglaterra, 1578–1700*, ed. Jordi Sanchez-Marti (Salamanca: Ediciones Universidad de Salamanca, forthcoming), chapter 11.

8 Arber, II, 383.

9 See the chapter by Elizabeth Evenden-Kenyon in this volume. For an important discussion of the range and means of censorship in this period, see also Simona Munari, "Translation, Re-Writing and Censorship during the Counter-Reformation," in *Translation and the Book Trade in Early Modern Europe*, ed. Jose María Pérez Fernández and Edward Wilson-Lee (Cambridge: Cambridge University Press, 2014), 185–200.

10 See Hamilton, *Anthony Munday and the Catholics*, xx.

11 While no copies of this first printing are extant, we can be quite certain the printing went forward. In 1585, Thomas Marsh recorded that among the books he had sold to Edward Wingfield, Esquire of Kimbolton Castle in Huntingdonshire, was "'Palmeryng,' [sic], 2 parts, 2s. 4d" (Henry R. Plomer, "Some Elizabethan Book Sales," *The Library*, ser. 3 vol. 7, no. 28 (October 1916): 328). Gerald R. Hayes, "Anthony Munday's Romances of Chivalry," *The Library*, ser. 4, vol. 6, no. 1 (June 1925): 57–81, 59). I am grateful to Jordi Sánchez-Martí for this reference. In 1593, Wingfield was a member of Parliament and would later be one of the four incorporators of the London Virginia Company in the Virginia Charter of 1606.

12 In 1616, *Palmerin* was again reprinted and for the first time including both Part 1 and Part 2. Part 1 repeated the paratextual material from the 1609 edition. In Part 2, Munday's dedication recalled how Alfonsus, King of Naples, seeking to recover his health, requested that he hear the deeds of Alexander the Great as told by Quintus Curtius, a Roman historian. Associating the romance with history and citing Aristotle, Munday declared that "History is the Schoolemistresse of Princes, and the onelie Trumpet that soundeth in the eares of all noble personages" (A3^v).

13 Questier, "Loyalty, Religion and State Power in Early Modern England: English Romanism and the Jacobean Oath of Allegiance," *Historical Journal* 40, no. 2 (1997): 320; Andrew Hadfield, *Lying in Early Modern English Culture: From the Oath of Supremacy to the Oath of Allegiance* (Oxford: Oxford University Press, 2017), 92.

14 Questier, "Loyalty, Religion and State Power," 320.

15 For a bibliography, see Peter Milward, *Religious Controversies of the Jacobean Age: A Survey of Printed Sources* (Lincoln: University of Nebraska Press, 1978), 86–119; W.B. Patterson, *King James VI and I and the Reunion of Christendom* (Cambridge: Cambridge University Press, 1997), 75–123; Hamilton, *Shakespeare and the Politics of Protestant England* (Lexington: University of Kentucky Press, 1992), 131–7.

16 Cardwell, *Documentary Annals of the Reformed Church of England* (Oxford: Oxford University Press, 1844), 2: 160–1.

17 See Hamilton, *Shakespeare and the Politics of Protestant England*, 134.

18 Patterson, *King James VI*, 122.

19 Evenden-Kenyon, in this volume. See also Brian Lockey, *Early Modern Catholics, Royalists, and Cosmopolitans: English Transnationalism and the Christian Commonwealth* (Farnham, UK: Ashgate, 2015).

20 Questier, "Loyalty, Religion and State Power," 323, also citing Clarence J. Ryan, "The Jacobean Oath of Allegiance and English Lay Catholics,' *Catholic Historical Review* 28, no. 2 (1942): 171. For records of recusancy and refusing the Oath of Allegiance, see *London Sessions Records, 1605–1685*, ed. Hugh Bowler (London: John Whitehead & Son for the Catholic Record Society, 1934), xxxvi–xlv, 1–100.

21 Ryan, "The Jacobean Oath," 177.

22 For this range, see Patterson, *King James VI*, 101n; Ryan, "The Jacobean Oath," 161.

23 Hugh Tootell, *Dodd's Church History of England from the Commencement of the Sixteenth Century to the Revolution in 1688* (London: C. Dolman, 1839–43), 4: 179–80.

24 Questier, "Loyalty, Religion and State Power," 324; Hamilton, *Anthony Munday and the Catholics*, 159.

25 Tootell, *Dodd's Church History*, 4: 179n.

26 See especially Questier, "Catholic Loyalism in Early Stuart England," *English Historical Review* 123, no. 504 (2008): 1138–43.

27 Ibid., 1143.

28 Ibid., 1147–50, 1153.

29 Ibid., 1155–6.

30 Questier, "Loyalty, Religion and State Power," 317.

31 Leticia Álvarez-Recio, "Translations of Spanish Chivalry Works in the Jacobean Book Trade: Shelton's *Don Quixote* in the Light of Anthony Munday's Publications," *Renaissance Studies* 33, no. 5 (2019): 707; Hamilton, *Anthony Munday and the Catholics*, 98–104.

32 Hamilton, *Anthony Munday and the Catholics*, 98–104.

33 Hill, *Anthony Munday and Civic Culture*, 144–6. This characteristic suggests that Munday was writing in part with an eye toward securing the commission to revise Stow's *Survey*. In the dedication to his 1618 edition of *The Survey*, Munday mentions that Montagu had reviewed *A Briefe Chronicle* along with his proposal for a revision of *The Survey*.

34 For a fuller account of these episodes, see Hamilton, *Anthony Munday and the Catholics*, 91–2. See also Álvarez-Recio's chapter in the present volume.

35 Patterson, *King James VI*, 81.

36 For a different but related reading of this material, see Lockey, *Early Modern Catholics*, 130.

37 See Questier, "Catholic Loyalism," 1139–40, 1164.

38 See Hamilton, *Anthony Munday and the Catholics*, 97–105. For recusant interest in chivalric romance, see Helen Cooper, *The English Romance in Time: Transforming Motifs from Geoffrey of Monmouth to the Death of Shakespeare* (Oxford: Oxford University Press, 2004), 38.

39 In 1589, John Wolfe's permission to print *Amadis*, Books 2–5, specified that the bishops reserved the right to look at "every of the iiii French bookes severally for alowance of the printinge thereof in English." See Hamilton, *Anthony Munday and the Catholics*, 93.

40 Hamilton, *Anthony Munday and the Catholics*, 98.

41 Ibid., 99–102.

42 Ibid., 99.

43 Ibid.; for Catholic details in *Palmendos*, see 92. For the network of printers interested in Spanish books, see Álvarez-Recio, "Translations of Spanish Chivalry Works," 16–17.

44 For the relationship between Munday's *A Briefe Chronicle* and his revisions of Stow's *Survey* (1618), see Helen Moore, "Succeeding Stow: Anthony Munday and the 1618 Survey of London," in *John Stow and the Making of the English Past: Studies in Early Modern Culture and the History of the Book*, ed. Ian Gadd and Alexandra Gillespie (London: British Library, 2004), 99–108.

45 Hamilton, *Anthony Munday and the Catholics*, 171.

46 Patrick Collinson, "John Stow and Nostalgic Antiquarianism," in *Imagining Early Modern London: Perceptions and Portrayals of the City from Stow to Strype, 1598–1720*, ed. J.F. Merritt (Cambridge: Cambridge University Press, 2001), 47.

47 Merritt argued that Munday's insertions of Protestant charity make Stow's text Protestant. See "The Reshaping of Stow's 'Survey': Munday, Strype, and the Protestant City," in Merritt, *Imagining Early Modern London*, 59.

48 See Hamilton, *Anthony Munday and the Catholics*, 172–3.

49 For these examples, see ibid., 173.

50 Ibid., 98–104; Álvarez-Recio, "'Translations of Spanish Chivalry Works," 16.

51 See Merritt, "Reshaping of Stow's 'Survey'"; Kenneth Fincham and Nicholas Tyacke, *Altars Restored: The Changing Face of English Religious Worship, 1547–c.1700* (Oxford: Oxford University Press, 2007); Hamilton, *Anthony Munday and the Catholics*, 181–3.

52 David Womersley, "Against the Teleology of Technique," in Kewes, *The Uses of History*, 102, 104.

53 Fincham and Tyacke, *Altars Restored*, 137.

54 Merritt, "Reshaping of Stow's 'Survey'," 59.

55 See Thomas Cogswell, *The Blessed Revolution: English Politics and the Coming of War, 1621–1624* (Cambridge: Cambridge University Press, 1989), 36–53, 285–301.

56 James F. Larkin and Paul L. Hughes, eds., *Stuart Royal Proclamations: Royal Proclamations of King James I, 1603–1625* (Oxford: Clarendon Press, 1973), 591–3, 599–600.

57 Michael C. Questier, "Introduction," in *Stuart Dynastic Policy and Religious Politics, 1621–1625*, ed. Questier (Cambridge: Cambridge University Press for the Royal Historical Society, 2009), 113.

58 Hamilton, *Anthony Munday and the Catholics*, 76–9.

59 See Christopher Highley, "Theatre, Church, and Neighborhood in the Early Modern Blackfriars," in *The Oxford Handbook of the Age of Shakespeare*, ed. Malcolm Smuts (Oxford: Oxford University Press, 2016), 616–32; Hamilton, *Anthony Munday and the Catholics*, 186.

60 Alexandra Walsham, "'The Fatall Vesper': Providentialism and Anti-Popery in Late Jacobean London," *Past and Present* 144 (1994): 36–87.

61 Arthur Freeman, "*The Fatal Vesper* and *The Doleful Evensong*: Claim-Jumping in 1623," *The Library*, 5th series, 22 (1967): 135, 129–30.

62 For the 1624–25 struggle to reach a point where Catholics might be assured toleration, see Questier, "Introduction," 72–114; and Questier, *Catholicism and Community*, 409–25. Questier refers to the disagreements about whether or not to make public any new leniency for Catholics.

63 See Eamon Duffy, *The Stripping of the Altars: Traditional Religion in England c. 1400–c. 1580* (New Haven, CT: Yale University Press, 1992).

64 Selden, *The Historie of Tithes* (1618), Ggg3^{r-v}; Montague, *Diatribae upon the First Part of the Late History of Tithes* (1621; STC 18037), G2^r, G5^r.

65 Duffy, *Stripping of the Altars*, 412.

66 For other examples, see Hamilton, *Anthony Munday and the Catholics*, 182–3.

67 John Baker, "Sanctuary and Abjuration," in *The Oxford History of the Laws of England, VI (1483–1558)*, ed. John Baker (Oxford: Oxford University Press, 2003), 541; Shannon McSheffrey, "Sanctuary and the Legal Topography of Pre-Reformation London," *Law and History Review* 27, no. 3 (2009): 483.

68 I.D. Thornley, "The Destruction of Sanctuary," in *Tudor Studies*, ed. R.W. Seton-Watson (London: Longmans, Green, 1924), 204n116.

69 Gervase Rosser, "Sanctuary and Social Negotiation in Medieval England," in *The Cloister and the World: Essays in Medieval History in Honour of Barbara Harvey*, ed. John Blair and Brian Golding (Oxford: Clarendon Press, 1996), 76. For the effectiveness of community support, of "neighborliness," see Shiels, "'Getting on'"; Lewycky and Morton, "Introduction"; Walsham, "Supping with Satan's Disciples"; Gibbons, "'When he was in France.'"

70 Thornley, "Destruction of Sanctuary," 203–5.

71 Rosser, "Sanctuary and Social Negotiation," 76–7.

72 McSheffrey, "Sanctuary and the Legal Topography," 484.

73 This folio page has been reproduced in Hamilton, *Anthony Munday and the Catholics*, 187. However, an error occurred in recording the accompanying citation. The folio page is incorrectly identified as originating in the 1618 edition of *The Survey*. This plat occurs only in the 1633 edition, a detail that underscores Munday's work on sanctuary for the later edition.

74 Anthony Milton, "Licensing, Censorship, and Religious Orthodoxy in Early Stuart England," *Historical Journal* 41, no. 3 (1998): 632. See also Sheila Lambert, "Richard Montagu, Arminianism and Censorship," *Past and Present* 124 (August 1989): 36–68.

75 See Anthony Milton, *Catholic and Reformed: The Roman and Protestant Churches in English Protestant Thought, 1600–1640* (Cambridge: Cambridge University Press, 1995), 85–7.

76 Ibid., 645–6.

77 For emphasis on the unity of Christendom, see Hamilton, *Anthony Munday and the Catholics*, 86–8, 175. Lockey, *Early Modern Catholics*, 8, also concluded that Munday's works "can be read as" aligning with "those Catholic exiles who sought to reintegrate the English realm into the transnational Christian commonwealth."

PART FOUR

The Impact of Iberian Chivalric Romance on English Prose Fiction

Chapter Nine

Iberian Chivalric Romance and the Formation of Fiction in Early Modern England

GORAN STANIVUKOVIC

In his book *The Man Who Invented Fiction: How Cervantes Ushered in the Modern World*, William Egginton argues that the publication of the first part of Miguel de Cervantes's *Don Quixote* in the winter of 1605 (IB B9296) represented a watershed moment "in a time of economic decline and political stagnation" in Golden Age Spain. The major shift, Egginton proposes, was a result of the rhetorical force of the "language of fiction" to weave irony into the narrative of sensations and connections, "without ever giving up the knowledge that we are, in fact, elsewhere," in the world of imagination.[1] The power of expression in Cervantes's fiction that produced and defied wonderment by exposing romance conventions to mockery and by using irony to subvert the conventions in turn, transformed the tone and narrative directions of his fiction and of romance as a literary type. Romance, which in the medieval period promoted the heroic ideal, became in Cervantes's writing a kind of fiction that humorously played with the heroic tone and narrative. Cervantes's refusal not only to imitate and imaginatively recreate the classics in his fiction but also to secularize, or at least moderate, the fictional world of his eponymous hero makes his work a peculiarly modern kind of romance. (This refusal should be distinguished from his occasional and isolated reference to a classical figure, which was an integral part of early modern writing style and literary aesthetics.) This element of Cervantes's fictional praxis shaped the modernity of his novel.[2] The modernity of *Don Quixote* is produced by its author's creation of a self-conscious distance between the fictional medium and the literary and cultural world imagined in fiction, in the comic transformation of romance conventions, and in the main hero's ironic take on chivalric actions. The long "debates" on commonplace matters in the novel are a further aspect of this modernity, and David Quint associates them with "a movement [of the setting of Cervantes's fiction] from an earlier feudal social formation to the modern, money-driven society of Cervantes's age."[3] And, so, Cervantes's fiction ushered modernity into the writing of romance in the early modern period through several doors. When *Don Quixote* was published, other Iberian chivalric romances were also moving romance fiction toward the modernity of self-reflective and self-regarding narrative expression. In this shift, the romances that I address here did not evince the same tenor as Cervantes's fiction, but they shared with *Don Quixote*, as Cervantes acknowledges, the same place in the literary history of fiction, not just late medieval and Renaissance Iberian chivalric fiction, which his romance transforms by leaving them behind.[4]

Don Quixote did not reimagine the writing of romance only at home, in Spanish literary culture, but it did so, and almost immediately upon its publication in Madrid in 1605, in England as well. A copy of the 1605 edition in the Bodleian Library, as Leticia Álvarez-Recio has argued recently, "bears witness to a long-standing interest in Spanish culture and literature, especially within courtly circles," in England.[5] This transnational traffic of romance fiction suggests further that Cervantes's fiction imbued new energy into the trade of romance fictions on the Jacobean book market, shedding new light, especially, on the role Anthony Munday played in expanding and shaping the marketplace of romance in print and in English translation.[6] The English book market of Iberian romances was not only vibrant and saturated by the printing of Spanish books, as Gustav Ungerer's research showed some time ago,[7] but the preponderance of the Iberian romance in the English market meant that the idea of romance was shaped largely by the availability of Iberian romances ready for printing and for sale.

This chapter shows how the availability of Iberian chivalric romances in English translation shaped the modernity of fiction writing more generally by balancing heroic and romantic material – that is, by shifting narrative focus from the exteriority of militant chivalry to the interiority of protagonists and their emotional lives. Building on the scholarship documenting the role Spanish books played in the writing of romance in England, this chapter focuses on *Amadis de Gaule*, an Iberian chivalric romance that looms large over the English romance in the early modern period, and that is also invoked in modern literature as a signifying tool. Indeed, D.H. Lawrence refers to *Amadis* when he speculates about the meaning of male folklore rituals in a veiled attempt to understand their implication for masculinity, which evidently drew his attention as he describes them in his travelogue *Sea and Sardinia* (1921).[8] Lawrence's book modifies the genre of travel writing by interweaving travel narrative with fictional writing, and by resorting to the language of fiction and of romance writing when the literary expression of realist explanation does not give him the meanings he searches for – or chooses not to search for. In such moments, for example, chivalric Amadis offers a hiding place for alluring masculinity, for Lawrence to admire young Sardinian men and their pseudo-heroic comportment in Sardinian folk dance. The literary afterlife of the figure of Amadis thus resonates long after the Renaissance and crops up in unfrequented places that evoke a wander-land through which Amadis moves in fiction – as Sardinia appeared to Lawrence.

In her critical edition of *Amadis de Gaule*, as the series of the nine books of this Iberian romance began to be known in English translation and in print, Helen Moore has argued that the "earliest reputation" of *Amadis* was associated with these books as "an exemplar of fine speaking and loving." This element of *Amadis* must have inspired its main English translator, Anthony Munday, to contribute to the narrative, which came to him from French, "his treatment of sexual encounters" and, as Moore states, to add "details which specify London, the Thames and the Tower of London."[9] While the amplified rhetoric of amorous exchanges and, especially, erotic passion puts emphasis on language and thoughts about interiority and intimacy, the topical references to London act as a vehicle for bringing the narrative of a foreign romance closer to the reading experience of the English reader. Long passages of prose depicting interiority and eroticism are an index of a change that literary romance underwent in Elizabethan England. The anachronism, improbability, implausibility, and wonder that imbue romance narrative became associated with the heroic quest of a chivalric hero and presented as narrative bridges between progressively longer sections depicting sensitive, and elaborate, explorations of love and erotic desire upon which romance increasingly focused. The evocative vitality and energy of such descriptions of interiority became a new way of engaging with the chivalric past, history, and royal discourse in Elizabethan England; a shift from heroic to romantic concerns became pronounced as patriotism started to be forged less on the battlefield and more within the royal court.[10] Romance, as a literary genre, then becomes more alive for its contemporary readers not as an imaginative account of battles and heroic victories (usually enabled by miracles) but as a model for emotional and sexual conduct of men and women alike. Consideration of the role that *Amadis* and other Iberian romances, like those from the *Palmerin* and *Mirrour of Knightood* cycles, played in the formation of the new fictions of interiority in the late Elizabethan period and during the Jacobean era has often been secondary to critical assessments of royalist, textual, gendered, and materialist readings. In their neo-chivalric narratives, Iberian romances, read in French by the educated or in English by all social classes – as Rocío G. Sumillera explains in her chapter in this volume – provided ways of expressing interiority as modernity of a literary character. They support John O'Connor's point that "*Amadís* and other [Iberian chivalric] romances offered not only national but a personal ideal."[11] The representation of interiority in these books' connection with humanist ideas about selfhood and virtue still calls for critical interpretation.

Don Quixote, Iberian Chivalric Romance, and *Amadis* in England

News of the publication of the neo-romance *Don Quixote*, which treated an old subject and narrative mode in a refreshingly ironic way, travelled quickly beyond the Iberian Peninsula. Seven years after its publication in Spain, Part One of *Don Quixote* was first translated into English, appearing in print in England in 1612. The book was translated from Spanish by Thomas Shelton (fl. 1598–1629) and entitled *The History of the Valorous and Wittie Knight-errant, Don-Quichote of the Mancha* (STC 4915). Some years later, in 1654, Edmund Gayton's (1608–66) *Pleasant Notes upon Don Quixote* became more than a translation. As Alex Davis has argued, Gayton's book was "the first English commentary on Cervantes – possibly the first anywhere in Europe." This volume, "rather than directly celebrating the talents of the Spanish author," Davis writes, "aim[s] to construct a cultural bridge to … [its] subject matter out of the material provided by native dramatic productions of some twenty or thirty years earlier" – productions of Jacobean and Caroline drama.[12] By the time *Don Quixote* ushered modernity into romance fiction across Europe, *Amadis*, another romance of transnational literary significance and appeal, had already paved the way towards the modernity of romance writing.

Shortly before the publication of *Don Quixote*, *Amadis* had already demonstrated how effectively modern imaginary fiction could violate verisimilitude and create pleasure, and how providing readers with probable narratives depicting situations that were examples of moral virtue and of actions that violated such virtue could make romance a fiction for exemplary agency.[13] *Amadis* is explicit in its refusal to make wonder the central motif of the chivalric narrative; instead, it makes reasoning or human agency the main vehicle for attempted resolutions within. This refusal is apparent in Book Two, chapter 2, in which the narrative depicts a woman who is keen to know whether "Amadis will go to the Firme-Island, to behold such strange and marvellous things as there are to be seene," and who introduces herself to Amadis as "the daughter of him that is Governor thereof." Amadis refuses: "I have oftentimes heard of the wonders of this Island, and I should account my selfe happy if I might proove then as I desire, but I repent that I adventured them no sooner."[14] His refusal is a story-telling strategy that mitigates the role of the marvellous when used against introspective self-exploration in credible situations that weigh existential options.

Amadis came to England by way of France, and individual books of it were translated from French by Anthony Munday, who, as various chapters in this volume have shown, was a prolific writer across different genres and a translator displaying Catholic sympathies, which may have attracted him to romances sometimes associated with Catholicism in post-Reformation England.[15] The earliest surviving edition of the known text of *Amadis*, by Garci Rodríguez de Montalvo, printed in Saragossa in 1508 (IB 16414), entered English reading culture by way of Nicholas de Herberay des Essarts's French translations of Books One to Eight, printed between 1540 and 1548 (FB 651–766), which educated English readers could read in French, and Thomas Paynell's selection from Herberay's translation (c. 1572; STC 545). The popularity of *Amadis* culminated in England with Munday's translation, providing readers of all social classes and both genders with the narrative models for exploring interiority, and also enhancing the erotic and the sensual within passages full of rhetorical flourish, as Moore has argued.[16]

Munday's translation was a publishing success, both in literary and commercial terms, judged by the four parts in which it was printed between 1590 and 1619 (STC 541–4). This success rests partly on Munday's fluent translation of an already translated text, a process in which Munday's text reads as an adaptation of the Spanish and Portuguese original text, as the endnotes in Moore's critical edition of *Amadis* explain. The success of Munday's translation also lies in the fact that he occasionally engaged in the process of new creation: while translating, he was also "producing [romance]" – a new romance, that is – as Joshua Phillips has proposed. Phillips further suggests that Munday's work as a translator ought to be regarded also as a work of a writer who fended off the disenchantment with the idea of "reforming romance" at a time when the genre was frequently attacked.[17] Moreover, Munday's work on *Amadis* was not only a labour of a translator-writer but also of a mediator between national literatures, languages, and cultures, spanning the Mediterranean and northwest Europe. The impression that *Amadis* left on different writers in different cultures and circumstances could not be discounted. Warren Boutcher, for example, has demonstrated that *Amadis* found its way into a document of a diplomatic dispute "concerning the textual interpretation of some remarks and some literary allusions."[18] Yet the process of this cross-linguistic mediation, which, as Phillips appreciates, was also a process of genre creation, balances the primacy of the familiar narrative of the Crusades and chivalric battles fought by knights from different Christian lands with lengthy introspective self-exploration of both men and women as romantic and sexual partners. In this new romance writing, the distant, the wondrous, and the chivalric juxtapose with the passionate, the erotic, and the emotional; at the same time, formulaic tableaux and descriptions of battles and chivalric clashes give room to depictions of sensuous and psychological explorations of interiority. Given such approaches, romance captures the attention of its readers with fictions that are closer to questions raised, and debates unfolding, in a culture that scrutinized love, the body, sex, fidelity, temperance and intemperance, and sexual violence with growing depth and intensity. With this movement toward the intimate, fiction started to read like a new kind of writing about private concerns, as well as politics, under the imaginative influence of romances that came from outside England.

The changing emphasis on romantic narrative and love, as opposed to chivalric rituals, battles, and heroic agency,[19] is a crucial transformation that romance as a literary type underwent in the early modern period. In the late medieval period, the genre of romance was associated as much with secular ideals of courtship as with the combined secular and religious underpinnings of chivalry and the Crusades that had provided its cultural background. Thus, in the early modern period, romance became increasingly tied to ideals different from that of knighthood, and to a broad audience, from nobility to commoners. In a culture in which knighthood was revived as an idealized story of the past at a time of growing Elizabethan nationalism, romance flourished as well as a kind of imaginary literature in which various secular ideals of the new Protestant society rooted in the Calvinist belief in an individual's responsibility for one's agency were reflected in romance narratives: the individual's choice of a mate, proto-imperial expansion of territories for trade, political and military overpowering of the Islamic foe in the eastern Mediterranean, the quest of youth (especially that of the younger son) for their own place and role in society after leaving the paternal household, erotic satisfaction, and woman's control of her amorous and erotic agency. Such themes illustrate that romance became a literary space of intellectual vibrancy and an exploration of interiority, often using the rhetorical strategies of deliberation characteristic of the humanist practice of crafting argument and exemplary stories.

As Donna Hamilton has stated, Iberian chivalric romances like *Amadis* "were being placed in dialogue with their Protestant counterpart."

Translations of such works by Munday and by Margaret Tyler "were regarded suspiciously for religious and political reasons."[20] Nonetheless, such romances shaped the English tradition of romance writing at the turn of the century and expanded the Anglo-European book trade. When European book production shifted from Venice to expanding centres for the printing and selling of (foreign) books in the northwest Europe, Louise Wilson claims, "Iberian romances were certainly beneficiaries of this increased confidence, which was partnered with new economic models of production and distribution in the French market."[21] England benefited from this expansion in book production and in the transcultural circulation of Iberian romance in translation and original, largely because of Munday's and Tyler's print translations of Iberian chivalric romances.[22] By contributing to the abundance of such material in the book market, Munday's and Tyler's translations also augmented and solidified the cultural impact that Munday's translations and his own work on romance writing was already having. Between 1588 and 1619, "at least twenty-three editions of [*Amadis* and *Palmerin*] romances" appeared in print, "making them a bestseller of early modern fiction,"[23] asserts Wilson. These translations by Munday and Tyler were published in cheap black-letter print quarto format, which made them both available and affordable. Such popular literature targeted both common and noble readers.

The *Amadis* volumes printed in England were illustrated only occasionally: they were hardly the handsome volumes produced in folio format in France. The English *Amadis* books also did not have the same linguistic impact on the language and style of literary prose written in England as the *Amadis* romance cycle had in France, where individual romances were regarded "as a prime vehicle for displaying the beauty of the French language by humanists occupied with the status of the literary vernacular."[24] However, English translations of Spanish chivalric romances, printed both before and at the time of the publication of the first English translation of *Don Quixote*, played a key role in redrawing the map of English imaginary fiction and the print and book trade in post-Reformation England. *Amadis* was instrumental in shaping both the narrative strategies and the content of romance writing in the sixteenth and seventeenth centuries, giving early English fictional writing a distinctive place in the formation of the post-Reformation modernity of fiction writing in England. Although *Amadis* and other Iberian chivalric romances look back in time, to the period of the first Christian Crusades and only occasionally invoke the classicism of antiquity – as when the narrator in *Amadis* observes features of "a high wall of black-marble, Dorick Colomnes of white marble,"[25] which evokes a Greek temple – the narrative of these romances is oriented toward the future, as the narrative produces ways for the protagonists to overcome obstacle and seek reward for their emotional effort, not just because of their heroic deeds.

This past and the future dimension of time in romances contributed to critics' reluctance to accept them. At the time of the growing renewal of chivalry as an ideal in romance literature and in the social practice of the Elizabethan Accession Day tilts, Roger Ascham (1514/15–68), once a tutor to the young Elizabeth, enjoyed the chivalric pageantry during her progresses in the country, yet he vehemently attacked romances for their "open mans slaughter and bold bawdrye: In which booke those be counted the noblest Knightes, that do kill the most men without any quarrel, and commit fowlest aduoulteres by sutlest shiftes."[26] Ascham wrote this in *The Scholemaster*, first published in 1570 and reprinted in 1589. Literary critics have often used this pronouncement as an argument to illustrate the period's frequent hostility toward romances, largely on moral grounds. Yet Ascham's attack on the romance as a kind of writing is part of his anxious hostility toward Catholic – or, as he writes, "Papist" – writing of the Reformation more broadly. Ascham labels papist writing "lewd," and he identifies it explicitly with an Italian rather than Spanish influence on the native tongue.[27] He does not target English translations of continental romances but channels his criticism at early medieval romance writing in England, at works like *"Morte Arthur"* and *"Syr Laucelote … Syr Tristram … [and] Syr Lamerocke."*[28]

Yet both despite and because of this literary and cultural climate of animosity toward romances, *Amadis* thrived in the book market, found its readers, and offered narrative models for the popularization of chivalry and, with such models, a new way of scrutinizing, understanding, and representing interiority and heroic action. For all its narrative infused with the wonders characteristic of the old romances of the medieval past, the neo-chivalric episodes based on a narrative in which probable and circumstantial chains of events challenge marvels associated with the old romance writing, *Amadis*, and the newly written romances it influenced, was a work of post-Reformation modernity and of the selfhood that was fashioned in that writing. *Amadis* became a model for a new kind of fiction that suited the romantic spirit of neo-chivalric discourses in which emphasis was on the self, love, and seduction, more than on chivalry and heroic combat.

Don Quixote, Amadis, and Diana

The proliferation of the newly translated books of *Amadis* contributed to the popularization of chivalric romance in England, as critics have already argued.[29] Yet the effect that *Amadis* had on the formation of English romance fiction and the English humanist idiom in fiction was not an isolated instance of the absorption of Iberian chivalric romance into English literary history. In 1596, Thomas Wilson translated *Diana de Monte Mayor* (1559; IB 13239), a romance written by Jorge de Montemayor (1520–61).[30] The translation was reprinted in 1598 (STC 18044), and there are numerous extant copies of this edition in libraries in Britain, on the Continent, and in North America, Australia, and New Zealand.[31] The 1598 reprint of Wilson's translation is exactly contemporaneous with Bartholomew Yong's translation.[32] The high survival rate of Wilson's reprint is a sign of the abundance of this book in the print market and confirms *Diana*'s popularity and influence in the sixteenth century. In 1617, Wilson made a manuscript copy of Yong's translation, which is now in the British Library.[33] In the short prefatory dedication in this copy to the poet and dramatist Fulke Greville, later Lord Brooke, Wilson admits that "it may be said of mee that I shewe my vanities enough in this title, that after 15 yeares painfully spent in universitie studies, I should bestow soe many ydle howres in translating vaine amorous conceipts out of an Exotique language," concluding that his was "chyldish exercises" and "toyees."[34] Spanish was hardly an exotic language from the perspective of the English, despite the political tension between England and Spain at that time. But it appeared so symbolically – and as an alien language (and in that sense beyond the familiar), especially in the context of romance writing and cultural transmission – because of its association with Catholicism. This perception of the Spanish language denigrated the status of romance as a literary genre. Wilson's text is a testimony to the ambivalent repute of Spanish romances in England, as influential and familiar as well as foreign and immoral. The language of vanity and idleness, which Wilson uses to describe the labour of the translator, echoes the vocabulary that writers and translators often employed to describe their work in rendering foreign romance into English, or, in the case of writers, of authoring new romances.

The history of Wilson's translation of *Diana* provides evidence that, despite their association with Catholicism and sensuality, Iberian romances found their way into the households of Reformation England, as texts avidly read by women, despite the fear that such texts were sources of moral impropriety.[35] One example of marginalia in the 1617 manuscript asserts that "patience overcometh all things," written by one of the readers through whose hands this manuscript book passed. The signatures of women as readers, which appear in the same copy, include Dorothy Greuell (Greville),[36] Mary Arron, Elizabeth Denbigh ("wife of Basil Fielding, 2nd Earl of Denbigh, 1703"), Katarine Astuly, and Anne Bourgchier. The book was also given as a gift to "the virtuous good Lady the Lady margaret [*sic*] Hambleton my very good Lady." And, to spice up the experience of reading this manuscript, a contemporary hand, dated 1643, wrote a recipe for almond and pistachio cake on the blank page after the romance, as if aligning the two activities of the everyday, reading and baking, with women's domestic labour. The long history of the 1617 manuscript book, which connected women as readers across at least one century, not only confirms what scholars have already documented – that romance was staple reading for women[37] – but affirms the fact that *Diana* paved the way for transmitting the literary and cultural value of the Spanish romance into the literary culture and the literary canon of romance fiction in early modern England. Furthermore, the role that this romance played in documenting women as readers of fiction completes the connection between *Don Quixote*, *Amadis*, and *Diana*, and highlights the influence these prose works exerted on the narrative of interiority and on the ideas about subjectivity in early fiction.[38] These three texts exist in an intertextual relationship with one another, and their cross-referencing confirms their literary and trans-cultural interconnectedness.

The ubiquity of *Amadis* and *Diana* on the print market and their wide circulation among early modern readers became one of the causes of Cervantes's parody of romance as a literary genre. In the well-known episode of book burning in *Don Quixote*, the novel's eponymous hero does not spare many romances from vanishing in the fire but saves *Amadis* and *Diana*. Yet, only parts of *Diana* are spared the flames, largely because the story of Christians crushing the Moors – illustrated by the episode of Abindaraz, a Moor taken by the Constable of Antequara, Roderick Naruaez – would have appealed to Cervantes's readers eager to see such a victory. This episode is narrated in chapter 5 in the 1612 translation of *Don Quixote* by Thomas Shelton.[39] As he is listing arguments for preserving the kind of books that were easily dismissed and threatened by the Puritans, Don Quixote says, "since we begin with the *Diana of Montemayor*, I am of opinion that it be not burned, but only that all that which treates of the wife of *Felicia*, and of the inchanted water be taken away, and also all the longer verses, and let him remaine with his prose, and the honour of being the best of that kind."[40] The burning of *Diana* and the selection of the parts of it to be preserved are critical acts, a commentary on the popularity of this popular fiction. By selecting what needs to be preserved and what eliminated from *Diana* in his act of literary purging, Don Quixote clears the literary scene for the arrival of his romance; he paves the way for a new manner of narrating romantic love, or for parodying it even more conspicuously than his fiction does, and, finally, for privileging love poetry over chivalric prose fiction. The emphasis on the amorous over the chivalric is a clear sign where priorities in this neo-chivalric fiction lie, and it shows how a kind of literary prose bent flexibly under the pleasant weight of love poetry that flourished across the vast plain of Renaissance love-writing. Neither *Diana* nor other romances that it influenced were purged of the longer verses and love poems. On the contrary, love poems embedded at almost regular frequency within prose became a staple of composing romance, before and after *Diana*.[41] Don Quixote's irony, evident in retaining only the heroic adventures that appear more entertaining than awe inspiring, is part of the modernity of Cervantes's novel as an anti-romance.

In his critical scrutiny of the world of romance writing, Cervantes's knight-errant does not stop at *Diana*. When in, chapter 6, he decides to preserve both "The Aduentures of Splandian Amadis of Gaules" (D3ʳ) and, as the Curate in his story adds, also the story of "Amadis of Greece" (D4ʳ), the expansive story of the Palmerin figure doubles the role *Diana* plays as a piece of literature worth saving because it offers instruction. Not only is *Amadis* saved from disappearance, but Don Quixote declares: "let *Palmerin of England* be preserued"[42] and reiterates that "*Amadis de Gaule* may be preserued from the fire."[43] Saving *Amadis* from the fire means preserving its literary legacy as a text, as a book, and as a literary signifier – or as "a certain brand of writing,"[44] which is a parody of romance heroism and amorous pursuit. In the preliminary pages in Shelton's translation, among "Certaine sonnets," the reader will also find a sonnet "Amadis of Gaule in Praise of Don Quixote." In chapter 5, another sonnet, this time by the squires accompanying the two knights will have a whole chapter, and a heading, "Amadis of Gaules Squire, Sanco Panca, Don-Quixote Squire,"[45] reflecting on the adventures of Don Quixote and his page. The romance stories of *Amadis de Gaule* and of Montemayor's *Diana* are, therefore, narratively embroidered upon in the fiction of *Don Quixote*. The self-conscious referencing of these stories by the narrator in Cervantes's novel and in different narrative scenarios and episodes underscores Cervantes's debt to the romance tradition, which he in turn wishes to leave behind in his novel. This referencing confirms that the modernity of his romance depends on the readers' expectation of romance conventions to provide entertainment and moral enlightenment, as well as on overturning such conventions, as a gesture of narrative modernity of romance writing, where a writer signals a self-conscious distance from the making of his own art, leading his readers to attempt the same. In a way, then, what romance as a mode of writing exerted on a diverse and multifarious literary production in centuries after the Renaissance, to the point that romance became an unavoidable inspiration for new writing across literary genres, not just fiction – a process that Patricia Parker has called the "inescapable romance"[46] – was a mode of writing in which love, adventure, heroism, gender, the wondrous, and the circumstantial narrative are shaped by the cultural memory of a neo-chivalric past and provide the narrative opportunity to examine that past.[47] *Don Quixote*, *Diana*, and *Amadis* are connected not merely by their roots in Iberian literary tradition but, more importantly, by their significance as constitutive texts that expanded meaning in romance writing in England.

Amadis and the Fiction of Interiority

In his trenchant study of early modern romance as a humanist genre, a kind of text in which humanist pedagogy becomes "a peculiar way to study the enterprise" of learning as a poetics of literary writing, Jeff Dolven employs the term "habitus" to "capture a form of life from the inside."[48] As a route toward an exploration of interiority understood as a life enhanced by learning, habitus in romance encompasses "scenes of instruction" conducted by "the poet-as-teacher" and "representational conventions" by which those scenes create a grid for this humanist goal.[49] This is a complex and original take on how romance works. As a form of life unfolding from within, then, habitus is transported and developed further in the English euphuistic fictions written by John Lyly. Habitus also describes the neo-chivalric romances of the 1590s, such as the prose fiction of Philip Sidney – the *Old* and *New Arcadia* – and Edmund Spenser's romance epic in verse, *The Faerie Queene*. However, understood broadly as a way of experiencing, living, and articulating selfhood in fiction, against the background of the humanist emulation of the classical ideas of virtue that underpin it, habitus can be said also to capture the counter-humanist yet prevalent current in romance narrative, one in which subjectivity and interiority express what Cicero calls *corporis voluptatem* ("sensual pleasure," 1.30.106) in the treatise *On Duties* (*De officiis*) in a lengthy analysis of the idea of one's own nature (*propria natura*, 1.30.110).[50] Cicero's text was foundational in the formulation of the neoclassical moral philosophy in the Renaissance and for crafting ideas about character, love, intimacy, and friendship, as well as conceptualizing the heroic roles of duty and justice. These Ciceronian currents of thought infused romance narratives and coded discourses of interiority within romance. They made romance not merely a genre of the past revived in the early modern period to serve the Elizabethan nationalism and, later, emerging Jacobean internationalism, but also a genre of modern fiction that questions the world outside romance by circumspectly engaging with one within romance.

In sixteenth- and seventeenth-century literature, selfhood and emotions were expressed in discourses of faith and love. The meeting point of this contact lay between freedom and what Michael Schoenfeldt has described as "a fear of emotion that resembles our own fear of repression."[51] The focus of Schoenfeldt's criticism is poetry, but his idea is useful for an analysis of fiction too. Yet, when Amadis tells Oriana, the woman he is courting, that "Love is sicknesse, and be it favourable or contrary, it cannot be without passion, working the like affect in other, which you reprove in me,"[52] romance fiction resonates with the same sentiment that charges selfhood with emotion; the character not only renders into the lovers' dialogue the Renaissance idea of love as sickness but also transforms the Ciceronian notion of ethical duty of a character into amorous agency that romance narrates in love episodes interlaced with heroic ones. Read against the background of *On Duties*, *Amadis* comes across as an anti-Ciceronian text written from within Ciceronian literary culture. Amadis echoes the period's belief that love is a form of sickness, causing a state of disorientation and producing melancholy. But his words also balance a lover's abjection with the necessity of desire that creates such a state. In the life- and eros-affirming power that passion is given in Amadis's formulation, the reader could see how romance was imbued with a new take on the familiar trope – love as sickness – and how the fiction that revealed itself before the reader's eyes was a fiction in which love was a source of power. In the episodes in which the narrative of chivalric heroic agency gives way to the story of "sensual pleasure," which, Cicero says, "is quite unworthy of the dignity of man and [something] that we ought to despise ... and cast ... from us"[53] – because pleasure so conceived takes away from the pursuit of duty and the propriety of a character rooted in reason – *Amadis* promotes emotion over knowledge and reason. *Amadis* reveals habitus embodied in emotion, not knowledge or reason. At the same time as it reimagines rather than embodies or emulates Ciceronianism, *Amadis* draws on the spirit of the Ciceronian text in so far as the narrative favouring the pursuit of the heroic ideal makes heroism the basis of the knight's virtue, together with loyalty and friendship, and with social and ethical ideals that romance promotes. In this regard, the re-envisaged Ciceronian ideals intersect with the cultural value of romance as a transhistorical genre. In other words, the private self that unfolds from within the subject in *Amadis* opens itself both to pleasing other characters (often a courted lady) and to encouraging the reader of Iberian romance to think of the self as a concept shaped by narrative circumstances. Those features of romance that enabled a model of habitus as an intimate, private, and interior way of "activating"[54] romantic and private selfhood that is different from heroic agency are the most authentic features of *Amadis*, emerging from the original, Iberian text and from Munday's intervention in it.

Barbara Fuchs has identified many "markers of identity"[55] in the two parts of *Don Quixote*, arguing more implicitly, and in a methodologically different way, than Egginton, that Cervantes's romance charted a new way of expressing identity. Yet, the scenes of sensual pleasure in *Amadis*, which gave Cervantes the cause to mock Don Quixote's heroic comportment and his ways of courtship, and out of which Don Quixote's identity as an anti-chivalric and anti-romantic knight emerges, are also the scenes that give *Amadis* narrative energy and conviction. Those moments in *Amadis* reduce the distance between the past in which scenes of interiority are narrated and the experience of reading romance in the present for the early modern reader.

Criticism of early modern literature has largely explored the ideas of selfhood and interiority in poetry, drama, and theatre, assessing embodiment and analysing the social practice of friendship and its literary representations and discourses.[56] While prose romance has offered material for an exploration of gender, it has rarely been interpreted as a source of ideas about early modern subjectivity, largely because romance protagonists are considered stock types rather than individually developed literary characters.[57] In the critical quest for ideas about interiority and selfhood, in a culture in which, as Katharine Eiseman Maus has stated, "truth is imagined to be inward and invisible,"[58] interiority produced in romance narrative is as available and rich as that in stage drama. Iberian chivalric romances in both French and English translations, especially, became popular not only because their stories travelled across the frontiers of chivalric culture in continental Europe and England, but also because the narratives of individual agency would have appealed to a variety of readers living and reading at a time that put emphasis on agency, emotions, and responsibility, as was the case in Calvinist England. *Amadis* engages not with the man and woman fallen in the garden, but with protagonists that struggle to act in the tempting early modern romance pastoral, a mode influenced by Edmund Spenser's *Shepheardes Calender* of 1579.[59]

A scene of courtship from *Amadis* illustrates the growing concern with the language and narrative depicting emotion and interiority within chivalric romance. In Book One, in the twenty-third chapter, the "wise and discreete" Mabila directs Amadis to sit between her and

Oriana. Mabila has "devised ... to bring the lovers [Amadis and Oriana] together ... to contend with their thoughts with secret communication."[60] Safely seated between the two women,

> Now beginneth Amadis to confer with his Ladie, and thinking to declare the great affection, which under good hope gave him life and essence: extreme love took from him and facultie of speech, yet his eyes not unmindful of their office, supplied the defect to his tongue, delivering testimony to their divine object, how farre the sad and languishing heart was transported by ease and pleasure. Which Oriana perceiving, she secretly tooke his hand under her mantle, and stringing him by the fingers sighing thus spake. My lord and friend, what dolour and griefe did the traytor procure in me, who brought hither tidings of your death? Never was poore maiden in greater peril, and not without cause: for never did woman sustain such a losse, as I should have done in loosing you. And as I am better loved then any other, so hath my fortune graciously favoured mee, that it should be by him who is of higher desert then any other. Herewith Amadis cast downe his looks as bashful to heare himself so praised, by her to whom all commendation was due.[61]

This passage demonstrates more than how the text uses the humility *topos* to narrate courtship. The narrator relates how emotion is exchanged and what its effect is on the lovers; the narrative emphasizes the transformation of the loving subject under the pleasant influence of an exchange of emotions, and captures the effect of being "unmindful" (*OED*, "indifferent," "heedless") at a moment of ease and pleasure. The effect of the narrative rhetoric is to lead the reader to contemplate what "life and essence" mean at a moment of "good hope." The passage has a didactic goal. At this point, *Amadis* gives the reader an opportunity to contemplate romance "as a way of thinking ... about what it meant to be created human in an age that had abandoned the established schemes of Roman Catholic doctrine."[62] In the process of this temporal, cultural, and religious negotiation of romance narrative between the past and the present, between the old Catholic faith and the newly reformed Catholic religion and ideology, which are moments in which romance exists as a literary text, *Amadis* offers a possibility for equalizing male and female romantic identity. Such an identity is subject both to emotional transformation of what "life" and the "essence" of it mean, and to how personal agency and consciousness are shaped in the narrative of a neo-chivalric world.

Out of this narrative background dominated by recounting chivalric affairs, another aspect of romance interrupts such public concern of

Amadis. Nandini Das has identified this aspect of romance as "youthful ambition," by which she means both a personal and public force associated with "youthful excess" of such ambitious youth.[63] This excess captures the sense of romance's affective anti-Ciceronianism. What Cicero refers to as the unworthiness of "sensual pleasure" is just what the narrative of *Amadis* presents as a moment worth waiting for.[64] In moments like this, *Amadis* gives the early modern humanist pedagogue a good reason to reject *Amadis*. To the early modern reader of *Amadis*, however, episodes that capture youthful excess as details in an erotic narrative would have appeared as opportunities to reinvent sexual intimacy in response and contrast to the renunciation of sexual desire in the old church doctrine in England. The modernity of *Amadis* also lies in providing such moments of pleasurable excess, moments in which the intimate, pleasurable, and affective privilege the narrative subject as an emotional type, pointing toward a creation of a literary character rather than a stock type.

Alone with his beloved Oriana, Amadis's "hands had been slow in unarming him, all his other members were in better state, for not one of them but did his duty." The narrator then proceeds to develop this erotic scene into an episode of soft pornography:

> [Amadis's] heart was ravished in thoughts, the eye, in contemplation of excellent beauty, the mouth, with sweete kisses, the armes, with kinde embracings: and no one mal content in any point, except the eyes, which wished themselves in number like the stares in heaven, for their better ability in function, thinking they could not sufficiently beholde so divine an object. In great paine were they likewise, because they were hindered from the pride of beauty, for the Princesse held her eyes closed, as well to disguise her desire of sleepe, as also for the discreet shame conceived by this pleasure, so that shee durst not boldly looke on him she must love. Hereupon, carelessly spreding her armes abroad, as though she slept in deed, and by reason of the exceeding heate, leaving her gorget open, two little alabaster bowles lively shewed themselves in her bosome, so faire and sweetly respiring, as Nature never shewed more curous workman-shippe. Now Amadis forgetting his former bashfulnesse, seeing Fortune allowed him to quaint a favour, let loose the reines of amorous desire with such advantage, as notwithstanding some weak resistance of the Princesse, she was enforced to proove the good and bad together, which maketh friendly maidens become faire women.[65]

This is the kind of "bawdrye" episode that provoked Ascham to voice his hostility against romance. Reacting to the relentless emphasis on chivalric combat and violence, which is a different kind of youthful excess, the narrative of *Amadis* indulges in a competing narrative strategy of excess. The narrator imagines the effect of emotional and sexual pleasure on the physical and cognitive reaction of the subject. This episode makes the knight both a bashful lover disarmed by the prospect of sexual satisfaction and a social agent who transforms a bashful woman from a maiden into a willing "fair woman" in a story of dynastic aspiration and achievement. The narrative strategy, which turns a woman into a man's object of pleasure, is both a sign of a literary love convention within the narrative of heteroerotic fantasy and a marker of the misogyny of such a narrative. An episode of soft pornography like this one might have been a marketing ploy to help the sale of romance. Yet a modern reader may find something revealingly Freudian in this account, in which the role the eye plays in the zone of pleasure, and in the narrated strategy of a visual foreplay, contributes to thinking of the erotic conquest as complementary to the heroic conquest.[66] This episode shows that in *Amadis* and other romances on which this Iberian romance left a strong imprint – like Emanuel Ford's *Ornatus and Artesia* (ca. 1599; STC 11168), a romance that brims with similar episodes – sexuality is not the Freudian "weak spot"[67] but a moment of unbridled energy of youthful excess. For the Elizabethan subject as a lover, embodied in Amadis, erotic experience expressed in detail and alongside the narrative of public achievement meant both recognizing and recording the openness of romance to sexual fantasy, which is both physical and cognitive. When the narrator concludes this episode of sexual maturity by giving voice to Oriana's thoughts – "Ah, how many repetitions made Oriana, of the paines she suffered in expectations of this day? Confessing those private particularities, which none but she and her desire were acquainted withal"[68] – the reader of *Amadis* is invited to contemplate subjectivity as depending upon a relationship between thinking and experience. The romance offers an example of thinking about selfhood as existing between a range of possibilities arising from fantasies and expressing the probability of re-living those fantasies in action.

The relationship between narrative and agency is explicitly addressed in another Iberian romance available in English translation, *The Second Part of the First Booke of the Myrrour of Knighthood* (1599; STC 18863). The translator's initials, "R.P." may stand for Robert Parry (active 1540–1612), the author of *Moderatus, the Most Delectable Historie of the Blacke Knight* (1595; STC 19337), a prose romance modelled on the Iberian chivalric romance from the *Myrrour of knighthood* (*Espejo de príncipes y caballeros*), a work of prose fiction written "prior to 1545" by Diego Ortúñez de

Calahorra and published in 1555, and translated by Margaret Tyler (fl. 1558–78).[69] This fiction, "now newly translated into our vulgar tongue,"[70] as the title page declares, is one of many romances in which the narrative of chivalry is presented also as the narrative of moral conduct. In romance narratives, "All ... records of Chiualrie tending to animate others vnto imitating the like, and being as a spur to instigate and prick vs [readers] forwards vnto prowess."[71] This suggests that translations of Iberian romances were understood to instil moral virtue in the recipient English culture. Not only does a translation of a foreign romance keep the text, which otherwise would "bee idle and lie in obscurity,"[72] alive in another language and in literary memory, but it is meant "to encourage dastards and to teach the readie minded what excellencie is in puissant and inuincible minds, passing common judgment" rather than "feede the reader with an untruth."[73] That romance can influence the reader's actions as well tells the modern critic that the early modern period placed significant emphasis on the instrumental function of such early fiction.

The main protagonist of Iberian romances never ceases to reflect upon and analyse his actions. Not being able to sleep is a state that often gives Amadis the space for self-examination. On one such occasion, "unable to sleep, his [Amadis's] thoughts laboured continually, how he might recover the credit he had lost: concluding with himself to runne a contrary bias, to the rash speeches rumored out against him."[74] The meaning implied by the metaphor "to runne a contrary bias," deriving from the game of bowls, as Moore explains, "is that Amadis will behave in a manner contrary to that expected of him by those who have set the rumours abroad."[75] The psychological and cognitive weighing of one's actions and assessing them against real threats in concrete situations turns sleeplessness into a state in which thinking and feeling transform the sleepless knight into a resolute man. In other words, the concern of romance as a genre at this point is with exploring consciousness and psychological effects of the subject's turning toward itself, not outwardly toward the pattern of actions in traditional romance narratives. Moments of such "psychological refinement"[76] are not rare in romances, as Erich Auerbach notes; he found them aplenty in French late-medieval romances. As the genre developed across time, and the aesthetics and ethics of the late Elizabethan age shaped the fictions and story-telling strategies of neo-chivalric romance, such moments became rhetorically amplified. In *Amadis*, such instances accommodate the breath of thought that goes with the eloquence; and they turn the stock figure of the knight into a thinking, sensitive, and reasoning protagonist who, unlike Don Quixote, does not use irony to dismiss agency but engages in self-analysis.

In his list of nine "certain characteristic differences between the novel and romance," Leonard J. Davis enumerates the familiar structural and thematic elements that are common to all romances and that distinguish them from the eighteenth-century novel.[77] However, psychological and cognitive authenticity characterizing the voice of the hero's inner thoughts is not on that list. Yet psychological self-awareness and the articulation of one's inner self are some of the features that shaped the eighteenth-century novel in the early phase of its development when the link with romance was still close. For the narrator of *Amadis*, moreover, this element missing from Davis's list becomes the foundation of new fiction. Iberian chivalric romances, including *Amadis*, did not invent interiority as a place from which a literary character emerges as something more than a stock figure. However, by giving rhetorical and narrative space to interiority, Iberian romances, including *Amadis*, contributed significantly to the constitution of literary culture in the English Reformation as an antithesis to confessional poetry, of which Fulke Greville's (1554–1628) poems of inwardness in the collection *Caelica* (1633; STC 12361) are a good example.[78] When, early in Munday's translation of *Amadis*, the narrator comments on the effect of desire on agency, it would not have escaped the attentive early modern reader that this fiction puts passion in tension with faith. In moments like this, the narrator formulates a new kind of agency and interiority for Oriana and Mabila. "If it seeme to the Reader," says the narrator, that their purpose was not according to affection but simply in response to their vehement passions:

> I answer, that they ought to excuse their age, likewise it often commeth passe, that they which thinke themselves most expert in those pleasing and amorous actions, have beene by this God so strongly bound, and lively attainted: as not only he deprived them of speech, but of judgment also, and it is necessary for such persons to use greater words, then these two who as yet had not learned them. But this new Knight being thoroughly furnished and ready to this journey by his Ladies consent: would in thanking the company, take a more secret conge of Oriana … Then rehearse he all that King Languines had told him, wherein she conceived very great pleasure: which done, they committed each other to God.[79]

The "new Knight" is reformed by the experience and exchange of love and desire, and the transformation of his selfhood has been limited by faith, showing that desire is governed by emotions but that knowledge is controlled and bound by God. The emotional extremes of youth give rise to "amorous actions," but, when one wants to employ reasonable judgment to make sense of one's passionate agency, one requires God's intervention and a new language; one needs "greater words" that come with knowledge. At this point in the narrative, *Amadis* challenges the idea that "the self is a region of limits rather than freedom," in the words of Brian Cummings from his exploration of the self in relation to reason and the knowledge of divinity.[80] But selfhood imagined as bound by God does not place the idea of individual agency and interiority outside the bounds of romance, a literary genre full of the excesses of youth, brimming with high emotions, and indulging in display of unabashed eroticism. Rather, testing the relationship between individual agency and emotions, and exploring the knowledge of faith that governs individual morality (and against the social background of royalist literature), *Amadis* takes its interlaced chivalric narrative closer to the modernity of the novel, a literary genre that will emerge fully in the eighteenth century.

The many roles the Iberian chivalric romance played in the process of the formation of a new fiction genre that transforms old narrative and stylistic formulas shows that critics still grapple to describe the resilient and capacious literary form of romance as modern literature in the making within the growing body of vernacular northwestern European literature. Ever since *Don Quixote* saved it from the flames, *Amadis* has captivated the literary imagination of the early modern fiction that came after, and out of, it, as its themes were reworked in other romance fictions written across the long period of early modernity.

NOTES

1 William Egginton, *The Man Who Invented Fiction: How Cervantes Ushered in the Modern World* (London: Bloomsbury, 2016), xv–xvi.
2 Behind this thinking lies Ivan Jablonka's discussion of how Cervantes become "a certain brand of writing" in the early modern period by creating fictional characters that are different from the ones shaped in imitations of the ancients. Jablonka, *History Is a Contemporary Literature*, trans. Nathan J. Bracher (Ithaca, NY: Cornell University Press, 2018), 29.
3 David Quint, *Cervantes's Novel of Modern Times: A New Reading of* Don Quijote (Princeton, NJ: Princeton University Press, 2003), 8.
4 The exploits of fictional Christian knights that Cervantes parodies in *Don Quixote* are a literary version of early fictions of the Crusades, which flourished in early modern Spanish literature, as compellingly explored in detailed in David A. Wacks, *Medieval Iberian Crusade Fiction and the Mediterranean World* (Toronto: University of Toronto Press, 2019).

5 Leticia Álvarez-Recio, "Translations of Spanish Chivalry Works in the Jacobean Book Trade: Shelton's *Don Quixote* in the Light of Anthony Munday's Publications," *Renaissance Studies* 33, no. 5 (2019): 691.

6 The centrality of Munday to the shaping of the English literary culture of romance writing influenced by the Iberian models is further, and importantly, documented in Álvarez-Recio's detailed analysis of the role Spanish chivalric romances played in the culture of translation of chivalric fiction in late Elizabethan and Jacobean England. See Leticia Álvarez-Recio, "Spanish Chivalric Romances in English Translation: Anthony Munday's *Palmendos* (1589)," *Cahiers Élisabéhains* 91, no. 1 (2016): 5–20.

7 Gustav Ungerer, "The Printing of Spanish Books in Elizabethan England," *Library*, 5th series, 20, no. 3 (1965): 177–229.

8 D.H. Lawrence, *Sea and Sardinia* (New York: Thomas Seltzer, 1921). Lawrence and his wife, Frieda, travelled in Sardinia in January 1921. References to *Amadis* and romance writing generally are largely responsible for critical thinking about how Lawrence bends the genre of travel writing in this book.

9 *Amadis de Gaule. Translated by Anthony Munday*, ed. Helen Moore (Aldershot, UK: Ashgate, 2004), xix.

10 Jablonka focuses on the epic as a literary form on which he tests his argument about a shift in heroic writing that took place in the early modern period. His idea in this regard is flexible enough to encompass other forms of the literary writing of history on which he elaborates in his book. See *History Is a Contemporary Literature*, 38.

11 John O'Connor, *Amadis de Gaule and Its Influence on Elizabethan Literature* (New Brunswick, NJ: Rutgers University Press, 1970), 8.

12 Alex Davis, *Chivalry and Romance in the English Renaissance* (Woodbridge, UK: D.S. Brewer, 2003), 99.

13 *Palmerin* romances, sometimes attributed to Francisco de Morais and Luis Hurtago, contributed to the same literary goal.

14 *Amadis*, ed. Moore, 311.

15 On Munday's Catholic sympathies, see the chapters by Donna Hamilton and Elizabeth Evenden-Kenyon in this collection.

16 *Amadis*, ed. Moore, xxv.

17 Joshua Phillips, "Chronicles of Wasted Time: Anthony Munday, Tudor Romance, and Literary Labor," *English Literary History* 73 (2006): 788.

18 Warren Boutcher, "Vernacular Humanism in the Sixteenth Century," in *The Cambridge Companion to Renaissance Humanism*, ed. Jill Kraye (Cambridge: Cambridge University Press, 1996), 193.

19 I thank the press's readers of this chapter, who suggested expanding this point in the direction I follow in this paragraph.

20 Donna B. Hamilton, *Anthony Munday and the Catholics, 1560–1633* (Aldershot, UK: Ashgate, 2005), 80.

21 Louise Wilson, "The Publication of Iberian Romance in Early Modern Europe," in *Translation and the Book Trade in Early Modern Europe*, ed. José María Pérez Fernández and Edward Wilson-Lee (Cambridge: Cambridge University Press, 2014), 202.

22 The publication of *Amadis* and *Palmerin* romances, and of the books of *Mirrour of Knighthood*, enriched an already extensive range of books in Spanish published in Elizabethan England. For an account of the printing of Spanish books, see Gustav Ungerer, "The Printing of Spanish Books in Elizabethan England," *Library*, 5th Series, 20, no. 3 (1965): 177–229.

23 Wilson, "The Publication," 210.

24 Ibid., 205

25 *Amadis*, ed. Moore, 745.

26 Roger Ascham, *The Scholemaster*, ed. John E.B. Mayor (London: Bell and Daldy; repr. New York: AMS Press, 1967), 81.

27 For more examples, see the introduction to this volume.

28 Ascham, *The Scholemaster*, 81.

29 This influence is explored in detail by O'Connor, *Amadis*, esp. 170–80, and by Mary Patchell, *The "Palmerin" Romances in Elizabethan Prose Fiction* (New York: AMS Press, 1966). The printing of the books of the late fifteenth-century Spanish romance *Cárcel de amor*, popularized in the French translation as *La prison d'amours*, is the subject of Emily C. Francomano, *The Prison of Love: Romance, Translation, and the Book in the Sixteenth Century* (Toronto: University of Toronto Press, 2017).

30 Sir Thomas Wilson (1560?–1629) translated *Diana* from Spanish during his travels in Italy and Germany, after fifteen years of studying civil law at Cambridge, and after, in 1594, a recommendation by Lord Burghley for his election as Fellow of Trinity Hall, Cambridge, failed. As the result of this failure, he turned to travel. Wilson had a connection with Spain, having been a consul there in 1604 until the ambassadors, the Earl of Nottingham and Charles Cornwallis, arrived in 1605. This information is based on Albert Frederick Pollard's entry on Wilson in *Dictionary of National Biography, 1885–1900*, ed. Sidney Lee (London: Elder and Smith, 1900), 136–8.

31 I am grateful to Leticia Álvarez-Recio for directing me to further explore the existence of this copy. The ESTC lists the following libraries where the 1598 copy of *Diana* (STC 18044) can be located. Britain: Cambridge University Library, Trinity College Library, Edinburgh University Library, Bodleian Library, Senate House Library of the University of London, University of Sheffield Library Special Collection, John Rylands Library of the University of Manchester, Special Collection of the University of Bristol Arts and Social Sciences Library; Spain: Universidad Complutense de Madrid; the United States: Bryn Mawr College, Rare Books and Manuscript Library of

Columbia University in New York, Duke University, Houghton Library of Harvard University (two copies), Folger Shakespeare Library (four copies), Henry E. Huntington Library, New York Public Library, Newberry Library of Chicago, University of Chicago, University of Iowa, Charles Patterson Van Polt Dietrich Library of the University of Pennsylvania, Harry Ransom Humanities Research Center of the University of Texas at Austin, and Beinecke Rare Book and Manuscript Library of Yale University (two copies); Canada:McGill University; Australia: Mitchell Collection in the State Library of New South Wales; and New Zealand: Alexander Turnbull Collections in the National Library of New Zealand.

32 I am grateful to one of the external assessors for the suggestion that I situate Yong's translation of *Diana* in the chronology concerning the Wilson manuscript translation of the same work.

33 "Diana de Monte Mayor done out of Spanish by Thomas Wilson," British Library Add.MS. 18,638. The story of *Diana* partially influenced Shakespeare's early comedy *The Two Gentlemen of Verona* (comp. 1588–94). The 1617 copy made by Wilson is the manuscript from which an edition was prepared by H. Thomas and published as *"Diana* de Monte Mayor done out of Spanish by Thomas Wilson (1596)," *Revue hispanique: Recueil consacré à l'étude des langues, des littératures et de l'historie des pays castillans, catalans et portugais* 50, no. 118 (1920): 36–418.

34 "Diana de Monte Mayor" (MS), fol. 5b–6a.

35 María Beatriz Hernández-Pérez explores female readership of romance in her chapter in this collection.

36 Dorothy Greville, who signed the book, seems to have been a daughter of the cousin who inherited the Brooke title, who lived from 1590 to 1650 and did not marry. I owe this information to Lori Humphrey Newcomb.

37 This has been documented by Lori Humphrey Newcomb, *Reading Popular Romance in Early Modern England* (New York: Columbia University Press, 2002); Helen Hackett, *Women and Romance Fiction in the English Renaissance* (Cambridge: Cambridge University Press, 2000); and Caroline Lucas, *Writing for Women: The Example of Woman as Reader in Elizabethan Romance* (Milton Keynes, UK: Open University Press, 1989).

38 Newcomb, *Reading Popular Romance*, provides ample evidence of women as readers of romance, especially on the example of Robert Green's fictions.

39 Cervantes, *History of the Valorous and Wittie Knight-errant, Don Quixote of the Mancha. The First Parte*, trans. Thomas Shelton (London: William Stansby for Ed. Blount and W. Barret, 1612; STC 4915), D1[r].

40 Ibid., chap. 6, D6[r].

41 For instance, Philip Sidney's *Old Arcadia*, written between 1580 and 1582, includes poems that spread over a page or two and appear at almost regular intervals throughout this long prose romance.

42 Cervantes, *History of the Valorous and Wittie Knight-errant*, chap. 6, D3^r.

43 Ibid., chap. 6, D5^r.

44 Jablonka, *History Is a Contemporary Literature*, 29.

45 Cervantes, *History of the Valorous and Wittie Knight-errant*, chap. 5, A5^r.

46 Patricia Parker, *Inescapable Romance: Studies in the Poetics of a Mode* (Princeton, NJ: Princeton University Press, 1979).

47 The essays in *Timely Voices: Romance Writing in English Literature*, ed. Goran Stanivukovic (Montreal and Kingston: McGill-Queen's University Press, 2017), explore transhistorical afterlives of romance from the late Middle Ages to the first half of the twentieth century, in English and Irish literatures, in many new directions.

48 Jeff Dolven, *Scenes of Instruction in Renaissance Romance* (Chicago: University of Chicago Press, 2007), 27.

49 Ibid., 29.

50 Cicero, *De officiis*, trans. Walter Miller (Cambridge, MA: Harvard University Press, 2005).

51 Michael C. Schoenfeldt, *Bodies and Selves in Early Modern England: Physiology and Inwardness in Spenser, Shakespeare, Herbert, and Milton* (Cambridge: Cambridge University Press, 1999), 16.

52 *Amadis*, ed. Moore, 120.

53 Ibid., 1.30.106.

54 My argument here is influenced by Kathy Eden's exploration of Ciceronian stoic philosophy as a discursive model for negotiating intimacy by way of an exchange of humanist discourses, which she explores in her book *The Renaissance Discovery of Intimacy* (Chicago: University of Chicago Press, 2012), esp. 26–30.

55 Barbara Fuchs, *Passing for Spain: Cervantes and the Fictions of Identity* (Urbana: University of Illinois Press, 2003), 7.

56 Francis Barker, *The Tremulous Private Body* (Ann Arbor: University of Michigan Press, 1995), and Jonathan Sawday, *The Body Emblazoned: Dissection and the Human Body in Renaissance Culture* (London: Routledge, 1996). For recent accounts of how selfhood and interiority unfolded through religion, see Ramie Targoff, *Posthumous Love: Eros and the Afterlife in Renaissance England* (Chicago: University of Chicago Press, 2014), and Ronald Huebert, *Privacy in the Age of Shakespeare: Evolving Relationships in a Changing Environment* (Toronto: University of Toronto Press, 2016).

57 See Richard Helgerson, *The Elizabethan Prodigals* (Berkeley: University of California Press, 1976); Constance C. Relihan, *Fashioning Authority: The Development of Elizabethan Novelistic Discourse* (Kent, OH: Kent State University Press, 1994); Relihan, *Cosmographical Glasses: Geographic Discourse, Gender, and Elizabethan Fiction* (Kent, OH: Kent State University Press, 2004); and Relihan, ed. *Framing Elizabethan Fictions: Contemporary*

Approaches to Early Modern Narrative Prose (Kent, OH: Kent State University Press, 1996); and essays in Thomas Keymer, ed., *Prose Fiction in English from the Origins of Print to 1750* (Oxford: Oxford University Press, 2017).

58 Katharine Eiseman Maus, *Inwardness and Theater in the English Renaissance* (Chicago: University of Chicago Press, 1995), 32.

59 Helen Cooper, *Pastoral: Mediaeval into Renaissance* (Ipswich, UK: D.S. Brewer; Totowa, NJ: Rowman and Littlefield, 1977), 115. Cooper says, though, that the influence of Spenser's work "was due less to the fact of innovation than to the fact of tradition" (115). The point here is that the Spenserian pastoral is used as a model and appropriated within its own tradition. But in new writing, the Spenserian pastoral did not change and was not innovated; rather, it is extended and embedded in new texts. Yet, the influence of Spenser and more generally of late medieval pastoral on Renaissance romance has yet to be examined in detail; new results of how it was adapted symbolically would reveal original uses of the pastoral in romance writing.

60 *Amadis*, ed. Moore, 217.

61 Ibid.

62 Helen Cooper, *The English Romance in Time: Transforming Motifs from Geoffrey of Monmouth to the Death of Shakespeare* (Oxford: Oxford University Press, 2004), 7.

63 Nandini Das, *Renaissance Romance: The Transformation of English Prose Fiction, 1570–1620* (Farnham, UK: Ashgate, 2011), 48.

64 Cicero, *On Duties*, trans. Walter Miller (Cambridge, MA: Harvard University Press, 2005), I.xxx.106.

65 *Amadis*, ed. Moore, 252–3.

66 I draw on some of the points, relevant to this episode, which Freud elaborates in several of his essays included in "Three Essays on the Theory of Sexuality," in Sigmund Freud, *On Sexuality*, trans. James Stratchey, ed. Angela Richards (London: Penguin Books, 1991), 222–3. The narrative produced by the pleasure of looking in this instance is different from one of the more familiar literary scenarios in which the eye is represented as the organ that incites love. Robert Burton describes this scenario memorably in *The Anatomy of Melancholy*, published in 1621, where he states that "The eye is a secret orator, the first bawd, *amoris porta* [the gate of love], and with private looks, winking, glances and smiles, as so many dialogues, they make up the match may times and understand one another's meanings before they come speak a word." Quoted from Robert Burton, *The Anatomy of Melancholy*, ed. Holbrook Jackson (New York: NYRB, 2001), 89–90. Burton illustrates his point by invoking the love of Euryalus and Lucretia, the lovers in one of the first epistolary novels, *Historia de duobus amantibus* (The Tale of Two Lovers), written in

1444 by Aeneas Sylvius Piccolomini (1405–65), who became Pope Pius II. Separated, the lovers wrote letters to each other in which they sometimes invoked the eyes and looks to give life to desire that they rendered rhetorically, as when "he asked her good will with his eyes," for which she "gave consent with a pleasant look" (90). But this is a scenario of amorous exchange based on reciprocity, whereas the romance describes an act of ocular ravishment of a sleeping beauty, which is both structurally and ethically a very different, and initially unreciprocal, use of the gaze as an instrument of love.

67 Freud, *On Sexuality*, 61.

68 *Amadis*, ed. Moore, 253.

69 Joyce Boro, "Introduction: 'Thou Have Here, Gentle Reader, The History': Margaret Tyler's *Mirror of Princely Deeds and Knighthood*," in Margaret Tyler, *Mirror of Princely Deeds and Knighthood*, ed. Boro, MHRA Tudor and Stuart Translations, Vol. 1 (London: Modern Humanities Research Association, 2014), 2.

70 *The Second Part of the First Booke of the Myrrour of Knighthood*, now newly translated into our vulgar tongue by R[obert] P[arry], London: Thomas Este, 1599; STC 18863.

71 Ibid., A2^r.

72 Ibid.

73 Ibid., A2^{r-v}.

74 Ibid., 571.

75 Ibid., 986–7.

76 Erich Auerbach, *Mimesis: The Representation of Reality in Western Literature* (Princeton, NJ: Princeton University Press, 2013), 132.

77 Leonard J. Davis, *Factual Fictions: The Origins of the English Novel* (New York: Columbia University Press, 1983), 40.

78 In his book *The Literary Culture of the Reformation: Grammar and Grace* (Oxford: Oxford University Press, 2002), Brian Cummings does not address prose romances, the literary genre that, granted, did not participate as deeply as poetry and drama in establishing the rhetorical and dialectic foundations of that literature. Yet both faith and rhetoric played a part in the transformation of romance as a literary genre as it evolved from forms that were prevalent in medieval feudalism to the fiction flourishing in Reformation England, under the influence of Elizabethan and Jacobean neoclassical humanism.

79 *Amadis*, ed. Moore, 40.

80 Brian Cummings, *Mortal Thoughts: Religion, Secularity and Identity in Shakespeare and Early Modern Culture* (Oxford: Oxford University Press, 2013), 60.

Chapter Ten

La *Celestina* and the Reception
of Spanish Literature in England

HELEN COOPER

A chapter on the *Celestina* of Fernando de Rojas (ca. 1470–1541) might seem out of place in this volume: the work is neither chivalric nor in any normal sense a romance. Far from being set far away and long ago, its action takes place in an urban setting of Rojas's present, or not far removed from it. Yet the first two English versions of it, dating from 1525–30 and 1631, embrace the great age of the early modern reception of Spanish romance in England and have the potential to reveal something about that age. These anglicizations offer in epitome a view of how extensively public taste changed over the century that separated them, changes, moreover, that are, arguably, at least partly due to the influx of Spanish romance itself. The English *Celestinas* offer not only a measure of those changes but epitomize what had become acceptable to an English reading public a hundred years after Rojas's work entered English consciousness.

Rojas's original was first published in its complete form in 1501, but not under the title by which it has become famous. The lengthy title page heads it as *Tragicomedia de Calisto y Melibea*, and adds a generous account of what its readers will find in it, including that it contains "de mas de su agradable & dulce estilo muchas sentencias filosofales: & avisos muy necessarios" (IB 16144). The 1631 translation, by James Mabbe (1572–1642?), renames it *The Spanish Bawd, represented in Celestina* (STC 4911) but then imports Rojas's whole title as its subtitle: *The Tragicke-Comedy of Calisto and Melibea. Wherein is contained, besides the pleasantness and sweetness of the stile, many Philosophicall Sentences, and profitable Instructions necessary for the younger sort: Shewing the deceits and subtilties housed in the bosomes of false servants, and Cunny-catching Bawds.*[1] Both title pages thus provide the names of the work's two lovers, though only Mabbe names Celestina; a generic description of the work as a tragicomedy; a recommendation of the work on grounds of its style; an advertisement for its "sentences" and pithy, wise sayings; and warnings against getting deceived into sin, especially by servants. The primacy Rojas gives to the conjoined names of the lovers, Calisto and Melibea, nonetheless makes it sound like other romances known widely across Europe, such as *Paris and Vienne* or *William and Melior* (the latter being the title given in various of its different language versions to the romance now most often known as *William of Palerne*). Yet Celestina herself is much the most striking character, so it is not surprising that the work became associated with her name. At the same time, the beginning of Mabbe's title, *The Spanish Bawd*, functions as a clear warning to its readers as to what they should, and should not, expect.

Rojas's work was something of a *succès de scandale* – or, at the very least, a *succès* – and its fame spread rapidly around Europe, along with translations into most European languages; an Italian translation appeared in 1506 (Edit16 56102), and in 1624 it was even translated into Latin (USTC reference no. 2135281).[2] The earliest reference to it in England comes from the humanist Vives (1492–1540), in a 1524 treatise he wrote for Catherine of Aragon, advising her on the education of the young Princess Mary, *De Institutione foeminae christianae* (USTC 403719). This work includes a list of books read across Europe that are bad for the young (*pestiferis libris*); here, Rojas's work appears under the title *Celestina* in a list that otherwise entirely comprises romances, including *Tristan, Amadis, Tirant lo Blanc, Lancelot, Paris and Vienne, Melusine,* the *Carcel d'Amor,* among others, plus the *Decameron* of Boccaccio. Celestina is singled out as especially bad: she is "nequitarium parens," the parent of wickedness.[3] The work figures again in Richard Hyrd's (d. 1528) English translation of Vives, which appeared in 1529 (STC 24856), and where the list of condemned romances is increased by a number of other works recently printed in England: *Parthenope, William and Melior,* Arthur (presumably by this date in Malory's version), *Bevis of Hampton,* and so on. Here too *Celestina* is differentiated from the rest by the additional health warning attached specifically to her, that she is "Celestina the baude mother of naughtynes."[4] The association of the work with romance continued throughout the sixteenth century. Francis Meres (1565–1647), in his 1598 *Palladis Tamia* (STC 17834) – the work famous for its praise of Shakespeare – incorporated the *Celestina* into his own list of works to be censured as being "no lesse hurtfull to youth than the workes of Machiavell to age," a list that consisted largely of chivalric romances: it included a good number of the recently translated Spanish romances, led by *Amadis de Gaule* and followed by *Primaleon, Palmerin, Palmendos,* and *The Mirror of Knighthood* (the *Espejo de principes y cavalleros* of Diego Ortuñez de Calahorra), alongside *Bevis,* King Arthur, and

Huon of Bordeaux.[5] If it was indeed Rojas's *Celestina* that Meres had in mind, and not an alternative version of *Primaleon* disguised under the Celestina name and probably written by William Barley (ca. 1565–1614),[6] his list again suggests how easily the work could be thought of as chivalric romance, despite the generic steer toward drama in the title of its English versions. Evidently Barley thought the name entirely appropriate for a Spanish romance.

The first English version of the *Celestina* does not name any of its characters in its title: at the time it was written, Celestina's name did not yet carry its own advertisement with it in England. This version takes the form of a play published by John Rastell (d. 1536), the brother-in-law of Sir Thomas More, around 1525 (STC 20721). It is anonymous, though it is possible that Rastell himself wrote the moralizing epilogue.[7] Vives too had spent time as part of the More circle, and it may have been through him that Rojas's work came to Rastell's attention. As was still common for English printed books at this date, where the title would have meant little to a browsing potential purchaser, the title page carries a description rather than a name: *A New Commodye in Englysh in maner of an Enterlude, ryght elygant and full of craft of rethoryk, wherein is shewd and dyscrybyd as well the bewte and good propertes of women, as theyr vycys and evyll condicions, with a morall conclusion and exhortacyon to vertew.* This description retains Rojas's emphasis on the work's rhetoric, but it emphasizes more the morality of the text to follow: it will show both what is directly instructive, and what is reprehensible, and the original warning against servants here becomes both a condemnation of female vice and a celebration of women's "beauty and good properties." The same distinction between instruction and condemnation appears in Rojas's and Mabbe's versions, too, but there it is held over to the prefatory material, a rhymed prologue in Rojas, a more emphatic warning in Mabbe's dedicatory epistle. "The reading of *Celestina*," Mabbe declares, "to those that are profane, is as poison to their hearts, but to the chaste and honest mind, a preservative against such inconveniences as occur in the world." "Her life is foul, but her precepts fair."[8] The interlude turns that warning against poison into the very substance of the action.[9] It is also, unlike Rojas's original or more faithful translations, clearly designed to be acted rather than just read. It runs for something over a thousand lines in 155 stanzas of seven-line Chaucerian rhyme royal, rhyme still being the universal medium of English drama at this period. In its entirety, it is roughly the same length as half of Act 1 of its original, and that original runs to twenty-one acts. The English author is therefore highly selective in his borrowings. He uses only parts of Rojas's Acts 1 and 4, and a few other small passages from later in the work.

The action runs continuously on the page, but for acting purposes it divides into three scenes as understood by the English definition of a cleared stage.

In contrast to the concision of the interlude, Mabbe's version was a translation of Rojas's lengthy text in its entirety, running to some 200 pages, as against the play's 155 stanzas. Mabbe was an Oxford don with considerable experience of Spain. He had been a member of an English diplomatic delegation there, and he translated Spanish works of just about every genre available, including picaresque fiction, *novelle*, and religious and political treatises. Some, including the *Celestina*, appeared under the pseudonym of "Don Diego Puede-Ser," a hispanizing riff on his name pronounced as "maybe". The lead title he chose for his version, *The Spanish Bawd*, decisively gives priority to wickedness rather than love; its first appeal is to the scandal of its contents – not only is Celestina a bawd, but she is Spanish too, with all its implication of continental and Catholic wickedness. Only after that does he add the names of Calisto and Melibea, and then the advertisement of the work's stylistic, philosophical, and moral usefulness, as quoted above. He makes a particular point about its "sentences," both here and in some of the elaborations he made to the text. Rojas comments in his prologue that it will provide good material for its readers' commonplace books, and Mabbe picks that up: "that they may transpose them into such fit places as may make, upon occasion, for their own use and purpose."[10]

Rojas, Rastell, and Mabbe all also offer generic definitions on their title pages. Rastell's, indeed, offers two – "comedy" and "interlude." The work would also fit with what the sixteenth century called a "moral play" – a "morality play," in more recent terminology – although it belongs to the generation of moral plays that demonstrated their ethical messages by means of exemplary characters rather than personified abstractions. It is the term "interlude" that defines it as drama: at this date, "comedy" applied more widely than the stage alone. In a dramatic context in English, "comedy" was a humanist technical term, with which Rastell would have been thoroughly familiar, used to describe the works of Terence and Plautus and other plays that followed the same model. In common usage in vernacular English, however, it most often meant a story with a happy ending, just as "tragedy" meant a narrative ending in grief, and the interlude does indeed, in marked contrast to its original, have at least a comparatively happy ending. The dramatic sense dominated in the context of Latin, but it was only later in the century that its primary association came to be with the stage. That the title offers both "comedy" and "interlude" ensures that potential purchasers of all levels of education would understand both that it was designed to be acted and that it had a happy ending.

The "tragicomedy" designation was Rojas's own choice, as he tells us in some detail in his prologue.[11] This too was a humanist dramatic term not yet familiar in Tudor England, though it had become so by the time Mabbe was writing. Rojas states that the first act, originally written by someone else, described it as a comedy; and that label was adopted for its initial printing in 1499, a text enlarged the following year for what is recognized as the first edition of the work. For that, Rojas changed "comedy" to "tragicomedy," in view of the multiple deaths at the end: there, everyone who has misbehaved (which is almost all of the cast list) is murdered or executed or commits suicide. "Tragicomedy" is, however, itself rather misleading, since it still implies drama, and, on account of its length, Rojas's *Celestina* is scarcely actable. Both Rojas and Mabbe supply an initial list of *dramatis personae* and further lists of the "interlocutors" (Mabbe's term) who appear in each act, but there is no evidence for either of their texts ever having been staged. Rojas himself thinks of it as appropriate for reading rather than performance. It would suit a reading aloud,[12] perhaps in a social gathering in which various participants read different parts, passing the book between them; and perhaps over twenty-one evenings, one for each act (though they vary greatly in length). The other generic term Rojas uses for the work is simply *historia* (story), expanded by Mabbe into "a history huddled, I know not how, together, a kind of hodgepodge or gallimaufry."[13]

Neither Spanish nor English vernacular literature cared too much at the start of the sixteenth century about precise generic taxonomies – they were much more of a humanist preoccupation, imported from the Classics – and, in any case, the most interesting things often happen at the borders or the cross-over points of literature. The *Celestina* is situated at a number of such intersections, as Rojas recognized when he relabelled it to remove it from the comedy category (although that category reappears as "comedia o tragicomedia" on the page following the title page, and Mabbe retains that).[14] Mabbe provides two further variations, once by the title page substitution of "tragicke-comedie" for tragicomedy, which perhaps indicates a small shift away from the increasingly well-recognized dramatic term; and again in the marginal notes to his manuscript draft (on which more below), where he notes that "the contention is not ended, for I should term it a Comicke-Tragedie" to match the structure of the plot.[15] It certainly does not fit the recognized understanding of tragicomedy as following a potentially tragic trajectory that yet ends happily; John Fletcher, for example, specifies, in his 1610 prologue to his *Faithfull Shepheardesse* (STC 11068), that a tragicomedy contains no deaths – a far cry from the *Celestina*. Those early generic labels have satisfied modern critical requirements even less. The question of genre has bedevilled this prose-fiction-in-dialogue throughout its existence, and drama has not figured extensively in the critical attempts to define it. It can be seen as a proto-novel, as a picaresque novel, or as a fabliau; it has also been argued that it is a parody of sentimental romance[16] – and, in view of how Vives and Meres seem to have thought of it, in association with the other Spanish romances, that makes good sense, even though they never suggest a parody element. The idea of it as parody works well for the early parts of the plot, but it does not adequately account for the grimness of the ending, which is not Tom-and-Jerry enough to be taken as funny in the way that parody implies. Comedy, with its happy ending, could be understood in England as equivalent to romance; the *Celestina* is more like a romance that goes very badly wrong.

Outside humanist circles, readers do not seem to have been unduly troubled by the generic definition of what they were reading, but they were certainly attuned to whatever horizon of expectation a work established, independent of any specific terminology.[17] Romances, for instance, were rarely labelled as such, but everyone was capable of recognizing them. Since literary works cannot be defined in terms of biological taxonomies – one cannot turn them upside down and count their legs, as one might distinguish insects from spiders – those expectations are the primary way in which genre is set. Romance is indeed exceptionally hard to define in any other way;[18] but the initial horizon of expectation set by Rojas's text comes very close indeed to romance in a way that could initially suggest to its readers that that is what they are reading. The opening of the Argument, as translated by Mabbe, describes Calisto as being "of lineage noble, of wit singular, of disposition gentle, of behaviour sweet, with many graceful qualities richly endowed"; Melibea is "of years young, of blood noble, of estate great," and an heiress to boot.[19] It sounds exactly like the way a romance would be set up, with an initially reluctant heroine poised to be won round – as happens, for instance, in the first chapter of *Amadis*. The Argument proceeds to give a warning about the disasters to follow, but the text itself opens with what looks like a scene of courtly wooing, enhancing those romance expectations.

The Rastell interlude varies that opening slightly. It begins with a soliloquy from Melibea, describing how Calisto is importuning her; but her very first line invokes "Franciscus Petrarcus the poet lawreate," with all that that suggests by way of love poetry, even though here the appeal to him is more as a moral philosopher – the function he serves in

Rojas's authorial prologue and silently elsewhere in the work.[20] Melibea cites him for how everything in nature is created from strife, and she sees her problems with Calisto as a further example: however much he may be "of grete worthynes" (l. 19), she wants to be rid of him. She plays, in fact, the part that in other romances is filled by the disdainful lady. Her soliloquy is followed by Calisto's attempts to woo her with a display of full courtly rhetoric. She is "Not yerthly, but aungellyke of lykelyhode, / In bewte so passyng the kinde of womanhood" (ll. 46–7), rather as Chaucer had described Criseyde. Calisto, however, goes further than Troilus, declaring that the reward of love would be better than the joy the saints receive from looking on God's face (ll. 50–4), and expounding his sufferings in even more extravagant terms, as comparable to the fires of purgatory (l. 133). Those are all characteristics already found in Rojas, but they acquire a much greater emphasis here by virtue of the proportion of the play they take up, as well as by the elimination of much of the sheer excess of the Spanish, along with its comedy and bawdiness. At the start, in fact, and given the absence of anything resembling Rojas's Argument, the original English audience might well have thought they were watching a dramatic romance of the kind that became so important later, from the 1570s forwards.

The chaste woman, as Melibea presents herself at the start of the interlude, was central to English romance in a way that she was not in Spanish. To generalize, Spanish chivalric romances (and French too) were very often about the *overcoming* of the would-be virtue of the heroine (chapter 1 of *Amadis* is an obvious example), quite apart from containing steamier sex scenes once that virtue had been overcome. Female virtue was a premise of most English romances throughout the medieval and much of the modern period, including in Shakespeare; and it was maintained through to its culmination in marriage, when chastity in the sense of virginity gave way to chastity in the sense of faithful married love.[21] Such a plot trajectory is often assumed to be associated with bourgeois values, but more to the point is how closely it is in keeping with that fundamental aristocratic concern, the preservation of the dynasty. In all the versions of the *Celestina*, Melibea initially repels Calisto's attempts to woo her, and those attempts are never presented in any terms other than seduction, not marriage: whatever her own intentions at the start, his are always both dishonourable and self-serving. She is induced to change her mind when Celestina persuades her to send to Calisto, supposedly so ill as to be at death's door, a miracle-working belt and a copy of a special prayer to St Apollonia (items paganized in Mabbe's version into a girdle that had once belonged to the Sibyl of Cumae, and a charm – on which more below).[22] Melibea hands over the girdle, but she asks Celestina to come back secretly the next day for the prayer – that "secretly" already carrying the implication that she is aware that she is overstepping bounds of propriety, which is the worst sin that the action of the Rastell version allows her. In Rojas and Mabbe, the implication of that adverb is picked up in an aside by the family maid Lucrecia, Mabbe adding an extra weight to it beyond the original (he elaborates on her dismay with "I like not this come secretly tomorrow");[23] the interlude lets it stand for itself.

In a complete break from Rojas, at the point in the action of the interlude when Celestina leaves with the girdle, Melibea's father comes in and recounts to his daughter a nightmare he has had, of a medicinal bath and its symbolic opposite, a foul pit of stinking water, and of how he imagined her being seduced by "a foule rough bitch" into going to the very brink of the pit.[24] She immediately realizes that the dream symbolizes herself and Celestina, repents, acknowledges her fault, and beseeches her father for forgiveness – so preserving her as being at least close to the typical English chaste heroine. The title description of the play as showing "the bewte and good propertes of women" as well as their wickedness thus keeps clear the gulf between Melibea and the "vycys and evyll condicions" of Celestina. Vives and Hyrd had coupled their lists of romances with indecent songs that "doo none other wyse than they that infect the common welles with poison," and the father's dream turns the simile into symbol. The interlude concludes with a long speech from him, the first stanza addressed primarily to Melibea on God's willingness to forgive sinners, the next seven to the presumed audience and its constituent virgins, maidens, parents, guardians, and rulers about the need to bring up children virtuously and instil wholesome principles, and the final verse addressed to God to influence all "governours" to introduce good laws. The dominant theme of the speech is that the best way to avoid temptation and vice is to have all young people given useful work: a much more middle-class instruction than one would find in a romance, but by this time the interlude is showing a very different face. It has been suggested that this speech was written by Rastell himself, since he had a strong interest in the education of young.[25] If it was written by the author of the whole interlude, it may perhaps have been that didactic potential that made this version appeal to him for printing. The anonymous author, endorsed by Rastell, transforms *Calisto and Melibea* into a morality play, a model of good parental discipline winning out over the temptation to vice and preventing the poison before it corrupts the well. That is not exactly what Rojas intended, nor what Spanish chivalric romance proper was about.

Mabbe's 1631 translation remains much more faithful to the original in both outline and detail. He had begun work on it some years earlier: a slightly abridged version survives in manuscript, as Alnwick Castle MS 510, entitled *Celestine, or the Tragick-Comedie of Calisto and Melibea*. Its dedicatory material can be dated to 1603–11, though it is possible that he started on it still earlier: there is an entry in the Stationers' Register for a work of the same title for October 1598, which, if it does not refer to a lost play or other unknown version, could possibly constitute an early record of Mabbe's own work.[26] The style in which both the manuscript and the print are composed is of the kind that was more in fashion at the end of the sixteenth century, incorporating as it does a number of euphuistic features – an abundance of synonyms and a fondness for comparisons and analogies, for instance. Mabbe made a number of revisions to the manuscript text for the 1631 print, besides inserting translations of the passages he had previously omitted, and these show some distinctive differences in his treatment of Rojas's text. He had provided his early version with marginal comments that delivered moral judgments on various topics, including love,[27] but he also expanded some of Rojas's more sexually suggestive dialogue; when it came to revising it for printing, he cut some of these out again but retained others.[28] If he was more relaxed about its bawdiness, he was much more sensitive about Rojas's blasphemy, altering the religious references of the original to make them pagan rather than Christian, as in the example mentioned above where a charm is substituted for a prayer. Rastell had been happy to print those as they stood, though Calisto's servant Sempronio does point out that his master's remark comparing his sufferings to the fires of purgatory has a "spyce of heryse" about it (136). Otherwise the playwright is entirely happy to offer exchanges such as this:

SEMPRONIO: Syr, God be with you.
CALISTO: Cryst make the strong!
  The myghty and perdurable God be his gyde,
  As he gydyd the thre kyngis in to Bedleme
  From the est by the starr, and again dyd provide
  As theyre conduct to return to theyre own reame. (ll. 296–300)

Mabbe retains this explicitly Christian frame of reference in his first version, but he attaches marginal comments to such passages deploring, variously, their idolatry (the adoration of one's mistress), atheism (the disprizing of heaven as well as purgatory), and profanity ("The text of Scripture profaned"), depending on their degree of Catholicism.[29]

Rather than retracting or disapproving of them in the margins of the print, however, Mabbe now reframes the whole narrative as if to give it a pagan setting. That change of setting has little effect on the story itself: it never reads like an attempt to summon up any kind of alternative Classical or heathen world, and the alterations are cosmetic, not substantive. Rojas's references to the Nativity story (quoted above from the interlude), God, Christ, Adam and Eve, and other Biblical figures, the beatific vision, the saints, and purgatory, thus disappear. Casual greetings such as the manuscript's "God prosper thee" become "So fortune befriend you."[30] The alterations may have been impelled by the 1606 Act of Abuses, which prohibited the naming of God or Christ on stage, but that covered only works intended for public performance, and references to the Catholic paraphernalia of saints or purgatory did not come under prohibition.[31] The act may have made Mabbe additionally cautious, or it may be that his additional squeamishness where religion was concerned was a result of maturity, or a reflection of changes in the attitudes to Catholicism by the royal party at court. The change in attitude might equally have been in Mabbe himself, as a result of translating various Spanish devotional works; we have no way of knowing.

Those differences in the English versions, from the interlude to the Alnwick manuscript and then to the 1631 print, represent more than just a reconfiguring of Rojas's text for a culture sensitized by the Reformation. In the manuscript, that is done by the addition of the moralizing marginalia; in the print, by the removal from the narrative of any Christian context at all, whether Catholic or Protestant. Collectively, the alterations in the 1631 version paganize the work in a way at odds with the urban grittiness of the story. The bawdiness and the violence are still all present in Mabbe, along with the retention of a rampant sexuality such as never came close to medieval English romance, which had always retained a marked level of sexual propriety. There, in marked contrast to French and Italian forms, violence is never radically displaced from chivalry, and even premarital sex is exceptional. Adultery in English literature is a marker for fabliau rather than romance. Chaucer's *Merchant's Tale* makes an instructive comparison with the *Celestina*, since it disguises an unashamed fabliau plot with a romance-style treatment such as likewise results in a rather distasteful presentation of urban sex; in contrast to Rojas's work, it also furnishes a parody of a happy ending. Romance adultery appears in England only in late translations from French: the affair between Lancelot and Guinevere, for instance, is barely hinted at before 1400 and does not get extensive treatment until Malory's *Morte Darthur*. That was published in 1485, and was the first treatment of Arthurian material in any language to see print – the French prose romances followed only later. English romances focus rather on courtship, as the *Celestina* appears at first glance that it is going to do, or else on the recuperation of the falsely accused wife, the pattern most familiar now from Shakespeare's "romances." The key factor in both those story patterns, of courtship and unwarranted calumny, is that the heroine is chaste, in the sense that she will not have sex with anyone other than the husband that she herself chooses, even if, like Melibea, she initially repels his advances. Of romances put into print by Caxton's successors in the decades before the interlude appeared, *Guy of Warwick* would be the most widely known English model of such a narrative, where the higher-born heroine Felice requires her suitor to go through a long series of chivalric tests before she agrees to marriage with him, and then spends the rest of her life, after he leaves her to devote his life to God, in deeds of charity performed in imitation of him. In others, the passionate heroine is prepared to undergo suffering of all kinds to remain faithful to her chosen partner. This is the model of the one romance to equal *Guy* in popularity, *Bevis of Hampton*. Premarital sex is not unheard of (*Sir Eglamour*, for instance, has the young couple make love after they have become betrothed to each other but while her father is forbidding their marriage) but is unusual. The shift away from those principles in the *Celestina* clearly did not disturb Mabbe in the way that the treatment of religion did, and he was happy to incorporate or even develop Rojas's uninhibited attitude to sex.

The one thing that never happens in English romance is that the heroine falls into bed with the hero at almost the first suggestion. The interlude was written within the period when the expectation of women's integrity was still paramount within English romance. Fabliau was of course a different matter, but the *Celestina* does not announce itself as a fabliau. Melibea is convinced at the start of the narrative that she is chaste in the full romance implication of the term – not in the sense that she has any intention of taking a religious vow of chastity, but rather that she resists all temptation to casual sex: that is not what nice girls *do*. The interlude's early audience or readers would have no reason to imagine otherwise of her for almost nine-tenths of the play, and she is rescued in the final tenth by her realization of just what it is she is embarking on. Mabbe, by contrast, follows Rojas's narrative through all its casual and unappealing erotic manoeuvrings to its gruesome end.

Sex is likely to be one of the reasons why Mabbe undertook the translation: sex sells, and especially Spanish sex as advertised in its new title, *The Spanish Bawd*. That was certainly the impulse behind a later adaptation of the work, John Stevens's (ca. 1662–1726) 1707 abbreviated novella "Celestina, The Bawd of Madrid," which appeared in a collection of stories enticingly called *The Spanish Libertines*. Another motive for Mabbe is likely to have been the Europe-wide fame of the *Celestina*; a third, the desire to cash in on the English fashion for Spanish romance. That new title for the 1631 print was perhaps an attempt to make the most of both, romance and the sex that accompanied it in its Spanish exemplars being commercially attractive. It has to be admitted, however, that the work did not, in the event, sell very well. There were enough unsold sheets left for them to be incorporated at the end of the fourth edition of his much more successful *The Rogue*, a translation of *Guzman de Alfarache*. The interlude likewise was less than a commercial success, and failed to sell up to expectations: 370 copies remained unsold at Rastell's death.[32] Mabbe shows no signs of knowing of the interlude, but the hope for a rather better outcome for his own work would have had sound reasoning behind it. Overt literary eroticism had become naturalized in England by the 1630s through the fashion for Spanish romance, as cultural expectations and conditions had been reset. What to Rastell's generation had been so shocking as to require elimination had effectively become normal. Rojas's *Celestina* does not seem to have been sufficiently widely known to have played any direct part in that shift, but the gulf between the interlude and Mabbe's print is a measure of the change in taste, and in both ethical and literary expectations, over the intervening century: a gulf bridged by *Amadis* and its successors.

NOTES

1 All citations from Mabbe come from *Fernando de Rojas: Celestina*, ed. Dorothy Sherman Severin, corrected ed. (Warminster, UK: Aris and Phillips, 1992) (hereafter *Celestina*, ed. Severin). Severin prints Rojas's original and Mabbe's translation in parallel, with his departures from the Spanish italicized (these are referred to below as Rojas and Mabbe, respectively).

2 For an account of these and an introduction to the knowledge of the *Celestina* in England and to Mabbe himself, see *Fernando de Rojas: Celestine, or the Tragick-Comedie of Calisto and Melibea, translated by James Mabbe*, ed. Guadalupe Martinez Lacalle (London: Tamesis, 1972), 1–24 (hereafter *Celestina*, ed. Lacalle); this is an edition of the manuscript version that preceded the 1631 printed text. For an introduction more specifically to the 1631 version, see José María Pérez Fernández, "James Mabbe, *The Spanish Bawd, Represented in Celestina: or, the Tragicke-comedy of Calisto and Melibea, 1631*," EEBO Introductions series (STC 4911 and 4911.2).

3   J.L. Vives, *De Institutione feminae Christianae*, ed. C. Matheeussen and C. Fantazzi, trans. C. Fantazzi, 3 vols (Leiden: Brill, 1996–68), I: 45–6.

4   Richard Hyrd, *A Very Frvteful and Pleasant Boke Callyd the Instrvction of a Cristen Woman* (1529), cap. v, Eiv^a.

5   Quoted by Pérez Fernández in his EEBO introduction; and see G. Gregory Smith, ed., *Elizabethan Critical Essays* (London: Oxford University Press, 1904), 2: 308–9. Meres notes that the comparison with Machiavelli comes from the *Discours politiques et militaires du Seigneur de la Noue*, which had been translated into English in 1587 (STC 15215). La Noue cites *Amadis* as the prime example of an immoral work, but he limits himself to romances proper and does not mention the *Celestina*.

6   Barley's version, published in 1596, was entitled *The Delightful History of Celestina the Faire* (STC 4910). Barley may have been attempting to promote it by means of the familiarity of the Celestina name, but it has nothing to do with Rojas.

7   Edited under the title by which it is usually known, *Calisto and Melibea*, in *Three Rastell Plays*, ed. Richard Axton (Cambridge: D.S. Brewer, 1979). Severin also prints the text in her *Celestina*.

8   *Celestina*, ed. Severin: Rojas's final stanzas to his prologue, 10–13; Mabbe 2–5, quotations from 2, 4.

9   On the "poison *topos*," see the introduction to this volume.

10   *Celestina*, ed. Severin: Rojas 18, Mabbe 19.

11   Ibid.

12   See also *Celestine*, ed. Lacalle, 37.

13   *Celestina*, ed. Severin: Rojas 18, Mabbe 19.

14   *Celestina*, ed. Severin: Rojas 20, Mabbe 21.

15   *Celestine*, ed. Lacalle, 114 (Mabbe's marginalia are printed as footnotes).

16   On critical disagreements, see *Celestina*, ed. Severin, viii–x. The most detailed argument for it as a parody of sentimental romance is Yolanda Iglesias, *Una nueva Mirada a la parodia de la novela sentimental en La Celestina* (Madrid: Iberoamericana; Frankfurt: Vervuert, 2009); and see also the review by Dorothy Sherman Severin in *Speculum* 87, no. 2 (2012): 565–7.

17   The definition is that of Hans Robert Jauss, *Towards an Aesthetic of Reception*, trans. Timothy Bahti (Minneapolis: University of Minnesota Press, 1982), 22–5, 79, 88–9.

18   Studies of romance attest generously to the difficulty; on recognition, see, for example, Helen Cooper, *The English Romance in Time: Transforming Motifs from Geoffrey of Monmouth to the Death of Shakespeare* (Oxford: Oxford University Press, 2004), 7–15.

19   *Celestina*, ed. Severin: Rojas 22, Mabbe 23.

20   *Celestina*, ed. Severin: xiii–xiv, Rojas 14, Mabbe 15, and A.D. Deyermond, *The Petrarchan Sources of* La Celestina (London: Oxford University Press, 1961).

21 See Cooper, *English Romance*, 218–74.

22 *Calisto*, ed. Axton, lines 833–9; *Celestina*, ed. Severin: Rojas 128, Mabbe 129.

23 *Celestina*, ed. Severin: Rojas 134, Mabbe 135.

24 This is the closest the *Celestina* comes to the story of the weeping bitch, which first appears in Europe in the work of Petrus Alfonsi. It was dramatized in Middle English as *Dame Sirith*, but no version was likely to have been known in Tudor England.

25 *Calisto*, ed. Axton, 18, and note at lines 1032–87.

26 *Celestine*, ed. Lacalle, 34.

27 *Celestine*, ed. Lacalle, 46–8; other topics for these maxims (or occasionally proverbs) include death, old age, virtue, friendship, repentance, time, and women (bad).

28 Lacalle supplies some examples from the manuscript, *Celestine*, 65–6; those cited are from 120, 9, and 172. For a removal of added material, compare Lacalle 195 with *Celestina*, ed. Severin: Rojas 192, Mabbe 193; and for a retention, compare Lacalle 197 with *Celestina*, ed. Severin: Rojas 196, Mabbe 197.

29 Discussed with examples by Lacalle, *Celestine*, 36.

30 Severin prints Mabbe's alterations and substitutions in italics, with the equivalent passage from the manuscript in square brackets: see, for example, 25, 31, 37, 45, and 129 (all retained in the interlude) and *passim*.

31 Lacalle, in *Celestine*, 37–9, sees the passing of the act between the composition of the manuscript and its revision as crucial to Mabbe's alterations.

32 *Calisto*, ed. Axton, 20.

Afterword

ALEX DAVIS

After words, action. Or, if one prefers, the inverse – violent action, succeeded by words. This afterword aims to draw together the chapters
collected in this volume around a reading of Iberian chivalric romance
as a literary form characterized by a distinctive understanding of the
relationship between deeds and words; and it does so in order to think
through questions about sixteenth-century romance's relationship
to the wider world of which it is a part, which are raised by all the
contributors here. My discussion takes its cue from the most extraordinary early modern commentator on the matter of Iberian romance,
the Huguenot soldier François de La Noue. In his *Discours politique and
militaires*, La Noue was emphatic. For all its indebtedness to the past –
indeed, because of that indebtedness – Iberian chivalric romance was a
distinctively *modern* literary form. I quote from the 1588 English translation by Edward Aggas:

> The auncient fables whose relickes doe yet remaine, namely, *Lancelot of the
> lake, Pierceforest, Tristran, Giron the courteous*, & such otheas [sic] doe beare
> witnesse of this olde vanitie. Herewith were men fed for the space of 500.
> yeeres, vntill our language growing more polished, & our mindes more
> ticklish, they were driuen to inuent some nouelties, wherewith to delight
> vs. Thus came yᵉ bookes of *Amadis* into light among vs in this last age.[1]

The itch for ticklish novelty demands new stories rather than old
ones, and, as Le Noue's discussion unfolds, it becomes clear that this
interplay between language and desire lies at its heart, for while the
Iberian romances represent a new version of old "vanitie," it would
not be right simply to describe them as ineffectual. On the contrary: the
worst thing about them is that they provide a spur toward action. The
Iberian romance prompts bad imitation.[2] The readers of romance may

think that they are learning to talk like ideal lovers and to fight like ideal fighters. The very opposite is the case: "those loues are dishonest, and almost all the combats full of falsehood, and not to be practised, so that the following of those rules is to walke in errour."[3] The hostility animating François de La Noue's account of the Iberian romance thus couples two foundational contradictions that he sees structuring these texts. The Iberian romance is both a version of the "auncient fables" of the Middle Ages and a format animated by an impulse toward novelty; and it is an utterly impractical fabric of verbal vanity that is nonetheless somehow directed toward action. It is a modern literature with an utterly implausible relationship to the modern world.

The chapters of this volume have all spoken in their different ways to the ticklish modernity identified by La Noue and to his sense of literary texts as historical actors. Drawing upon some of the most up-to-date work being done in the field of early modern studies, they locate Iberian chivalric romance at the heart of several key zones of cultural transformation. In the first place, we have the Iberian romance as a transnational entity. Very often this theme involves attention to the details of translation, but, on a broader scale, it involves an awareness of the Renaissance as a pan-European phenomenon. Whatever national histories may be evoked within these texts, the matter of romance cannot ultimately be held fully separate from a continental and even global perspective. The chapters by Helen Cooper, Rocío G. Sumillera, Timothy D. Crowley, and Goran Stanivukovic all look at the migration of stories across national and linguistic boundaries throughout the sixteenth and seventeenth centuries; while Elizabeth Evenden-Kenyon specifically considers Anthony Munday's engagement with the matter of Britain from the perspective of an early modern cosmopolitanism. Second, we have book history and material culture. If romance and its sources and analogues circulated, they did so along the lines of transmission opened up by the early modern book trade. Iberian romance is a phenomenon of print. More generally, questions of material mediation and the historicity of objects are a recurring presence in these chapters, as is the English hub for book production and commodity production, London. In this vein, Jordi Sánchez-Martí offers a detailed investigation of the London book trade, Donna B. Hamilton considers the historical culture of early modern London, and Louise Wilson looks at the "polytemporal" character of the objects imagined within the civic institutions of the early modern capital. Third, we have the transformations of value that were driven by this whirl of material and textual circulation. María Beatriz Hernández Pérez, Crowley, and Cooper all take in questions of gender and women's sexuality, with the law of clandestine marriage a recurring motif; Donna Hamilton focuses in particular on religious history and the divisions of the Reformation; while Leticia Álvarez-Recio opens the collection outwards toward world history by considering the ways in which Iberian romance might speak to an emergent international order of colonial expansion. Romance, then, is fully part of the world of sixteenth-century Europe, and its words reach out to engage with the world of which they are a part – they act. Jean Maugin's *Le premier livre de Palmerin d'Oliue* seems to have it just right: in the Iberian romance, we encounter fiction "à la modern."[4]

Romance "à la modern" is a way of seeing these texts positioned at nodes of transformation in a variety of spheres – and not just as reflectors but also as drivers of historical change. All I want to add in this afterword is something of the sense, powerfully articulated by François de La Noue, that the relationship between words and deeds instantiated by Iberian chivalric romance might also have something about it of the fantastical, even of the perverse. La Noue is clear about Iberian romance's modernity. At the same time, he exemplifies an early modern discourse that powerfully insists upon the sheer impossibility of romance's relationship with the world. In texts such as *Don Quixote* and *The Knight of the Burning Pestle,* the coexistence of chivalric matter and modern life issues into comedy; it is construed as absurd. How might this claim be factored into the analyses offered here? Without at all affirming its satirical take on romance, we can admit the possibility that relation can also be a matter of incongruity, and it is this option that I aim to explore here. What has Amadis de Gaule to do with the baffling, unwholesome figure of Antony Munday? Quite a lot, as it turns out; the contributors to this volume show that. This afterword aims to think through the implications of this and other such affinities for the Iberian romance as a structure of values.[5] It follows François de La Noue in understanding this issue to be one of deeds and words, and I take as my starting point the way in which their relationship is presented within the romances themselves. What do they have to say on the matter?[6]

In the eighteenth chapter of Margaret Tyler's translation of *The Mirror of Knighthood,* the Gentleman of the Sun is welcomed to the city of Babylon with an oration that anticipates the heroic deeds he will perform in the service of its people:

> Oh, how well may Babylon rejoice since he is thither brought whose glory shall no less glister through the earth than the bright sun shineth in the world, who deserveth to have his biding among the demigods for his valour and mightiness! Oh, how he shall erase out of the memory of Ninus,

and Xerxes, and all the praise of the Assyrian monarchs! From henceforth, Assyria, for being only the cradle of his gentleman's nursery, shall be famous throughout the whole world. From henceforth, men shall have so much to do to put in writing the worthiness of this gentleman that all monuments of our ancestors shall quite die, and this man only shall be our table talk.[7]

There is just a hint of something comic in the speaker Lirgandeo's self-abasing enthusiasm for the obliteration of his nation's past. Nonetheless, the very extremity of his speech suggests a buried ideal, which is that of action so exceptional as to confound the celebration that it elicits. We are asked to imagine memories erased, monuments falling into desuetude, historical writing and familiar conversation both monopolized by the same impossible task of commemoration. Meanwhile, the heroism that prompts this activity is understood on analogy with a natural phenomenon, the shining of the sun; it acts non-discursively. Deeds, here, have decisively established their superiority to words.

The *Mirror*'s fantasy of historical eclipse represents an extreme, and it would not be at all correct to suggest that Iberian romances simply discard words in favour of action. On the contrary: they are full of oaths, letters, prophetic inscriptions, vengeful imprecations, passionate declarations of love, expressive failures of speech. Even in Lirgandeo's oration, "table talk" has its part to play. But the episode may be helpful in opening up to view some of the distinctive preoccupations of these narratives. The *Mirror*'s Babylonian history imagines the relationship between words and deeds as one of subordination. At other times, the favoured option is one in which the former take on something of the character of the latter. Later in Tyler's translation, the Gentleman of the Sun taunts Raiartes: "hitherto I have had more experience of thy vain and foolish words than thy great and valiant prowess."[8] Words unsupported by deeds are empty. More than that, though: their optimal state is one of verbal action. In the first book of Anthony Munday's translation of *Amadis de Gaule*, the Gentleman of the Sea ("the Prince") encounters the guards of a rapist knight:

I meane, quoth the Prince, to revenge her wrong if I can. Go to, said the Knight, I shall see then what kinde of revendge you use. So giving the Spurs to his Horse, ran as fiercely as he could against the Prince, yet he failed in the attaint: but the Prince meeting him with full carire, gave him such a greeting with his Launce through the Sheeld, as the armour being unable to resist it, let passe the yron through both his shoulders, whereby he fell downe dead in the place.[9]

This episode opens with an exchange of words in which verbal defiance is presented as fully continuous with the act of killing. First Amadis tells his enemy what he means to do, as a prelude to doing it. Then, when the knight replies "Go to," his response is construed as a bridge to action. He speaks, and then, "So giving the Spurs to his Horse," he charges – the conjunction "so" implying that the action was entailed by the words. The ideal of language here is performative: the word that is like a deed.

Another aspect of this ideology of chivalric language is the propensity of the heroes of romance to tangle themselves up in oaths, a habit that elicited the derision of François de La Noue:

> This likewise was another custome of the knights of those daies, *That if any one had made promise to goe about any aduenture with one of these pilgrimes, who alwaies trauailed alone with them:* though their soueraigne Lord, or their father or mother should command them euen with lordlike authoritie & fatherly power, to desist therefro to the end to serue in some other necessarie seruice, yet if they gaue it ouer, it was a perpetuall infamy to them, for they were bound by the order of knightood to folow their gentlewoman, who somtimes was of a reasonable disposition.[10]

The oath is one of J.L. Austin's key examples of performative utterance, of words endowed with the character of an action.[11] In the romances it is given a distinctively future-oriented spin, functioning as earnest of the chivalric hero's willingness to match deeds to words. It is this impulse to offer proof of one's integrity that La Noue criticizes. But here we might glimpse the possibility of a line of connection between the worlds conjured by Iberian romance – its absurd artificial universes, with their specialized conventions of speech and action – and the world of which they are a part, because La Noue's discussion situates the narrative clichés of romance in relation to a kind of modernity. In sixteenth- and seventeenth-century culture, frivolous vows, or indeed vowing generally, might be condemned as impious.[12] La Noue highlights a different issue, which is that the incontinent promiser arrogates to himself a "lordlike authoritie" in defiance of reason and necessity. That makes sense: very often in the romances it is a king who commits himself in this way. Many an Arthurian narrative opens up from a royal pledge to assist petitioners. In *Amadis de Gaule*, King Lisuart seems particularly prone to inept oath-making; a key episode involves the abduction of his daughter Oriana consequent upon a rash vow.[13] Interestingly, though, La Noue's focus is on the oath made in *defiance* of sovereign or familial authority. He seems to identify within the narrative machinery of Iberian romance something inimical to royal and parental power.

La Noue's is a striking reading – and in many ways an odd one, given its complex resonances with his own career as a Huguenot general, which might also be described as one of opposition to a purported "lordlike authoritie."[14] But the point to draw out here is that of the possibility of a relationship – however odd or back-to-front it may seem – between the verbal detail of romance and a larger historical movement. The sixteenth century sees a number of attempts to theorize the nature of sovereign power, often in relation to questions of familial authority. Jean Bodin's is among the most influential. "Wherefore as a familie well and wisely ordered," Bodin writes, "is the true image of a Citie, and the domesticall gouernment, in sort like vnto the soueraigntie in a Commonweale: so also is the manner of the gouernment of an house or familie, the true modell for the gouernment of a Commonweale."[15] François de La Noue's discussion of chivalric oaths strikingly imagines in the words of Iberian romance something recalcitrant, something that – however unrealistic in itself – nonetheless offers a moment of resistance to processes of state formation.

Are there aspects of these texts that push in the opposite direction – moving more in harmony with the dominant forces of historical change that we might identify in this period? I propose to approach this question by considering how deeds are represented in Iberian romance. In their chapters in this volume, Rocío Sumillera and Goran Stanivukovic have commented on Iberian romances' sensitive depictions of their protagonists' inner lives. But now: fighting. The following passage from Anthony Munday's translation of *Amadis de Gaule* describes an encounter between Amadis and the giant Balan:

> Clasping downe their Beavers, and couching their Launces, they ranne each against other with such swiftnesse, as if lightning had carried them. Amadis met Balan so strongly, that hee pierced both his shield and coate of Male, directly upon the stomacke bone, which was so painefull to him, that he fell downe on the ground, when as he had charged Amadis, and ran his Launce so farre into his horses head (the paine he felt much qualifying the vigour of the blow) that the horse fell downe dead, and his Master under him … Then they began to hack and hew one another, that whomsoever had heard and not seene them: would rather have thought the noyse to bee hammers on an anvile, then swords on Armour.[16]

Iberian chivalric romance is full of such scenes. They formed a central element of their appeal for readers, or were imagined to do so. The innkeeper in *Don Quixote* is an enthusiast, commenting of his favourite author that "when I hear him describing all those furious and terrible blows that the knights deal one another I feel like doing the same thing myself, and I could go on listening day and night."[17] This seems plausible. So too, though, does the opposite reaction: that far from holding the attention, day and night, Iberian romances' descriptions of knightly violence are actually a bit dull. Certainly they exhibit an extraordinary variety – being staged between all kinds of combatants, using an arsenal of different weapons, and taking place in any number of different locations. Yet one is struck by an underlying similarity. They often seem unindividuated, substitutable. One could, one feels, transpose the details of the battle between Amadis de Gaule and the retinue of the rapist knight Galpan (from toward the start of the *Amadis*) with that between Bruneo de Bonne Mer and two knights of Alumenta (from toward its end) without generating any significant narrative consequences.[18] What ties these scenes together and makes them feel interchangeable is the shared descriptive machinery that was so appreciated by Cervantes's innkeeper. It is the representation of combat as a succession of "furious and terrible blows."

This narrative technology subtly distinguishes the Iberian chivalric romance from its predecessors. Certainly it has its medieval antecedents. The encounter between Lancelot and Meleagant at the climax of Chrétien de Troye's *Chevalier de la Charette* offers a good comparison; or one might look at the final encounter between Arthur and Mordred in Malory's *Morte Darthur*. Elsewhere, though, Malory can be brisk in a way that Iberian romance would rarely permit. Consider this crucial narrative turning point: "Ane anone at the first stroke [Lancelot] slew sir Aggravayne, and anone aftir twelve of his felowys."[19] Alternatively, contrast the following passage, again from Chrétien's *Chevalier de la Charette*:

> Angrily they pay one other with blows exchanged as if in a deal. But very often their swords are deflected on to the horses' cruppers and slake their thirst in their blood, of which they drink their fill, being driven right into their flanks until they fell both of them dead. Then, when the combatants have fallen to the ground, each attacks the other on foot; and had they shared a mortal hatred, they could certainly not have set upon one another more ferociously with their swords. They rain down their blows more thick and fast than the dice-player stakes his coins when he keeps playing on and on, doubling at every losing throw. But this was a very different game, consisting not of losing throws but of blows and hard, savage, fierce combat.[20]

For our purposes, D.D.R. Owens's prose translation usefully narrows the distance between Chrétien and his Iberian descendants, and the relationship between the medieval romance and its "modern" equivalent is certainly clear enough. At the same time, though, Chrétien's descriptions open out the scene of combat to the imagination in a way that feels subtly different from the sixteenth-century romance. The passage playfully evokes commerce, gaming, the weather. It invites us to imagine the intentionalities of objects and the suffering of animals. Even while it stays tightly focused on the performance of aristocratic violence, it surrounds knightly rage with a penumbra of other affects and preoccupations. This is writing rendered compelling by a kind of deliberate internal drift, such as its Iberian successor typically lacks.

The point, then, would not be the absolute novelty of the Iberian romance's treatment of combat (since parallels with earlier texts abound), nor any absolute loss of aesthetic integrity, but rather the systematization of a set of descriptive conventions, generating a method of writing that aims to grip its readers precisely through a kind of narrowness of intent. Across the board, Iberian chivalric romances offer scenes of action that are more relentlessly exact, more precisely specified in their delineation of violence, more consistently *blow-by-blow*, than their medieval predecessors. Strokes are isolated as fights are broken down into patterns of action and response; body parts are named; wounds enumerated; equipment – arms and armour – is granted unusual prominence, usually as it is being whittled down into uselessness through the prodigious efforts of the combatants. Similes typically measure frequency and magnitude or indicate intent, but otherwise offer little to the imagination. For all their extravagance and even absurdity, these descriptions of combat respond to an internal principle of extreme efficiency. Their focus is action, directed to foreseen results.

We might perceive an affinity between this regimentation of narrative description and one of the key impulses in sixteenth- and seventeenth-century culture. The early modern period sees, across a variety of fields, an outpouring of books that exploit the medium of print in order to systematize and propagate various kinds of specialized technical knowledge. *A Table of Good Nurture. An Hundred Godly Lessons. A Helpe to Discourse. The Secretarie's Studie. The Ground of Arts*. This was the age of the handbook.[21] Plainly the Iberian romance bears no straightforward relation to this literature. Only an idiot would try to master the arts of war by reading *Palmerin d'Oliva* or *Amadis de Gaule*. That, after all, is the joke of every anti-chivalric satire. Perhaps significantly, though, it *is* the principal joke of that satire, and to be an absurd manual of instruction is not quite the same thing as to have nothing to do with the form at all. It is a common critical manoeuvre to link the Iberian romance to the courtesy books of the sixteenth century, to Castiglione and Giovanni della Casa and Stefano Guazzo, on the understanding that the Iberian romance possesses a relationship – possibly a provocative and contested one, but a relationship nonetheless – to writing that sought to offer opportunities for self-improvement.[22] Rocío Sumillera's chapter is astute in noting that inset epistles, reproduced in full, are a feature that formally distinguishes the Iberian romance from its medieval predecessors. Furthermore, this feeling that these texts were in some sense writing as a model or template was also a sixteenth-century perception. One of François de La Noue's principal complaints against books like *Amadis* was that they were bad teachers, "instruments for the corruption of maners."[23] La Noue was a real-life soldier and was witheringly scornful about the romances' scenes of violence. But we might note how his complaint about their practical imbecility – that "When a man hath bestowed all his time in reading the bookes of *Amadis,* yet wil it not all make him a good soldiour or warrior" – modulates almost instantly into stylistic critique, homing in on the descriptions of "these mightie blowes that cleaue a man to the waste, or cut asunder a *Vantbrasse* arme and all."[24] That is: La Noue implies that the Iberian romances' fantasy of the deed, of learning to fight like an Amadis or an Esplandian, is underpinned by a verbal technology that is practical, repeatable, and systematic in a way that the actions it describes could not ever be.

We might also note that the early modern period sees a notable systematization of actual military practice, a shift that plays a key role in the historiography of the "military revolution" of the seventeenth century.[25] Here we find ourselves returned to questions of state power and centralization, since the suggestion is that the revision of soldiers' training implies that warfare might have functioned as a testing ground for and impetus toward new, concentrated forms of administrative power. Thus, Anthony Giddens argues that Maurice of Nassau's military innovations portended a wider pattern of transformations within modernity:

> Maurice helped initiate two connected administrative changes seen later in all more bureaucratized organization – the formation of a body of experts holding exclusive knowledge of certain essential administrative techniques, and the simultaneous creation of a "de-skilled" population of ordinary soldiery ... Maurice divided the technical aspects of the work of soldiery into specific, regular sequences of single activities. Thus, building upon what had already been accomplished by the Spanish commanders, he produced flow charts for the handling of the musket and the pike, each part of the sequence of acts being clearly specified ... Rather than being treated as "craftsmen," skilled in the use of weaponry, recruits were regarded as having to be drilled to acquire the necessary familiarity with handling military equipment.[26]

Alternatively, one might think of the connection between canons of bodily regimentation and wider processes of classification and control explored in Michel Foucault's *Discipline and Punish*, the key section of which on "discipline" leads off with a discussion of the early modern soldier.[27] And lest this all seem too much like theory formulated with the benefit of hindsight, we might note that La Noue drew a similar line of connection between questions of military discipline and those of sovereign authority. He wrote: "It is in my opinion a poore excuse to say, *The Souldier will not do this or that*: for although in ciuill warre it must many tymes passe for payment: yet in a tyme of rule and reformation it is meete to commaund with authoritie, so to make the Souldiers more readie to frame themselues to whatsoeuer is conuenient."[28]

Does the Iberian romance perform similar work? The prodigious feats of arms accomplished by an Amadis or a Don Belianis must seem unlikely harbingers of professional deskilling, and indeed the romances retain an unshakeable commitment to the unique value of aristocratic identities. But even as they entertain a fantasy of achievements so superhuman as to rewrite history and utterly subordinate language to the heroic deed, as in the Knight of the Sun's welcome to Babylon, the representational conventions of these texts – their own management of words – pull in a fractionally different direction. The final battle of *The Mirror of Princely Deeds and Knighthood* culminates in a quartet of blows. Aridon strikes the Knight of the Sun on the headpiece; then the Knight of the Sun makes Aridon stagger; then Aridon strikes the Knight of the Sun on the headpiece again; and finally the Knight of the Sun "stretching himself and following his blow with all his might" hits Aridon so hard that he falls to the ground motionless.[29] "Those furious and terrible blows that the knights deal one another" and other such feats of arms are often extravagantly unrealistic, yet by isolating actions and organizing them into legible sequences of cause and effect, the narrative conventions that frame them do echo something of the military Taylorism of which Giddens speaks. They do so at the level of what is described, and of how they describe. What, after all, is a cliché but a reproducible unit of narrative?

Descriptive convention, therefore, hints at an affinity between the words of romance and the deeds performed in the wider world of sixteenth-century Europe. Something in these narratives speaks to themes of regimentation and repeatability. Certainly La Noue was clear that the romances offered, if not useful guides to fighting, then models of discourse. Their readers learn, he claimed, "to Amadize in speech."[30] We might pause to consider the implications of the -ize suffix, which transforms nouns into verbs that indicate processes of making. When the noun is a proper name, we are shifted from a zone inhabited by particulars into one of generalities. The possibility of "Amadizing" must in some measure dissolve the uniqueness of Amadis the son of Perion and Elisena. Or consider the pluralization of the hero's name. Ben Jonson refers disparagingly to "Esplandians, Arthurs, Palmerins," and Cervantes to "Amadises, Esplandians and Belianises."[31] Not one Amadis, but many Amadises. We might contrast this habit with Philip Sidney's advice to aspirant poets in his great work of humanist poetics, the *Apology for Poetry*, which is that they should "bestow a Cyrus upon the world to make many Cyruses." Sidney's is a vision of unfolding rhetorical efficacy, contingent upon an understanding of the ends of poetic creation ("to make many Cyruses," he continues, "if they will learn aright why and how that maker made him").[32] The conversion of Amadis into many Amadises, or the process of Amadizing, suggests something different. Both knit together monotony and invention in ways that upend the values inculcated within the humanistic rhetorical culture that dominated sixteenth-century thinking about fiction and invention. Circulating through Europe along the trading networks brought into being by the new technology of mechanical reproduction, the Iberian romances propagate a fantasy of unique heroic achievement and erode it, both at the same time.

∽

If Iberian romance has within it something of a routinizing force, that perception shouldn't obscure the fantastical character of these books. The central joke of satires such as *Don Quixote* and *The Knight of the Burning Pestle* concerns the romances' ludicrous incompatibility with real life, and François de La Noue makes the same point. But we might reflect that La Noue's own analysis is not free from its own kind of absurdity. What place, after all, does *Amadis de Gaule* deserve in a collection of Plutarchian moral essays? A mention, certainly; several, even. But a whole chapter? La Noue's vision of the apocalyptic social harm wrought by Iberian romance is itself completely unreal. It seems that even the sixteenth-century's most penetrating diagnostician of romance's irrationality must find himself caught up in scenes that are in some sense crazed or disproportionate. The final movement of this afterword explores this amalgam of the perverse and the systematic as it plays out in the literature of humanistic self-improvement, of sound common sense and practical application.

Much of the most interesting recent scholarship on Iberian romances has put together the world they imagined and the world that read them by exploring questions of language acquisition, by focusing on a polylingual European scene in which stories moved across borders to be adapted to local contexts and uses.[33] This moment sees the publication of Thomas Paynell's *Treasurie of Amadis of Fraunce*, a translation of the *Trésor des livres d'Amadis de Gaule*. The *Trésor* compiled extracts of speeches and letters drawn from the French *Amadis*, offering them to the reader as templates for practical discourse; Paynell's *Treasurie* "Englishes" the text for an audience that had, as yet, no access to *Amadis de Gaule* in the vernacular. (The first English translation of *Amadis* appeared in 1590; the *Treasurie* is undated, but was probably printed around 1572.) The best description of Paynell's volume has been offered by Helen Moore, who aligns it with the ambitions of a vernacular humanism that "seeks to engage profitably with the everyday lives of readers."[34] It is another instance of the affinity between chivalric romance and the handbook. And yet, for all that, the *Treasurie* is also a deeply peculiar, wildly impractical text.

The intention, as Thomas Hacket explains in his dedication of the volume to Thomas Gresham, is that these "pleasant orations, fine epistles, [and] singular complaintes" should offer "matter mixt so fitly and aptly to serue the turne of all persons."[35] To facilitate the business of everyday application, the *Treasurie* prefaces its extracts with "A Table of the principall matters of this Booke, reduced into common places for the more speedie and easie finding of the maner to write Letters missiues, according to the minde and argument of him that writeth." This table consists of thirty "formes," in which the suggestion is that the extracts from *Amadis* can be generalized and more-or-less directly redeployed into parallel situations. It begins:

> A Forme to declare his aduice, to aske or to giue counsell of any thing to Lords, friends, parents, alies, or subiects.
>
> 2 A forme to write, or to say, that they accepte the counsell giuen.
>
> 3 A forme to aske, or to declare to any man his deliberation and minde concerning some businesse.
>
> 4 A forme to pray and to desire a man to do a thing, or to shewe him selfe fauourable.
>
> 5 A forme to commende a thing to one, and to recite some thing that is chaunced.[36]

As Helen Moore shows, Paynell's attempt to commonplace *Amadis de Gaule* is fully consonant with his practice elsewhere, which characteristically translates, compiles, and digests in order to produce "profitable" books of practical utility for mid-Tudor readers. Still, we might wonder how exactly his book was meant to be used. How to make the connection between the words and deeds depicted in romance and action in real life?

It is not easy to say. Very often the *Treasurie*'s examples feel just too embedded in their local narrative contexts to be exported into alternative circumstances. The second extract Paynell offers is "The oration of Lisnarde [sic] the King of England vnto his subiectes and freendes, exhorting them to giue him counsell." This is presumably an instance of Paynell's first form, and learning how to nicely ask for advice sounds useful. The speech itself opens: "My freendes, there is none of you that is ignorant of the graces that it hath pleased God to shew me, making me the greatest earthly Lorde that is this day in al the Iles of the Occean."[37] That isn't something that just anybody might say, and although Lisuart's oration does indeed include some generalizable content, the obligation of subjects to offer counsel to their lord remains the motif that organizes his speech. Is this really verbal matter available "to serue the turne of all persons"? Only if you are a king. A careful reader of Philip Sidney's *Apology* might respond that it is recognition of the oration's deep rhetorical structure – what lies beneath the contingencies that seemingly motivate it – that can truly expand our verbal resources. When we understand how Lisuart's discourse is organized in relation to the authority of a commonplace formulation (loyal subjects should offer counsel), then we will "learn aright why and how that maker made [it]." This is true, but it is not how Paynell's volume sells itself. His table declares that we are getting direct models for how to ask for or to receive counsel; to expound, or plead, or praise. But as a "form" for soliciting advice, Lisuart's speech looks fairly useless.

It is true that some of Paynell's extracts are much more abstract. Still, we might feel that any might struggle to bridge the gap between one set of circumstances and another. The generality of his forms can't interact with the specificity of the extracts in a productive way. It might be hard, therefore, to imagine anybody actually using Paynell's *Treasurie* without venturing into the territory occupied by a Don Quixote. Indeed, it is hard at points to imagine Paynell imagining it. The final entry in the table reads: "A forme to write, or to pronounce any thing in maner of a prophecie." Furthermore, Paynell's "table" omits to key its forms to individual extracts. If you are looking for a template for how to accept counsel given – well, the *Treasurie* might be able to help, but not to the extent of telling you where the letters or speeches that exemplify this second form are actually to be found, because, unlike its French equivalents, the English table doesn't tag its forms to the pages on which they appear.[38] It is a bizarrely self-sabotaging omission in what is otherwise a quite well-produced volume, but the effect is to underline the way in which, throughout the book, words and deeds are constantly at risk of floating apart from each other. To this extent, the *Treasurie* might be taken to exemplify the diagnosis of a deep-lying division between humanistic and chivalric attitudes to language. Yet while the material Paynell gathers from the *Amadis* certainly does embody a kind of recalcitrance, it's the volume's paratextual apparatus – that is, an element of its "humanistic" makeup – that is most profoundly engaged in obstructing the movement from words to deeds. The final oddity about this book is that it precedes the appearance in English of any of the volumes of the text it digests. Did Thomas Paynell's readers actually buy his *Treasurie* not to improve their speechmaking but in order to sample a narrative that wasn't yet available in the vernacular? Possibly – although we might wonder whether anybody could satisfyingly reconstruct *Amadis de Gaule* from the *Treasurie*'s fragmentation of the original. On a variety of fronts, Paynell's *Treasurie of Amadis of Fraunce* is a fascinatingly useless volume, even while it insists upon its ability to "serue the turne of all persons."

∾

As with the *Treasurie*, so with the romances it excerpts. This afterword has followed François de La Noue in giving an account of the Iberian romance as a modern literary form. The modernity that it has invoked is one marked by processes such as formalization, exchange and substitution, bureaucratic organization and administrative control. It is the modernity of Max Weber and Theodor Adorno and Michel Foucault, each in his different way. This feels like the right historiography to conjure in this context – the off-centre way in which the Iberian romance speaks to these themes notwithstanding. Needless to say, any relation between individual texts and the very broadest of historical movements must have something about it that is speculative and uncertain. This is all the more so with the Iberian romance, where so many people involved spend so much time insisting that the fact of relation can only take forms that are absurd. But the resonance is real. The modernity I have invoked is one defined by an ever-more meticulously controlled direction of the human capacity for action, to which Iberian romance, as the literature of deeds that can never be performed but only ever described, must bear an oblique relation. So this afterword has been about (to misapply Cervantes's parody of Feliciano de Silva, quoted in Timothy Crowley's chapter in this volume) "la razón de la sinrazón" of Iberian chivalric romance's relationship to the modernizing process, which is itself construed as one of rationalization. This is writing that is at once – as François de la Noue insisted – vain or absurd, and imbued with a formidable organizing energy; that is utterly resistant to use, but that constantly gravitates toward the form of a template. It is this ambivalent relationship to the first stirrings of the administered life in which we are now so thoroughly caught up that must account for at least part of the Iberian romance's enduring interest today.

NOTES

1 François de la Noue, *The Politicke and Militarie Discourses*, trans. E.A. (London: Thomas Orwin for T.C. and E.A., 1588; STC 15215), G4ᵛ.
2 See Colin Burrow, *Imitating Authors: Plato to Futurity* (Oxford: Oxford University Press, 2019), 199–203.
3 La Noue, *Discourses*, G5ʳ.
4 *Le Premier Livre de Palmerin d'Oliue*, trans. Jean Maugin (Paris: Jeanne de Marnef for Jean Longis, 1546), A2ᵛ.
5 This afterword therefore represents an adjustment to the argument made in my first approach to this material, which was that the relationship between chivalric romance and early modern history is broadly rationalizable; it wants to add the irrational into that account. See Alex Davis, *Chivalry and Romance in the English Renaissance* (Cambridge: D.S. Brewer, 2003).
6 I have been also guided by the questions raised in Lorna Hutson's account of Iberian chivalric romance in her book *The Usurer's Daughter*. In the context of this afterword, I would pick out the way in which Hutson neither offers the too-simple division between chivalric literature as a literature of the deed and humanistic fiction as that of the word, nor collapses the two together under the shared heading of "romance." See Lorna Hutson, *The Usurer's Daughter: Male Friendship and Fictions of Women in Sixteenth-Century England* (London: Routledge, 1994), 91–8.
7 Margaret Tyler, *Mirror of Princely Deeds and Knighthood*, ed. Joyce Boro (London: Modern Humanities Research Association, 2014), 90.
8 Ibid., 102.
9 *Amadis de Gaule*, trans. Anthony Munday, ed. Helen Moore (Aldershot, UK: Ashgate, 2004), 52.
10 La Noue, *Discourses*, G7ʳ⁻ᵛ.
11 J.L. Austin, *How to Do Things with Words: The William James Lectures Delivered at Harvard University in 1955*, 2nd ed., ed. J.O. Urmson and Marina Sbisà (1962; Oxford: Oxford University Press, 1976).
12 See John Kerrigan, *Shakespeare's Binding Language* (Oxford: Oxford University Press, 2016).
13 On "boon tricks" in *Amadis*, see John J. O'Connor, *Amadis de Gaule and Its Influence on Elizabethan Literature* (New Brunswick, NJ: Rutgers University Press, 1970), 69.

14 Le Noue's *Discourses* are not untouched by Protestant resistance theory. His incomplete tenth discourse argues against the proposition "that although the Prince command things vniust to his subiect, he must neuerthelesse put them in execution" (I8ᵛ). In general, though, the book looks toward a polity unified under the king, recommending the establishment of a standing army and an end to private quarrels.

15 *The Six Bookes of a Common-weale*, trans. Richard Knolles (London: [Adam Islip] for G. Bishop, 1606; STC 3193), B4ᵛ.

16 Munday, *Amadis*, 909–10.

17 Miguel de Cervantes Saavedra, *Don Quixote*, trans. John Rutherford (London: Penguin, 2003), 290. Cervantes seems to have particularly associated the romance of *Don Belianis* with this way of describing combat. "Who," it is asked, "[is] readier to hack and be hacked than Don Belianis?" (494); and earlier we have a reference to "the wounds that Sir Belianis kept on inflicting and receiving" (26).

18 Compare Munday, *Amadis*, 52 and 879–80.

19 Thomas Malory, *Works*, ed. Eugène Vinaver (Oxford: Oxford University Press, 1971), 678.

20 Chrétien de Troyes, *Arthurian Romances*, trans. D.D.R. Owen (London: J.M. Dent, 1993), 221.

21 See Louis B. Wright, *Middle-Class Culture in Elizabethan England* (Chapel Hill: University of North Carolina Press, 1935), chap. 5, "Handbooks to Improvement," 121–69, which discusses all the texts listed here.

22 See, for example, O'Connor, *Amadis de Gaule*, chap. 4, "*Amadis* as a Courtesy Book," 61–83.

23 La Noue, *Discourses*, G4ʳ.

24 Ibid., G7ʳ.

25 See Geoffrey Parker, *The Military Revolution: Military Innovation and the Rise of the West, 1500–1800*, 2nd ed. (Cambridge: Cambridge University Press, 1996). Maurice of Nassau's innovations in drill are described on 20–1.

26 Anthony Giddens, *The Nation State and Violence*, vol. 2, *A Contemporary Critique of Cultural Materialism* (Cambridge: Polity Press, 1985), 113–14. I first encountered this passage as part of a longer exploration of the meanings of modernity in Fredric Jameson, *A Singular Modernity: Essay on the Ontology of the Present* (London: Verso, 2002), 87–8.

27 See Michel Foucault, *Discipline and Punish: The Birth of the Prison*, trans. Alan Sheridan (1977; London: Penguin, 1991), 135–6. And see also the breakdown of actions into a narrative of body parts as an "instrumental coding of the body" in military drill on 153.

28 La Noue, *Discourses*, M7ᵛ.

29 Tyler, *Mirror*, 231.

30 La Noue, *Discourses*, G4ᵛ.

31 See "An Execration upon Vulcan," l. 30, in *The Cambridge Edition of the Works of Ben Jonson*, ed. David Bevington, Martin Butler, and Ian Donaldson, 7 vols. (Cambridge: Cambridge University Press, 2012), 7: 167; and Cervantes, *Don Quixote*, 743.

32 Sir Philip Sidney, *An Apology for Poetry (Or, The Defence of Poesy)*, ed. Geoffrey Shepherd, rev. R.W. Maslen (Manchester: Manchester University Press, 2002), 85.

33 See, for example, Emily C. Francomano, *The Prison of Love: Romance, Translation, and the Book in the Sixteenth Century* (Toronto: University of Toronto Press, 2018); or Joyce Boro, "Multilingualism, Romance, and Language Pedagogy; or, Why Were so Many Sentimental Romances Printed as Polyglot Texts?" in *Tudor Translation*, ed. Fred Schurink (London: Palgrave Macmillan, 2011), 18–38.

34 Helen Moore, "Gathering Fruit: The 'Profitable' Translations of Thomas Paynell," in Schurink, *Tudor Translation*, 40, 43.

35 Thomas Paynell, *The Moste Excellent and Pleasaunt Booke, Entituled: The Treasurie of Amadis of Fraunce* (London: Henry Bynneman for Thomas Hacket, 1572?), ¶2ᵛ.

36 Ibid., ¶¶2ʳ.

37 Ibid., A1ʳ.

38 Helen Moore's account of the *Treasurie* argues that the table is Paynell's addition to the French *Thresor*, which was first printed in 1559. Many editions of the French text lack the table. However, the 1571 *Thresor* issued by Jeanne Bruneau does contain one, and it probably predates Paynell's volume. Paynell's *Treasurie* is undated. It was entered into the Stationers' Register in 1567–8, but it ends with an extract from the thirteenth book of *Amadis*, which was published in 1571. The English Short Title catalogue conjecturally dates the *Treasurie* to 1572, which seems plausible (STC 545). At any rate, the contrast between French and English tables is clear. We can compare Paynell's first form with the first entry in the 1571 *Thresor*, which opens: "Maniere de declarer son advis, de demander au donner conseil de quelque chose à ses seigneurs, amis, parens, alliez ou subiets. fuie [i.e., 'fueillet'] 4.b. 26.a. 29.a. 39.b. 44.a ..." These page numbers are omitted from the English table. See *Le thresor des livres d'Amadis de Gaule* (Paris: J. Bruneau, 1571; FB 935), *iiiʳ.

Contributors

Leticia Álvarez-Recio is an associate professor of English literature at the University of Seville.

Helen Cooper is professor emeritus of medieval and Renaissance English at the University of Cambridge, a Life Fellow of Magdalene College, Cambridge, and an Honorary and Emeritus Fellow of University College, Oxford.

Timothy D. Crowley is an associate professor at Northern Illinois University.

Alex Davis is a senior lecturer of English at the University of St Andrews.

Elizabeth Evenden-Kenyon is an Honorary Research Fellow at the Faculty of Medieval and Modern Languages of the University of Oxford.

Donna B. Hamilton is professor emeritus of English at the University of Maryland.

María Beatriz Hernández Pérez is an associate professor of English literature at the Universidad de La Laguna.

Jordi Sánchez-Martí is an associate professor of English literature at the University of Alicante.

Goran Stanivukovic is a professor of English at Saint Mary's University in Halifax.

Rocío G. Sumillera is an associate professor of English literature at the University of Granada.

Louise Wilson is a lecturer of English literature (medieval to early modern) at Liverpool Hope University.

Index

Toronto Iberic

Co-editors: Robert Davidson (Toronto) and Frederick A. de Armas (Chicago)